Lost beyond Telling

Lost beyond Telling

REPRESENTATIONS OF
DEATH AND ABSENCE IN
MODERN FRENCH POETRY

Richard Stamelman

CORNELL UNIVERSITY PRESS

Ithaca and London

First published 1990 by Cornell University Press.

International Standard Book Number 0-8014-2408-9
Library of Congress Catalog Card Number 90-55127
Printed in the United States of America
Librarians: Library of Congress cataloging information appears on the last page of the book.

⊗ The paper in this publication meets the minimum requirements of the American National Standard for Information Sciences— Permanence of Paper for Printed Library Materials, ANSI Z39.48-1984.

For Emily and Jeremy

CONTENTS

Perhaps an angel looks like everything
We have forgotten, I mean forgotten
Things that don't seem familiar when
We meet them again, lost beyond telling,
Which were ours once.

—John Ashbery, "Self-Portrait
in a Convex Mirror"

Preface

What do modern poets imagine when they look toward the past, when they peer into what Prospero calls "the dark backward and abysm of time"? The sight is chilling, for the past is a frozen scene of death, exile, absence, incompletion, dispersion, ruin, fragmentation, effacement, and lack. The angel of history, according to Walter Benjamin, looks back to the past and sees a scene of disorder and destruction: "one single catastrophe which keeps piling wreckage upon wreckage." Benjamin's angel tries to reach out to repair or to make whole again what has been smashed, but a wind blows him into the future, putting an unbridgeable distance between him and a past that will unceasingly present image upon image of loss.

The poetic confrontation with the past is an encounter with the signs and traces of loss. Poetry is a contemplation of what Baudelaire in "Le Cygne" described as "ce qui ne se retrouve / Jamais, jamais! ("what is never, never / Found again!"). It is an acceptance of the "neverness" of recovery and a hope that, failing all else, the scope and nature of the loss, at the very least, can be rescued for poetic expression. Modern French poets, from Charles Baudelaire in the nineteenth century to Yves Bonnefoy and Edmond Jabès in our own, do not resist loss. They refuse to hide the signs of its devastation behind the perfect mask of artistic illusion or to take refuge in a benighted aestheticism where unwavering faith in poetry's power of figuration overcomes the incompleteness and finitude of temporal existence. Loss is the *fait accompli* of the modern poem, the experience from which poetry emerges into being; it is the raison d'être of poetic language. While a past event, a lost object of pleasure, or a distant homeland may be literally "lost beyond telling," as the poet John Ashbery writes, the reality—the very fact and occurrence—of loss is not. The way in which an experience was (and is) lost can be articulated, even if the experience—in the fullness, immediacy, and presence it once had—cannot. Loss, then, is the cause as well as the subject of the modern poem.

Because loss is intrinsic to the human condition, the history of literature and art reflects the history of humanity's experience with loss of one kind or another. Absence, death, lack, exile, nonbeing, dispossession, alterity, passage, distance, separation, evanescence, effacement, ruin, dispersion, insufficiency, incompleteness, deprivation, depletion, emptiness, void, nothingness, dissolution, grief, mourning, melancholy, regret, nostalgia, longing, forgetting, loneliness, disillusionment, suffering, pain—the glossary of loss is practically inexhaustible. If events were everlasting, if sensations remained forever immediate, if perceptions were reexperienced with the same burning intensity and compelling immediacy the second time as the first, would writing, or other forms of artistic representation for that matter, be necessary? If things did not disappear or die, if they were not forgotten or lost, if they were continuously enveloped in a never-ending presence, as luminous and whole at one moment as at another, would there be any need to struggle to recover them through images of artistic recuperation? If perceptions remained forever present, who would feel the desire to *re*-present them? There would, in fact, be no desire. The strategies of representation as they have developed in art and literature through the centuries are motivated by the powerful longing to recapture the past. Representation strives to repossess what nature, history, and the world have removed from the human sphere. The need for figuration derives from the reality of loss. It expresses the desire to return to a past moment in order to make it once again fully present; similarly, it is the wish to preserve the intensity of a present perception so that it will not disappear. Representation longs for the recovery of presence. But, in truth, representation involves images and traces, never origins. Loss of the original fuels the fires of artifice. Possessing an origin, what need would there be to represent it? Dispossession makes possible the creation of images, and negativity, as embodied in absence, death, and loss, animates the quest of writing and other forms of figuration.

The experience of loss creates the drama of human existence, and the history of literary and artistic representation is the history of the struggle to confront and resolve that loss. But how does one ever come to terms with loss? How does one ever succeed in describing it in words or giving it form in art? How can the blankness, the void, and the nothingness of loss be figured? Is not the figuration of loss a contradiction in terms, because no forms can be found to encompass and re-create what, because it is missing, is formless and figureless? If things are truly "lost *beyond* telling," what relationship do words and images have to this "beyond"? Are they condemned to revolve around a center of emptiness into which they can never enter, because to do so would be to become empty themselves? Moreover, how does one designate the truth of a loss, when to speak it, to make it the subject of a discourse, is to speak of something that by the very fact of its having been uttered, of its having become a "something," is no longer fully lost? Every speaking of loss is thus a misspeaking, because loss is truly beyond figuration. Every utterance, striving to express an experience of loss, will have to leave something out, will have to leave unspoken what remains beyond all telling. Every discourse on loss will, thus, itself be subject to loss.

The words I write at this moment and that are present before my eyes on the paper are already invaded by loss. The "telling" of my text circles around a subject it will never seize, never exhaust, never fully speak. To write about loss is to acknowledge from the start that the very nature of the subject thwarts capture. A book titled *Lost beyond Telling* is itself beyond telling, containing at its heart the vacancy of a subject that no language can signify and no writing encompass. Several of the poets studied designate this emptiness by means of the white page surrounding their words. But a work of criticism cannot designate what the poet A. R. Ammons calls "the hum of omissions," "the chant of vacancies." It cannot impose large gaps of blank and open space between words or sentences. It can, however, admit that its discourse is perpetually circling its subject, that it is in exile from what it strives to represent, and that it is always distant from the truth and the source of what its speaking evokes. Regarding its origin, every text is marginal; it remains at the periphery of an originating moment that it cannot remember and whose configuration it cannot even imagine; it exists outside the orbit of its subject. Every text is in exile from the untraceable origin and the lost source on which it continuously focuses its vision and desire. Each of the thousands and thousands of words that writing spews forth into the void of loss, seeking to recover meaning and presence, is ultimately no more than the incarnation, the figuration, of loss, for as the poet Robert Hass writes, "a word is elegy to what it signifies."

The concern of modern French poets—including Charles Baudelaire, Guillaume Apollinaire, Pierre Jean Jouve, Yves Bonnefoy, Philippe Jaccottet, Jacques Dupin, André du Bouchet, Edmond Jabès—of an artist such as Alberto Giacometti, and of a critic such as Roland Barthes is with the nature of loss: with the signs that absent things leave of themselves, with the desires that past encounters kindle in those who are compelled to feel an essential lack; with the fundamental alterity of one's perception of the world; with the lost homeland that the exiled person longs to regain; and with the distance that otherness establishes between human beings. These poets recognize that the poem can never compensate for what has been lost. For the poem is desire— "désir demeuré désir," in René Char's remarkable phrase—never the fulfillment of desire. It is the quintessential expression of a longing so powerfully embodied that only its fundamental incompleteness and unfulfillment are revealed. "Although we know that after . . . a loss the acute state of mourning will subside," Freud wrote Ludwig Binswanger after the death of Binswanger's son, "we also know we shall remain inconsolable and will never find a substitute. No matter what may fill the gap, even if it be filled completely, it nevertheless remains something else." The poem is this "something else," this paradoxical otherness trying to fill the gap. It is essentially allegorical, as we shall see. For allegory sets in motion an excessive, decentered, unstable language, unleashed in reaction to the loss that suddenly separates the poet from an object or being that words will never fully signify or recover. Allegorical discourse is always incomplete and imperfect, because it evokes some meaning, some image, some figure lying beyond the horizon of its signification, some "otherness" that it can designate but not join. It is a failed figuration. The allegorical sign invokes a totality that can never be possessed, an origin that can never be found again, and a referent that can never be represented. It is a figure in exile. The allegorical representation of death, lack, or ruin makes loss textually present but only as the absence, the "something else," it really is. Loss in poetry, as this book demonstrates, is expressed, therefore, in the melancholic discourses of allegory and alterity.

In the chapters that follow I examine the poetry and the poetics of loss in the works of eight French poets, in the art of one French artist, and in the writings of one French critic, starting with Charles Baudelaire in the nineteenth century and concluding with Roland Barthes in the late twentieth. Part 1 of the book presents a theoretical discussion of the nature of poetic loss in general, especially its relation to writing, representation, and interpretation and to the poetics of presence and absence. The different ways particular French poets confront experiences of loss, otherness, and melancholy are studied in part 2. Chapter 2 examines how loss—experienced as the withering away of matter,

memory, and the body, as the passage of time, as the paralyzing inactivity of "spleen," and as the relentless confrontation with the ineluc-
tability of death—becomes for Baudelaire the initiatory experience for
the allegorical incarnation and lyrical "presencing" that constitute poetic creation. Chapter 3 discusses the enigma of otherness as expressed
by Guillaume Apollinaire in an orphic poetry, where the desire for the
wholeness of a unified self perfectly fused with the world coincides with
the sorrowful recognition of the loss and impossibility of such undifferentiated being. The central role that loss and absence play in love,
in particular Pierre Jean Jouve's lyrical eroticization of a lost object of
love through a process of melancholic incorporation, is considered in
chapter 4. In chapter 5, I examine Yves Bonnefoy's poetry as a writing
that hides within itself a secret calligraphy, an *écriture autre,* which,
because of its very alterity—an otherness expressing the openness and
finitude of mortal existence—negates the closure that all representations, poetic and artistic, pretend to achieve. In chapter 6, the poetry of
Jacques Dupin and André du Bouchet, who along with Yves Bonnefoy
were referred to at one time as the poets of *L'Ephémère,* is considered
and their poetic theories compared to the aesthetic notions of the
painter and sculptor Alberto Giacometti. The poetry of *L'Ephémère* is
subject to the same erosion, fragmentariness, and effacement as being
itself, for art offers no haven from the ravages of time and death which
literally invade the work of art in the form of a discontinuous syntax,
an unorthodox *mise-en-page,* a unique interplay of writing and white
space, and, in the case of Giacometti, a dialectical struggle between
construction and destruction, between the building up of the artwork
and its reduction to nothingness. Chapter 7 discusses the way the
alterity of the real provokes, in the writings of Philippe Jaccottet, a
poetics of passage, of passing through, as Jaccottet, trying to understand the opposition between the limits of language and the limitlessness of the world, wanders through the unseizable landscape and the
elusive discourse in which he dwells.

Chapters 8 and 9 constitute part 3 of the book, which is devoted to a
study of the poetic narrative of loss. They concern two writers of what
may be called the poetic *récit* of loss, in which language comes undone
under the strain of collective and personal histories of exile, absence,
and mourning: first, Edmond Jabès, who blends poetry and prose, lyric
and narrative, into works where the life of exile is conceived of as the
life of a book, one composed of unending, ever-renewed questions,
commentaries, interpretations, aphorisms, quotations, and fragments,
which symbolically and mimetically reproduce the wandering of an

exiled people (and of a language) across the empty sands (and pages) of a desert (a book); and second, Roland Barthes, who in the last work of his life, *La Chambre claire*, a meditation on photographic representation and the death of his mother, reveals how the structures of critical discourse break down under the weight of an impossible grief, as he turns away from the constraints of impersonal theory and toward a new, not yet fully realized, form of affective writing. This is a form of elegiac prose somewhere between criticism and poetry, a lyrical narrative of mourning that searches vainly to recover what is, ultimately, "lost beyond telling."

Although this is a book about loss, I have not been at a loss in writing it. To the contrary, I have been rich in friends on both sides of the Atlantic who have helped to mitigate the ordinary losses and absences that one experiences in everyday life. I am most grateful to them for having deepened my knowledge of modern French poetry and thus my understanding of human existence. Conversations with them over the years on different aspects of French poetry and poetic theory have helped inspire and develop many of the ideas and interpretations presented in this book. Their insights have been invaluable and their encouragement unflagging.

For their generosity of spirit and their willingness to share ideas and thoughts, which even the distance of a great ocean could not hinder, I thank Odile Bombarde, Lucy Bonnefoy, Yves Bonnefoy, Didier Cahen, Dominique Combe, Georges Formentelli, Nadine Fresco, Claude Garache, Hélène Garache, Mortimer Guiney, Arlette Jabès, Edmond Jabès, Daniel Lançon, James Lord, Jérôme Thélot, and, in London, Anthony Rudolf. I also express my gratitude to those closer to home— Margaret Brose, Mary Ann Caws, Laurie Edson, Gérard Gasarian, Robert W. Greene, Josué Harari, Edward Kaplan, Berel Lang, James Lawler, George Nama, John Naughton, Ronnie Scharfman, Paul Schwaber, Khachig Tölölyan, Richard Vernier, and Hayden White— for having richly and warmly shared with me their ideas on modern poetry and contemporary literary theory. The manuscript benefited from meticulous readings by David Konstan, Robert W. Greene, and Stephen Ungar, whose suggestions and criticisms were of immense value. I am very grateful to them for their assistance.

Without the generous research support of Wesleyan University this book could not have been completed in as timely a fashion as it was. To the Wesleyan University Center for the Humanities and its past and present directors—Louis O. Mink, Jr., Richard Vann, and Richard

Ohmann—I owe a special debt of gratitude for the opportunity of working over several years with scholars from various disciplines and different institutions. With skill, patience, and considerable grace under pressure, the administrative staff of the Center, in particular Patricia Camden and Jaqueline Rich, tirelessly typed and corrected several versions of the manuscript. I cannot thank them enough for their generosity and selflessness. To Steven D. Lebergott, Head of Interlibrary Loan, and the staff at Olin Memorial Library, who searched, sometimes against all hope, in this country and in France for hard-to-find articles and collections of poetry, I express my thanks. To the students in my courses on nineteenth- and twentieth-century French poetry and on Roland Barthes, I am particularly grateful for what they taught me about poetic and critical texts I thought I already understood.

I thank as well the staff of Cornell University Press—in particular Carol Betsch, Burl Barr, Cynthia Gration, Richard Rosenbaum, Marilyn M. Sale, Kay Scheuer, and Linda Wentworth—for their expert advice and generous assistance in the preparation of the manuscript for publication, and especially Bernhard Kendler for the wisdom of his counsel and for his encouragement. I am also extremely grateful to Jane Warth for her meticulous and skillful copyediting of the manuscript, and to Emily Stamelman for having spent many a sweltering summer afternoon checking sources and verifying quotations.

For the support his loyal friendship has given me for over three decades, I thank Walter A. Brown. Finally, for having endured with patience, understanding, and compassion the absences and distances that the solitary work of writing has necessitated, my deepest gratitude and affection go to my wife—and to my two children, to whom this book is lovingly dedicated.

Some of the chapters of this book first appeared—in whole, or in part, or in different versions—in various books and journals, to whose publishers and editors I gratefully acknowledge permission to use them here. Chapter 2 was published as "The Shroud of Allegory: Death, Mourning, and Melancholy in Baudelaire's Work," in *Texas Studies in Literature and Language* 25 (Fall 1983). Chapter 3 appeared as "The 'Fatal Shadow' of Otherness: Desire and Identity in the Poetry of Guillaume Apollinaire," in *French Forum* 8 (May 1983). Chapter 5 was published as "'Le Cri qui perce la musique': Le Surgissement de l'altérité dans l'oeuvre d'Yves Bonnefoy," in a special number of *Sud* 15 (1985) devoted to the proceedings of a colloquium on Yves Bonnefoy held at the Centre Culturel International de Cerisy-la-Salle, France, in August 1983. The first part of chapter 6 appeared as "The Syntax of the Ephemeral," in *Dalhousie French Studies* 2 (October 1980), and the second part as "The Art of the Void: Alberto Giacometti and the Poets of *L'Ephémère*," in *L'Esprit créateur* 22 (Winter 1982). Chapter 7 was published under the title "The Unseizable Landscape of the Real: The Poetry and Poetics of Philippe Jaccottet," in *Studies in Twentieth-Century Literature* 13 (Winter 1989). Chapter 8 first appeared in *The Sin of the Book: Edmond Jabès*, edited by Eric Gould, and is published here by permission of the University of Nebraska Press. Copyright 1985 by the University of Nebraska Press.

Acknowledgment is gratefully made as well to the following publishers: Carcanet Press Limited and Viking Penguin, a division of Penguin Books USA Inc., for permission to quote from *Self-Portrait in a Convex Mirror* by John Ashbery. Copyright © 1972, 1973, 1974, 1975 by John Ashbery. All rights reserved; Farrar, Straus & Giroux, Inc., for permission to reprint "One Art" and excerpt from "The End of March" from *The Complete Poems* by Elizabeth Bishop. Copyright © 1979, 1983 by Elizabeth Bishop and Alice Helen Methfessel; Alfred A. Knopf, Inc., for permission to reprint the poem "Old Hat" from *Hundreds of Fireflies* by Brad Leithauser. Copyright © 1981 by Brad Leithauser; and Mercure de France (and its rights and permissions editor, Nicole Boyer), first, for the right to use passages from Pierre Jean Jouve, *Oeuvre* (© 1987), and, second, for the permission to reprint selections from Yves Bonnefoy's *Poèmes* (© 1978) and his *Ce qui fut sans lumière* (© 1987).

A Note on Translation: All translations from the French are my own, unless otherwise indicated. Whenever I use translations by others, two page numbers are given, separated by a slash: the first number refers to the French edition and the second to the English translation. In a very few instances, I have slightly modified translations by others, when I thought it necessary.

RICHARD STAMELMAN

Portland, Connecticut

PART ONE

Thε Poεtics of Loss

Savoir que l'écriture ne compense rien, ne sublime rien, qu'elle est précisément *là où tu n'es pas*—c'est le commencement de l'écriture.

[To know that writing compensates for nothing, sublimates nothing, that it is precisely *there where you are not*—this is the beginning of writing.]

—Roland Barthes, *Fragments d'un discours amoureux*

Voir, penser, différencier l'univers, le pressentir dans sa vraie figure, c'est aussitôt, puisque nous parlons—quelle découverte!—le perdre.

[To see, to imagine, to find differences in the world, to intuit it in its true light is, because we speak—what a revelation!—immediately to lose it.]

—Yves Bonnefoy, *Le Nuage rouge*

"Il ne peut y avoir de langue pour l'unité; il n'y a de langue que pour la séparation," disait-il.

["There can be no language for unity; there is only language for separation," he said.]

—Edmond Jabès, *El, ou le dernier livre*

CHAPTER 1

THE REPRESENTATION of LOSS

> It is the image in the mind that links us to our lost treasures; but it is the loss that shapes the image, gathers the flowers, weaves the garland.
>
> —Colette, *Mes Apprentissages*

A man dies and is mourned by family and friends. A young woman, exiled from the country of her birth, longs to return. A growing child asserts his independence, taking distance from his mother and yet unconsciously desiring the lost sense of oneness with her which in infancy sustained his fragile life. A woman, having forgotten the look of a room in the house of her childhood, examines innumerable photographs for clues that might bring back the memory. A widow finds herself talking to a husband who has been dead for almost a year. A painter, trying to capture the extraordinary play of light on a model's face, loses the vision and abandons the painting. An elderly man remembers a cherished toy, companion to many hours of childhood play, and wonders with a tinge of regret what has become of it. A woman returns near the end of her life to the pastoral landscape of her adolescence to find it dotted with tract houses. A young boy, before falling asleep, recalls the bedtime stories his dead father used to read to him.

That we live in a state of unending loss, grieving for lost childhoods, absent homelands, departed loved ones, destroyed objects, and eroded images of the past, is abundantly clear. From the moment we take notice of the world and become aware of our place in it, we become painfully conscious of the loss that shadows all human activity. For to be human is to know loss and to struggle with it. Yet we do more than confront and wrestle with loss. We also struggle to undo it, to reverse its actions, to find ways around it. We fill the hole that it opens in our lives with something meaningful, as if this tear in the fabric of human

3

existence could ever be completely repaired. We strive to regain the feeling of intimacy associated with things or beings no longer physically proximate. We work to overcome the gulf separating us from a past we remember, often mistakenly, as a moment of blissful oneness and immanence or as a time of certain knowledge and understanding.[1]

Thus, we try to overcome loss by naming it, by representing it, and by finding new forms and images through which to retell, recall, remember, and resuscitate what has disappeared. We invent objects, icons, talismans, memories, and phantasms to mediate the loss: transi-

---

1. In his poem "The Lost Children," Randall Jarrell suggests that memory of the past is in itself no guarantee against the reality of loss, which is so much a part of living and growing. A mother attempts to remember the childhood of her two daughters—one dead, the other married. Recalling her closeness to them, she now sadly acknowledges that their relationship has undergone change, because over the years distance and separateness have grown:

> The young person who writes once a week
> Is the authority upon herself.
> She sits in my living room and shows her husband
> My albums of her as a child. He enjoys them
> And makes fun of them. I look too
> And realize the girl in the matching blue
> Mother-and-daughter dress, the fair one carrying
> The tiny lunch box with the half-pint thermos bottle
> Or training her pet duck to go down the slide
> Is lost just as the dark one, who is dead, is lost.

These childhood photographs have a reality that floods the mother with "all the old sure knowledge," and she remembers the past. Yet, such knowledge and memory are not enough to dissipate the loss of intimacy and distance which the growing up of her children has demanded:

> . . . when I put the album down
> I keep saying inside: "I *did* know those children.
> I braided those braids. I was driving the car
> The day that she stepped in the can of grease
> We were taking to the butcher for our ration points.
> I *know* those children. I know all about them.
> Where are they?"

To know is not to possess. The mother's closeness to her children has become part of her memory, and it is remembering that makes the loss more painful and the longing greater. At the poem's end, the mother imagines playing hide-and-seek with dream images of her absent daughters; it is, however, no longer a child's game, but the reality of her life: the hiding of what is lost and the persistent, vain seeking to recover it at all costs:

> The dark one
> Looks at me longingly, and disappears;
> The fair one stays in sight, just out of reach
> No matter where I reach. I am tired
> As a mother who's played all day, some rainy day.
> I don't want to play it any more, I don't want to.
> But the child keeps on playing, so I play.

(*The Complete Poems* [New York: Farrar, Straus and Giroux, 1969], pp. 301–3).

tional objects, such as corners of blankets or pillows, that, bridging the gap between what was and what now is, ease the pain of separation; surrogate objects that, standing in the place of what has disappeared, simultaneously memorialize its significance and mourn its loss; verbal and visual objects that, representing in words or images the truth of what is absent, struggle to repossess it through the thereness of a human artifact or a work of art; memory objects that, by tapping the psychic energy of the melancholic imagination, become symbolic incarnations for what has been lost; and, finally, fetish objects that, as unconscious, sometimes hallucinatory constructions, attempt to deny that the loss ever occurred. Each of these inventions of unconscious desire indicates our distance from a lost object of love, and each, despite its efforts to reverse or compensate for the loss, inadequately represents and signifies that lost object. It is inadequate because the referent it designates is, and will forever remain, absent. That referent, that lost object or being, becomes part of the lack that loss establishes; it is swallowed up by the "hole in the real," as Jacques Lacan calls it, the gaping void, which death, exile, and loss create.[2]

Through various strategies of mediation, such as painting, music, writing, and memory, which attempt to restore the lost object in the present moment of a representation, we work to change an irreversible absence and shape it into a tangible presence. We substitute the here-and-now reality of an image, a figure of speech, or a work of art for the absent object of desire. But to make what is lost *re*-present itself endowed with the immediacy and fullness that it once possessed is beyond the powers of imagination. It is beyond the power of language and of mimetic representation. The immediacy of experience is unseizable; it is already past, already lost, even as we begin to represent and record it. To write about experience is to lose it, for the self-consciousness that makes possible the change from living in the world to speaking or writing about the world is fatal to the immediacy of being, as Yves Bonnefoy has affirmed: "Voir, penser, différencier l'univers, le pressentir dans sa vraie figure, c'est aussitôt, puisque nous parlons—quelle découverte!—le perdre" ("To see, to imagine, to find differences in the world, to intuit it in its true light is, because we speak—what a revelation!—immediately to lose it").[3] The word or the artistic image cannot

2. "Desire and the Interpretation of Desire in *Hamlet*," *Yale French Studies* (*Literature and Psychoanalysis: The Question of Reading: Otherwise*) 55–56 (1977): 37. Lacan also writes that "the one unbearable dimension of possible human experience is not the experience of one's own death, which no one has, but the experience of the death of another" (ibid.)

3. "La Poétique de Mallarmé," in *Le Nuage rouge* (Paris: Mercure de France, 1977), p. 187.

establish presence. The poet, for whom the highest goal of poetry is, according to Paul de Man, "not only to speak *of* Being, but to say Being itself,"[4] recognizes eventually the sad truth that "as soon as the word is uttered, it destroys the immediate and discovers that instead of stating Being, it can only state mediation." And, de Man continues, "for us, . . . the sorrow of mediation lies in finitude, and we are able to conceive of it only under the form of death."[5] The words we write or speak only name what is absent or in the process of becoming absent. Language is a condition of mediation designating the frailty of our relationship with the world and naming the loss that undermines all being.[6] Our

4. "Les Exégèses de Hölderlin par Martin Heidegger," *Critique* 12 (September–October 1955): 810 ["Heidegger's Exegeses of Hölderlin," in *Blindness and Insight: Essays in the Rhetoric of Contemporary Criticism*, 2d ed., rev. (Minneapolis: University of Minnesota Press, 1983), p. 256].

5. Ibid., pp. 812/259 and 816/262, respectively.

6. The fundamental consciousness that language expresses is, de Man writes, the consciousness of loss; it is the presence of nothingness, which language tries to name: "Poetic language names this void with ever-renewed understanding and, like Rousseau's longing, it never tires of naming it again. This persistent naming is what we call literature" (*Blindness and Insight*, p. 18). J.-B. Pontalis goes a step further in asserting that all language, because it is born of loss, is voracious desire wildly seeking what it has lost:

> Il est dans sa nature même d'aller vers ce qui n'est pas lui. Puisqu'il est né de la perte et qu'il n'a rien qui soit à lui, son appétit est énorme! Il peut, il doit, pour vivre, tout "incorporer" jusqu'au corps et plus que lui: il séduit mieux qu'un sexe, il émeut plus profondément que les larmes, il convainc plus fort qu'un coup de poing, il blesse, il endort, il assomme . . . il a tous les pouvoirs. Dans ce mouvement qui le porte de la maîtrise, de la magie, à la conscience de sa vacuité essentielle, il va osciller entre le triomphe maniaque et la mélancolie. Mais la mélancolie révèle sa nature, la manie seulement son effort. . . . [Le langage] est à la fois un deuil qui se fait et un deuil qui ne s'achève pas.

> [It is of the very nature of language to go towards what is not it. Since it is born from loss and has nothing that is truly its own, its appetite is enormous! It can, it must, in order to live, "incorporate" everything, including the body and more: it seduces better than sexuality; it moves more deeply than tears; it settles things more assertively than a punch; it wounds, it anesthetizes, it overwhelms . . . it has all the powers. In its movement from mastery and magic to the consciousness of its own essential emptiness, it alternates between manic triumph and melancholy. But melancholy reveals its nature, mania only its effort. . . . [Language] is at the same time a mourning that takes form and a mourning that remains incomplete.] (*Perdre de vue*, Collection Connaissance de l'inconscient [Paris: Gallimard, 1988], pp. 194–95)

Loss is, for Julia Kristeva as well, the precondition for language. Behind our words are a wound, a deprivation, a pain, which in themselves make speech possible:

> Notre don de parler, de nous situer dans le temps pour un autre, ne saurait exister ailleurs qu'au-delà d'un abîme. L'être parlant, depuis sa capacité à durer dans le temps jusqu'à ses constructions enthousiastes, savantes ou simplement amusantes, exige à sa base une rupture, un abandon, un malaise.

> [Our ability to speak, to situate ourselves in time for another person, could not exist anywhere else but on the other side of an abyss. The being who speaks—

relation to the past, to what has disappeared from the present, is, therefore, a continuously mediated one. Images, words, and texts are what we depend on in order to take note of what has passed away. These representations may reflect the past as well as reflect upon it, but they are without the power to re-create the living sensation of that past, as Hayden White observes:

> By definition, we might say, a datum is *past* only in the extent to which it is *no longer* something to which I can be referred as *a possible object of living perception.* The historically real, the past real, is that to which I can be referred only *by way of* an artifact that is textual in nature. The indexical, iconic, and symbolic notions of language, and therefore of texts, obscure the nature of this indirect referentiality and hold out the possibility of (feign) direct referentiality, create the illusion that there is a past *out there* which is directly reflected *in* the texts. But even if we grant this, it is the reflection that we perceive, not the thing reflected.[7]

The past is irrevocably and irreversibly lost. From the point of view of the present, it is an unchanging absence enveloped in the immobility of a no longer existent temporal moment, the pastness of which can never be removed. The past is, as Vladimir Jankélévitch writes, "the realm of the impossible," because the fact of a life as a reality that has existed cannot be undone or reversed.[8] Being can be destroyed but not the *fact* of being. Death can end life but never cancel "le fait d'*avoir-vécu*" (p. 202). It is thus the pastness of the past—the very fact of its having existed and become the past—which is inherently irreversible. The past is beyond resurrection; it is precisely that which cannot return, that which cannot again become present: "For that which belongs to the past everything is permitted except precisely the essential, the actual making present, for it is 'too late!' The 'no longer at all' [*le déjà plus*] lends itself only to remembrance, itself an imaginary presentification. The past points to that impassible limit placed on our

from his or her capacity to live in time to his or her enthusiastic, clever, or simply amusing constructions—must have, as the basis for existence, a rupture, an abandonment, a malaise.] (*Soleil noir: Dépression et mélancolie* [Paris: Gallimard, 1987], p. 54)

7. "Method and Ideology in Intellectual History: The Case of Henry Adams," in *Modern European Intellectual History: Reappraisals and New Perspectives,* ed. Dominick LaCapra and Stephen L. Kaplan (Ithaca: Cornell University Press, 1982), p. 305.

8. *L'Irréversible et la nostalgie,* Collection Champs (Paris: Flammarion, 1974), p. 181; page references are hereafter cited in the text.

power" (p. 177). When we remember, we experience a certain truth about the lost and absent past, but our experience is only a fragment of the original truth, a mere trace of the original presence. Memory may resemble the truth, but it can never coincide with it:

> Vestige and ideal symbol of the present, spectral and nebulous image superimposed on perceived reality, memory intensifies, by its very inadequacy or . . . weakness, our hunger and thirst for reality: memory, far from compensating for what returns, sharpens nostalgia and confirms the irreversible. . . . In highlighting the pastness of the past, memory makes us, alas, sensitive to all that we have lost: the irreplaceable fragrance of the present and the incomparable savor of presence—the flesh and blood tangibility of the real. (P. 26)

Memory compares the past to the present and reveals the impoverishment of the latter, thereby disclosing the extent of what has been lost. It measures "the ravages of becoming" (p. 312) and points to its own failure as a conservator of the unpreservable past. Nostalgic memory calls attention to itself as a faded copy of a lost reality, for, as Jankélévitch writes, "in leaving us memories, that is to say, substitutes for presence, passing time throws us a meager bone to gnaw on: unsatisfied, we still remain hungry. Such is the impoverishment of memory" (p. 314).[9]

9. The anguish of memory is generated by the impossible demand for temporal reversibility. "Return," Jankélévitch writes, "is the medication for nostalgia, as aspirin is the medication for migraine" (ibid., p. 340). For a fascinating study of nostalgic desire, see Susan Stewart, *On Longing: Narratives of the Miniature, the Gigantic, the Souvenir, the Collection* (Baltimore: Johns Hopkins University Press, 1984), pp. 22–24 and 132–69. According to Stewart, the nostalgic longs to reexperience a time—before knowledge and self-consciousness and predating his or her own narrative of nostalgic reconstruction—that *faute de mieux* can only exist in the self-consciousness and loss that narrative engenders. Confronted by the gap between signifier and signified, the nostalgic longs for absolute presence. Thus, the souvenir or memento becomes a metonymic object, which is made to stand in the place of a no-longer-present event to which it was at one time related. The souvenir signifies the loss of that event. But because the trace of the event is concentrated in it, the souvenir is also a condensation, a node, of mnemonic energy. The souvenir charges the emptiness of the lost past with a burst of meaning, a "surplus of signification," like Freud's fetish object. Existing in the space between present and past—the space of separation and distance—the souvenir remains partial and incomplete, so it can recall the wholeness, now lost, to which it perpetually refers and so it can be supplemented by the narrative discourse, now present, to which it makes appeal, a discourse that activates the endless play of desire. For Stewart, nostalgia is established on loss and is sustained by the unrecoverability and irreversibility of this loss: "The nostalgic is enamored of distance, not of the referent itself. Nostalgia cannot be sustained without loss. For the nostalgic to reach his or her goal of closing the gap between resemblance and identity, *lived* experience would have to take place, an erasure of the gap between sign and signified, an experience which would cancel out the desire that is nostalgia's reason for existence" (p. 145).

The sense of loss, for Jankélévitch, derives from "the despair at never combining being and having been" (p. 336). The past is fixed and unchangeable; we cannot go back and relive it except through imagination, illusion, dream, or hallucination. It is beyond the reach of life and of present experience. We cannot return because becoming ("le devenir effectif"), which animates living and being, which moves us ineluctably toward futureness ("la futurition toute-puissante") and away from pastness ("le rêve de la prétérition impuissante"), prevents a return (p. 240). In the flux of becoming, the idea of return can only be dreamed or imagined; it is what Jankélévitch calls "un revenir fantomal" ("a phantasmatic returning"; p. 240). Because every moment that drops out of the present to fall into the past is both a first and last moment, it is fundamentally not only irreversible but also unrepeatable. Such moments are unique. Once experienced, they are englobed within a pastness that is also their lostness: "With the first time-last time quality that lost life has, all hope of recuperation has left us, for we live but once. . . . Once, and never again! Time regained? What folly!" (p. 337).

Yet, an assurance against the absolute triumph of nothingness lies in the fact that, although lost and unrecoverable, the past nevertheless does exist. It continues to have a certain identity as a past. It is precisely that which cannot be revoked, changed, or effaced, for it has the "character, if not *indestructible,* at least *interminable,* of the fact-of-having-occurred" (p. 337). This past is a monument to its existence as that which once was; it is a marker or sign designating its identity as a lost, but still real, event; it is what Jankélévitch describes as "the flash of a forgotten past, blinking in the night of nonbeing" (p. 337). What the light from this dead star of the past illuminates is the reality of its having been, which nothing can abolish, not even loss itself.

At best, then what we achieve when we look nostalgically and retrospectively at the past is the calling back into the present, the "presencing," of an absence that remains frozen and stilled by the fact or event of loss, which had propelled it into this *other* temporal dimension where it now dwells. From the moment the object or being disappears, time stands still, because it enters a realm of temporal alterity that makes it radically and eternally different from the present world of the living. Efforts to remember, to memorialize, to re-create, or to represent something or someone that has been lost succeed in resuscitating an image of the lost object or person. The image indeed returns, but it emerges from a past whose pastness, adhering to it like some dark shadow, accompanies it into the present. The past, returning to the present through representation, is haunted by loss, ineffaceably colored by it, as old photographs are tinged yellow. An irreversible past-ness, like a halo of difference, encircles the past event or lost being as its one and only reality, as its unique identity, testifying that what has been recalled, relived, or remembered through representational illusion is dead, lost, or vanished. The returning image invariably designates the past from which it has come. No matter what new meaning it is made to convey in the present moment of its utterance or representation, no matter what new context it becomes part of in its new moment of time, the image perpetually emits signals from a lost, unfindable, and distant past. It announces the radical and menacing otherness of the wide gulf that death, absence, and loss excavate in the world of the living.[10]

Like a moth circling a flame in an arc of fatal fascination, the image moves in a frenetic, always circular, self-repeating pattern around the event of the past it wishes to carry back into the present. Its relent-less attempts at recuperation multiply the forms and meanings it ex-presses. This quest to repossess the past produces a proliferation of signs and an excess of meaning that seek to compensate for the inade-quacy of the representational process. The image is always impover-ished when compared to the loss it is trying to signify. The dance that representation performs around the lost object becomes all the more

---

10. A certain negativity and mortality adhere to the image or metaphor, as Eugenio Donato observes in an important essay on Flaubert's writing: "To write is to turn back towards an irrecoverable past, not so much to recover that past to try to give it presence, and permanence, but on the contrary, to bid it farewell. The moment of writing is caught in between a dead past and a dead future" (p. 10). Language "*is the metaphor of an absence*" (p. 11). The origin of language was long ago erased, but this loss forces language to search for the absent traces that may have been left when that erasure propelled it into being. Thus, a conflict arises within language between the law of metaphor and the exiled reality of language. This tension produces a representational metaphoricity, which causes language to exceed "the 'objects' or 'meanings' that it displays" (p. 12). Language nostalgically seeks an "original object," either a transcendental signifier or the truth of Being, the loss of which "constitutes its origin as primary metaphor." But language also refuses to take up the nostalgic quest and accentuates its own playfulness and the subversive unruliness of its own tropes. Thus, within language, Donato affirms, there is an "original violent play of an original displacement, of an original metaphor. . . . This original tear or wound—which could also be read as the original complicity of language and negativity, of language and death as the necessary inscription of death in language—cannot be closed or healed. Because of it language will be in a constant drift that will always mark and define a space which separates it from any possible resting place in any object or intention. The law to which metaphor subordinates language is the law of the same as different and the order of language is not one of identity and presence but of absence and difference" (p. 11). There can be no mastery over the constant play and errancy of language, despite the impossible desire of literary and philosophical discourses to dominate it, Donato writes. Ultimately, these discourses have to confront the reality of "an original loss in language that triggers the open-ended play of its representational metaphoricity" (p. 12) ("The Idioms of the *Text:* Notes on the Language of Philosophy and the Fictions of Literature," *Glyph* 2 [1977]: 1–13).

intense and desperate as the loss resists restoration. It is as if Eurydice had refused Orpheus's efforts to lead her out of the underworld, provoking him to redouble his efforts, to increase a hundredfold his words of entreaty. Faced with the event and the reality of loss, humanity has no other instrument of expression but the endlessly proliferating, always different, forever ephemeral image: sign, surrogate, and memorial for what lives no more.

The Fullness and Emptiness of Loss

Psammenitus, the king of Egypt, is captured by the king of Persia, Montaigne tells us, and forced to watch as his noble daughter becomes a slave and his son is led off to be killed. While his entourage weeps inconsolably, Psammenitus "se tint coy sans mot dire, les yeux fichez en terre" ("neither moved nor spoke a word, his eyes fixed on the ground"). But when his servant is made captive, the king's reaction changes dramatically: "il se mit à battre sa teste et mener un dueil extreme" ("he began to beat his head and manifest extreme grief"). Asked later why his reaction to the suffering of his family differed so greatly from his reaction to that of his servant, Psammenitus replies that "'ce seul dernier desplaisir se peut signifier par larmes, les deux premiers surpassans de bien loin tout moyen de se pouvoir exprimer'" ("'this last grief alone can be signified by tears; the first two far surpass any power of expression'").[11] Similarly, a Greek painter's representation of the sacrifice of Iphigenia also indicates, according to Montaigne, the ultimate inexpressibility of sorrow. The reaction of each witness to Iphigenia's death is painted differently, the faces and bodies depicted in different stages of horror, lamentation, and sadness. But in representing the grief of Iphigenia's father, the painter portrays him "le visage couvert, comme si nulle contenance ne pouvoit representer ce degré de dueil" ("with his face covered, as if no countenance could represent that degree of grief").[12]

Both of Montaigne's examples reveal the fundamental unrepresentability of deep mourning. Psammenitus and Iphigenia's father express a grief too large for words, a sorrow that only silence can adequately render. Stupefaction, speechlessness, facelessness ("le visage couvert"),

11. "De la tristesse," in *Oeuvres complètes*, Bibliothèque de la Pléiade (Paris: Gallimard, 1962), pp. 15–16 ["Of Sadness," in *The Complete Essays of Montaigne*, trans. Donald M. Frame (Stanford: Stanford University Press, 1958), p. 6].
12. Ibid., p. 16/6.

and muteness are the only signifiers for this inexpressible sadness. A loss of such monumental proportions can be translated only through the blank, the gap, the zero-degree that characterize the loss itself. The emptiness of loss is matched by the emptiness of expression on the part of the bereaved. A strange mimetic correspondence is evident here, for the unrepresentability of loss can be "shown" only by a loss of affect. It can be "represented" only by absences: by missing words, gestures, movements, expressions. What is finally "represented" is the defeat of representation. The nothing of death, having invaded the image, makes it express nothing itself. Such loss is beyond telling, beyond representing. The mimesis of loss can only generate loss itself. This explains, Montaigne continues, why Niobé, lamenting the death of her sons and daughters, is described by Ovid and others as "en fin trans-muée en rochier . . . pour exprimer cette morne, muette et sourde stupidité qui nous transit, lors que les accidens nous accablent sur-passans nostre portée" ("having been at last transformed into a rock . . . to represent the bleak, dumb, and deaf stupor that benumbs us when accidents surpassing our endurance overwhelm us").[13]

Grief effaces the body; it erases gesture, speech, and movement, immobilizing the face, hands, and limbs. One becomes one's loss in the sense that one begins to incarnate that loss, to take on its character of absence, numbness, and emptiness. The survivor mimes the quality of the loss he has witnessed. He is filled by it in such a way that his identity no longer belongs to him but to the lack he is experiencing. He barely lives, breathes, thinks, or feels. He is hollowed out by the death for which he grieves, but in such a way that the interior emptiness is immediately filled with loss itself. Herein lies the paradox of loss. It is an emptiness of such vast magnitude, a lack of such great proportion, an absence of such irreversibility that it has the reality, the *thereness*, of a presence. It is an absence that takes over one's entire being. One comes to live it until one is united with it. Loss even comes to take on a body of its very own, for it seems to inhabit, to find a place of dwelling, in the body of the one it afflicts. If "for a man who no longer has a homeland, writing becomes a place to live," as Theodor Adorno said,[14] then for a man or woman who has lost a loved one, grief becomes a place to dwell, a space in which to experience the fullness of what has been lost.

Mourning encourages and nourishes the afterlife of the lost being who has died. It commemorates the dead person by giving her a new

13. Ibid., p. 16/7.
14. *Minima Moralia: Reflections from Damaged Life*, trans. E.F.N. Jephcott (London: NLB, 1974), p. 87.

body in which to continue her existence. The body of the mourner becomes the expression and embodiment of the dead person, whose identity now coincides with that of the bereaved. By her actions, movements, and gestures, the mourner designates a lost being whose death has suddenly come to determine her own life and for whom in the world of the living she is now the unique sign. The mourner is dominated by a grief that makes the dead person as fully present as the plenitude of the loss itself will permit. Everything about the person and the body of the mourner signifies the presence of loss at its fullest. Mourning runs to excess because it strives to be a plenitude, to represent, by the intensity of an expressed grief, the absence that has suddenly occurred. It is mimetic in the sense that mourning strives to substitute the fullness of a present grief for the lost plenitude of an absent being. Thus does loss come to find a place of habitation in the here and now of existence. What we have lost defines us. And that identity, marked by the vestiges of absence and lack, is the history of a survival, the history of what is left behind.

Loss may be beyond telling in that the object of loss cannot be fully represented; but grief for that loss is its sign. Emptiness becomes *significant*. The silence of grief that Montaigne describes in Psammenitus, in Iphigenia's father, and in Niobé is, literally, a *telling* silence; it speaks volumes. While loss may be felt as beyond telling, grief is not. It is the way that loss speaks. The emptiness left by the absence of a beloved is filled with the grief that loss creates. Mourning is the legacy of loss, and in the wake of this vacancy and depletion comes the fullness of grief, as Constance, mourning the imminent loss of her imprisoned son, eloquently observes in Shakespeare's *King John:*

> Therefore never, never
> Must I behold my pretty Arthur more.
> .   .   .   .   .
> Grief fills the room up of my absent child,
> Lies in his bed, walks up and down with me,
> Puts on his pretty looks, repeats his words,
> Remembers me of all his gracious parts,
> Stuffs out his vacant garments with his form;
> Then have I reason to be fond of Grief.
> Fare you well. Had you such a loss as I,
> I could give better comfort than you do.
> I will not keep this form upon my head
> When there is such disorder in my wit.

O Lord! My boy, my Arthur, my fair son!
My life, my joy, my food, my all the world!
My widow-comfort, and my sorrows' cure!

(3.4.88–105)

Grief concretely and physically replaces the lost object of love; it becomes its surrogate. Constance's new child is grief itself cast in her son's image. It takes on his appearance, speaks his words, wears his clothes. The emptiness of Arthur's absence is occupied and filled in by the grief it has caused; mourning "Stuffs out his vacant garments with his form." It is the child's new body. In Constance's melancholic imagination, so completely identified is the child with the reality of loss that to think of her son Arthur is to think of Arthur-as-absent. Grief is his new incarnation, as it is Constance's new identity. She has herself become coterminous with her mourning; her being is penetrated through and through by her loss.[15]

The Writing of Loss

What is the relationship between an event or experience of loss and its description in language? If it is true that the meanings and nuances

---

15. On the power of mourning to represent excessively the vacancy of loss and on the nature of grief to be at once a fullness and an emptiness, see chapter 2 below. The intensity of Constance's identification with her grief, provoking her to imagine that loss is now the child she nurtures, contrasts sharply with elegies in which a poet expresses the fear of losing intimacy with his or her grief. The desire to hold onto one's mourning is great because it supports a continuing relationship with the lost other. There is concern that in the course of passing time, as the feeling of intense loss abates, the presence of the lost other and the immediacy of his or her absence will vanish. In his elegy "Old Hat," Brad Leithauser writes about the effort to resist what in the wake of the death of a loved person is yet a second loss—the fading away of memory and mourning:

It was like you, so considerate a man,
to have your papers in order, to leave
your belongings neat; while compelled to grieve,
we were spared the hard, niggling tasks that can
clutter and spoil grief. Yet not even you
understood how a mere cap on its hook,
companion on those outings you still took,
would hang so heavily now for those who,

like you, would keep a tidy house. We've tried
to sort your things, but where are we to hide
those in which some living threads remain?
What we want is to store such things outside
the slow, spiraling loss of love and pain
that turns you, day by day, into a stranger.

(*Hundreds of Fireflies* [New York: Alfred A. Knopf, 1982], p. 62)

of a poem may be lost in translation, is it equally true that all attempts at representation suffer from a similar loss and that metaphors and figures, elegies and threnodies do not have the power to recuperate or evoke the lost presence of being?[16] What can it mean to "write" loss when it is possible that loss may be fundamentally unwritable, resistant to the language that searches to encompass and express it? What, then, is the role of language when confronted by the extremities of human experience?

In Elizabeth Bishop's poem "The End of March" the narrator and some friends are walking along a beach, when suddenly they come upon a strange and intriguing series of traces:

> We came on
> lengths and lengths, endless, of wet white string,
> looping up to the tide-line, down to the water,
> over and over. Finally, they did end:
> a thick white snarl, man-size, awash,
> rising on every wave, a sodden ghost,
> falling back, sodden, giving up the ghost . . .
> A kite string?—But no kite.[17]

The narrator and her companions search for the source of the string. They follow the trail left by the meandering lengths in the sand and by the wet coils bobbing in the waves, until they come to the beginning, or the end, of the string. But there is no enlightenment in this discovery; something is still lacking: namely, the object to which the string was once attached. What the poet and her friends have discovered is the absence that lies at the end of figuration. They have been following the trail of a kind of writing inscribed by accident on the shoreline of a beach. They find the trace (a complex one with convoluted and overlapping lines, swerving arcs, concentrated knots) of an absence. Like writing, the lengths, turns, and strands of the kite string weave back and forth across a white surface—running free here, snarling there,

---

16. On the history and poetics of the elegy as a genre, see Peter M. Sacks's excellent book *The English Elegy: Studies in the Genre from Spenser to Yeats* (Baltimore: Johns Hopkins University Press, 1985). More than a detailed description of the genre, Sacks's study examines the connections between language and the pathos of human consciousness, analyzing the ways the forms of elegy relate to experiences of loss and consolation. In particular, see the opening chapter (pp. 1–37) on elegy and the work of mourning, which discusses the conventions of the genre and, more important, its mythopoetic, psychoanalytic, and ritualistic dimensions.

17. *The Complete Poems, 1927–1979* (New York: Farrar, Straus and Giroux, 1979), p. 179.

almost lifelike and human in size, yet more ghostlike than real—whose only function is to designate the missing origin, and the raison d'être, of its existence: namely, the lost kite. As the poem makes clear, writing is a trail of lines which finally loses the subject it "carries," or lets fly in the air. Writing leads to interruption, to a tearing away, to a broken end. It is attached to something lost whose reality can only be known by the void, lack, or absence it leaves behind. As the absent kite is signified by the coils and loops of string that once had tied it to a certain earthly presence, so the language of a poem—weaving, running, turning, meandering, performing an acrobatics of figuration on the white space of a page—signifies a lost experience it tries to recall and recapture, but that it can only evoke as a lack.

Writing is the "presentification" of absence. On the one hand, there are the kite string and the poem, present in the here and now of a representation; they can be touched, picked up, examined, unsnarled, uncoiled. On the other, there is the kite, the lost referent, the absent object, without which the poem, the *string* of words, would not have existed. As the string still continues to "look up to" the kite lost somewhere in the sky, so the poem continues literally to designate the absent experience lost somewhere in the past that its presence as writing commemorates, signifies, and, finally, mourns. Words give form and shape to absence, as the kite string makes present the emptiness at its end.

For Bishop, a poem is a representation of loss. Like the kite string, poetry is a vestige, a trace. It is that which is left behind in place of an absent person, object, or event. It both remembers and mourns. Poetic representation does not for Bishop offer the consolation of a full return of the past or the repossession of the presence of a lost moment. Yet her poetry is most definitely informed by faith in the power of memory to recall what has been lost. In "Poem," for example, she describes a small painting of the Nova Scotia landscape made by a great-uncle she never knew: "Useless and free, it has spent seventy years / as a minor family relic / handed along collaterally to owners / who looked at it sometimes, or didn't bother to." Bishop is struck by the coincidence between her own childhood memory of the scene ("Heavens, I recognize the place, I know it!") and her great-uncle's much earlier perception of it:

> Life and the memory of it cramped,
> dim, on a piece of Bristol board,
> dim, but how live, how touching in detail

—the little that we get for free,
the little of our earthly trust. Not much.[18]

Bishop is aware that what is rescued from the loss of the past is not very significant, that it is "the little" and the "not much" that our living in the world ultimately leaves us. But this legacy is sufficient to make a poem. The "little" and "not much" of memory are the "enough" from which a poem or painting can be made; they allow for a certain possession of the world. Nevertheless, her great-uncle's representation as well as her own poem exist only an inch or two away from nothingness and insignificance. They only barely salvage an image from the passing of time. Knowing how to represent things in painting and poetry involves, Bishop suggests, a mastery of the art of losing. Writing is always the writing of loss. It is the inscribing and circumscribing of the losses and absences of human life by means of a precarious form that is only barely able to encompass them, as Bishop makes so vividly clear in the beautiful villanelle "One Art":

The art of losing isn't hard to master;
so many things seem filled with the intent
to be lost that their loss is no disaster.

Lose something every day. Accept the fluster
of lost door keys, the hour badly spent.
The art of losing isn't hard to master.

Then practice losing farther, losing faster:
places, and names, and where it was you meant
to travel. None of these will bring disaster.

I lost my mother's watch. And look! my last, or
next-to-last, of three loved houses went.
The art of losing isn't hard to master.

I lost two cities, lovely ones. And, vaster,
some realms I owned, two rivers, a continent.
I miss them, but it wasn't a disaster.

—Even losing you (the joking voice, a gesture

18. Ibid., pp. 176 and 177, respectively.

I love) I shan't have lied. It's evident
the art of losing's not too hard to master
though it may look like (*Write* it!) like disaster.[19]

Loss haunts the poet's life. It is the art at which she is particularly
talented, one perfected by many years of practice. In "One Art" Bishop
presents herself as a virtuoso of losing, giving master classes in her art,
offering advice and instruction. "Lose something every day," she coun-
sels. "Accept the fluster" of lost things, and then "practice losing farther, losing faster." Mastery of the art of loss is essential. But the poem's
irony conceals the truth that we are all good at losing because we have
to be. The poem's refrain is indeed true: "The art of losing isn't hard to
master." Survivors are by nature and by necessity masters at the art of
losing. Having overcome the absence and separation of a loss attenu-
ates the disaster. Through the competing rhymes of "master-disaster,"
which orient this formally complex poem, Bishop oscillates between
the extremes of order and chaos, the human and the nonhuman, the
controllable and the uncontrollable, life and death, to assert the power
of men and women to remember and survive their losses.

Loss is what surrounds and penetrates human life. Things seem
made and born for loss: they are, Bishop writes, "filled with the intent /
to be lost." The catalogue of losses the poet herself has experienced is
long: objects, hours, places, names, roads not traveled, a watch, loved
houses, cities, rivers, continents. In the final stanza, however, it is not a
thing or a place that is perceived as absent, but a loved person. No
longer is the disaster of loss as confidently negated as it had been in earlier stanzas. The mastery is less sure. The refrain is slightly changed; it
is introduced by an all too confident and overcompensating "It's evident. . . ." More important, for the first time in the poem the word
"disaster" is not accompanied by a neighboring negative. Whereas
earlier stanzas negated the connection between loss and disaster by
asserting that "loss is no disaster" (stanza 1), or "None of these will
bring disaster" (stanza 3), or "it wasn't a disaster" (stanza 5), the last line
of the final strophe abandons negation. It withdraws ever so slightly
from asserting the difference between loss and disaster and moves
(through simile) toward the affirmation of a possible resemblance: "the
art of losing's not too hard to master / though it may look like (*Write* it!)
like disaster." Although loss may seem like a disaster, may resemble a
disaster, may even have the form of disaster, Bishop subtly and paren-

19. Ibid., p. 178.

thetically asserts that the writing of loss may neutralize it, may prevent it from descending into the total nonbeing and nothingness of catastrophe. Writing is an act of survivorship; it is what the survivor does in order to keep on going, to understand what has happened in his or her life, and to give form, shape, and sound to the pain of losing. The experience itself is a disaster until it is transformed into words, until the sorrow and pain are expressed in a representation, an image, a figure that name and speak the loss. In the poem's last line, what the poet fears may be a disaster, may even "look like . . . like disaster," is suddenly interrupted by the italicized, exclamatory, although parenthetical, presence of writing: "(*Write* it!)," she commands. Through an act of writing, whereby images, metaphors, analogies, and other forms are found to express an event of catastrophic proportions, what had looked like disaster, Bishop suggests, is suddenly transformed into the mastery of art.

Yet, this transformation is neither all that easy an accomplishment nor all that permanent a triumph; it poses a serious challenge to the poet. The writing of the pain of loss, the mastering of it, is a constant struggle. Bishop's command—"(*Write* it!)"—cuts two ways. It holds out the promise of mastery through writing, but it also suggests that such mastery, when compared to the vastness of loss, is no more than mere writing, the tracing of letters on sand. There is loss and the art of losing, on the one hand, and the art of telling about that loss, of writing it, of "italicizing" it, on the other. For Bishop, however, the two arts go hand in hand, the way "master" and "disaster" alternate with such ease in her poem. She does not imagine that artistic representation could ever eclipse the event of loss; rather, she envisions art and loss working together. Through art, disaster is temporarily mastered, although its reality is never effaced or forgotten. The rhyming words of the villanelle thus resound with the rhyme of being.[20]

20. Similarly, in Bishop's lyrical, semi-autobiographical story "In the Village," the struggle between the experience of disaster and the art of a master is expressed through the conflict in a child's imagination between the piercing scream of a mad mother and the rhythmic clang of a blacksmith's hammer—between a disordered, destructive, uncontrollable wail and a beautiful, creative, world-ordering sound, which momentarily dominates the Nova Scotian landscape and silences the din of loss echoing in the child's memory:

Clang.
Clang.
Nate is shaping a horseshoe.
Oh, beautiful pure sound!
It turns everything else to silence.
. . . . .

Writing is loss as it comes to exist in another form. Supporting and nourishing the poetic representation is the never-forgotten catastrophe that has engendered it. Loss is present in the poem as its origin. Transformed by writing, it is no longer *experienced* as the disaster it once was, but rather *remembered* as an event of separation and void. Writing moves the poet from the immediacy of perception to the mediacy of memory. For Bishop, poetry and loss are, as the poem's title states, "One Art." The *art* of the art of losing commemorates loss and recalls its vacant darkness. Writing reverberates with the long-echoing thunder of the lightning of disastrous change, the rumblings of the emptiness of loss continuing to resound in the fullness of language.[21]

"One Art," as well as Bishop's moving short story "In the Village," make clear that an event of loss leaves an indelible trace across the landscape of a life, that it cuts a swathe through the space of memory. Loss echoes down through the seasons of one's existence. The aftershocks, after-sounds, and after-images, characterizing the life of the survivor who outlives the loss, mark the passage of hours, days, and years with their presence. All signs point back to an *ur*-event, for loss is indeed the origin. This is clear in the mother's scream, which hangs

---

Now there is no scream. Once there was one and it settled slowly down to earth one hot summer afternoon; or did it float up, into that dark, too dark, blue sky? But surely it has gone away, forever.
It sounds like a bell buoy out at sea.
It is the elements speaking: earth, air, fire, water.
All those other things—clothes, crumbling postcards, broken china; things damaged and lost, sickened or destroyed, even the frail almost-lost scream—are they too frail for us to hear their voices long, too mortal?
Nate!
Oh, beautiful sound, strike again!
            (*The Collected Prose*, ed. Robert Giroux [New York: Farrar, Straus and
                                                    Giroux, 1984], p. 274)

The blacksmith's clang is the sound of artistry, skill, and manual labor momentarily drowning out the screams of past losses, absorbing them into its own pure music, but never totally dominating them. The control over formlessness, the triumph over disorder, the craft and labor of the hand, in which blacksmith, dressmaker (the mother's scream comes during the fitting of a dress), and writer excel, assist them in their struggle with the darkness of the mother's world. The hand that hammers, sews, and writes struggles to transform absence into presence, pain into beauty, and loss into art. The world of "things damaged and lost, sickened or destroyed" is replaced for a brief moment by the tentative mastery of a fiction, by the "clang" of writing.

21. For interesting discussions of loss in Bishop's work, see David Kalstone's "Elizabeth Bishop: Questions of Memory, Questions of Travel," in his *Five Temperaments* (New York: Oxford University Press, 1977), pp. 12–40; Bonnie Costello, "The Impersonal and the Interrogative in the Poetry of Elizabeth Bishop," in *Elizabeth Bishop and Her Art*, ed. Lloyd Schwartz and Sybil P. Estess (Ann Arbor: University of Michigan Press, 1983), pp. 109–32; and Lloyd Schwartz, "One Art: The Poetry of Elizabeth Bishop, 1971–1976," in *Elizabeth Bishop and Her Art*, pp. 133–53.

over the Nova Scotian landscape in Bishop's "In the Village." It flows into the nooks and crannies of the countryside as it seeps into the recesses and folds of the narrator's memory; it is "a slight stain in those pure blue skies." It is there, and yet it is not there: "No one hears it; it hangs there forever."[22] It is both a presence that is absent and an absence that is present. As such, it resembles a delicate set of china teacups, which fascinate the child in the story. On the side of each cup are tiny, pale-blue windows made from grains of rice, which in the firing process have disintegrated, leaving behind the traces of what are exquisite empty spaces. "Could you poke the grains out?" the child asks her grandmother. "No, it seems they aren't really there any more," she answers. "They were put there just for a while and then they left something or other behind" (p. 256). From the lost, invisible grains of rice, a trace, a stain, a "something or other" remain. A blank space survives as evidence that a loss has occurred but at the same time as an affirmation that something beautiful has been created from this loss. The grains of rice are present in their very absence, and present in a way that manifests the delicate beauty created by that absence. The grains of rice cannot be seen; only an imprint, a trace, is visible. The thing is gone, but its after-image survives, exactly as formed by the loss that was its cause. "It is the image in the mind," writes Colette, "that links us to our lost treasures; but it is the loss that shapes the image, gathers the flowers, weaves the garland."[23]

---

22. *The Collected Prose*, p. 251; page references are hereafter cited in the text.

23. *Mes Apprentissages*, quoted in *In the Midst of Winter: Selections from the Literature of Mourning*, ed. Mary Jane Moffat (New York: Vintage Books, 1982), p. 193. ("Nous tenons par une image aux biens évanouis, mais c'est l'arrachement qui forme l'image, assemble, noue le bouquet," in Colette, *Oeuvres*, 3 vols. [Paris: Flammarion, 1960], 3:427.) A striking image of the spatialization of loss and the imprinting of absences is found in Georges Perec's novel *La Vie, mode d'emploi* (Paris: Hachette, 1978) [*Life: A User's Manual*, trans. David Bellos (Boston: David R. Godine, 1987)]. It concerns a "cluster of coral," a calcified residue, produced when Grifalconi, a cabinetmaker, injects a liquid solution of lead, alum, and asbestos fibers into the tunnels that termites have bored in the base of an old wooden table. Removing the wood that remains, Grifalconi discovers

> cette fantastique arborescence, trace exacte de ce qu'avait été la vie du ver dans ce morceau de bois, superposition immobile, minérale, de tous les mouvements qui avaient constitué son existence aveugle, cette obstination unique, cet itinéraire opiniâtre, cette matérialisation fidèle de tout ce qu'il avait mangé et digéré, arrachant à la compacité du monde alentour les imperceptibles éléments néces-saires à sa survie, image étalée, visible, incommensurablement troublante de ce cheminement sans fin qui avait réduit le bois le plus dur en un réseau impalpable de galeries pulvérulentes.

> [the fabulous arborescence within, this exact record of the worms' life inside the wooden mass: a static, mineral accumulation of all the movements that had constituted their blind existence, their undeviating single-mindedness, their obsti-

The Poetics of Presence and Absence

The art of mastering loss is a schizophrenic art: on the one hand, there is mastery; on the other, loss. One feels two contradictory emotions, because presence and absence in an absolute sense clash. They coexist in a stubborn confrontation, neither giving ground to the other. There is no synthesis of or resolution to their antagonism. As image, the lost person is present, but as living being he or she is absent. The lost object is enveloped in the coincidence of absence-presence. Whether one gives the upper-hand to art ("mastery," in Bishop's terms) or to loss (what she calls "disaster") depends on how one unconsciously perceives the contest. It depends on whether one believes in an ideology that places faith in the recuperative power of art and language to recall what has vanished, or whether one accepts an ideology that refuses to see strategies of figuration as anything but fictions, masking—behind illusory myths of wholeness, coherence, and totalization—the reality of the lack upon which all representation rests.

Both the lost being and its surrogate, whether a representation, an image, or a metaphor, coexist. Every work of art and of literature forces a confrontation between absence and presence. The work exists in order to make present certain formal and aesthetic realities (words, images, colors, forms), whose existence is possible only because what they designate is absent. Every work is established on this contradiction: namely, that the compelling, self-centered brilliance of a text blots out the world to which it refers; that the full expression of a painting is only a different and inadequate representation of the artist's original perception; that a word only partially names what is ultimately unnameable; and that a metaphor figures an absence that no artistic imagination can shape into a true presence. Because it is established on lack, every representation is invariably *other* than the world or the

---

nate itineraries; the faithful materialisation of all they had eaten and digested as they forced from their dense surroundings the invisible elements needed for their survival, the explicit, visible, immeasurably disturbing image of the endless progressions that had reduced the hardest of woods to an impalpable network of crumbling galleries.] (P. 163/123)

Salvaged from the table is the trace of lost life, now transformed into a palpable, visible substance, into the matter of loss itself. Lack becomes an object. Emptiness is preserved in the fullness of its vacancy. Of loss itself, nothing has been lost. Absence becomes present as absence. Allegorically, Perec's image reveals the way language preserves both the form and the fact of loss. Injected into the experiences of deprivation, despair, and death, language, as it solidifies, takes on the very shape of what is no longer present. Molded by loss, language becomes its ossified residue, its unique trace, its one and only sign.

experience to which it refers. Despite the "being-thereness" of its self-presentation, the presence of its textuality and rhetoricity, or the immediacy of its painterliness, the representation designates an absence, which, despite its efforts, it never succeeds in transforming into a presence. The representation lies on the other side of existence, separated from it by the passage of time and by forgetfulness, loss, and belatedness.

In giving presence to images and metaphors, language points to its own inadequacy at ever being able to express the void of absence. The contradiction lies in the hopeless trap of our having no other means by which to refer to events of absence and loss other than the words and images we must use. Mediation and the metaphoricity that accompanies it are a curse. We are hounded by failure because we must always speak by analogy: that is, imprecisely, imperfectly, and indeterminately. But traditional theories of language do not recognize the inadequacy of linguistic or artistic signification. Metaphor has often been perceived as having the power to recuperate a fixed and stable set of meanings. It views language as "a means towards a recovered presence that transcends language itself," as Paul de Man has argued.[24] Against metaphor, de Man poses the *figure*, which is the tropological mode of loss. Through figuration, the nature of loss as that which is unrecoverable and unrepresentable is respected. Unlike the metaphor, which strives to recover what is absent, the figure expresses loss by its acceptance of the very loss of referentiality that gives the figure its existence; it reveals the void that informs its own structure and identity. It internalizes loss as its very mode of being. Thus, the figure, according to de Man, "designates the impossibility for the language of poetry to appropriate anything, be it as consciousness, as object, or as a synthesis of both."[25] The loss of reference and the new primacy given to rhetoricity are liberating, because figuration "triggers the play of rhetorical reversals and allows them the freedom of their play without being hampered by the referential constraints of meaning."[26] Moreover, the experiences that the poet may wish to convert into figures must already contain a void or lack.[27] They must be made ready for figuration by the experience of loss.

To see how the figuration of loss can occur in a manner that pre-

24. *Allegories of Reading: Figural Language in Rousseau, Nietzsche, Rilke, and Proust* (New Haven: Yale University Press, 1979), p. 46.
25. Ibid., p. 47.
26. Ibid.
27. Ibid., p. 50.

serves the essential reality of the loss and that protects it from being swept away in a cascade of metaphors, it is instructive to examine the passage from Proust's *Sodome et Gomorrhe* in which the narrator, suddenly remembering his dead grandmother, is overwhelmed by grief. What strikes Marcel is the gulf between the present of his remembering and the past of his loss. A struggle is waged in his consciousness between fantasies of recuperation and restoration, on the one hand, and the painful realities of deprivation and lack, on the other. Marcel suffers from the contradiction that the coincidence of absence and presence initiates. Proust represents the equilibrium between possession and loss by describing the relationship between the presence of the grandmother, as reexperienced in the narrator's memory, and her real absence, as acknowledged by his consciousness.

On the first night of his return to Balbec, Marcel, while unbuttoning his shoes, is suddenly swept away by the memory of his grandmother undressing him as a child on the first evening of his last visit to Balbec so very long ago. The longing for his grandmother, mixed with memories of her love and tenderness, makes him sob uncontrollably, his first real acknowledgment and acceptance of her death. The act of rediscovering and repossessing the fullness of the past through memory occurs simultaneously with the recognition that this past is lost forever. Presence and absence coincide cruelly, as do intimacy and distance, plenitude and void. Marcel's desire brings together the illusion of mnemonic recuperation and the irrefutable reality of loss, but in such a way that the feeling of repossession fights to repress the recognition of loss, overwhelming it with an excessive (and phantasmatic) sense of immediacy and intimacy. The intensity of the memory is so strong that Marcel reexperiences the events of the past as a presence so real and authentic that he fantasizes being a child held in his grandmother's arms. Against this hallucinatory presence, the reality of loss struggles to gain the upper hand; it fights not to be forgotten in this moment of fictive restoration which memory and desire have created:

> Je me rappelais comme, une heure avant le moment où ma grand'mère s'était penchée ainsi dans sa robe de chambre vers mes bottines, errant dans la rue étouffante de chaleur, devant le pâtissier, j'avais cru que je ne pourrais jamais, dans le besoin que j'avais de l'embrasser, attendre l'heure qu'il me fallait encore passer sans elle. Et maintenant que ce même besoin renaissait, je savais que je pouvais attendre des heures après des heures, qu'elle ne serait plus jamais auprès de moi, je ne faisais que de le découvrir parce que je venais, en

la sentant, pour la première fois, vivante, véritable, gonflant mon
coeur à le briser, en la retrouvant enfin, d'apprendre que je l'avais
perdue pour toujours. Perdue pour toujours.[28]

[I remembered how, an hour before the moment when my grandmother had stooped in her dressing-gown to unfasten my boots, as I
wandered along the stiflingly hot street, past the pastry-cook's, I had
felt that I could never, in my need to feel her arms round me, live
through the hour that I had still to spend without her. And now that
this same need had reawakened, I knew that I might wait hour after
hour, that she would never again be by my side. I had only just
discovered this because I had only just, on feeling her for the first
time alive, real, making my heart swell to breaking-point, on finding
her at last, learned that I had lost her for ever. Lost for ever.]

Proust describes the simultaneity of presence and absence, in particular the way the two phenomena overlap and coincide. Marcel discovers at the very moment that he feels most close to recovering the
presence of his grandmother—"en la sentant, pour la première fois,
vivante, véritable, gonflant mon coeur à le briser, en la retrouvant
enfin" ("on feeling her for the first time alive, real, making my heart
swell to breaking-point, on finding her at last")—that she is lost forever
("perdue pour toujours"). Marcel remembers how difficult it was for
him as a child to wait a mere hour to embrace his grandmother. Little
did he realize then that one hour of waiting would expand to become
an infinity of hours. The child's anticipation and desire are oriented
toward the future; all that had separated him from a moment of bliss
and intimacy had been one hour. But for the adult Marcel the same act
of unbuttoning his shoes, which has triggered the memory of the
childhood scene and has rekindled a similar need for intimacy with the
grandmother, has now lost its futurity. His desire can move only backward, not across the short span of sixty minutes, but across a wide,
unbridgeable gulf of thousands of empty hours. What had been the
child's joyful anticipation of an imminent future has now become the
adult's doleful regret of a distant and lost past. Prospective desire has
now become retrospective and impossible to satisfy, because the only
person able to fulfill it is dead. Between the adult Marcel and the

28. *A la recherche du temps perdu*, 3 vols., Bibliothèque de la Pléiade (Paris: Gallimard,
1954), 2:757–58 [*Remembrance of Things Past, 2: The Guermantes Way, Cities of the Plain*,
trans. C. K. Scott Moncrieff and Terence Kilmartin (New York: Random House, 1981),
p. 785]; page numbers are hereafter cited in the text.

grandmother lies a gulf of irreversible pastness. The child's desire, which had only to wait a short while to be satisfied, although it may have seemed an eternity, has turned into a truly eternal longing, which will never be fulfilled or, conversely, which can be fulfilled only in imaginary ways through the fantasizing mechanisms of desire.

Linking together these two moments and these two different desires is an act of unbuttoning. The whole scene unravels at the moment Marcel touches his shoe: "Mais à peine eus-je touché le premier bouton de ma bottine, ma poitrine s'enfla, remplie d'une présence inconnue, divine, des sanglots me secouèrent, des larmes ruisselèrent de mes yeux" ("But scarcely had I touched the topmost button than my chest swelled, filled with an unknown, a divine presence, I was shaken with sobs, tears streamed from my eyes"; 2:755/783). But he touches more than his shoe; it is the whole process of mourning that is unbuttoned here. An object opens the past, revealing an unexpressed grief over the loss of that past. The shoe expresses metonymically the lost presence of the grandmother. It returns the grandmother to reality but only as memory. It touches her again, as she had at one time touched it. Within the present it embodies her. But because it is only Marcel who can now unbutton this past, it represents a grief he can share with no other person.

Through the medium or agency of the shoe button the grand-mother is present as memory and as sorrow. As memory, she can be re-visualized as she was in the narrator's childhood. As grief, she reinhab-its the space of the narrator's adulthood; she becomes the expression of her loss, her absence speaking through Marcel's sorrow. Through his mourning, he gives her body and substance, for he has two very different images of his grandmother: one, the image of a recovered presence; the other, the image of an irreversible lack. In both instances, an excessive representation gives meaning to the lost woman. Both the memory and grief are overdetermined in the sense that it is through the excessiveness of remembering or of mourning that Marcel tries to restore a feeling of closeness to his grandmother.

It is this difficulty in understanding the juxtaposition or, as he calls it, the "contradiction" of fullness and emptiness, of presence and ab-sence—"that contradiction of survival and annihilation, so strangely intertwined within me"; "the agonizing synthesis of survival and an-nihilation, once more reformed"; "that incomprehensible contradic-tion between memory and non-existence" (2:759/786; 760/787; 769/796)—that most troubles Marcel. Most painful of all is his experience of the coincidence of familiarity and strangeness: the intimacy with the grandmother transformed into an alienated and distant reality. Proust's understanding of the devastation of loss reveals the schizophrenic nature of the experience: one remembers a closeness to someone who has become alien; one feels tenderness toward someone who, having by death been robbed of all sensation and feeling, no longer responds. For the survivor that Marcel has become the realization of the juxtaposition of light and shadow, of living and dying, of past and present, of memory and nothingness, of presence and absence, of person and image, darkens the very site of his existence. He has come face to face with the nonbeing that loss declares:

Je ne pouvais comprendre, et je m'exerçais à subir la souffrance de cette contradiction: d'une part, une existence, une tendresse, survivantes en moi telles que je les avais connues, c'est-à-dire faites pour moi, un amour où tout trouvait tellement en moi son complément, son but, sa constante direction, que le génie de grands hommes, tous les génies qui avaient pu exister depuis le commencement du monde n'eussent pas valu pour ma grand'mère un seul de mes défauts; et d'autre part, aussitôt que j'avais revécu, comme présente, cette félicité, la sentir traversée par la certitude, s'élançant comme une douleur physique à répétition, d'un néant qui avait effacé mon image de cette tendresse, qui avait détruit cette existence, aboli rétrospectivement notre mutuelle prédestination, fait de ma grand'mère, au moment où je la retrouvais comme dans un miroir, une simple étrangère qu'un hasard a fait passer quelques années auprès de moi, comme cela aurait pu être auprès de tout autre, mais pour qui, avant et après, je n'étais rien, je ne serais rien.

[I could not understand, and I struggled to endure the anguish of this contradiction: on the one hand an existence, a tenderness, surviving in me as I had known them, that is to say created for me, a love which found in me so totally its complement, its goal, its constant lodestar, that the genius of great men, all the genius that might have existed from the beginning of the world, would have been less precious to my grandmother than a single one of my defects; and on the other hand, as soon as I had relived that bliss, as though it were present, feeling it shot through by the certainty, throbbing like a recurrent pain, of an annihilation that had effaced my image of that tenderness, had destroyed that existence, retrospectively abolished our mutual predestination, made of my grandmother, at the moment when I had found her again as in a mirror, a mere stranger whom chance had allowed to spend a few years with me, as she might have done with anyone else, but to whom, before and after those years, I was and would be nothing.] (2:758/785)

The narrator's narcissistic interiorization of the grandmother through memory, by which she becomes so fused and identified with his being that to see her is also to see his own reflection ("au moment où je la retrouvais comme dans un miroir"), enables the grandmother's image to survive as an immediate presence. Her image is restored, made complete and whole, by his desire: "tout trouvait tellement en moi son complément, son but, sa constante direction" ("a love which found in me so totally its complement, its goal, its constant lodestar"), he writes. More intense still in this fantasy of an internalized and permanent presence is the narrator's desire, so vital to his narcissism, that he continue to occupy the center of the doting grandmother's world. But this is only one pole of the "contradiction" of loss. For on the other side of the presence that memory and desire construct, on the side of grief and loss, lies the image of the grandmother as effaced, abolished, destroyed, and foreign. Where there had been interiorization, now there is exteriorization. Where once he had felt the return of intimacy with the grandmother, he now feels only her distance, strangeness, and radical otherness. No longer is he the alpha and omega of her universe. The certainty of *le néant* has abolished her image and his own narcissistic desire to live a totalized, unified relationship with her. She has lost her uniqueness as a being related to him. Her ties to him are severed. She is an anonymous stranger with whom he was brought into contact by mere chance, because, Marcel reasons, she could have just as easily been a grandmother to any other little boy. Her uniqueness as a loving relation and her essentiality as *his* grandmother are abolished. He has truly lost possession of her. The loss of the grandmother, then, is a loss of his own identity, or at least that part of his being that was tied to hers. In contrast to his having been everything to her, and her having become internalized in his being, he now finds that he is nothing ("je n'étais rien, je ne serais rien"). He mourns, thus, not only her passing but also his own: the loss of that closeness to a loved being, that undivided oneness with the other, which had shaped and formed his own individuality. To mourn the loss of the other is also to mourn the loss of the self.

As the presence of the other defines who we are, so does the absence of that other. In the "afterward" that death initiates and mourning realizes, everything is different. The loss of the grandmother, which

Marcel mourns for the first time during his visit to Balbec, forces him to live in a state of otherness. Even Balbec is different. Strolling in the parks or walking along the beach, Marcel looks at a landscape whose beauty is hollowed out by lack. Even the shimmering, crashing waves, which his grandmother once loved to watch, speak of loss:

> L'image nouvelle de leur beauté indifférente se complétait aussitôt par l'idée qu'elle ne les voyait pas; j'aurais voulu boucher mes oreilles à leur bruit, car maintenant la plénitude lumineuse de la plage creusait un vide dans mon coeur.

> [The fresh image of their heedless beauty was at once supplemented by the thought that she could not see them; I should have liked to stop my ears against their sound, for now the luminous plenitude of the beach carved out an emptiness in my heart.] (2:762/789)

The plenitude of this image, like the fully present memory of the grandmother, is undone by the reality of loss. Presence seeps away through the fissures and holes that death opens in existence. Everything Marcel sees, feels, or lives whispers to him—as it once did when, as a child, he had lost the grandmother in the alleys of a public garden—that "'Nous ne l'avons pas vue'" ("'We haven't seen her'"; 2:762/790). The doubleness of Proust's vision keeps in focus the two aspects of the experience of loss: first, as a presence restored through memory but always remaining other than what it once had been; second, as an irreversible absence enveloping memory with the indelible signs of lack and otherness. Either as presence or absence, loss invariably makes what is remembered and mourned fatally different.

The Interpretation of Loss

If writing expresses the loss of its origin and the unrecoverability of the fullness of its referent, if it ultimately fails to coincide with the world it expresses, if it looks from afar into the promised land of presence but can never cross the frontier, if it is in mourning for an immediacy of life and experience it can never possess, and if it replaces the lost object it cannot represent with the very language of its grief, then what relationship exists between writing and the discourses of criticism which surround, confront, and interpret it? How can interpretation take possession of a writing that avoids taking hold of anything, except perhaps its own decentered, indeterminate movement away from possession? Can criticism wrest meaning from the loss of meaning? Can it transform into presence what in writing is ultimately absence? What lies beyond the reach of interpretation and, conversely, what is within its grasp? How, finally, is one to interpret the writing of loss?

Certainly, one could answer, "With more writing." Loss frees texts from referentiality. It opens them to the proliferation of figures, images, and meanings, all equally able to stand in for one another. Loss foregrounds the endlessness and the excess of interpretation, because what is lost, since it can neither be replaced nor recovered, provokes an excessive questioning and an unending search for meaning. In an effort to understand what has been lost, the critic returns repeatedly, sometimes obsessively, to the "hole in the real" that loss has opened. The intractability of the loss, its resistance to representation, its rejection of strategies of compensation and consolation, and its irreducibility and unrecoverability produce an endless stream of signs. Because the hole in the real is bottomless, this cascade of writing falls into a void, which, because it can never be filled, intensifies the demand for more and more writing.

Every work hides something that it keeps silent, that it leaves unspoken. This is the void that constitutes the work, the originary loss that has propelled the writing into being but that remains beyond language. Imprecise traces and fragments of this loss are expressed in the work's silence. This lack or void, unexpressed because covered over by the perceivable expression of the writing, yearns to be spoken. The work moves to express it by appealing to what Maurice Blanchot calls the "infinite word of commentary."[29] Commentary, because of its inextinguishable nature, may possibly end the lack at the heart of the work by filling it with endless signifiers. But it cannot fill in all the interstices of the text. To do so would be to deplete the energy, fueled by the loss itself, that powers and mobilizes the work. Unable to reverse the originary lack, criticism is reduced to repeating the text, rephrasing it again and again. Thus, having remained faithful to the distance and absence that constitute the work's unexpressed truth, criticism expresses or

29. *L'Entretien infini* (Paris: Gallimard, 1969), p. 571. Blanchot suggests that the relationship of criticism to the work upon which it comments is one of self-effacement. The more the work of criticism develops and asserts itself, the more it must disappear or break apart. It accomplishes its tasks by vanishing. It is like snow falling on a bell. As the snow melts, it causes the bell to vibrate lightly, imperceptibly. Criticism is thus an almost-nothing; but it is a nothing that, before vanishing, animates the work ("Qu'en est-il de la critique?" in his *Lautréamont et Sade* [Paris: Editions de Minuit, 1963], p. 11).

rewrites the work's fundamental lack. Commentary respects the text's void by carrying into critical discourse the same emptiness that secretly defines the work. Commentary is *another* writing of loss, its rewriting. It expresses an ambiguity that further enhances and deepens the ambiguity already inherent in the work. It does not clarify or explain loss, but rather gives it a new textual home, in which it grows in different and mysterious ways.

The failure to acknowledge loss leads to overconfidence in the human ability to interpret. If nothing is accepted as lost, then everything can ultimately be recovered by whatever means possible. There is in the will to interpretation a will to coherence and recuperation. Interpretation shuns absence; it lives in horror of the vacuum. It struggles to fill in, supplement, repress, mask, construct, synthesize, and unify. Over the abyss of loss, it constructs elaborate and coherent structures of truth designed to hide the meaningless void below and to conceal the subversive fact that its very existence rests on this ground, or lack of ground. In front of the ruins of loss, it builds an elegant Potemkin village of meaning and significance. The very presence of the construction and the very massiveness of the interpretation are designed to give convincing evidence that the loss has been repaired, the origin rediscovered, and the past resurrected in an unchanging form of truth and beauty.

Loss is the precondition of interpretation. But much writing represses that truth, and the will of much interpretation is a will to forget loss. A representation can seek to depict death and, through the very act of representing it, deny its reality. Through interpretation one succeeds in neutralizing the power of death, in dissipating through words and images its brutally physical presence. An interpretation or a representation by its very existence signifies that a forgetting has transpired: one forgets the original sting of loss. It has been masked by an image or a figure, and one's efforts to interpret it move one further away from the immediacy of the pain. "Decipherment, the fate of an endless interpretation," writes Louis Marin in his analysis of Poussin's painting *The Arcadian Shepherds*, "is in its very indecidability the way in which living people neutralize the anxiety of an originary loss and liberate themselves from death."[30] The identity of a dead person is forgotten, the inscription of an epitaph effaced, and the meaning of a life lost, despite the representations given it. A poem written in memo-

30. "Toward a Theory of Reading in the Visual Arts: Poussin's *The Arcadian Shepherds*," in *The Reader in the Text*, ed. Susan Suleiman and Inge Crosman (Princeton: Princeton University Press, 1980), pp. 317–18.

rium cannot capture the uniqueness of the deceased; it leaves out so much about his or her life that it becomes more a forgetting than a commemorating. The painting of a portrait depicts only one pose among many, only one moment selected among thousands in a lifetime. It suppresses the temporal experience of the sitter—where she was born, where she lives, whom she loves—which the frame of the portrait keeps out. As John Ashbery describes in his poem about Parmigianino's *Self-Portrait in a Convex Mirror,* every representation encloses, sequesters, and immobilizes the soul or the self, which "has to stay where it is, / Even though restless, hearing raindrops at the pane, / The sighing of autumn leaves thrashed by the wind, / Longing to be free, outside, but it must stay / Posing in this place."[31]

Representations are thus monuments to forgetfulness, to what had to be omitted from the speaking or portraying, to what was inadvertently or unconsciously left out. They designate an otherness that is central to the identity or nature of what is depicted. Although something is forgotten, an awareness of the forgetting seeps into the representation. The word we rack our brains trying to remember takes on in our consciousness the power of a lack, even when we do finally recall it. The forgotten word exists forcefully in the blank it has established; it is present as a meaningful absence. "When we are at a loss to remember a forgotten word," Blanchot observes, "it becomes identified with this loss; it comes to us as forgotten, and thus we reaffirm it in that absence."[32] One of the three shepherds in Poussin's painting, for example, is depicted turning to the shepherdess, the Memory figure, who stands beside him as he points inquisitively to the words "Et in Arcadia ego," inscribed on the tomb. Having forgotten their meaning, he calls on her to assist him in remembering them. The three shepherds examine the worn, cracked letters for some clue to the identity of the "I," the "ego," of the epitaph. Now dead, the remains watched over by a tombstone that is all that is visible and readable, the man or woman of yesteryear, with no name but the pronoun "I," is a being enveloped in otherness. That person is very different from the "I" that is the speaking subject of the inscription. There is a scission, as Marin observes, between the "I" that writes and the "I" that is written, between the person in the past composing an epitaph, and thus imagining the future when he or she will be dead, and the person as inscribed after

31. *Self-Portrait in a Convex Mirror* (New York: Viking Press, 1975), p. 69. For further discussion of the poem and of Ashbery's poetics of otherness, see my "Critical Reflections: Poetry and Art Criticism in Ashbery's 'Self-Portrait in a Convex Mirror,'" *New Literary History* 15 (Spring 1984): 607–30.
32. *L'Entretien infini,* p. 289.

death on the tombstone from which he or she addresses all those who come upon these words. What the person's name was, what kind of life he or she might have led, what feelings he or she had, these things are not revealed by the epitaph, which is now the sole enunciation of this life. The person no longer has an existence outside of the representation that the four Latin words give. All the shepherds can learn from the representation of a life, as these epitaphic words express it, is that "'I (who speak here and now to you) lived in Arcadia.'"[33] They are confused not only by the fissures and erasures that time has left on the surface of the inscribed words but also by the holes in the text opened by the grammatical shifters ("I," "here," "now," "you"), which designate referents that to these Arcadian readers stand empty and unknowable.[34] In destroying life, death and loss have destroyed reference. The deictics of the inscription, therefore, point to a referent that has been emptied of meaning.

The shepherd's unsuccessful efforts at decipherment indicate how much a representation reduces life and death to forgetfulness and ignorance. The epitaphic writing inscribes not the memory of the lost being but the person's nearly total oblivion; it signifies his or her lack. A representation is a blank space that can signify only by designating the hole or void left by an act of forgetting. The shepherdess seems to respond to the questioning glance of the uncomprehending shepherd, Marin explains, by answering, "'You, reader, are condemned to decipher, and nevertheless, you will not know anything. You remember only one thing: that you have always already forgotten everything.'"[35] Representation, according to Marin, dramatizes and theatricalizes the forgetting that loss is; it makes the blank space of death and absence the very subject of its activity. It points to a forgetting that demands greater and greater efforts of decipherment, as one tries vainly to remember what it is that has been forgotten, barred, and thus lost beyond telling.

The forgetting of the meaning or the content of a loss, as dramatized

33. "Toward a Theory of Reading," p. 321.

34. For a discussion of how the role of the "I" in a text, as characterized by Emile Benveniste, is not a mark of tautology, but rather "a hole in the discourse indicating the place of an empty subject [*un actant vide*]," see Jean Louis Schefer, *L'Espèce de chose mélancolie* (Paris: Flammarion, 1978), p. 190.

35. "Toward a Theory of Reading," p. 317. The poet A. R. Ammons makes a similar, more lyrical point (about letters inscribed and names forgotten) in his long poem "Tombstones": "the stone-name signifies / what it can find to mean / in some living head: / when the heads / are empty, / the stone's name names emptiness, / not the one / now neither a thing that is nor was // as if the name were not / already nothing, / stone, chipped away, // leaves the name nothingly / present, / grooves of absence" (*Sumerian Vistas: Poems* [New York: W. W. Norton, 1987], p. 48).

by the representation, neutralizes the reality of death and absence. A representation invests so much energy in presenting what has been forgotten, what it can not recall or signify, that it appears, Marin argues, to take death out of the realm of the living and to put it on a stage, where it designates what cannot be remembered. To represent what has been forgotten is a way of not remembering the real presence of a loss. One substitutes, *faute de mieux*, the forgetting for the lost content of the forgotten; this takes the sting out of death: "The obliteration of the name and the verb in the inscription [*Et in Arcadia ego*] points out the operation enacted by the representational-narrative process and represents it as the concealment of the 'enunciative' structure itself, thanks to which the past, death, loss, can come back here and now by our reading—but come back as representation, set up on its stage, the object of a serene contemplation exorcising all anxiety."[36] Thus does representation perform the neutralization of death through

36. "Toward a Theory of Reading," p. 322. On the tendency of representational strategies to dramatize and neutralize death and thus to conceal its brutal reality, while paradoxically designating its presence, see Michel Foucault's essay "Language to Infinity," in *Language, Counter-Memory, Practice: Selected Essays and Interviews*, ed. Donald F. Bouchard (Ithaca: Cornell University Press, 1977). According to Foucault, death engenders language. "It is quite likely," he writes, "that the approach of death—its sovereign gesture, its prominence within human memory—hollows out in the present and in existence the void toward which and from which we speak" (p. 53). Having made language its space of habitation, death unleashes an infinite play of signifiers whose endless activity testifies to the finality they wish to avoid: "The gods send disasters to mortals so that they can tell of them, but men speak of them so that misfortunes will never be fully realized, so that their fulfillment will be averted in the distance of words, at the place where they will be stilled in the negation of their nature. . . . Headed toward death, language turns back upon itself; it encounters something like a mirror; and to stop this death which would stop it, it possesses but a single power: that of giving birth to its own image in a play of mirrors that has no limits" (p. 54). The presence of death forces language to be excessive. This excess is the only way to keep mortality at bay: "The figure of a mirror to infinity erected against the black wall of death is fundamental for any language from the moment it determines to leave a trace of its passage" (p. 55). Representation exists only in reaction to the inescapable reality of death. We speak to avoid a direct encounter with nothingness, to avert our glance from the mortification of death. In every word we utter, death is present as that which has initiated our speaking and that sustains its being. Death is ever present in discourse as the great absence we necessarily speak against. The play of images, the self-mirroring of figures, and the self-repeating gestures of speech are all established by the fundamental relationship between language and dying. Never can words forget that their origin derives from the void; silently, they speak of nothing but death (and loss). It is the limit, Foucault writes, "to which language addresses itself and against which it is poised" (p. 57). Speech becomes impossible without the void of death to support it: "Death is undoubtedly the most essential of the accidents of language (its limit and its center): from the day that men began to speak toward death and against it, in order to grasp and imprison it, something was born, a murmuring which repeats, recounts, and redoubles itself endlessly, which has undergone an uncanny process of amplification and thickening, in which our language is today lodged and hidden" (p. 55).

the agency of forgetting. The figuration of loss reveals that figuration *is* loss. The process by which writing preserves things causes those things to vanish. Interpretation is an effort to unwrite (to reverse and to supplement) a loss through writing. But it ends up repeating the loss through a representation that in the effort to signify this loss succeeds only in forgetting it. Representation, therefore, only increases the distance between the present and an originary moment of lost presence.

The Writing of Death/The Death of Writing

There is no denying that writing is a form of death, originating in loss and reenacting death's ultimate unrepresentability. For Blanchot, death is the space of writing, the essence of what he calls "l'espace littéraire." In his criticism, novels, and *récits*, with their love of paradox and their physical, almost sensual, involvement with contradiction, death is not a subject or a theme, but a source and a site; it is the place where the work lives and dwells. Death is also not an end, but a beginning. It is an initiating event, what Georges Poulet calls "the initial catastrophe" from which language is born.[37] Death is "the hope of language," Blanchot writes.[38] It leads to the creation of being, for, as he suggests,

le néant même aide à faire le monde, le néant est créateur du monde en l'homme qui travaille et comprend. La mort aboutit à l'être: telle est la déchirure de l'homme, l'origine de son sort malheureux, car par l'homme la mort vient à l'être et par l'homme le sens repose sur le néant.

[nothingness itself helps to make the world, nothingness is the creator of the world in man as he works and understands. Death ends in

37. "Maurice Blanchot, critique et romancier," *Critique* 229 (June 1966): 492.
38. "La Littérature et le droit à la mort," in *De Kafka à Kafka,* Collection Idées (Paris: Gallimard, 1981), p. 51 ["Literature and the Right to Death," in *The Gaze of Orpheus and Other Literary Essays,* trans. Lydia Davis (Barrytown, N.Y.: Station Hill, 1981), p. 54]; cited in the text as *LDM.* (This essay was originally published in *La Part du feu* [Paris: Gallimard, 1949], pp. 291–331.) Other quotations from Blanchot's works are cited in the text according to the following abbreviations (in each instance, the work was published in Paris by Gallimard): *A: L'Amitié* (1971); *EI: L'Entretien infini* (1969); *EL: L'Espace littéraire,* Collection Idées (1955) [*The Space of Literature,* trans. Ann Smock (Lincoln: University of Nebraska Press, 1982)]; *FP: Faux pas* (1943; reprint, 1975); and *LV: Le Livre à venir,* Collection Idées (1959).

being: this is man's laceration, the source of his unhappy fate, since by man death comes to being and by man meaning rests on nothing-ness.] ("La Littérature et le droit à la mort," 60/62)

The work of writing is founded on the void, *le néant,* of death; it makes visible the absence that death is. Writing speaks with the voice of nothingness. It is a force of pure negation, which, like death, destroys the existence of what it represents. The writer derives his or her power of expression from an anticipated relationship with death; he or she achieves understanding by making death "possible" (*LDM,* 60/62). Death holds out the greatest hope for humanity, because it offers the possibility of establishing a "rapport de liberté." By means of a life never forgetful of and continuously oriented toward death, we possess the freedom to create our own existence. Death is perceived as some-thing that has to be "finely crafted," as Rilke would say; it is "not a given, it must be achieved" (*L'Espace littéraire,* 115/96). Death estab-lishes the domain of the human, according to Blanchot, because it foregrounds mortality as humanity's only mode of being-in-the-world. It humanizes life by lending pathos to it. Yet, the paradox of existence is that at the moment we die we lose not only the world but also death itself, both of which have defined our lives. Dying robs us of the anticipation of death. We lose the mortality ("la mort en devenir") that has shadowed and anchored our lives from the beginning. Having passed beyond death, we encounter for the first time ever the impos-sibility of dying:

Tel est le paradoxe de l'heure dernière. La mort travaille avec nous dans le monde; pouvoir qui humanise la nature, qui élève l'existence à l'être, elle est en nous, comme notre part la plus humaine; elle n'est mort que dans le monde, l'homme ne la connaît que parce qu'il est homme, et il n'est homme que parce qu'il est la mort en devenir. Mais mourir, c'est briser le monde; c'est perdre l'homme, anéantir l'être; c'est donc aussi perdre la mort, perdre ce qui en elle et pour moi faisait d'elle la mort. Tant que je vis, je suis un homme mortel, mais, quand je meurs, cessant d'être un homme, je cesse aussi d'être mor-tel, je ne suis plus capable de mourir, et la mort qui s'annonce me fait horreur, parce que je la vois telle qu'elle est: non plus mort, mais impossibilité de mourir.

[That is the paradox of the last hour. Death works with us in the world; it is a power that humanizes nature, that raises existence to being, and it is within each one of us as our most human quality; it is death only in the world—man only knows death because he is man, and he is only man because he is death in the process of becoming. But to die is to shatter the world; it is the loss of the person, the annihilation of the being; and so it is also the loss of death, the loss of what in it and for me made it death. As long as I live, I am a mortal man, but when I die, by ceasing to be a man I also cease to be mortal, I am no longer capable of dying, and my impending death horrifies me because I see it as it is: no longer death, but the impossibility of dying.] (*LDM,* 52/55)

Because death is man's vocation, the end (in both senses) of his life, it gives him, Blanchot argues, the opportunity to create a death that is entirely his own. As constructions that look to the future for their definition and perfection, death and writing coincide. Man is not only a creature who knows he will disappear but also one who in saying "yes" to this disappearance transforms it into song and poem. In him, death and loss become word. Paraphrasing Kafka, Blanchot writes: "I write to die, to give death its essential possibility, through which it is essentially death . . . ; but at the same time, I cannot write unless death writes in me" (*EL,* 195/149). Writing, therefore, begins with the consciousness of an ever-present end, void, and nullity that track the movement of human life. Speaking involves a constant awareness of death, which alone leads to understanding:

> Pour parler, nous devons voir la mort, la voir derrière nous. Quand nous parlons, nous nous appuyons à un tombeau, et ce vide du tombeau est ce qui fait la vérité du langage, mais en même temps le vide est réalité et la mort se fait être.

> [If we are to speak, we must see death, we must see it behind us. When we speak, we are leaning on a tomb, and the void of that tomb is what makes language true, but at the same time void is reality and death becomes being.] (*LDM,* 51/55)

For Blanchot, being therefore only exists because it is grounded in nothingness.

Language cannot preserve what disappears. It even hastens the effacement of what it signifies. When one pronounces the word "woman," Blanchot observes, one takes from that person her reality of flesh and blood; she becomes different, other, absent. As living being and presence, she is abolished: "Le mot me donne l'être, mais il me le donne privé d'être" ("The word gives me the being, but it gives it to me deprived of being"; *LDM,* 36/42). And, he continues,

> quand je dis "cette femme," la mort réelle est annoncée et déjà présente dans mon langage; mon langage veut dire que cette personne-ci, qui est là, maintenant, peut être séparée d'elle-même, soustraite à son existence et à sa présence et plongée soudain dans un néant d'existence et de présence; mon langage signifie essentiellement la possibilité de cette destruction; il est, à tout moment, une allusion résolue à un tel événement. Mon langage ne tue personne. Mais, si cette femme n'était pas réellement capable de mourir, si elle n'était pas à chaque moment de sa vie menacée de la mort, liée et unie à elle par un lien d'essence, je ne pourrais pas accomplir cette négation idéale, cet assassinat différé qu'est mon langage.

> [when I say, "This woman," real death has been announced and is already present in my language; my language means that this person, who is here right now, can be detached from herself, removed from her existence and her presence and suddenly plunged into a nothingness in which there is no existence or presence; my language essentially signifies the possibility of this destruction; it is a constant, bold allusion to such an event. My language does not kill anyone. But if this woman were not really capable of dying, if she were not threatened by death at every moment of her life, bound and joined to death by an essential bond, I would not be able to carry out that ideal negation, that deferred assassination which is what my language is.] (*LDM,* 37/42–43)

The law that language obeys is that of negation. It not only abolishes the being things have in the world but also negates its own power to recuperate or repossess the meaning of those annulled things. Language renounces the power to preserve the things it represents in the afterlife of figuration, as formed by image, memory, and metaphor:

> C'est vainement que nous prétendons maintenir, par nos paroles, par nos écrits, ce qui s'absente; vainement, que nous lui offrons l'attrait de nos souvenirs et une sorte de figure encore, le bonheur de demeurer au jour, la vie prolongée d'une apparence véridique. Nous ne cherchons qu'à combler un vide, nous ne supportons pas la douleur: l'affirmation de ce vide.

[In vain, do we claim, by our words, by our writings, to hold onto what disappears; in vain, do we offer it the lure of our memories and a kind of image: namely, the happiness of dwelling in the light of day, the prolonged life of a truthful appearance. We seek only to fill a void; we do not endure the pain: the affirmation of this void.] (*L'Amitié*, 326)

Indeed, by replacing the reality it designates, the word in its new presence causes that reality to vanish. To speak of something, to name it, is to recognize that as a thing it is now lost. The appearance of the word, which comes into being in order to express a reality, is established on the negation of that reality. The word cannot find its voice until the loss of the thing it expresses is assured. The world, thus, is suspended and bracketed by language:

Lorsque je parle, je reconnaîs bien qu'il n'y a parole que parce que ce qui "est" a disparu en ce qui le nomme, frappé de mort pour devenir la réalité du nom. . . . Quelque chose était là, qui n'y est plus; comment le retrouver, comment ressaisir, en ma parole, cette présence antérieure qu'il me faut exclure pour parler, pour la parler? Et, ici, nous évoquerons l'éternel tourment de notre langage, quand sa nostalgie se retourne vers ce qu'il manque toujours, par la nécessité où il est d'en être le manque pour le dire.

[When I speak, I fully recognize that the word exists only because what "is" has disappeared in what names it, has undergone death in order to become the reality of the word. . . . Something was there that no longer exists; how to find it again? How to recapture in my speech this anterior presence that must be excluded if I am to speak, if I am to speak it? And we think of the eternal torment of our language, when nostalgically it turns back towards what it constantly lacks, for it must, of necessity, itself be lack in order to articulate lack.] (*L'Entretien infini*, 50)

It is to absence that Blanchot wishes to remain faithful. The word he speaks obliterates the immediacy of the thing it expresses. It envelops that thing in a void, which makes it both absent and distant. Language signifies, thus, not the thing but the absence of the thing and so is implicated in the loss. It must become silence and lack in order best to express the faraway absence of what it designates. A word such as "cat," for example, signifies not only the nonexistence of the cat but, Blanchot writes, "a non-existence made *word*" (*LDM*, 39/44). Words are under pressure to designate the void, the negative emptiness underlying all language, in which they, like everything else in the world, are mired, and which, like everything else, they are incapable of changing or suppressing. The goal for Blanchot, thus, is to express the void while allowing it to remain the nothing that it is. The writer inhabits the space of the nothing. His subject is "le rien." It is the "material" with which he works. Like Beckett, who associates the noble failure of art with the artist's belief that "there is nothing to express, nothing with which to express, nothing from which to express, no power to express, no desire to express, together with the obligation to express,"[39] Blanchot sees the writer in the tragicomic situation "of having nothing to write, of having no means to write it, and of being forced by extreme necessity to never stop writing it" (*Faux pas*, 11). The writer may have nothing to say, but he does have the obligation to speak this nothing. He has to write "le rien," but in a way that nothing (not even a negative "something") is expressed. His words must express "'the need to express nothing'" (*FP*, 15). Inexpressibility is the end of all figuration, because it alone embodies the lack, loss, and void that writing strives to express as silently, absently, and inexpressively as it can.

Loss, death, silence, and interruption play an essential role in Blanchot's conception of language and writing. No dialogue or conversation, for example, can occur without discontinuity. When two people converse, one of them must interrupt the other in order to speak his or her mind. Only through interruption can an exchange take place. More generally, Blanchot observes, "interruption must be present in every sequence of words" (*EI*, 107). It represents in language the distance that separates two beings. In this respect, interruption is mimetic, because it is the sign in a discourse of the strangeness, separation, and otherness of two individuals whose speaking engages them in dialogue. It brings into writing the distance and the loss that define being. For Blanchot, even friendship is founded on remoteness, but of a unique kind: namely, "infinite distance, that fundamental separation in which estrangement becomes attachment" (*A*, 328). In this simultaneously absent and present friendship the void plays an essential role; it binds two beings together in a rapport of distance. According to Blanchot's poetics of separation, what truly separates also truly connects. One person is linked to another by the ever-present gulf of absence, which keeps them both apart.

39. Samuel Beckett and Georges Duthuit, "Three Dialogues," *Transition* 5 (1949): 98.

Often, however, we forget the reality of separation. Our faith in the coherence and unity that we believe representations create has caused us to lose sight of loss and death. We have suppressed their reality by designing a language that denies absence, that "reveals, in what 'is,' not what disappears, but what perpetually endures" (*EI*, 47). This is a subterfuge that kills death by pretending that certain aesthetic strategies of figuration have the spiritual or symbolical power to recuperate lost things. The thick, black reality of death is dissolved; it is neutralized and denaturalized. But this retreat from death is a retreat from reality, Blanchot argues, for when we fail to signify death, we also fail to express life.

For Blanchot, language has the power to assassinate. The reality a word designates vanishes as a living presence. Writing destroys being-in-the-world, replacing it with being-in-language. But if the word is the agent of death, in its death-dealing it has an important rapport with what it has killed. It is the agent of the thing's disappearance and thus is linked to the absence it has caused. The word creates a distance between itself and the thing, but through this separation it continues to be connected to the lost thing. By becoming absent the thing is endowed with the meaning that only language can bestow. The disappearance of the object, of the referent, is the precondition for the appearance of the word. At the moment it declares the birth of the text, writing announces the death of the world, because "language can only begin with the void; no fullness, no certainty can ever speak. . . . Negation is tied to language" (*LDM*, 38/43).

When the writer speaks, death speaks in her: "My speech is a warning that at this very moment death is loose in the world, that it has suddenly appeared between me, as I speak, and the being I address" (*LDM*, 37/43). But the individual to whom the writer addresses her words is not the only person to disappear. The power of the word to create absence touches the writer as well. In naming herself, in finding words to express the ideas that belong to her, she becomes separated from herself. She loses her own being. Supplanted by the words she speaks, she no longer has a self apart from the one that language gives her. She is now "other" to herself. She exists by means of the impersonality of writing. No longer does her language express a self or a life or a feeling. Rather, it reveals the void of the self. Writing is the effacement of the subject in favor not of the universal but of the impersonal.[40]

---

40. Françoise Collin, *Maurice Blanchot et la question de l'écriture* (Paris: Gallimard, 1971), p. 35.

Thus, the entry of language into existence coincides with its retreat from the world it abolishes. The being of language is thus established on the reality of loss.

This does not mean, however, that Blanchot renounces the quest to recover what has been lost. To the contrary, he envisions language trying to rediscover what was once present but that its very existence had destroyed. The goal is to return to the moment of silence before speech changed everything, and death appeared. The language of literature searches for this first moment, for this presence, which its coming into existence had abolished. The only possibility of rediscovering the presence of things in the world as they existed before the advent of words is by letting language itself become a thing, a physical presence in its own right, which like the bark of a tree, or a rock, or a clump of clay expresses the materiality of the earth. A language in which the physical has precedence—in the rhythm, weight, mass, and matter of words, in the paper and leather of the book, in the trace of ink on a page—and in which words are coterminous with being has the power of incantation; it is a language that is a thing among things. To rediscover this presence, language must become an autonomous mode of expression, independent of the consciousness that formed it. It must exist as a discourse of pure impersonality—"the language of no one, the writing of no writer, the light of a consciousness deprived of self"— an impersonal language proclaiming that "'I no longer represent, I am; I do not signify, I present'" (*LDM*, 43/47).

A language of this kind is no longer prisoner to the illusions of mimesis. It no longer represents what already exists, but rather presents perceptions and events, the existence of which coincide with their appearance in language. Through its decentered impersonality, this language of pure presentation would express the reality of absence: namely, that intractable absence of vanished things which continues to adhere to the words that displaced them. From the first appearance, the word internalized the absence it had initiated, harboring within itself the vacancy of the thing it had replaced. Loss was given a home, stored away within the word as a memory-trace of the originary event that had brought the word into being. The negating of the world, which language accomplished, became part of the inscribing of that language. The afterlife of lost things, especially the vacancy that has become their new reality, resides in words. When language names things, Blanchot observes, "whatever it designates is abolished; but whatever is abolished is also sustained, and the thing has found a refuge (in the being which is the word) rather than a threat" (*LDM*, 43/48).

Blanchot's "literary space" is neither the expression of the reality of the world nor the opening of another, more harmonious, more authentic world. Writing is not the space of evasion but that of exile. The text does not open onto the world but onto what Blanchot calls "le Dehors" ("the Outside"), a space that is neither interior nor exterior, nor even a synthesis of the two.[41] Exile, indeed, names the poetic state; put simply, "the poem is exile." The poet is perpetually on the outside, excluded from his native place and inhabiting a strange domain that is "the outside [*le dehors*], which knows no intimacy or limit" (*EL*, 322/ 237). In exile, the poet is a perpetual wanderer, "he to whom the stability of presence is not granted and who is deprived of a true abode" (*EL*, 322/237). His errancy also forces him to encounter error, because the poet has no true place of habitation or being: "the wanderer's country is not truth, but exile; he lives outside, *on the other side, separated*" (*EL*, 323/238). In the work of exile, in which the poet is compelled to err, truth is missing. Writing, for Blanchot, is not an activity through which something is projected into truth, but rather one in which everything is lost. Writing is the errant movement of loss. It dissipates truth; it establishes the nomadism of error. And it is perpetual repetition. Because writing is always partial and incomplete, always making and then unmaking itself, it is forced to repeat again and again the emptiness that lies at its core. Language ultimately subverts its own will. Forces of disintegration work at fragmenting and then at reconstructing a work, so it becomes a field of metamorphic activity and indeterminacy. Any net of coherence or meaning can be unstrung by the fundamental instability of the writing itself. Language can turn against itself and destroy the text it has constructed, making it "a work of unhappiness and ruin"; but it can just as quickly heal its self-inflicted wounds and turn its power of disintegration into the force by which "anguish turns into hope" (*LDM*, 59/61).

One of Blanchot's more eloquent discussions of loss, and one of the texts most central to his *oeuvre,* involves the retelling of the myth of Orpheus and Eurydice.[42] The Greek myth is a story of loss: of an object of love lost, recovered, and then lost again. Orpheus's gaze is the gaze that annihilates, abolishes, and makes absent. The myth is an allegory about the failure of art and representation to recover and repossess

41. Ibid., pp. 37–38.
42. "Le Regard d'Orphée," in *EL*, 227–34 ["The Gaze of Orpheus," in *The Gaze of Orpheus,* pp. 99–104]; hereafter cited in the text as "Le Regard." For a probing and extensive analysis of Blanchot's recasting of the Orpheus myth—what he calls "the most original transformation of the Orpheus theme in the twentieth century"—see Walter A. Strauss, *Descent and Return: The Orphic Theme in Modern Literature* (Cambridge: Harvard University Press, 1971), pp. 251–61.

what has been lost. Orpheus's descent into the underworld represents the writer's descent into the darkness and death of what Blanchot calls "l'Obscur" in order to bring back what is unrecoverable. Art tries to achieve the impossible: namely, to put the ineffability of death and nothingness into words. Orpheus attempts to lead Eurydice to daylight and to return to her the form, figure, light, and reality she once possessed. But because of her stay in the realm of nonbeing, Eurydice has become "the center of the night in the night" ("Le Regard," 227/99). She has been contaminated by the essence of the void. She cannot be seen with mortal eyes, because she no longer has mortal being. Orpheus, therefore, can lead Eurydice, this incarnation of nothingness and of difference, back to light only if he refrains from looking at her.

According to Blanchot's dialectical logic—whereby separation is a form of attachment, distance an aspect of proximity, and absence a form of presence—Orpheus's act of turning his gaze away from Eurydice is an attempt to approach and possess her; recoil and distance lead to proximity. According to Blanchot's allegorical perspective, the work of art can attempt to restore what is lost, but only if it agrees to the dissimulating gesture of not looking at what it has recaptured, only if it blinds itself to its discovery. The restoration of a loss is thus accomplished by the artifice of a dissimulation. But because the intimacy, and proximity, of the past (for example, the face-to-face encounter of two lovers) is no longer possible during the act of repossession, what is achieved is a recapturing that still involves great loss. Orpheus has lost a certain "type" of Eurydice. The woman he leads back is different from what she had been. She is a Eurydice of obscurity and darkness, a negative Eurydice, whom he does not know, because he has never looked at her and whom, should he decide to gaze at her, he will never have the opportunity of knowing. Like writing, Orpheus's gaze abolishes what it touches. To look at something in the world, to possess it, to name it, to touch it, are all acts that ultimately lead to its loss. The work of art masquerades as a possession, as a presence; but in reality it is dispossession and absence.

For Blanchot, Orpheus is a tragic hero who knows from the start of his journey that he can bring Eurydice back to the world of presence and light only through artifice and dissimulation. The averting of his glance is a trick of imagination and intelligence designed to enable him to snare his prey. Orpheus knows, moreover, that once he and Eurydice have left the entrance to the underworld, and she stands again in the bright light of day, she will no longer be the mysterious Eurydice, icon of death and nothingness. She will be immediately transformed into a normal, mundane, mortal being. The aura of death will have dissipated. Having lost the radiant, flesh-and-blood Eurydice of the long-ago past, the woman he had known and loved, he will now experience a second loss: that of the shadowy Eurydice who had been transformed by the underworld into a symbol of negativity and absence. Orpheus's desire not to lose this dark Eurydice and his curiosity to see her just once as she truly exists, marked by death and nothingness, compel him to look at her, although he knows that he will pay for this gaze with her loss. From Blanchot's perspective, Orpheus refuses the dissimulation of art (and of all strategies of representation that aim at recuperation) in order to gaze upon the obscurity and otherness of death. He abolishes the work he is in the act of performing, the work of recuperation which involves the return of Eurydice. To see death as it really is, in its strangeness and nullity, Orpheus, according to Blanchot's revisionary reading, is willing to lose the work of art. This is because he knows that all forms of figuration and representation are by necessity tricks of mediation. In order to give the illusion of presence and to vaunt art's triumph over loss and mortality, these forms must "close their eyes to," or turn away from, the reality of nothingness:

> En se tournant vers Eurydice, Orphée ruine l'oeuvre, l'oeuvre immédiatement se défait, et Eurydice se retourne en l'ombre. . . . Ainsi trahit-il l'oeuvre et Eurydice et la nuit. Mais ne pas se tourner vers Eurydice, ce ne serait pas moins trahir, être infidèle à la force sans mesure et sans prudence de son mouvement, qui ne veut pas Eurydice dans sa vérité diurne et dans son agrément quotidien, qui la veut dans son obscurité nocturne, dans son éloignement, avec son corps fermé et son visage scellé, qui veut la voir, non quand elle est visible, mais quand elle est invisible, et non comme l'intimité d'une vie familière, mais comme l'étrangeté de ce qui exclut toute intimité, non pas la faire vivre, mais avoir vivante en elle la plénitude de sa mort.

> [By turning around to look at Eurydice, Orpheus ruins the work, the work immediately falls apart, and Eurydice returns to the shadows; under his gaze, the essence of the night reveals itself to be inessential. He thus betrays the work and Eurydice and the night. But if he did not turn around to look at Eurydice, he still would be betraying, being disloyal to, the boundless and imprudent force of his impulse, which does not demand Eurydice in her diurnal truth and her everyday charm, but in her nocturnal darkness, in her distance, her body closed, her face sealed, which wants to see her not when she is visible, but when she is invisible, and not as the intimacy of a familiar life, but

as the strangeness of that which excludes all intimacy; it does not want to make her live, but to have the fullness of her death living in her.] ("Le Regard," 228/100)

Orpheus thus sees Eurydice without artifice and free of mediation. He gazes at an enigmatic woman who in her veiled presence does not dissimulate her absence, but rather offers to his view the "presence of her infinite absence" ("Le Regard," 229/100). It is outside of art that Orpheus experiences this vision. In some respects, his glance is a refusal of his identity as poet and of the power of lyric and song. Up to now, his only task had been to sing of Eurydice; that is, to experience her indirectly and with eyes averted. Only through song could he have had the illusion of mastery over her. But the song he now sings expresses the loss of Eurydice; it is not a song of dawn, of a rising sun, but of night, mourning, and death. Having lost the center of his existence, Orpheus wanders aimlessly. His act has carried the work of literature into the realm of loss, indeterminacy, and negativity, which characterizes what Blanchot calls "le neutre" ("the neuter"). But this realm is essential to the work, Blanchot argues. It represents the disintegrative undoing and the silent, passive inactivity (what he calls "le *désoeuvrement*," "work-lessness") that lie at the heart of every work of literature. Orpheus loses Eurydice, because his desire for her goes beyond the bounds of telling, beyond "the measured limits of the song" ("Le Regard," 230/101). And Orpheus loses himself, as well. But the loss of self and other, Blanchot writes, is necessary to the creation of the impersonal, inactive, and unraveling work: "this desire, and Eurydice lost, and Orpheus scattered are necessary to the song, just as the ordeal of eternal worklessness [*le désoeuvrement*] is necessary to the work" ("Le Regard," 230/101). By the fact of its having been undone and lost, the work has the possibility, Blanchot suggests, of going beyond itself into the world of nonbeing, and there of "uniting with its origin and of establishing itself in impossibility" ("Le Regard," 232/102). Through the Orphic glance that effaces the work, the work has the possibility of recovering its own impossibility, of rediscovering the void that is the uncertainty of its origin. All writing begins with Orpheus's gaze, a writing that glances at its object and sees an imminent blankness. Writing-as-the-gaze-of-Orpheus establishes the absence that language creates not only when it names and thus displaces the things of the world but also when, losing the object of its desire, it effaces itself. Writing is a death that, unleashing its nullifying powers onto its own being, creates a space disfigured by loss and deprivation, an "espace littéraire."

PART TWO

The Poetry of Loss

Il est vrai . . . que ce qui fait défaut appelle la poésie et que celle-ci a pour terrain par excellence l'endroit où quelque chose manque.

[It is true that what we lack calls out for poetry, which has as its preeminent domain the place where something is missing.]
— Michel Leiris, in *A quoi bon des poètes en un temps de manque?*

Parler alors semble mensonge, ou pire: lâche
insulte à la douleur, et gaspillage
du peu de temps et de forces qui nous reste.

[To speak is to lie, or worse: a craven
insult to grief or a waste
of the little time and energy at our disposal.]
— Philippe Jaccottet, *Chants d'en bas*

Poetry can repair no loss, but it defies the space which separates. And it does this by its continual labour of reassembling what has been scattered.
— John Berger, *The Sense of Sight*

Il y a un chant de ce qui s'use, est blessé, décline ou s'en va. Peut-être même n'y a-t-il proprement de chant que là.

[There is a song of what wears away, is wounded, wanes, or departs. Perhaps no other song really exists.]
— Roger Munier, *Le Visiteur qui jamais ne vient*

CHAPTER 2

UNdER thE SiGN of SATURN:
AllEGORiES of MOURNiNG ANd
MElANCholy iN ChARlES BAUdElAiRE

> The only pleasure the melancholic permits himself, and it is a power-
> ful one, is allegory.
> —Walter Benjamin, *The Origin of German Tragic Drama*

When at the end of the fourth act of *Macbeth* Macduff learns
that his wife and children—"all my pretty ones," as he calls them—
have been murdered, he can find no words, no signifying speech, to
express his grief at this horrible death; he is literally dumbfounded,
deprived of the consoling release that language alone can give.[1] Only
Malcolm's prodding reminder of the need to speak dislodges Macduff
from his paralyzing muteness and calls him back to the world:

> Merciful Heaven!
> What, man! Ne'er pull your hat upon your brows.
> Give sorrow words. The grief that does not speak
> Whispers the o'erfraught heart and bids it break
>
> (4.3. 208–11)

To "give sorrow words" is to insert language into an experience of
unendurable loss so that grief can come to speak itself. Death is a void
out of which language—the language that consoles, the language that
offers catharsis, the language that strives to compensate, the language
that desires, the language that seeks meaning—emerges. The experi-

---

1. As the poet Joseph Brodsky writes concerning the realness of death in Anna
Akhmatova's poetry, "from a figure of speech it became a figure that leaves you speech-
less" (*Less Than One: Selected Essays* [New York: Farrar, Straus and Giroux, 1986], p. 49).

49

ence of death initiates a stream of unending words, detached signifiers circulating and sliding one over the other as they errantly search for the lost signified, the lost other, to which they once were joined but with which they can no longer coincide; for death has taken that signified out of the realm of language, making it transcendental and unreachable. There where the loved being no longer exists, there where a gap opens up in the world, there where dialogue can no longer occur and silence prevails, it is there that speech—imperfect, allegorical speech— can begin.[2] Sadness, grief, mourning, and melancholy in the wake of death are languages of loss, experiences translated into signs whose originating event and referent lie beyond the power of signification. "The work of mourning," writes Jacques Lacan, "is accomplished at the level of the *logos* . . . [It] is first of all performed to satisfy the disorder that is produced by the inadequacy of signifying elements to cope with the hole that has been created in existence, for it is the system of signifiers in their totality which is impeached by the least instance of mourning."[3]

All that remains after the event of a loss, such as death, is the incomplete signs in which grief, desire, and language coincide. Curiously, the expression of grief and melancholy may lead to a state where the experience of loss takes on a life of its own, coming to replace, even to eclipse, the absent object. The words, the sorrow, the unappeased desire may seem more real, more present, and more immediate than that being whose death has occasioned them. Loss, the very experience of deprivation, of subtraction, succeeds paradoxically in adding something to the image of the dead or absent object: an aspect, an identity it never possessed before. The object comes to be known uniquely by and through its absence. Loss penetrates the being of language, filling it

2. Language is born from absence and sustained by it, as Roland Barthes remarks in *Fragments d'un discours amoureux* (Paris: Seuil, 1977) [*A Lover's Discourse: Fragments*, trans. Richard Howard (New York: Hill and Wang, 1978)]: "Endlessly I sustain the discourse of the beloved's absence; actually a preposterous situation; the other is absent as referent, present as allocutory. This singular distortion generates a kind of insupportable present; I am wedged between two tenses, that of the reference and that of the allocution: you have gone (which I lament), you are here (since I am addressing you)" (pp. 21–22/15). "To know that writing compensates for nothing, sublimates nothing, that it is precisely *there where you are not*—this is the beginning of writing" (p. 116/100). Similarly, Julia Kristeva identifies loss as the unique precondition for language. It is "the unseizability of this *Thing [cette Chose]*, necessarily lost," that ensures that "the 'subject' separated from the object will become a being who speaks. . . . To take up language, to place or establish oneself within the statutory fiction that constitutes all acts of symbol-making, is in effect to lose the Thing [*la Chose*]" (*Soleil noir: Dépression et mélancolie* [Paris: Gallimard, 1987], p. 157).

3. "Desire and the Interpretation of Desire in *Hamlet*," *Yale French Studies (Literature and Psychoanalysis: The Question of Reading: Otherwise)* 55–56 (1977): 38.

with a sorrow so abundant and, as we shall see in Baudelaire's poems, so fecund that the worded grief displaces the loved object, its source. One need only think of the personification of sorrow in Baudelaire's poem "Recueillement" to realize how the death or absence occasioning such grief is eclipsed by the forceful and intimate presentness of the sorrow, whom the poet fondly, paternally, lovingly, tenderly, and caringly watches over: "Ma Douleur, donne-moi la main; viens par ici, / . . . . / Entends, ma chère, entends la douce Nuit qui marche" ("My Sorrow, give me your hand, come this way, /. . . . / Listen, my dear, listen to the soft Night that stirs").[4]

Unable to repossess the being who is dead, the mourning or melancholic person develops a strategy for clinging to the loss, enveloping himself in the all-encompassing sorrow that now signifies that lost being. Love for the object is replaced by love for the *loss* of the object. Intimacy with what has disappeared is preserved by an obsession, a fascination, with the ostensible and ostentatious signs of loss: with the gestures, mannerisms, words, and aesthetic forms that attempt to represent absence. Melancholy, as the psychoanalyst Pierre Fédida observes, is "less the regressive reaction to the loss of the object than the phantasmatic (or hallucinatory) capacity to *keep it alive as lost object.*"[5] The being who has died continues to live in the pain and grief he or she leaves behind. In varying degrees, people who have experienced a loss through death come to identify with their loss, to embody and incorporate it, and to drape themselves in its excessively, sometimes sumptuously, dark colors; mourning is an attire that "becomes" them only because they long to become it.

In the work of mourning, Freud explained in his classic study of 1917, "Mourning and Melancholia," the libido is forced to withdraw its attachments, its cathexes, from a loved object that has passed out of existence, that has either died or disappeared. During the process of pulling away, "the existence of the lost object is continued in the mind," until the libido finally relinquishes its attachments and is liberated. But in the state of melancholy, in contrast to mourning, the attachment to the lost object remains unsevered. The loss of the object, due either to injury, neglect, abandonment, or disappointment, initiates a withdrawal of the libido into the ego, an internalization establishing, as

4. *Oeuvres complètes*, 2 vols., Bibliothèque de la Pléiade (Paris: Gallimard, 1975), 1:141; cited in the text as *OC*. All translations of Baudelaire are mine.
5. "Le Cannibale mélancolique," *Nouvelle Revue de psychanalyse* 6 (Fall 1972): 126; reprinted in his *L'Absence*, Collection Connaissance de l'inconscient (Paris: Gallimard, 1978), pp. 61–67.

Freud wrote, "an *identification* of the ego with the abandoned object. Thus the shadow of the object [falls] upon the ego, so that the latter [can] henceforth be criticized by a special mental faculty like an object, like the forsaken object."[6] The superego, venting its rage against the loved object for having disappeared and avenging the hurt and anger the abandonment has caused, attacks the object in the only place it now survives, in the ego itself, in which it has been incorporated. "The loss of the object," Freud wrote, becomes "transformed into a loss in the ego."[7] Thus, "by taking flight into the ego love escapes annihilation."[8]

It is under the sign of loss, therefore, that the dead being or the absent object exists. The work of melancholy, as Freud showed, keeps the lost object alive, preserving an intimate relationship, often an identification, between this object and the subject who desperately desires to repossess it. As more and more words are spewed forth to fill the hole created in the real by the death of the loved being and as greater and greater numbers of signs are created to signify and thus compensate for a loss that can never be satisfied, the languages of mourning and melancholy run to excess and are overdetermined. Despite the plethora of signifiers, no plenum of signification is ever reached. The experience of death occasions an exorbitant proliferation within the signifying process, which in the realm of poetic representation takes the form of *allegory*, the literary mode that posits an unbridgeable distance between itself and a referent it can never fully signify or recover. As Walter Benjamin, the great theorist of modern allegory, observes in his study of the German tragic drama, the seventeenth-century baroque *Trauerspiel* (sorrow play), mourning and melancholy, because they are experiences that follow in the wake of death, are "at once the mother of . . . allegories and their content." And, he affirms, "the only pleasure the melancholic permits himself, and it is a powerful one, is allegory."[9]

6. *General Psychological Theory: Papers on Metapsychology*, ed. Philip Rieff (New York: Macmillan, 1963), pp. 166 and 170, respectively.

7. Ibid., p. 170. The superego desires, as Kristeva observes, to destroy the loved object "so as all the better to possess it alive. Rather carved up, shredded, cut, swallowed, digested . . . than lost" (*Soleil noir*, p. 21).

8. *General Psychological Theory*, p. 178.

9. *The Origin of German Tragic Drama*, trans. John Osborne (London: NLB, 1977), pp. 230 and 185, respectively; hereafter cited as *Origin*. Pleasure, Kristeva remarks, is a fundamental element in the allegorical presentation of melancholy. Allegory "confers a signifying pleasure upon the lost signifier, a resurrectional jubilation upon even the stone and the corpse, thus affirming itself as coextensive with the subjective experience of a melancholy that is named, of melancholic bliss [*la jouissance mélancolique*]" (*Soleil noir*, p. 114).

For studies of Benjamin's theory of allegory and its relationship to melancholy, see

Allegory could be called the trope of death: the language of fragmentation, decay, and erosion which death speaks or writes. It is, to quote Benjamin, "the incomparable language of the death's head: total expressionlessness—the black of the eye-sockets—coupled to the most unbridled expression—the grinning rows of teeth."[10] Allegory is a richly ambivalent and highly dialectical form juxtaposing a profound vacancy of expression with a savage expressivity, the latter fueled by the intense force of unfulfilled desire. In allegory, an absent and unrecoverable meaning is joined to an excessive and overdetermined language. There is a doubleness of vision in allegorical representation (like that, for example, inherent in Baudelaire's ambivalence over *spleen* and *ideal*) that remains unresolved, because allegory, unable to synthesize opposites—the way symbol, for example, in its will to totality and fusion can—is compelled to present contraries in the full force of their dialectical reality. Allegorical discourse, moreover, is always

Timothy Bahti, "History as Rhetorical Enactment: Walter Benjamin's Theses 'On the Concept of History,'" *Diacritics* 9 (Fall 1979): 2–17; Christine Buci-Glucksmann, *La Raison baroque: De Baudelaire à Benjamin* (Paris: Galilée, 1984); Bainard Cowan, "Walter Benjamin's Theory of Allegory," *New German Critique* 22 (Winter 1981): 109–22; Terry Eagleton, *Walter Benjamin, or Towards a Revolutionary Criticism* (London: Verso and NLB, 1981); Jürgen Habermas, "Consciousness-Raising or Redemptive Criticism—The Contemporaneity of Walter Benjamin," *New German Critique* 17 (Spring 1979): 30–59; Geoffrey Hartman, *Criticism in the Wilderness: The Study of Literature Today* (New Haven: Yale University Press, 1980), pp. 63–85; Fredric Jameson, *Marxism and Form: Twentieth-Century Dialectical Theories of Literature* (Princeton: Princeton University Press, 1971), pp. 60–83; Michael W. Jennings, *Dialectical Images: Walter Benjamin's Theory of Literary Criticism* (Ithaca: Cornell University Press, 1987); Henri Meschonnic, "L'Allégorie chez Walter Benjamin, une aventure juive," in *Walter Benjamin et Paris*, ed. Heinz Wismann (Paris: Cerf, 1986), pp. 707–41; J. Hillis Miller, "The Two Allegories," in *Allegory, Myth, and Symbol*, ed. Morton W. Bloomfield, Harvard English Studies, no. 19 (Cambridge: Harvard University Press, 1981), pp. 355–70; Pierre Missac, "Walter Benjamin: De la rupture au naufrage," *Critique* 395 (April 1980): 370–81; Charles Rosen, "The Ruins of Walter Benjamin," *New York Review of Books*, 27 October 1977 and 10 November 1977, pp. 31–40 and 30–38, respectively; Lloyd Spencer, "Allegory in the World of the Commodity: The Importance of *Central Park*," *New German Critique* 34 (Winter 1985): 59–77; and Richard Wolin, *Walter Benjamin: An Aesthetic of Redemption* (New York: Columbia University Press, 1982). For a general discussion of Benjamin's theories of language, see Irving Wohlfarth's two important essays—"On the Messianic Structure of Walter Benjamin's Last Reflections," *Glyph* 3 (1978): 148–212, and "The Politics of Prose and the Art of Awakening: Walter Benjamin's Version of a German Romantic Motif," *Glyph* 7 (1980): 131–48—as well as Rodolphe Gasché's "Saturnine Vision and the Question of Difference: Reflections on Walter Benjamin's Theory of Language," *Studies in Twentieth-Century Literature* 11 (Fall 1986): 69–90. Finally, for a redefinition of allegory, which has been seminal in contemporary studies of the trope, see Paul de Man, "The Rhetoric of Temporality," in *Blindness and Insight: Essays in the Rhetoric of Contemporary Criticism*, 2d ed., rev. (Minneapolis: University of Minnesota Press, 1983), pp. 187–228, as well as his *Allegories of Reading: Figural Language in Rousseau, Nietzsche, Rilke, and Proust* (New Haven: Yale University Press, 1979), esp. pp. 57–78 and 188–220.

10. *One-Way Street and Other Writings*, trans. Edmund Jephcott and Kingsley Shorter (London: NLB, 1979), p. 70.

incomplete and imperfect, because it evokes some meaning, some image, some figure lying beyond the horizon of its signification, some "otherness" that it can designate but not join. The allegorical sign invokes a totality that can never be possessed, an origin that can never be found again, and a referent that can never be represented. Allegorical discourse, to use words from Baudelaire's poem "L'Irréparable," is "un théâtre où l'on attend / Toujours, toujours en vain, l'Etre aux ailes de gaze!" ("a theatre where one awaits, / Always, always in vain, the Being with gossamer wings"; *Oeuvres complètes*, 55).

As the trope of death, allegory is, to speak metaphorically, Baudelaire's shroud, the thick winding sheet he mentions at the end of the poem "Un Voyage à Cythère": "Hélas! et j'avais, comme en un suaire épais, / Le coeur enseveli dans cette allégorie" ("Alas, I had, as in a thick winding-sheet / My heart enshrouded in this allegory"; *OC*, 119). It enfolds his consciousness, turning his vision of the world perpetually toward death. Baudelaire's "thanatotropic" imagination persistently confronts the realities of death, decay, and temporality. Even in moments of sublime, transcendental evasion or meditation, as, for example, in poems such as "Rêve Parisien," "La Chambre double," "Le Gâteau," or "Le Masque," where the poet envisions a sumptuous, timeless paradise of quiet ecstasy, or ontological plenitude, or aesthetic perfection, Baudelaire causes the sordid, mortal world to return and disrupt his reverie.[11] In the prose poem "Une Mort héroïque," he shows the fatal consequences of an artistic performance that suppresses the consciousness of death in order to lose itself in the perfection of a symbolic, ideal art. Death for Baudelaire, as Yves Bonnefoy has remarked, is a form of consciousness, a way of coming to know and apprehend the world and of seeing it as through a glass darkly.[12] Death becomes a mode of subjective thought and perception for Baudelaire.

11. For a discussion of "Le Masque" as an allegory of the unmasking of allegorical figuration, see my "L'Anamorphose baudelairienne: L'Allégorie du 'Masque,'" *Cahiers de l'Association Internationale des Etudes Françaises* 41 (May 1989): 251–67.
12. See his essay "Les Fleurs du mal," in *L'Improbable*, followed by *Un rêve fait à Mantoue*, new ed., corrected and augmented (Paris: Mercure de France, 1980), pp. 29–38. In *Les Fleurs de mal*, Bonnefoy observes, there is a striking convergence of temporality, as encountered in forces of decay and ruin, and of poetic language: an intimate conjoining "of the wounded body and of immortal language" (p. 34). For an examination of other ways Baudelaire poetically envisions and confronts death, see Marc Eigeldinger, "Baudelaire et la conscience de la mort," in his *Poésie et métamorphoses* (Neuchâtel: La Baconnière, 1973), pp. 137–54; John E. Jackson, *La Mort Baudelaire: Essais sur* Les Fleurs du mal (Neuchâtel: La Baconnière, 1982), and his "Rilke et Baudelaire," *Stanford French Review* 3 (Winter 1979): 325–41; Edward K. Kaplan, "Baudelaire and the Battle with Finitude: 'La Mort,' Conclusion of *Les Fleurs du mal*," *French Forum* 4 (September 1979): 219–31; and Ross Chambers, "Baudelaire's Street Poetry," *Nineteenth-Century French Studies* 13 (Summer 1985): 244–59.

It invades his memory, transforming it, as he writes in "Spleen," into "une pyramide, un immense caveau, / Qui contient plus de morts que la fosse commune" ("a pyramid, an immense vault, / Containing more dead than a potter's field"; *OC*, 73). His inner being, his psyche and soul, become "un cimetière abhorré de la lune" ("a cemetary the moon abhors"). So completely does Baudelaire's imagination internalize death that mortality comes to govern the natural, circadian rhythms of his body; his heart is "plein de choses funèbres" ("filled with lugubrious things") ("Brumes et pluies," *OC*, 101), containing "Chambres d'éternel deuil où vibrent de vieux râles" ("Chambers of eternal mourning where old death cries resound") ("Obsession," *OC*, 75).

To give concrete substance to these theoretical speculations, I will focus attention on images of melancholy and mourning as inspired by death in Baudelaire's poetry. That Baudelaire was obsessed with the subject of loss and sadness; that he developed a taste for despair, a "goût du néant" as he called it (*OC*, 76); that he was barely able, and then only because of poetry, to overcome experiences of hopeless horror; that he waged perpetual and vain war against time, the great destroyer of human desire; that he identified melancholy with the essential condition of human existence; that he recognized suffering as a permanent, and not an intermittent, state of being, the only arena in which man could find dignity; that he found neither reprieve nor escape in experiences of love or beauty, knowing all too well the pain, suffering, and evil they promised; that he perpetually manifested a need to fail, to be unsatisfied, to receive punishment; and that he imagined life as eternally and universally desperate, writing in "Le Gouffre" that "tout est abîme,—action, désir, rêve, / Parole!" ("everything is abyss—action, desire, dream / Word!"; *OC*, 142)—these are the dolorous commonplaces, the saturnine realities of the Baudelairean world.[13] And yet, against this dark background great poetic beauty and

13. Baudelaire was not "un mélancolique" in the strict and perhaps clinical meaning of that term; rather, as Jean Starobinski observes, "he imitated admirably—with the help of what he called his 'hysteria'—the attitudes of melancholy, and its hidden movements" (p. 143 n.1) ("Les Rimes du vide: Une Lecture de Baudelaire," *Nouvelle Revue de psychanalyse* 11 [Spring 1975]: 133–43). For a general discussion of melancholy's "alchemical" power of changing bile into ink, sadness into writing (melancholy "establishes *lack* . . . for which the melodic word becomes at the same time the symbolic compensation and the sensitive translation" [p. 419]), see Starobinski's "L'Encre de la mélancolie," *Nouvelle Revue française* 21 (1 March 1963): 410–23, in which he argues that the poetic expression of melancholy transforms "the impossibility of living into the possibility of speaking" (p. 422), and his *La Mélancolie au miroir: Trois lectures de Baudelaire* (Paris: Julliard, 1989). For a study of the relationship of death, melancholy, and art, see Marie-Claude Lambotte, *Esthétique de la mélancolie* (Paris: Aubier, 1984), and, on the identification of beauty with melancholy, see Sarah Kofman, *Mélancolie de l'art* (Paris: Galilée, 1985), pp. 9–33.

sublimity stand out. All is not somber and black in Baudelaire's fallen world, because his poetry expresses a fundamental ambivalence about human existence; it vacillates between a courageous acceptance of the temporal world of sadness, despair, and death and a profound longing to escape into an eternal universe of "Luxe, calme et volupté" (*OC*, 53), to rediscover the pristine place he called "le vert paradis des amours enfantines" ("the green paradise of child-like loves"; *OC*, 64). Out of the very negativity that lies at the heart of *Les Fleurs du mal* and *Le Spleen de Paris* and at the center of Baudelaire's dualistic experience of the world emerges a radiance which is that of the poetic work itself. It is the illumination these dark poems written under the sign of Saturn give: a night-bounded light that Baudelaire calls, alluding to the stars, "ces feux de la fantaisie qui ne s'allument bien que sous le deuil profond de la Nuit" ("these fires of fantasy that flare only beneath the deep mourning of the Night") ("Le Crépuscule du soir," *OC*, 312).[14]

The Extravagance of Mourning

In his aimless wanderings, his *flânerie*, through the streets of Paris Baudelaire is drawn to signs and figures of loss. Poets, he explains, like philosophers, "se sentent irrésistiblement entraînés vers tout ce qui est faible, ruiné, contristé, orphelin" ("feel themselves irresistably pulled towards whatever is weak, ruined, saddened, or orphaned") ("Les

---

For a discussion of Baudelaire's kinship to Dürer and the similarities between his melancholic vision and that of the German artist, see James S. Patty, "Baudelaire and Dürer: Avatars of Melancholia," *Symposium* 38 (Fall 1984): 244–57; and William Hauptman, "Baudelaire, Michelet, and Dürer's 'Melencolia I': A Problem in Meaning," *Studi Francesi* 64 (January–April 1978): 106–10, and his "Manet's Portrait of Baudelaire: An Emblem of Melancholy," *Art Quarterly*, n.s. 1, vol. 3 (Summer 1978): 214–43.

14. For a discussion of the sometimes dialectical, sometimes synthetic, but always coincident relationship of light to darkness in Baudelaire's imagination, see Georges Poulet, *La Poésie éclatée: Baudelaire/Rimbaud* (Paris: Presses Universitaires de France, 1980), pp. 53–65. The poetic expression of melancholy itself seems to share a similar quality of paradoxical illumination, as Jean Starobinski observes. From the somber tones of melancholic poetry emanates a mysterious radiance. The darkness of the written word possesses a unique glow: "Melancholy, having become ink, finally becomes the tain of the mirror that allows the image to shine" ("L'Encre de la mélancolie," p. 423). Allegory also is a radiance of meaning bounded and hidden by obscurity, a veiled light, as Gerald L. Bruns has remarked: "We may figure allegory as the curtain that conceals (in order to be made radiant by) a sanctuary. The curtain mediates the light of what is hidden—*mediates*, because the light would blind us if we were able to look at it directly. Without the curtain we would be unable to see anything at all: it would be as if nothing were there. Allegory is an instance of darkening by means of words. . . . Imagine a world or text that darkens and is radiant and you have allegory: a darkening radiance" ("Allegory and Satire: A Rhetorical Meditation," *New Literary History* 11 [Fall 1979]: 121–32).

Veuves," *OC*, 292). And the image of loss, the sign of deprivation and lack, that strikes him as the most telling, the most expressively poignant, is that of a woman in mourning, a figure that at least four of Baudelaire's poems ("Le Cygne," "Les Veuves," "Les Petites Vieilles," and "A une Passante") evoke. The mourning woman clothes herself in her sorrow, wearing her grief like a sign; she is the very incarnation of the reality and power of loss.[15] Passing across her face in the present moment is "Le nuage affreux du passé" ("The ghastly cloud of the past") ("Madrigal triste," *OC*, 138), for she is inherently nostalgic. In her posture, her movement, her unsharable grief, and her wanderings through the great modern metropolis, Baudelaire discovers an emblem for absence made present, for unsatisfied desire in pursuit of the dead being, the unrecoverable other, that would have been its completion and fulfillment. The widow is a peripatetic sign, a poem in motion, because she expresses in the form of her person and her dress what the poet seeks to reveal about loss in and through the form of his words: namely, that it is a memory occurring within a world beset by forgetfulness; that it is a past resurrected within the narrow limits of an obliterating, uncaring present; that it is a tenuous identification with a lost being but in the full awareness that the loss is irreversible. No wonder that the wandering poet watches for these mournful creatures and comes to love them, for they are soul mates. They suffer the universal misery that defines the human condition. In their person, the past is alive and dead simultaneously; the image of a lost object is resuscitated and annulled at once. The lives of these women are turned invariably toward the same catastrophe—a death in the past—which they represent and embody to the fullest within the present. Mourning is an excess, a nostalgic excess, invented to compensate for an awesome experience of deprivation. All of their being is concentrated so perfectly, so intently, and so totally on the death, which has given them their identity as widows, that this loss appears as a fullness. It is this dialectical coalescence of mournful emptiness and ecstatic plenitude that Baudelaire evokes, for example, in the figure of Andromache in

---

15. As were all Parisians who dressed in black. In his essay "De l'héroïsme de la vie moderne" (in *Salon de 1846*), Baudelaire calls on people who consider themselves "modern" to wear the black of mourning, for only a black suit has a truly *modern* (and "dandy") beauty. It is a dress of mourning for an age in mourning, "l'habit nécessaire de notre époque, souffrante et portant jusque sur ses épaules noires et maigres le symbole d'un deuil perpétuel" ("the necessary costume for a tormented epoch that carries on its thin, black shoulders the symbol of perpetual mourning"; *OC*, 2:494). On the dominance of black in nineteenth-century bourgeois male clothing, see Valerie Steele, *Paris Fashion: A Cultural History* (New York: Oxford University Press, 1988), pp. 79–96.

the poem "Le Cygne." Widowed and exiled, she is shown mourning "Auprès d'un tombeau vide en extase courbée" ("Leaning over an empty tomb entranced"; *OC,* 86).

The majesty and nobility of mourning women, the profound, incisive manner they have of looking at things, the dazzling contrast between them and the frivolous, indifferent Parisian crowds that pass them by, and the mysterious, almost sacred, aura enveloping them point to Baudelaire's fascination with images of a radiance bounded by obscurity, with the kind of dark light that in his imagination death and loss emit. The blackness of mourning can be dazzling, luminous, singular, and resplendent, as he points out in his prose poem "Les Veuves."[16] But the finest, the most noble and evocative, description of the radiant poetry of mourning is found in the sonnet "A une Passante" ("To A Passerby"), written in 1860 and included in the "Tableaux parisiens" section of *Les Fleurs du mal.* Baudelaire's momentary encounter with what is an apparition of mourning is epiphanic, one of those shock experiences which, Benjamin observes, the modern city gives to the poetic being whose consciousness is attuned to the mystery and melancholy of a street:

> La rue assourdissante autour de moi hurlait.
> Longue, mince, en grand deuil, douleur majestueuse,
> Une femme passa, d'une main fastueuse
> Soulevant, balançant le feston et l'ourlet;
>
> Agile et noble, avec sa jambe de statue.
> Moi, je buvais, crispé comme un extravagant,
> Dans son oeil, ciel livide où germe l'ouragan,
> La douceur qui fascine et le plaisir qui tue.
>
> Un éclair . . . puis la nuit!—Fugitive beauté
> Dont le regard m'a fait soudainement renaître,
> Ne te verrai-je plus que dans l'éternité?
>
> Ailleurs, bien loin d'ici! trop tard! *jamais* peut-être!
> Car j'ignore où tu fuis, tu ne sais où je vais,
> O toi que j'eusse aimée, ô toi qui le savais![17]

16. For an interesting study of the widow as an allegorical figure of the poet, see Edward K. Kaplan, "Baudelaire's Portrait of the Poet as Widow: Three Poëmes en Prose and 'Le Cygne,'" *Symposium* 34 (Fall 1980): 233–48.

17. Compelling, although different, interpretations of this poem are found in Donald Aynesworth, "A Face in the Crowd: A Baudelairian Vision of the Eternal Feminine,"

[The deafening street around me roared.
Tall, slender, in deep mourning, her sorrow majestic,
A woman passed, with splendid hand
Lifting, balancing, the embroidered hem of her dress;

Lithe and noble, her leg like sculpted marble.
With the strained intensity of an extravagant man I drank
In her eye, livid sky where storms brew,
The sweetness that charms and the pleasure that kills.

A lightning flash . . . then night!—Elusive beauty
Whose sudden glance gave me new life,
Will I not see you again except in eternity?

Elsewhere, far from here! too late! *never* perhaps!
I do not know where you flee, you do not know where I go,
O you whom I might have loved, o you who knew it well!]

(*OC*, 92–93)

The woman in the poem is an ideal emblem or icon of sublime, baroque mourning. She wears her grief lavishly, even stylishly. She is "en grand deuil" ("deep mourning"); she expresses a "douleur majestueuse" ("majestic sorrow"). There is a regal elegance and ostentatiousness to the appearance of her sorrow. She embodies an aesthetics of mourning. An attention to the gestures and movements of mourning preoccupies her, as she walks gracefully along the street,

---

Stanford French Review 5 (Winter 1981): 327–39 (which studies the traumatic power of the woman's apparition on the poet's consciousness and identity and on his perception of the urban landscape); Hartman, *Criticism in the Wilderness*, pp. 67–72 (which considers the poem from the perspective of Benjamin's aesthetic and philosophical theories); and Irving Wohlfarth, "*Perte d'auréole:* The Emergence of the Dandy," *MLN* 85 (1970): 529–71 (which relates *la passante* to Baudelaire's conception of the dandy). Other critics who briefly, although quite interestingly, discuss the poem are: Ross Chambers ("Pour une poétique du vêtement," *Michigan Romance Studies* 1 [1980]: 18–46), who sees the woman as representing the fascination of death, disguised and enhanced by beauty; J. D. Hubert (*L'Esthétique des* Fleurs du mal: *Essai sur l'ambiguïté poétique* [Geneva: Pierre Cailler, 1953], pp. 184–86), who points to the metaphysical terror Baudelaire experiences when confronted with a feminine Doppelgänger; and Karlheinz Stierle ("Baudelaire and the Tradition of the *Tableau de Paris*," *New Literary History* 11 [Winter 1980]: 345–61), who draws attention to the dramatic juxtaposition in the poem of familiarity and strangeness, identity and anonymity. See also Ross Chambers, "The Storm in the Eye of the Poem (Baudelaire's 'A une Passante')," in *Textual Analysis: Some Readers Reading*, ed. Mary Ann Caws (New York: Modern Language Association, 1986), pp. 156–66; John Jefferson Humphries, "Poetical History or Historical Poetry: Baudelaire's *Epouvantable Jeu* of Love and Art," *Kentucky Romance Quarterly* 30 (1983): 231–37; and Jérôme Thélot, "A une Passante," *Berenice* 7 (March 1983): 45–51.

raising the hem of her dress from time to time. She expresses the essence of mourning, into which her entire being has been folded. Everything about her denotes loss. Her sorrow, grief, and misfortune even seem to precede her, especially in the way Baudelaire chooses to describe her apparition in the second and third lines of the poem; she has already become a personification by the time she even appears as a person, as "une femme [qui] passa." She is, moreover, an elusive, enigmatic being whose only reality, beyond her infolded, self-referential mourning, is her passage, her movement into oblivion. In the way she passes in and then out of the poet's consciousness, in the way she is possessed and then lost by him, she dramatically enacts an allegory of loss and death.[18] We see the poet engaged in an experience of intimacy followed by separation, of ecstatic union followed by emptiness, of fulfillment followed by unappeasable desire. "A une Passante" presents an allegorical representation of how loss—as an experience of deprivation, distance, and difference and as a fragmentation of being—occurs. The poet's contemplation of this personification of mourning ultimately results in his becoming himself a figure of melancholy.

With an extravagance not different in its self-centered intensity from the ostentatious grandeur of the woman's mourning, the poet in the second stanza of "A une Passante" internalizes her inner being, experiencing through this union an enigmatic and erotic pleasure (ll. 6–8): "Moi, je buvais crispé comme un extravagant, / Dans son oeil, ciel livide où germe l'ouragan, / La douceur qui fascine et le plaisir qui tue" ("With the strained intensity of an extravagant man I drank / In her eye, livid sky where storms brew, / The sweetness that charms and the pleasure that kills"). This moment of intimacy is one of intense centering, a moment of concentrated ecstasy when the external world disap-

18. Hartman remarks that the woman "does not complete time but rather defers or ruins it. Fulfillment is projected onto a plane that is infinite or empty, perhaps both. She is originally, from eternity, elsewhere: *allegorical*" (*Criticism in the Wilderness*, p. 71). For studies of Baudelairean allegory and its representation of loss (loss of meaning, of transcendence, of unity), see Barbara Johnson, *Défigurations du langage poétique: La Seconde Révolution Baudelairienne* (Paris: Flammarion, 1979); Ross Chambers, "'Je' dans les Tableaux Parisiens de Baudelaire," *Nineteenth-Century French Studies* 9 (Fall–Winter 1980–81): 59–68; Richard Klein, "'Bénédiction'/'Perte d'auréole': Parables of Interpretation," *MLN* 85 (1970): 515–28; Jean Starobinski, "Sur quelques répondants allégoriques du poète," *Revue d'histoire littéraire de la France* 67 (April–June 1967): 402–12; and his "'Je n'ai pas oublié . . .'" (Baudelaire: Poème XCIX des *Fleurs du Mal*)," in *Au Bonheur des mots: Mélanges en l'honneur de Gérard Antoine* (Nancy: Presses Universitaires de Nancy, 1984), pp. 419–29; Nathaniel Wing, "The Danaides Vessel: On Reading Baudelaire's Allegories," in *The Limits of Narrative: Essays on Baudelaire, Flaubert, Rimbaud, and Mallarmé* (Cambridge: Cambridge University Press, 1986), pp. 8–18; and my "Allegory of Loss and Exile in the Poetry of Yves Bonnefoy," *World Literature Today* 53 (Summer 1979): 421–29.

pears, all distance is annulled, time is suspended, and the poet loses himself in a phantasmatic internalization. Curiously, he introjects the object of his desire at the very moment it is about to be lost. The identification with the soon-to-be-lost other reveals an interesting form of incorporation, for Baudelaire consumes, drinks in, the loved object primarily in order to prevent its loss. This ingesting of the other momentarily appropriates the loved object, making it disappear inside the poet's being, where it continues to live. The woman disappears, but the love relation between poet and object continues for the moment. By placing the object in the closest possible proximity to himself, he has avoided what he most fears: separation. Any difference between the poet and the woman is negated; otherness is thoroughly destroyed, and the poet achieves a momentary oneness with the loved being.[19]

Baudelaire's retention of the soon-to-be-lost object by installing it in the inner world of his being is, of course, a fantasy, one that expresses the love of a melancholic temperament; the poet phantasmatically keeps the lost object alive, importing it into his ego. While the woman disappears (symbolically dies), leaving a void in her place, the image of the woman continues to live within the poet. Thus, it becomes clear why the woman's glance, her last look as she passes out of existence, has suddenly rejuvenated the poet (ll. 9–10): "Fugitive beauté / Dont le regard m'a fait soudainement renaître" ("Elusive beauty / Whose sudden glance gave me new life"). Because the glance is the last image the poet has of her, he cherishes it. It is the trace she leaves behind in his ego, the final vision he is given of what is about to disappear, thus confirming Benjamin's observation that what Baudelaire experiences is love "not at first sight, but at last sight."[20] And yet loss has not been reversed. Although the central moment of the poem—the poet's internalization of the woman—appears to represent a possession of sorts, it is important to remember exactly what the poet has succeeded in

19. In Baudelaire's poetry, melancholy often negotiates acts of poetic internalization. The fantasy of an ingestive assimilation of the other, by which the lost object of desire is kept alive and present in its very absence, is a common image of Baudelairean intimacy. See, for example, the fourth stanza of "Le Balcon" (*OC*, 37); the opening lines of "Le Cygne" (*OC*, 85), in which the poet's mind is filled to overflowing with thoughts and memories; and the striking conclusion to "La Chevelure," in which the beloved becomes "l'oasis où je rêve, et la gourde / Où je hume à longs traits le vin du souvenir" ("the oasis where I dream, and the gourd / From which with long draughts I drink the wine of memory"; *OC*, 27). For an insightful study of the poetics of otherness and desire in Baudelaire, in particular the confrontation between the other and an "essential Alterity," see Jérôme Thélot, "Critique du crime: Le poème XXIV des *Fleurs du Mal*," in *Baudelaire, Les Fleurs du Mal: L'Intériorité de la forme* (Paris: SEDES, 1989), pp. 93–103.
20. "On Some Motifs in Baudelaire," in *Illuminations*, trans. Harry Zohn (New York: Schocken Books, 1969), p. 169.

preserving from the experience: not the woman, but her image; not the object as loved, but the object as lost; not the thing, but its shadow. The poet's image and memory of the woman do not exist in isolation from his consciousness of her absence. Loss surrounds the loved object like an aura; it is the new reality, the only dimension, by which the object can now be known.

The tercets of the sonnet describe the "hole in the real," as Lacan calls it, which the woman's disappearance has opened up. They indicate the distance, the separation, the interruption, the dispossession, and the lack of knowledge and union that are now present. The loss and death have become final; the darkness has swallowed the light. "Un éclair . . . puis la nuit!" ("a lightning flash . . . then night"), the poet says in line nine, and the entire encounter with the passing woman seems to disappear into the three dots of that ellipsis. A gap between two words ("éclair"-"nuit"), between an image of radiance and an image of darkness, is all that remains of the experience. The "hole" in the text mimetically represents the hole that has opened up within the poet's experience of the real.

In the first tercet the poet wonders whether he will be able to reencounter the lost object of love, whether he will see her again during his lifetime or in the beyond. "Ne te verrai-je plus que dans l'éternité?" ("Will I not see you again except in eternity?"), he asks. And his answer in the last stanza indicates the extent of his despair and loss: "Ailleurs, bien loin d'ici! trop tard! *jamais* peut-être!" ("Elsewhere, far from here! too late! *never* perhaps!"). The woman now occupies a region defined by its distance. In relation to wherever the poet may be in place and time, she will always be "elsewhere" ("ailleurs"), in a space invariably different from and other than his. She inhabits an "adverbial" region outside the finite temporality of human activity.[21] It is a realm that only allegory can express, because the otherness that alle-

---

21. For Baudelaire, adverbs express the uncertainty of a future time and the mystery of unknown or obscure places. In an interesting essay on sculpture from the *Salon de 1859* (in which he describes two allegorical statues, *Melancholy* and *Mourning*), Baudelaire meditates on man's reaction to the unknown realities of death, to

> ce je ne sais quoi que personne n'a nommé ni défini, que l'homme n'exprime que par des adverbes mystérieux, tels que: peut-être, jamais, toujours! et qui contient, quelques-uns l'espèrent, la béatitude infinie, tant désirée, ou l'angoisse sans trêve dont la raison moderne repousse l'image avec le geste convulsif de l'agonie.

> [this unknown that no one can name or define, that man expresses only through mysterious adverbs, such as "perhaps," "never," "always!"; this unknown that contains, one hopes, the infinite bliss we so much desire, or the endless suffering whose image modern-day reason rejects with a convulsive gesture of anguish.] (*OC*, 2:669)

gorical representation signifies is precisely that place—of oblivion, of death, of absence—wherein the lost object dwells.[22] Allegory represents an alterity with which it can never coincide. It indicates the place of union and oneness with the other which the poet desires, that always *other* region of presence refound, of origin recaptured. But allegory can not cross into that promised land; it cannot represent that fusion and immediacy of signifier and signified, that presence of word to thing, which symbolic language expresses.[23] It can only signify from afar. It is a writing in exile: decentered, dispersed, and errant.

I have already commented on the excess that language brings to the representation of loss and the abundant, often fecund, nature that sadness and mourning have in Baudelaire's poetry. There is an art to expressing mourning, and the passer-by in "A une Passante" has mastered this art to an exuberant degree.[24] Allegory can also be perceived as a rhetorical mode of exuberant representation whose signs, because they can never reach the object they designate, move in random, arbitrary, and extravagant patterns. These signs run to excess because a coincidence with the inaccessible and anterior referent is impossible.[25] They are signifiers cut off from the signified and free to go their

22. On the relation of the rhetoric of mourning to alterity, in particular the otherness of the lost other, see Jacques Derrida, *Mémoires, for Paul de Man,* trans. Cecile Lindsay, Jonathan Culler, and Eduardo Cadava (New York: Columbia University Press, 1986), pp. 31–34.

23. Benjamin acknowledges a radical difference between symbol and allegory. The fusion of subject and object, the indivisible unity of form and content, and the intimation of transcendental eternity, which are characteristic of symbolic representation, are beyond the powers of allegory. For Benjamin, allegory is the trope of negativity through which fragmentation, discontinuity, physicality, time, and death are figured in both language and art. The "will to symbolic totality" is undone by allegorical language; "it is as something incomplete and imperfect," Benjamin asserts, "that objects stare out from the allegorical structure" (*Origin,* p. 186).

24. As has Baudelaire, for, according to Benjamin, "Baudelaire's genius, which drew its nourishment from melancholy, was an allegorical one. . . . The allegorist's gaze which falls upon the city is . . . the gaze of alienated man" (*Charles Baudelaire: A Lyric Poet in the Era of High Capitalism,* trans. Harry Zohn [London: NLB, 1973], p. 170).

25. Commenting upon Croce's observation that allegory is " 'an expression externally added to another expression,' " Craig Owens writes that "allegory is conceived as a *supplement. . . .* Allegory *is* extravagant, an expenditure of surplus value; it is always *in excess.* Croce found it 'monstrous' precisely because it encodes two contents within one form. Still, the allegorical supplement is not only an addition, but also a replacement. It takes the place of an earlier meaning, which is thereby either effaced or obscured" ("The Allegorical Impulse: Toward a Theory of Postmodernism," part 1, *October* 12 [Spring 1980]: 67–86; see also part 2, *October* 13 [Summer 1980]: 59–80). Nathaniel Wing uses the myth of the Danaides' vessel (as figured in Baudelaire's "Le Tonneau de la haine") to describe metaphorically the endless excessiveness of allegorical interpretation. The open-ended nature of allegory and its deferral of signification demand desperate, over-determined gestures in the vain attempt to fill a container that is continuously losing its meanings: "This overfilling . . . is both an excess (there is too much to be contained) and

own way. No coincidence with an origin controls them or keeps their meanings from slipping, blurring, or sliding. Allegorical signs are fragments of a lost wholeness. Abandoned like derelict ships, they wander on uncharted seas, always in movement, always in search of an elusive, easily effaced meaning. The allegorical process of signification is arbitrary and plural. "Any person, any object, any relationship," writes Benjamin, "can mean absolutely anything else" (*Origin*, p. 175). Death has emptied the object of permanent meaning. Signification comes undone because the link between signifier and signified has been broken and cannot be restored.[26] This means that allegory is characterized by a writing whose aim is not to establish a univocal meaning but to multiply the conjunctions and substitutions, the comings and goings, of its signifiers so that a polyvalent meaning is created.[27] In its polysemy and mobility, and especially in the originating lack or loss that calls it into being, allegory resembles desire: primarily, the decentered, displaced desire that seeks a lost experience of pleasure through a series of changing representations, each of which is an allegorized fantasy of the absent, original satisfaction.[28]

Thus, "at one stroke," Benjamin writes, "the profound vision of allegory transforms things and works into stirring writing" (*Origin*, p. 176). This writing bestirs itself to action and movement; it stirs the multifarious fragments and chips of lost experience into an unstable, always incomplete representation; it emits a stirring call for the return

---

a deficiency (the container cannot fully enclose)." In poems such as "Le Cygne," "Les Sept Vieillards," and "Le Tonneau de la haine," images of endless proliferation suggest a "threatening indeterminacy" because they figure a "loss of the illusion of meaning": "Containment, fullness, completion are necessary, since the buckets are themselves being filled and continually being emptied into the vat, but the process is inadequate to the task. Allegory thus inscribes the impossibility of figurative language to contain what it would hold" (*The Limits of Narrative*, p. 17).

26. See Eric Gans's discussion of the irreversible separation between signifier and signified in Baudelaire's poetry, which distinguishes it from romantic and symbolist verse, in his article "Baudelaire et la douleur de la signification," in *Essais d'esthétique paradoxale* (Paris: Gallimard, 1977), pp. 195–220.

27. "The stock of [allegory's] visual requisites," Benjamin remarks, is "unlimited. With every idea the moment of expression coincides with a veritable eruption of images, which gives rise to a chaotic mass of metaphors" (*Origin*, p. 173).

28. See Leo Bersani's excellent study *Baudelaire and Freud* (Berkeley: University of California Press, 1977), pp. 60–62, 86, and passim. In an important essay on the theory of allegorical representation, Joel Fineman discusses the insatiability and errancy of allegorical desire: "Distanced at the beginning from its source, allegory will set out on an increasingly futile search for a signifier with which to recuperate the fracture of and at its source, and with each successive signifier the fracture and the search begin again: a structure of continual yearning, the insatiable desire of allegory" ("The Structure of Allegorical Desire," in *Allegory and Representation*, Selected Papers from the English Institute, 1979–80, n.s., no. 5, ed. Stephen J. Greenblatt [Baltimore: Johns Hopkins University Press, 1981], pp. 26–60).

and repossession of a lost other. Allegory incarnates loss and exile, because it is the perfect postlapsarian form. "As a faculty of the spirit of language itself," Benjamin observes, the allegorical "is at home in the Fall" (*Origin*, p. 234). The loss of a paradisiacal speech is the originating event that brings melancholy into language. From this moment on, language begins to mourn and lament the loss of oneness with the pure language of God. Once mourning and melancholy become embedded in language and the fusion of word and thing is destroyed, then language is put in exile. It is now subjected to uncertainty and polysemy; it becomes, in other words, allegorical. From the Fall, therefore, dates the overnaming (the naming without end) that all writing enacts. "In the language of men," writes Benjamin, things "are over-named."[29] Having lost the knowledge of a divine, Edenic language, man unknowingly renames things of the world that already have proper names in the lost language of God; his words are no more than supplements. Thus, what Benjamin calls "overnaming" (and what I have been describing as the allegorical tendency toward excess in signification) is "the linguistic being of melancholy,"[30] the way grief and loss come to dwell in language.

The woman in "A une Passante" oversignifies her bereavement by the theatrical, ornamental manner of her mourning, as, in some respects, the poet oversignifies his internalization of her being. In regards to an anterior object that has been lost, every word that comes afterward can be seen as an overnaming, an excess of signs manufactured to make up for the lack. (No wonder the poet gives us in line twelve so many adverbs to designate the future times and places he might meet the woman.) But because of the nature of the lack, every word is also an undernaming: a breath of air, a frail sound, trying vainly to cover the vast emptiness or to fill the bottomless void or to embody the substanceless absence that have been brought into being by the experience of loss. As an expression of lack, language is *de trop*, being supplementary, redundant, and repetitive. But as the repossession of the lost object, it is consistently unsuccessful and impoverished. Thus, language is at once a plenitude (of sorrowful, melancholic expression) and an emptiness (of meaning and of the power to restore). In the poetry of loss, therefore, excess and scarcity dialectically coexist. This is strikingly evident, for example, in the opening stanza of Baude-

29. "On Language as Such and on the Language of Man," in *Reflections: Essays, Aphorisms, Autobiographical Writings*, trans. Edmund Jephcott (New York: Harcourt Brace Jovanovich, 1978), p. 330. See chapter 4 below.
30. Ibid.

laire's "Le Cygne," in which the poet, his mind swelling with thoughts and memories, describes mourning (that of the exiled Andromache) as an experience both of abundance and of lack, or more precisely, as a lack that expands and grows over time into a fullness:

> Andromaque, je pense à vous! Ce petit fleuve,
> Pauvre et triste miroir où jadis resplendit
> L'immense majesté de vos douleurs de veuve,
> Ce Simoïs menteur qui par vos pleurs grandit,
>
> A fécondé soudain ma mémoire fertile,
> Comme je traversais le nouveau Carrousel.[31]

> [Andromache, I think of you! This small river,
> Poor sad mirror where once shone
> The immense majesty of your widow's grief,
> This deceptive Simois which grows with your tears,
>
> Suddenly enriched my fertile memory,
> As I crossed the new Carrousel.]

(OC, 85)

In a similar way, "A une Passante," whose title indicates that the poet is both addressing the departed woman and dedicating the poem to her, can be seen as a work in which the poet implicitly turns his thoughts toward the passer-by, fills his mind with her memory, and through an excessive naming attempts to resuscitate what has been lost, what cannot be recalled through nomination. Little is saved from the passing away that the poem describes. The final stanza tallies the loss, pointing to the absence of knowledge on the one hand—"Car j'ignore où tu fuis, tu ne sais où je vais" ("I do not know where you flee, you do not know where I go")—and to a hypothetical otherness, a longing vision of what might have been, on the other—"O toi que j'eusse aimée, ô toi qui le savais!" ("O you whom I might have loved, o you who knew it well!").

31. For an excellent analysis of "Le Cygne" which shows how memory and melancholy function in the poem as "symptoms of an *historical* identity" and as "signs of a modernity corresponding to the irony of the sign," see Ross Chambers, *Mélancolie et opposition: Les Débuts du modernisme en France* (Paris: José Corti, 1987), pp. 167–86. See also Victor Brombert, " 'Le Cygne': The Artifact of Memory," in *The Hidden Reader: Stendhal, Balzac, Hugo, Baudelaire, Flaubert* (Cambridge: Harvard University Press, 1988), pp. 97–102.

Thus, "A une Passante" commemorates an encounter with an emblematic figure of loss and evokes the poet's consequent experience of melancholy. It is a poem in which memory (seen as a process of internalization involving the poet's identification with the other) and its opposite, oblivion (as represented by the poet's lack of knowledge about the woman's past and future life and the possibility that she is lost forever), share the same stage. It is a poem in which intimacy and distance, joy and sorrow, possession and loss, light and darkness, eternity and time, plenitude and emptiness—the ambivalences of Baudelaire's dualistic world view—coexist.

The Shroud of Allegory

"Je sais l'art d'évoquer les minutes heureuses" ("I know the art of evoking happy moments"), writes Baudelaire in "Le Balcon" (*OC,* 37). But he also knows that such poetic nostalgia may detemporalize the experiences of the past, turning them into frozen, lifeless memories. To be relived in the full resonance of nostalgic recall, moments of felicity must be evoked in time, and through change, and with a consciousness of death. The art of evoking moments of happiness is a temporal one; it is allegorical. By lyrically expressing the past as something different from, and radically other than, the present—as a moment lost forever in time though momentarily resuscitated in mind—the poet experiences a paradoxical feeling of distance and intimacy. He speaks of the past, which he brings back to life, in the same breath as he mourns its loss, its perpetual absence. His poem is a *Trauerspiel,* composed of words in mourning. On one level, the past lives again, shining with the radiance of poetic recall; on another, it is lost forever, its light extinguished by the night of forgetfulness and death. But what keeps both allegory and mourning from descending into nothingness, into the gray misery, the spleen, of inaction and hopelessness, is the cathartic release of language. The poet, literally, gives sorrow words: words that are in excess; words that constitute a dispersed and endless writing; and words that, like transitional objects—the bits of cloth or corners of blankets little children cling to—replace, if only imperfectly, absent, loved things.

The allegorical sign, by designating what is not there, by making present in language what is absent from life, is a sign perpetually in mourning. It is also a sign of melancholy, of that saturnine longing and sadness which arise when the poet internalizes a lost object in the hope of prolonging his love and satisfying his desire for possession. The ambivalence between what is lost and what remains, between absence and recovery, in Baudelaire is never resolved. An aura of loss englobes each recaptured image. The poet sees his memories against the dark backdrop, the black canvas, the night sky of death and absence. Loss initiates language, originates desire, engenders mourning, and gives birth to the form that incorporates and precariously joins all these realities into one: the poem.

Baudelaire's poetry—mournful, melancholic, allegorical—is the one ephemeral possession that can be forged from death, the one frail light in the englobing darkness. The shroud of allegory that envelops the lost beings, the absent loved ones, the corpses of the past possesses a unique originality, which is the very reflection of the loss it embodies and mourns. This originality keeps suffering alive, giving it evocative and sublime expression. By means of a dialectical interplay of mourning and memorialization, Baudelaire's poems come to signify the loss that death has created. They make present on the level of the poetic text what in the poet's existential experience is, and will forever remain, absent: "ce qui ne se retrouve / Jamais, jamais!" ("what is never, never / Found again!"; "Le Cygne," *OC*, 87). Thus, Baudelaire's poems of death and mourning represent the expressiveness and the vacancy—the grinning teeth, the hollow, black eye-sockets—of a death that has been recast and reinscribed as allegory. His poems are poetic corpses enshrouded by the endless folds of allegorical writing.

In his study of photographic representation and its relation to his mother's death, Roland Barthes writes that

> it is said that mourning, by its gradual labor, slowly erases pain; I could not, I cannot believe this; because for me, Time eliminates the emotion of loss (I do not weep), that is all. For the rest, everything has remained motionless. For what I have lost is not a Figure (the Mother), but a being; and not a being, but a *quality* (a soul): not the indispensable, but the irreplaceable. I could live without the Mother (as we all do, sooner or later); but what life remained would be absolutely and entirely *unqualifiable* (without quality).[32]

A poetry that attempts to express the bereavement and loss of death, therefore, represents not the absent loved object but the brutal, un-

32. *La Chambre claire: Note sur la photographie* (Paris: Gallimard, Seuil, "Cahiers du cinéma," 1980), p. 118 [*Camera Lucida: Reflections on Photography*, trans. Richard Howard (New York: Hill and Wang, 1981), p. 75].

changing reality of its death, of its disappearance as a quality defining all other qualities in a life. In particular, it affirms that nothing can ever take the place of the lost being: that no word, no figure, no poem, no consoling speech or language can ever ultimately close the bottomless chasm that has now opened at the center of existence. The closure of a text—its drive toward a completed, synthesized meaning, its assertion of symmetry and unity, and its confidence in mimetic representation— is therefore perpetually thwarted by the infinite openness of loss, which allegory alone can express. Thus, to "give sorrow words" is to know that the words will have to go on forever and to accept the unbridled expressiveness of death's grinning rows of teeth.

CHAPTER 3

The "Fatal Shadow" of Otherness: Guillaume Apollinaire

Il n'y a d'absence que de l'autre.

[The only absence is that of the other.]
—Roland Barthes, *Fragments d'un discours amoureux*

There is a parlor game, more popular in the past than today, in which a sentence whispered from one person to another in a large group of people makes the tour of the room and undergoes a complete transformation. The speaking of the words, or rather the misspeaking of them, changes the sentence into a different utterance.

Perhaps in a similar way, Apollinaire's efforts to whisper his own being to the words and phrases of his poems—to speak lyrically in *Alcools* and *Calligrammes* of his loves, his failures, his despair, his hopes for poetry in the twentieth century, his memory of the historical and mythical past, and his Orphic identification with the universe—result in a kind of misspeaking. The self-portrait that finally does emerge differs considerably from the image of self that Apollinaire may have intended or wished to present. In the telling, the self-portrait becomes curiously distorted and strangely other. It is not surprising, then, that Apollinaire is a man anxiously awaiting the appearance of a true and unified self: "Un jour / Un jour je m'attendais moi-même / Je me disais Guillaume il est temps que tu viennes / Pour que je sache enfin celui-là que je suis" ("One day / One day as I invited my soul / I said to myself William it's time to come / So I at last may find out who I am").[1] But

---

1. "Cortège," in *Oeuvres poétiques*, Bibliothèque de la Pléiade (Paris: Gallimard, 1959), p. 74; cited in the text as *OP* [*Alcools*, trans. Anne Hyde Greet (Berkeley: University of California Press, 1965), p. 67; cited as *A*]. Translations of poems from Apollinaire's *Calligrammes* are cited as *C: Calligrammes: Poems of Peace and War (1913–1916)*, trans. Anne Hyde Greet (Berkeley: University of California Press, 1980).

does this "time" ever come? Does Apollinaire ever succeed in surprising the elusive self, grasping it, wrestling it to the ground, and holding it in place? Is he repeatedly fated in each successive attempt at poetic self-expression and self-examination to discover always different and always *other* versions of himself, until finally—the changing rhythms of being and the protean forms of self having been immobilized for all time by death—Apollinaire appears, to quote Mallarmé, "Tel qu'en Lui-même enfin l'éternité le change" ("Such as eternity changes him finally into Himself")?[2]

The Enigma of Otherness:
"Ce mystère fatal fatal d'une autre vie"

Whatever intentions the poet may have, his efforts at self-expression and his search for identity invariably involve the discovery of a fundamental difference. The singularity of one's being is established by the extent to which one differs from others and differs as well from the image of self that one may have. In speaking, we invariably make ourselves different and in looking at ourselves—in the specular images of a mirror, in the reflections of contemplative thought, in the works of artistic creation, and in the confrontations of psychoanalysis—we cannot help but perceive a fundamental otherness. "Is there anything / To be serious about," asks Ashbery in his poem "Self-Portrait in a Convex Mirror," "beyond this otherness"

> That gets included in the most ordinary
> Forms of daily activity, changing everything
> Slightly and profoundly, and tearing the matter
> Of creation, any creation, not just artistic creation
> Out of our hands, to install it on some monstrous, near
> Peak, too close to ignore, too far
> For one to intervene? This otherness, this
> "Not-being-us" is all there is to look at
> In the mirror, though no one can say
> How it came to be this way.[3]

A coherent and complete definition of self must include the reality of otherness, of this "Not-being-us." It has to take account of what the

2. "Le Tombeau d'Edgar Poe," in *Oeuvres complètes*, Bibliothèque de la Pléiade (Paris: Gallimard, 1945), p. 70.
3. *Self-Portrait in a Convex Mirror* (New York: Viking Press, 1975), pp. 80–81.

philosopher Hannah Arendt calls "a difference . . . inserted into my Oneness."[4] That difference is an integral and constitutive part of what the self is and determines the uniqueness of its identity. "Everything that exists among a plurality of things," writes Arendt, "is not simply what it is, in its identity, but it is also different from others; this being different belongs to its very nature. When we try to get hold of it in thought, wanting to define it, we must take this otherness (*altereitas*) or difference into account. When we say what a thing is, we must say what it is *not* or we would speak in tautologies: every determination is nega- tion, as Spinoza has it."[5] Thinking—the act by which we reflect, medi- tate, contemplate, or take counsel with ourselves in a silent interior dialogue, in which one self questions and another responds—actual- izes and activates difference. Ultimately, difference and otherness are, asserts Arendt, "the very conditions for the existence of man's mental ego."[6]

Alterity is a fundamental fact of existence and an inescapable condi- tion of self-expression and self-consciousness. The question of the *moi* is also a question of the *autre*, for one cannot look upon oneself without seeing in that reflection the face of the other. I show in this chapter that alterity is an essential phenomenon of Apollinaire's search for self through poetry. Because it gives dramatic and lyrical form to interior states of being and because it exteriorizes these states in the form of the poem, poetry has the power to transform the self into a distant other. It creates an estrangement, which paradoxically initiates a dialogue be- tween the poet and those distanced, specular images that give form to his otherness. The writing of a poem, Apollinaire suggests in "Ombre," resembles the casting of a shadow. The light or illumination emanating from the poet's imagination or being is broken by the presence of an object or body and is darkened, creating an "Ecriture de ma lumière" ("Handwriting of my light"; *Oeuvres poétiques*, 217/*Calligrammes*, 137). When cast against the white surface of the page, the self is embodied as an "ombre fatale" ("fatal shadow") of otherness, a palpable sign or trace of alterity (*OP,* 125).

To the Orphic poet who desires to sing powerfully enough to make the sun rise and who wishes to fuse the song of the self with a world- chant—to a poet, that is, such as Apollinaire, who asserts with poetic immodesty "je chante toutes les possibilités de moi-même hors de ce

4. *The Life of the Mind,* 1: *Thinking* (New York and London: Harcourt Brace Jovano- vich, 1978), p. 183.
5. Ibid.
6. Ibid., p. 187.

monde et des astres / Je chante la joie d'errer et le plaisir d'en mourir" ("I sing of my own possibilities beyond this world and the stars / I sing the joy of wandering and the pleasure of the wanderer's death"; *OP*, 188/*C*, 71)—otherness is an enigma. Whether the poet's self moves centrifugally in the direction of the exterior world or prefers to follow a centripetal path toward a nucleus of essential selfhood, it consistently faces the irreducible reality of the other. No matter if Apollinaire tries to draw the world into himself, thus merging its multifarious elements with the personal joy and suffering of the lyrical self; or, to the contrary, no matter if he attempts to disperse fragments of the self in the universe, where they invade the otherness of objects and imperialistically take possession of them in the name of the self: in each case, he cannot avoid confronting the resistance of the other. The goal of his desire and thus of his poetry is the transcending of alterity, the obliteration of difference, and the simultaneous coexistence of both the other and the self. Only a poetic vision such as Apollinaire's, with its faith in the power of the synthetic imagination and in the creative force of simultaneity, could conceive the possibility of such a state of non-differentiation.[7] Apollinaire desires to create a world-self in which there would be no separation, no distance, and above all no difference between subject and object. His is a dream of oneness and plenitude, which is to be perpetually frustrated because the wholeness he yearns for is not possible. Yet, the strength of this desire is the energizing and motivating force of his poetry, his aesthetic theory, and his subjectivity. What frustrates Apollinaire's effort to totalize the self, and to make poetry generate the *plenum* of an uninterrupted oneness with the world, is the unassimilable "mystère fatal fatal d'une autre vie" ("fatal fatal mystery of another life"; *OP*, 150/*Alcools*, 201). The otherness of the objects of the poet's perception, desire, and memory causes these objects to escape the gravitational pull of the poetic ego. Otherness cannot be integrated in any completely satisfying way into the poetic self.

7. Clemens Heselhaus has pointed out that in Apollinaire's "simultaneity poems," multiple experiences, observations, and sensations are presented as if fused together within the poet's self: "The lyric author no longer reports or narrates, nor does he describe his own 'experiences' as a succession of events; he experiences the simultaneity of what enters into him. . . . What remains determinant is the fact that simultaneity represents a new structural principle within which the relation of parts to whole and whole to parts can be newly formulated. . . . The lyric *I* . . . as the *I* of the simultaneity poem keeps the heterogeneous associations together" (Hans Robert Jauss et al., "Group Interpretation of Apollinaire's *Arbre* (From *Calligrammes*)," in *New Perspectives in German Literary Criticism: A Collection of Essays*, trans. David Henry Wilson and others, ed. Richard E. Amacher and Victor Lange [Princeton: Princeton University Press, 1979], p. 199).

Apollinaire's thirst for the world—so passionately expressed in lines such as "J'ai soif villes de France et d'Europe et du monde / Venez toutes couler dans ma gorge profonde" ("I am thirsty come to me cities of France Europe and the world / Flow down my deep throat"; *OP*, 149/*A*, 199)—is destined to remain forever unquenched. Similarly, although in the opposite direction, the centrifugal movement of the dispersed myriads of mobile, partial selves, looking for havens in the world—expressed in a line such as "J'ai creusé le lit où je coule en me ramifiant en mille petits fleuves qui vont partout" ("I have hollowed out the bed where I flow and branch in a thousand small streams going everywhere"; *OP*, 272/*C*, 259)—does not have any greater success in overcoming the haunting alterity of an estranged and distant other. Apollinaire's poems express repeatedly the desire for the wholeness of a unified self completely and perfectly fused with the world; but they also reveal the failure of this desire for undifferentiated being. In the poems to be considered it will become evident how Apollinaire's poetry describes the movement between self and world as following either a centrifugal or a centripetal trajectory—the self invading the world or the world moving into the self—but never a coincidence of the two, even though such coincidence is the ultimate goal of the poet's desire for a unified and total self. The movement to fusion is always in one direction only and is thus fundamentally incomplete. With the exception of the "poems of fire" ("Le Brasier" and "Les Fiançailles"), in which an uninterrupted union between self and world is envisioned as a future ideal, the poems that will be discussed in the following pages express the poet's failure to supplement the lack of a lost object and to arrive at the full and undifferentiated possession of the other.[8]

"Qui parle ombre parle vrai"

In Apollinaire's poetic world, the shadow represents several things, many of them contradictory: life, death, the past, memory, mystery,

---

8. For studies that deal in part with the question of self in Apollinaire's work and with the nature of Apollinairean desire, see Margaret Davies, "Poetry as the Reconciliation of Contradictions in Apollinaire," in *Order and Adventure in Post-Romantic French Poetry: Essays Presented to C. A. Hackett*, ed. E. M. Beaumont, J. M. Cocking, and J. Cruickshank (London: Basil Blackwell, 1973), pp. 176–91; Raymond Jean, *Lectures du désir* (Paris: Seuil, 1977), pp. 7–28 and 105–41; and Dennis G. Sullivan, "On Time and Poetry: A Reading of Apollinaire," *MLN* 88 (May 1973): 811–37. In addition, see Michel Décaudin, "Apollinaire à la recherche de lui-même," *Cahiers du Sud*, no. 61 (January–March 1966): 3–12; James R. Lawler, "Music in Apollinaire," in *The Language of French Symbolism* (Princeton: Princeton University Press, 1969), pp. 218–62; Henri Meschonnic,

elusiveness, permanence, fate, exile, separation, the interruption of light, the continuing of light.[9] As Paul Celan writes, "Qui parle ombre parle vrai."[10] Primarily, however, the shadow is an image for the elusiveness of alterity. The insubstantial, impalpable trace of a distant object whose shape it adopts and to which it has an imperfect, if not incomplete, resemblance, the shadow is the sign of an absence, the trace of the physical body from which it is separated. It is the projected embodiment of a distant object whose uniqueness and singularity have been lost in the conversion to shadow-life. Thus, in the poem "Ombre" Apollinaire laments the loss of particularity, which the indifferent shadow represents:

Vous voilà de nouveau près de moi
Souvenirs de mes compagnons morts à la guerre
L'olive du temps
Souvenirs qui n'en faites plus qu'un
Comme cent fourrures ne font qu'un manteau
Comme ces milliers de blessures ne font qu'un article de journal
Apparence impalpable et sombre qui avez pris
La forme changeante de mon ombre
Un Indien à l'affût pendant l'éternité
Ombre vous rampez près de moi
Mais vous ne m'entendez plus
Vous ne connaîtrez plus les poèmes divins que je chante
Tandis que moi je vous entends je vous vois encore
Destinées
Ombre multiple que le soleil vous garde
Vous qui m'aimez assez pour ne jamais me quitter
Et qui dansez au soleil sans faire de poussière
Ombre encre du soleil
Ecriture de ma lumière

"Apollinaire illuminé au milieu d'ombres," in *Pour la poétique III: Une parole écriture* (Paris: Gallimard, 1973), pp. 55–107; and my *The Drama of Self in Guillaume Apollinaire's* Alcools, North Carolina Studies in the Romance Languages and Literatures, no. 178 (Chapel Hill: University of North Carolina Press, 1976).

9. For a comprehensive study of the different meanings of the shadow image, see Marie-Jeanne Durry, *Guillaume Apollinaire:* Alcools, 3 vols. (Paris: SEDES, 1964), 3:191–212. See also Maryann De Julio, "The Drama of Self in Apollinaire and Reverdy: Play of Light and Shadow," *French Forum* 6 (May 1981): 154–62, for a different reading of Apollinaire's "Ombre."

10. "Enonce" ["Sprich auch du"], in "De Seuil en Seuil," trans. Jean-Claude Schneider, *Nouvelle Revue française* 28 (1 December 1966): 1012.

Caisson de regrets
Un dieu qui s'humilie

[Here you are near me once more
Memories of my comrades dead in battle
Olive of time
Memories composing now a single memory
As a hundred furs make only one coat
As those thousands of wounds make only one newspaper article
Impalpable dark appearance you have assumed
The changing form of my shadow
An Indian hiding in wait throughout eternity
Shadow you creep near me
But you no longer hear me
You will no longer know the divine poems I sing
But I hear you I see you still
Destinies
Multiple shadow may the sun watch over you
You who love me so much you will never leave me
You who dance in the sun without stirring the dust
Shadow solar ink
Handwriting of my light
Caisson of regrets
A god humbling himself]

(*OP*, 217/*C*, 135–37)

If the shadow is the calligraphic inscription of the self onto the landscape (an "Ecriture de ma lumière"), then it represents some thing that is missing and irretrievable. The body that casts the shadow and the poet's self that "casts" the words of the poem cannot be recovered from the incomplete and substantial traces left behind. The origin is absent. Apollinaire's dead companions are indiscriminately reduced to a somber, homogeneous mass. The uniqueness and the complexity of the body or the self are not captured in the incompletely formed shadow. Apollinaire appears to suggest in this poem that poetry cannot express the idiosyncratic and essential being of the self. The poem is always incomplete and always different. It posits an irreversible alterity. The poet can only try to overcome it by the writing of another poem, which in turn will require yet another, and so on. Because poetry is the very place of otherness, no poem can ever get beyond this inescapable condition, this fate of always being other.

The shadow, then, is the sign of a difference, the trace of an absent, unpossessable other to which the shadow has a certain, although only partial, resemblance. The shadow stands apart from the poet. Incomplete and distant, it is an elusive aspect of the poet's self that he cannot approach, let alone embrace. Every step he makes toward it causes it to move farther ahead. As the image for an unpossessable part of the poet's being, the shadow represents all forms of otherness—mirror images, poems, friends, lovers—which, despite their closeness, ultimately elude his universal embrace and defeat his longing for an undifferentiated self. The shadow represents the failure of the desire for universal identification and the perpetual deferral of plenitude. In an earlier poem, from *Alcools,* Apollinaire calls attention to the mournful absence of life that the shadow represents and to the experience of nothingness that it imparts to the poet: "Ténébreuse épouse que j'aime / Tu es à moi en n'étant rien / O mon ombre en deuil de moi-même" ("Shadowy wife that I love / Your are mine and you are nil / My shadow that mourns for me"; *OP,* 54/A, 31).

Apollinaire desires the end of otherness, the negation of difference, the cessation of absence, and the simultaneous fusion of ego and world; only then will loss, separation, and incompleteness be denied. He expresses this dream of synthesis in a text that deals not with poetry (although resemblances are implied) but with the nature of modern painting. In his essay "Les Trois vertus plastiques," Apollinaire glorifies the synthetic power of the painter's imagination, which derives its creative energy from light (the medium of all painting), which he likens to the purity of fire:

> La flamme a la pureté qui ne souffre rien d'étranger et transforme cruellement en elle-même ce qu'elle atteint.
>
> Elle a cette unité magique qui fait que si on la divise, chaque flammèche est semblable à la flamme unique.
>
> Elle a enfin la vérité sublime de sa lumière que nul ne peut nier.[11]

[Flame has a purity which tolerates nothing alien, and cruelly transforms in itself whatever it touches.

Flame has a magical unity; if it is divided, each fork will be like the single flame.

Finally it has the sublime and incontestable truth of its own light.]

11. *Les Peintres cubistes: Méditations esthétiques,* ed. L. C. Breunig and J.-Cl. Chevalier, Collection Miroirs de l'art (Paris: Hermann, 1965), p. 46 [*The Cubist Painters: Aesthetic Meditations, 1913,* trans. Lionel Abel, Documents of Modern Art, no. 1 (New York: George Wittenborn, 1970), p. 10].

Apollinaire's longing to be the one and the many, the *je* and the *tu*, ego and world is fulfilled in this description. The flame destroys the categories of otherness and difference. The dividing of the flame does not change its nature; rather, it initiates a repetition that annuls difference. The flame's identity is untouched and its intensity undiminished by any kind of separation, distance, or fragmentation. The "flammèche" is no different from the original flame it embodies and duplicates. For Apollinaire, fire represents an ideal state—a condition of future rebirth—in which division will produce no difference, alterity will be abolished, and the poetic self, like the fire, will come to possess an irreducible "magic unity." In the image of a rejuvenating fire, Apollinaire expresses the goals of his desire: first, to reverse the experiences of loss and separation encountered in a temporal existence; second, to reduce the otherness that makes life incomplete; and third, to supplement the lack that alone has made desire necessary. The aim of desire, ultimately, is the end of desire, the complete and perfect satisfaction of longing through the artistic creation of a unified, undifferentiated self. But this is an ideal, the phantasm of a fervently desiring poetic will. By being itself absent and unfulfilled, this ideal creatively nourishes desire, which is the life force of Apollinaire's poetry.

Desire and the Poetic Imagination

Apollinaire's poetry demonstrates two kinds of alterity. There is first an otherness that can be called *autotropic* (meaning, literally, turned toward the self) because its referent is the poetic *I*, expressed either by first- and second-person pronouns (*je* and *tu*) or incarnated in various *personae* (Merlin, Pan, Icarus, Amphion). There is a second kind of otherness whose referent is not the Apollinairean self, but those individuals of verifiable existential reality with whom Apollinaire was friendly or intimate. Looking as it does toward other people, this form of otherness can be called *allotropic*. Whether functioning "allotropically" or "autotropically" and whether as an allotrope (sign of the other) or an autotrope (figure for the self), the other in Apollinaire's poetry demonstrates considerable resistance, for it is in perpetual flight from the poet's advances. A never-diminished gap exists between the poet and the object of his longing.[12] Desire emerges from this gap.

---

12. Regarding the irreducible distance between self and other and the absence that characterizes all states of otherness, Barthes writes in *Fragments d'un discours amoureux* (Paris: Seuil, 1977) [*A Lover's Discourse: Fragments,* trans. Richard Howard (New York: Hill

Thus, the perpetual existence of desire is assured, and the being of the desiring subject is established. As long as Apollinaire yearns for the impossible state of nondifference, which will put an end to the other as an independent subject and will unite the self to it, desire will not abate; the poem will continue to be, in René Char's aphorism, "désir demeuré désir" ("desire remained desire").[13]

It is Apollinaire's destiny—the "fatal shadow" falling on his life—to be forever in a state of indefinite displacement as his desire moves from object to object and among different forms of otherness. Desire, as Freud and Lacan have shown, moves from one substitute image to another in an endless and fruitless pursuit of a loved object, a transcendental Other, which can never be fully represented, let alone possessed. Language is the locus for this search and poetic language, the means whereby the poet tries to bridge the gap between the self and the distant other. Through the imagined possession of the other, the poet attempts the recovery of a lost intimacy and plenitude. But the fundamental *manque-à-être*—the lack and primal loss of oneness with another in which language, desire, and subjectivity have their origins—can never be fulfilled. Only surrogates that substitute momentarily for the lost object or experience can be found. The fulfillment of the lack can be imagined, but only partially; it can never be fully or completely represented. The word, according to Lacan, is "already a presence become absence." Desire reproduces "the relationship of the subject to the lost object," but it can never restore that object.[14] This relation can be expressed in terms of absence only. Of the lost object, only the quality of absence (and thus of difference and otherness) which defines it can be signified. The object of desire is powerfully present to the poet's consciousness and in his poetry, but only insofar as it is recognized as being lost and unrecoverable.

"La grande force est le désir" ("The supreme force is desire"), writes Apollinaire in "Les Collines" (*OP*, 173/*C*, 37), and this desire is uninterruptible, perpetual, and insatiable. It burns with a fierce intensity

---

and Wang, 1978)]: "Absence can exist only as a consequence of the other: it is the other who leaves, it is I who remain. The other is in a condition of perpetual departure, of journeying; the other is, by vocation, migrant, fugitive; I—I who love, by converse vocation, am sedentary, motionless, at hand, in expectation, nailed to the spot, *in suspense*—like a package in some forgotten corner of a railway station. Amorous absence functions in a single direction, expressed by the one who stays, never by the one who leaves: an always present *I* is constituted only by confrontation with an always absent *you*" (p. 19/13).

13. "Partage formel," in *Fureur et mystère*, Collection Poésie (Paris: Gallimard, 1962), p. 73.

14. *Ecrits* (Paris: Seuil, 1966), pp. 276 and 853, respectively.

because it draws its strength from an object perpetually *in absentia*. Its insatiability can reach universal proportions, as in a poem such as "Vendémiaire" when, after having ingested the cries, voices, and liquified outpourings of different cities, countries, and rivers, the still-parched Apollinaire announces:

> Mondes qui vous ressemblez et qui nous ressemblez
> Je vous ai bus et ne fus pas désaltéré
> . . . . .
> Ecoutez-moi je suis le gosier de Paris
> Et je boirai encore s'il me plaît l'univers
>
> [Worlds that resemble us and yourselves
> Though I have drained you I am thirsty still
> . . . . .
> Hear me I am the gullet of Paris
> I shall drain the universe again if I wish]
>
> (*OP*, 153–54/*A*, 209)

But the most striking acknowledgment of the powerlessness of the poet's desire to bridge the gap separating it from its object is the war poem "Dans l'abri-caverne" (*OP*, 259–60/*C*, 235–37). This poem, while paradoxically affirming the impotence of desire, insists on its power as a source of creative energy. It is characteristic of many of Apollinaire's World War I poems addressed to a distant other, a *donna lontana*. "Dans l'abri-caverne" opens with a passionate embrace of the two lovers, rendered all the more ardent because of the great distance that separates them:

> Je me jette vers toi et il me semble aussi que tu te jettes vers moi
> Une force part de nous qui est un feu solide qui nous soude
>
> [I project myself toward you and I think that you too project
>   yourself toward me
> A force issues from us it's a solid fire welding us together]

The élan of this initial union suddenly ceases. Apollinaire becomes aware of a "contradiction" inherent in every love poem that tries to recreate the presence of an absent or lost beloved. He acknowledges the illusoriness and factitiousness of an imaginative creation that fails to accept the reality of absence and to confront the presence of otherness:

Et puis il y a aussi une contradiction qui fait que nous ne pouvons
    nous apercevoir
En face de moi la paroi de craie s'effrite
Il y a des cassures
De longues traces d'outils traces lisses et qui semblent être faites
    dans de la stéarine
Des coins de cassures sont arrachés par le passage des types de ma
    pièce

[And yet paradoxically we can't see each other
Facing me the chalk wall crumbles
Filled with fractures
Long traces of tools sleek traces that appear to be made of stearin
Edges of fractures are torn by the fellows in my room passing by]

Apollinaire's passionate desire comes face to face with the reality of
absence and loss. It is not enough to imagine the woman one loves. The
poet must also imagine her distance. He must represent the otherness
that defines her relationship to him and that constitutes her identity at
this particular moment in time. Desire has its origins in a no man's land
between the poet and the other. It originates in alterity but then works
to abolish that otherness. The signs of his separation—the crumbling
chalk wall, its chips, cracks, and scratches, his vision, now blocked so he
no longer contemplates embracing the woman but rather stares for-
lornly at the wall facing him—these signs of material erosion and
decomposition forcefully suggest the impotence of his desire. Love
cannot stop the powers of loss or death at work in nature or in a world
at war.

    "Dans l'abri-caverne" is one of those poetic works of despairing
insight into the self which characterize some of Apollinaire's finest
lyrical poems. ("La Chanson du Mal Aimé," "Zone," and "A la Santé"
are other examples.) But it offers a rare topographical view of the inner
world of the Apollinairean self, which, because it is described by the
poet as a void, seems closer to Baudelaire's "paysages d'âme" than to
Apollinaire's earlier poetic representations of the interior "soulscape":

Moi j'ai ce soir une âme qui s'est creusée qui est vide
On dirait qu'on y tombe sans cesse et sans trouver de fond
Et qu'il n'y a rien pour se raccrocher
Ce qui y tombe et qui y vit c'est une sorte d'êtres laids qui me font
    mal et qui viennent de je ne sais où

Oui je crois qu'ils viennent de la vie d'une sorte de vie qui est dans
l'avenir dans l'avenir brut qu'on n'a pu encore cultiver ou
élever ou humaniser
Dans ce grand vide de mon âme il manque un soleil il manque ce
qui éclaire

[As for me tonight I have a soul that's hollow and empty
You could say in my soul someone keeps falling and finding no
bottom
And there's nothing to grab onto
What keeps falling and living inside me is a crowd of ugly beings
that hurt me I don't know where they come from
But I think they come from life from a kind of life still in the
future a raw future not yet refined or exalted or humanized
In the huge emptiness of my soul there isn't any sun there's
nothing that gives light]

Apollinaire, poet of light and of fire, who boasts in a poem that "c'est moi seul nuit qui t'étoile" ("Night I am the one who constellates you"; *OP,* 98/*A,* 115), has here lost his creative power. The poet's inner world reveals only a *manque-à-être.* Art or poetry is of no avail because the emptiness he feels comes from an inhuman, future world, as yet uncivilized by the light of truth or by the imagination. Apollinaire consoles himself in "Dans l'abri-caverne" with the realization (or maybe the rationalization) that his feeling of emptiness is short-lived and will disappear by morning: "C'est aujourd'hui c'est ce soir et non toujours / Heureusement que ce n'est que ce soir" ("It's today it's tonight but it's not for always / Luckily it's just for tonight"). Yet, he cannot quite free himself from the knowledge of the contradiction that has interrupted his erotic revery: namely, the awareness that the other is a beloved who can never be possessed, because her absence demands, *faute de mieux,* the use of poetry, which is always already, from the very beginning, the inscription of absence and the fiction of presence. The art of poetry cannot overcome distance. At best, it expresses the phantasms of a creative imagination, the fantasies that offer no intimacy and that permit no union other than the one fabricated narcissistically by the dreaming poet:

Les autres jours je me rattache à toi
Les autres jours je me console de la solitude et de toutes les
horreurs

En imaginant ta beauté
Pour l'élever au-dessus de l'univers extasié
Puis je pense que je l'imagine en vain
Je ne la connais par aucun sens
Ni même par les mots
Et mon goût de la beauté est-il donc aussi vain
Existes-tu mon amour
Ou n'es-tu qu'une entité que j'ai créée sans le vouloir
Pour peupler la solitude
Es-tu une de ces déesses comme celles que les Grecs avaient douées
    pour moins s'ennuyer

[Luckily it's just for tonight
Most days I cling to you
Most days I console myself for loneliness and all kinds of horrors
By imagining your beauty
And raising it above the ecstatic universe
Then I start wondering if I imagine it in vain
For I can't know your beauty by my senses
Or even by words
Then is my fondness for beauty also in vain
Do you really exist my love
Or are you only a being I created involuntarily
So that I might people my loneliness
Are you a goddess like those the Greeks instated so as to feel less
    weary]

In answer to these questions, and in a final reversal of the despair and doubt that he has been struggling with, Apollinaire affirms passionately not that poetry has the power to compensate for loss (it does not), but rather that desire has the power to create: to form images and phantasms for the elusive, unreachable other. Apollinaire asserts that the poem is the locus of desire, of *creative* desire, and as such will be the inexhaustible source of revery. In the poem's final verse, he celebrates the creativity of the poetic imagination: its inventiveness in finding new signs for presenting absence; its power to suggest new ways for tracing the elusiveness of the distant beloved; and its ingenuity in multiplying the diverse images that are the necessary surrogates for the unpossessable other: "Je t'adore ô ma déesse exquise même si tu n'es que dans mon imagination" ("I worship you my delicate goddess even if you are only the creature of my thought").

"L'Unique Lumière": The Dream of Otherness Denied

In "Dans l'abri-caverne," Apollinaire wonders whether the woman he loves and thinks about is real or "une entité que j'ai créée sans le vouloir / Pour peupler la solitude" ("a being I created involuntarily / So that I might people my loneliness"). This same question might be asked of the images of self Apollinaire presents in his poetry. Are they false and imaginary entities, fictions, that is, created by the poet in order to give himself an identity, a substantial reality? The poem "Cortège" (*OP*, 74–76/*A*, 67–71) offers a response; it expresses the tenacity of Apollinaire's desire to discover finally who he is: "Je me disais Guillaume il est temps que tu viennes / Pour que je sache enfin celui-là que je suis" ("I said to myself William it's time to come / So I at last may find out who I am"). While Apollinaire asks in "Dans l'abri-caverne" whether he can truly know the beauty of the woman he imagines—"Je ne la connais par aucun sens / Ni même par les mots" ("I can't know your beauty by my senses / Or even by words"), he writes—he does not have such doubts about knowing the other in "Cortège": "Moi qui connais les autres / Je les connais par les cinq sens et quelques autres" ("I who know the others / I know them by five senses and by some others"). It is the poet's strategy to re-create those others who once lived in a historical and folkloric past. By reconstructing them through imagination, memory, and the senses, a self may possibly be created. From bits and pieces the poet reconstructs the others, and they return the favor, piling up fragments, which finally coalesce into a complete self:

Le cortège passait et j'y cherchais mon corps
Tous ceux qui survenaient en n'étaient pas moi-même
Amenaient un à un les morceaux de moi-même
On me bâtit peu à peu comme on élève une tour
Les peuples s'entassaient et je parus moi-même
Qu'ont formé tous les corps et les choses humaines

[The procession marched by and I looked for my body there
All those who arrived and were not myself
Brought one by one the fragments of myself
They built me little by little as one raises a tower
The nations huddled together and I myself appeared
Formed by all bodies all human concerns]

Alterity generates the poetic self. Pieces combine to fabricate a whole self according to the poetics of accumulation evident throughout Apollinaire's poetry. The goal of the poet's desire—to join self and other in a union of nondifference and to reverse the incompleteness of existence—seems to have been realized. But has it really? In "Dans l'abri-caverne," Apollinaire wondered about the fictionality of poetry and about the imaginary, phantasmatic beings it creates. In "Cortège," and especially in its two concluding stanzas, the power of art is acclaimed, an art that turns away from the future to seek refuge in an unchanging, perfectly formed past synonymous with the poet's self:

Temps passés Trépassés Les dieux qui me formâtes
Je ne vis que passant ainsi que vous passâtes
Et détournant mes yeux de ce vide avenir
En moi-même je vois tout le passé grandir

Rien n'est mort que ce qui n'existe pas encore
Près du passé luisant demain est incolore
Il est informe aussi près de ce qui parfait
Présente tout ensemble et l'effort et l'effet

[Time past   time that has passed away   You gods who shaped
          me
I live only passing by as you passed by
And turning my eyes from the empty future
In myself I see arising all the past

Nothing is dead but what has not yet existed
Tomorrow is dim beside the shining past
And formless beside an achieved perfection
That displays at once the effort and the effect]

The condition for achieving wholeness (that perfection of effort and effect) is a movement into the self, a shutting out of the world of the future, which the magical bird in an earlier stanza of the poem prefigures by the lowering of its eyelid:

Oiseau tranquille au vol inverse oiseau
Qui nidifie en l'air
A la limite où brille déjà ma mémoire
Baisse ta deuxième paupière
Ni à cause du soleil ni à cause de la terre
Mais pour ce feu oblong dont l'intensité ira s'augmentant
Au point qu'il deviendra un jour l'unique lumière

[Calm bird on inverted wing   bird
Nesting in mid-air
At the limit where already my memory gleams
Lower your second eyelid
Neither for the sun or the earth
But for that oblong flame whose strength will increase
Until it becomes one day the unique light]

At the end of "Cortège," the "passé luisant" ("the shining past"), in which all experiences and events are preserved—because nothing is considered dead except that which does not yet exist—translates Apollinaire's desire for undifferentiated being. But this desire is only partially fulfilled. In the stanza in which he addresses the bird, Apollinaire speaks of "ce feu oblong dont l'intensité ira s'augmentant / Au point qu'il deviendra un jour l'unique lumière" ("that oblong flame whose strength will increase / Until it becomes one day the unique light"). This singular light, as yet neither fully nor dominantly radiant, is part of the unformed "vide avenir" ("empty future"). It is thus something still to be desired and still to be hoped for by the poet who experiences its absence.

"Cortège" suggests a possible, although limited, union between the self and the other. But the dream of a totalized self, a "unique lumière," can come only in the future. The past is presented as perfect, although it is a perfection of a limited and incomplete kind. It is indifferent to the future and to the otherness of a self moving toward its destiny in that future. In "Cortège" Apollinaire does possess the otherness of the past; remembering it enables him to make it his own. He joins with the shades of the past, which, as he reveals in the story "La Promenade de l'ombre," survive beyond death: "ceux qui sont morts ne sont pas des absents" ("those who are dead are not absent").[15] Death does not create absence; only the unformed nonexistence of the future does. Because "Cortège" indicates that the "unique lumière" of totalized selfhood belongs to an as yet unrealized future, the poem presents another vision, albeit an attenuated one, of an unfulfilled lack and of the indomitable desire that struggles through poetry to abolish it.

The Imperfections of Being

Desire traces its origins to lack. Thus, the representation of the imperfection to be found in a seemingly flawless or marvelous event,

15. *Contes retrouvés*, in *Oeuvres complètes de Guillaume Apollinaire*, 4 vols. (Paris: André Balland and Jacques Lecat, 1965), 1:461.

evident, for example, in a war poem such as "Merveille de la guerre" (*OP*, 271–72/*C*, 257–59), reveals Apollinaire's profound sensitivity to the presence of incompleteness in all things. In "Merveille de la guerre" Apollinaire glorifies the beauty of the battlefield sky—"Que c'est beau ces fusées qui illuminent la nuit" ("How lovely these flares are that light up the dark")—whose explosive and mercurial charms he compares to dancing women. But the marvel and wondrousness are not sufficient; they do not create perfection:

> Comme c'est beau toutes ces fusées
> Mais ce serait bien plus beau s'il y en avait plus encore
> S'il y en avait des millions qui auraient un sens complet et relatif
>   comme les lettres d'un livre

> [How lovely all these flares are
> But it would be finer if there were still more of them
> If there were millions with a full and relative meaning like letters
>   in a book]

Although beautiful, the festive scene is not beautiful enough. It lacks sublimity, even though the rockets create a "daily apotheosis" and even though the beautifully adorned women Apollinaire sees metaphorically dancing in the sky belong "to all times and all races." A coalescence of the universal and the particular—"un sens complet et relatif"—is missing. Such a meaning, simultaneously total and relative, would negate difference because it would be capable of containing abstractions as well as concrete particulars, of referring to what is essential as well as to what is accidental. The "letters in a book" have both a universal and a particular reality. Considered individually as vowels and consonants, or looked at in their changing interactions with one another in a word or series of words, the letters of a book are concrete marks inscribed on a page; yet, they are also the essential components of a world-expressive whole. In the book, the part and the whole, like the flame and the "flammèche" in Apollinaire's description of painting, are not seen as being different.

In "Merveille de la guerre" Apollinaire yearns for the "plus encore," which will render what he perceives "plus beau encore." And this applies as well to the final dispersed image of the ubiquitous, ramified self, flowing through the landscape and participating in whatever it encounters:

> Je lègue à l'avenir l'histoire de Guillaume Apollinaire
> Qui fut à la guerre et sut être partout

Dans les villes heureuses de l'arrière
Dans tout le reste de l'univers
Dans ceux qui meurent en piétinant dans le barbelé
Dans les femmes dans les canons dans les chevaux
Au zénith au nadir aux 4 points cardinaux
Et dans l'unique ardeur de cette veillée d'armes

[I bequeath to the future the story of Guillaume Apollinaire
Who was in the war and knew how to be everywhere
In the lucky towns behind the front lines
In all the rest of the universe
In those who died tangled in the barbed wire
In women in cannons in horses
At the zenith at the nadir at the four cardinal points
And in the unique ardor of this eve of battle]

But this union of the self with others in the world does not escape the incompleteness Apollinaire has perceived all along. Poet and world are not simultaneously present to each other:

Et ce serait sans doute bien plus beau
Si je pouvais supposer que toutes ces choses dans lesquelles je suis
    partout
Pouvaient m'occuper aussi
Mais dans ce sens il n'y a rien de fait
Car si je suis partout à cette heure il n'y a cependant que moi qui
    suis en moi

[And of course it would be finer
If I could imagine that all these things in which I dwell
Invaded me too
But in this sense there's nothing doing
For if I am everywhere at this hour there is only myself who is in
    me]

Part of the problem has to do with the self-consciousness of poetic creation, which rules out the possibility of the lyric self flowing ubiquitously in the world and telling about it poetically at the same time. Concern with the outside world, Apollinaire suggests, cuts short the exploration of the inner world. The failure is due in large part to the poet's inability to be simultaneously the I-in-the-I and the I-in-the-you.

"L'Ombre enfin solide"

The "fatal shadow" haunts Apollinaire's poetry as the sign of an otherness that cannot be appropriated. Its distance, difference, and incompleteness thwart the desire for a totalized self. But the "fatal shadow" of otherness experiences an ideal and hypothetical transformation in the fifth part of "Les Fiançailles," Apollinaire's great poem of purification, self-metamorphosis, and resurrection:

> Mais si le temps venait où l'ombre enfin solide
> Se multipliait en réalisant la diversité formelle de mon amour
> J'admirerais mon ouvrage
>
> [But if the time came when finally solid the shadow
> Multiplied by achieving my love's diverse forms
> Then I would admire my labors]
>
> (*OP*, 132/A, 175)

No longer is the shadow portrayed as a wispy, insubstantial wraith. In its ideal state, it has acquired concreteness and solidity. Most importantly, this shadow does not reduce its components to one undefined, homogeneous mass, as its counterpart did to Apollinaire's soldier friends in the poem "Ombre." The shadow, which "Les Fiançailles" announces for the future, will be simultaneously singular and multiple. Each of its many forms will exactly resemble the unique shadow, the source, that created it in the same way that the "flammèche" adopts the identity of the original flame in Apollinaire's description of the pure fire of creative inspiration. Thus, in this poetic dream of self-immolation and of subsequent resurrection—a true "betrothal" in which desire overcomes alterity in the simultaneous union of the poetic self with all that is not itself—the "fatal shadow" of otherness becomes the perfectly and "finally solid shadow" of wholeness.[16]

"But no one gets beyond / the other, and so world returns once more"—Rilke

There is no escaping otherness; its "fatal shadow" falls on all domains of human activity, as Rilke has observed.[17] The very nature of

16. For a detailed and subtle analysis of this poem and of the "multiplicity-into-unity principle" upon which it and Apollinaire's aesthetic renewal are based, see L. C. Breunig, "Apollinaire's 'Les Fiançailles,'" *Essays in French Literature* 3 (November 1966): 1–32.
17. Rainer Maria Rilke, "The Eighth Elegy," in *Duino Elegies*, trans. J. B. Leishman and Stephen Spender (1939; reprint, New York: W. W. Norton, 1967), p. 69. In this elegy,

speech is founded on alterity, for to speak is to envision and to designate an other to whom the message is destined. The locution of an *I*
involves by its very reality the allocution of a *you*.[18] But if the language
of self-expression is projected forward toward the other, it also points
backward to the otherness of an absent origin, an original signified that
it cannot name or possess. In this respect, texts are *allegorical*, for
behind an apparent meaning is hidden yet another meaning, whose
nonbeing the text vainly attempts to represent; "the 'now' of a text,"
writes one critic, "necessarily refers to the 'always already' of an 'Other
Text.'"[19] Otherness, then, is the alpha and omega of self-expression
through language. The text is confined at its source and at its destina-
tion by alterity—by the unsignifiable absent origin to which it refers
and by the unassimilable human presence to which it appeals and
speaks. Any formulation of self will by nature be incomplete, because
our identity is perpetually other than what our expression of it can
possibly suggest.

The primordial estrangement that otherness represents has its gen-
esis in a primal lack, in an initial experience of loss which language tries
to express and to mitigate. Poetry is, in many respects, a game of *fort/da*,
to use Freud's famous example of a child attempting to come to terms
symbolically with the anguish of an irreversible separation (the loss of
undifferentiated oneness with the mother) and of otherness. The child,

---

Rilke laments the physical presence of the other partner in the experience of love ("were
not the other present, always / spoiling the view!"; p. 69). This lover is an obstacle
blocking one's access to an unknown, invisible region and interfering with one's "gathering out-leap" into the angelic space of true being: a place of transcendental openness and
wholeness.

18. Self-consciousness is impossible without the presence of the other, which permits
the *I* to become aware of itself insofar as it contrasts with, and differs from, the *you*, its
"echo." In his important essay "De la subjectivité dans le langage," Emile Benveniste
writes:

> Nous n'atteignons jamais l'homme réduit à lui-même et s'ingéniant à concevoir
> l'existence de l'autre. C'est un homme parlant que nous trouvons dans le monde,
> un homme parlant à un autre homme, et le langage enseigne la définition même
> de l'homme.

> [We shall never get back to man reduced to himself and exercising his wits to
> conceive of the existence of another. It is a speaking man whom we find in the
> world, a man speaking to another man, and language provides the very definition
> of man.]

> (*Problèmes de linguistique générale*, 2 vols., Bibliothèque des sciences humaines
> [Paris: Gallimard, 1966, 1974], 1:259) [*Problems in General Linguistics*, trans.
> Mary Elizabeth Meek, Miami Linguistics Series, no. 8 (Coral Gables:
> University of Miami Press, 1971), p. 224]

19. Eugenio Donato, "Topographies of Memory," *Sub-Stance* 21 (1978): 38.

Freud writes, "had a wooden reel with a piece of string tied round it. . . . What he did was to hold the reel by the string and very skilfully throw it over the edge of his curtained cot, so that it disappeared into it, at the same time uttering his expressive 'o-o-o-o' [a sound representing the German word *'fort'* ('gone')]. He then pulled the reel out of the cot again by the string and hailed its reappearance with a joyful *'da'* ['there']."[20] Through the words *fort* and *da*, which accompany the disappearance and reappearance of the reel, the child plays with and *re*plays the loss of his mother. Language symbolizes and fills in the emptiness.[21] It permits the child to come to symbolic terms with the lack that, according to Lacan, coincides with the formation of subjectivity and the expression of desire. It is, he writes, "as desire for the Other that human desire finds form."[22] Similarly, poetic expression empowers a symbolic refiguring of loss—its reenactment through substitution—by which the experience of lack or absence is momentarily and phantasmatically overturned. But the desire for the absent other is ultimately unsatisfiable and thus endless, because no word, no metaphor, no symbol can restore what has been lost.

The recognition of otherness and the awareness of separation from a necessary but absent other are therefore primal experiences of loss, in which both desire and language have their origin. To this desire and language, which work in concert to abolish difference and to repossess the being of the distant other, Apollinaire gives a fervent, Heraclitean command: "Passe et dure sans t'arrêter" ("Pass on endure and never end"; *OP*, 172/*C*, 35). Such is the destiny of poets who, powerless to embrace the always-advancing "fatal shadow" of otherness, are fated to pursue endlessly its dark contour and elusive trace, to desire what

20. *Beyond the Pleasure Principle*, ed. and trans. James Strachey (New York: W. W. Norton, 1961), p. 9.

21. Barthes points out that because the absence is permanent and will not disappear, the child (as well as the abandoned lover, who is in the same position as the child) contends with the loss through a creative use of language. He begins to manipulate it, to "transform the distortion of time into oscillation, produce rhythm, make an entrance onto the stage of language (language is born of absence: the child has made himself a doll out of a spool, throws it away and picks it up again, miming the mother's departure and return: a paradigm is created). Absence becomes an active practice, a *business* (which keeps me from doing anything else); there is a creation of a fiction which has many roles (doubts, reproaches, desires, melancholies). This staging of language postpones the other's death: a very short interval, we are told, separates the time during which the child still believes his mother to be absent and the time during which he believes her to be already dead. To manipulate absence is to extend this interval, to delay as long as possible the moment when the other might topple sharply from absence into death" (*Fragments d'un discours amoureux*, p. 22/16).

22. *Ecrits*, p. 813.

Baudelaire, in a different although not unrelated context, calls "ce noir océan où l'autre est enfermé" ("this black ocean where the other lurks").[23]

23. "La Chevelure," in *Les Fleurs du mal,* in *OC,* 1:26 ["The Head of Hair," in *Les Fleurs du Mal/The Flowers of Evil,* trans. Richard Howard (Boston: David R. Godine, 1982), p. 31].

CHAPTER 4

THE EROS OF LOSS:
PIERRE JEAN JOUVE

Adieu. La nuit déjà nous fait méconnaissables
Ton visage est fondu dans l'absence.

[Adieu. Already, night has made us unrecognizable
Your face melts into absence.]
—Pierre Jean Jouve, "Adieu," *Mélodrame*

La poésie c'est la vie même du grand Eros morte et par là survivante.

[Poetry is the very life of sublime Eros, dead and for that reason surviving.]
—Pierre Jean Jouve, "Inconscient, spiritualité et catastrophe"

It could be said that writing opens a dialogue with death. Letters, words, and sentences force the writer into a relationship with something that has disappeared, with an absence that writing initiates and ultimately comes to signify. The word, Maurice Blanchot observes, "may give me its meaning, but first it suppresses it. For me to be able to say, 'This woman' I must somehow take her flesh and blood reality away from her, cause her to be absent, annihilate her. The word gives me the being but it gives it to me deprived of being. The word is the absence of that being, its nothingness, what is left of it when it has lost being—the very fact that it does not exist."[1] Writing establishes, thus, the absence of what it represents. It signifies the nonbeing of what, in order to be expressed, must withdraw from existence. Every word is

1. "La Littérature et le droit à la mort," in *De Kafka à Kafka*, Collection Idées (Paris: Gallimard, 1981), p. 36/42.

93

grounded in a lack. To come into being, language must be preceded by loss. Strategies of representation not only work to make realities of the world present through formal means but also call attention to the difference that the process of representation has created: a difference made all the more striking by having been created by the loss or absence of the object represented. In trying through writing, as one tries through love, to take hold of some thing or some being, one comes face to face with *l'impossédable*, with what is unpossessable. All words, therefore, are tombs, funerary monuments erected as signs of, and memorials to, an irreversible loss.

The experience of loss, as the poet and novelist Pierre Jean Jouve expresses it, gathers its strength from a melancholic and erotic attachment to a mysterious, absent woman, whom he calls "l'Abolie," "la Disparue," "l'Absente." Eros for Jouve is melancholic because it is founded on the loss or the inaccessibility of a beloved. Women in Jouve's work wear the halo of death. "Dans toutes les périodes du travail jusqu'à ce jour," he writes in his autobiographical work *En Miroir: Journal sans date* (1954), "il y a le passage de la Morte—la seule sous des vocables différents" ("In all periods of my work to this day, there is the passing of a dead Woman—only one, but under different names").[2] The beloved woman, whatever her name (and she has many names, as we shall see), is always a dead woman; she exists under the sign of a loss that Jouve associates sometimes with punishment, sometimes with salvation, and sometimes with poetry itself. Because in Jouve's work Eros and Thanatos sustain each other in ways both reciprocal and contestative, erotic love becomes the precondition for the disappearance of the beloved: "Forte couleur d'éros; forte couleur de mort" ("Strong color of eros; strong color of death"), he writes in *Les Beaux Masques* (*Oeuvre*, 2:1637). To make love is to lose the other. In the novella *Dans les années profondes*, Hélène de Sannis suffers a fatal heart attack after she and her adolescent lover, Léonide, make love with such abandon that their pleasure has the quality of an "orgie d'abîme" (*O*, 2:1040). And Dorothée, the "fausse morte-fausse vivante" (*O*, 2:1095) of the tale "La Victime," having died while making love to Waldemar, is magically brought back to life as a beautiful corpse.[3]

2. *Oeuvre*, 2 vols., ed. Jean Starobinski (Paris: Mercure de France, 1987), 2:1102; referred to as *O*.

3. The power of love to cause the loss of the beloved at the very moment that possession occurs is also affirmed by Georges Bataille in his writings on eroticism: "Eroticism does not represent by any means the point where the human being finds himself. It represents, to the contrary, the point where he loses himself. Life becomes erotic in the same way it dies, and this book, which describes erotic life, will necessarily

Indeed, the beauty of a woman is associated in Jouve's imagination with her " 'véritable *cadavérisation*' " (*O*, 2:953). The woman is beautiful only after her destruction, her transformation into a lost or absent object of love. "Que tu es belle maintenant que tu n'es plus," Jouve writes in "Hélène" ("How beautiful you are now that you no longer exist"; *O*, 1:282). Similarly, in "La Victime" the narrator observes that "Dorothée was, even in death, more beautiful" (*O*, 2:925). And of Hélène de Sannis, Léonide remarks that "Never, since the first hour of our meeting, had I adored her as much as when I saw her dead" (*O*, 2:1047). Death enhances passion; it intensifies the fascination, the attraction, and the eros of what has been lost, in both senses of the word: the individual lost to death and the soul lost to sin. The woman, who inhabits a place that is for Jouve the very center of mortal transgression, wears a halo of somber, guilt-ridden light. Eros and Thanatos are never without a third partner, *la Faute* ("sin"), in what is a tragic *ménage à trois*.

In contemplating the woman, Jouve cannot imagine her except as lost. Loss is an aura encircling her beauty; it defines her identity; and it is also the lens through which the poet sees the world. For example, before the end of his liaison with Elisabeth V., affectionately named "Lisbé," who died from cancer at the end of 1936, Jouve, in *Dans les années profondes* of 1934 and the Hélène poems of May 1936, imagines

---

have about it an odor of death" (*L'Histoire de l'érotisme*, in *Oeuvres complètes*, 10 vols. [Paris: Gallimard, 1976], 8:527). Although many differences of temperament, style, formation, and belief separate Jouve and Bataille, they appear to agree on several (though by no means all) points concerning the nature of eroticism. For both, eros is a form of human knowledge to which also corresponds the knowledge of death, although the relation of Christian sin to the erotic experience, so important to Jouve, is rejected by the more secular Bataille. Eros reveals human nature at its most noble and its most abject, illustrating (as Bataille expresses it, in accordance with his notion of "expenditure" [*la dépense*]) that "what we desire is what exhausts our forces and resources and puts our lives, sometimes necessarily, in danger" (p. 90). For Bataille, as well as for Jouve, love and loss are inseparable: "Desire demands the greatest loss possible," the former writes (p. 123). Such loss is nowhere more evident, he asserts, than in the example of the prostitute, in whom "*loss* takes the form of an object" (p. 123), an object of fascination and excess quickly consumed by masculine desire. The prostitute symbolizes for Bataille, and again for Jouve—"I admit an attraction for the prostitute," the latter writes (*O*, 2:1128)—the essence of an ephemeral *jouissance*, in which the veil of eros quickly parts to reveal the ugly face of death (or, as Jouve says, "le malheur"). The seductive prostitute, Bataille writes, is the "figure in whom death can be transparently read in the aspects of an excessive life . . . , figure of death behind the mask of life insofar as it expresses the meaning of eroticism, which is itself the place where life and death merge" (p. 124). Similarly, Jouve believes that the prostitute, more than any other being, can reveal "the secret, innermost heart of the erotic" (*O*, 2:1137). In Yanick, the prostitute with whom he fell in love and who inspired several of his poems before, like all Jouvean woman, disappearing forever, Jouve discovers "the features of Eros itself" (*O*, 2:1137; see also pp. 1131–37 and the prose poem "Nature prostituée," p. 1251).

her from a perspective both nostalgic and melancholic, as if death had already carried her away. Jouve literally prefigures Lisbé's death because, sensitive to the traces of mortality and sin lying beneath the surface of her erotic beauty, he has a particular need to see her as a figure of loss, as *the* Figure of Loss. Where carnality and sensuality reveal their charms, there is found the imminence of loss. The body is all the more mortal because it is voluptuous. It inspires love and passion as much as disease and decomposition. "One day," Jouve writes in *En Miroir* apropos of Lisbé, who several months later would succumb to cancer, "lightly touching her left breast, I had the sensation of feeling a small, hard point" (*O*, 2:1099), an observation that the prose poem "La Douce Visiteuse" clarifies further: "If he had touched her breast that day, he would have already felt the hard lump of death" (*O*, 2:1213). As the incarnation of erotic and transgressive love, the woman is destined to be swallowed up by death and nothingness. Her body is, for Jouve, the site of Eros and Thanatos, of fulfillment and destitution, of health and disease. Essentially erotic by nature, she only lives to be annihilated by death. It already inhabits her body, which is contaminated by a loss that is contagious.[4]

Nevertheless, loss in Jouve's world can also lead to salvation. The death of the woman represents a first step toward the deliverance of the world, which only divine grace can accomplish. The nothingness (*le rien*) of loss becomes the everything (*le tout*) of possession; the Fall is transformed into ascension, and death becomes resurrection:

Le péché remontant jusque dans son sourire
Défait la terre et la transforme en air
Jusqu'au bleu sans forme éternel et très bleu
Ciel et coupole froide des lumières

[Sin rising until it meets her smile
Destroys the earth, turns it into air
Reaching to the formless blue, the eternal and very blue,
Sky and the cold cupula of light]

("Ma Beauté," *O*, 1:296–97)

4. It is clear from some of Jouve's more blatantly erotic writings that he imagines the body of the passionately aroused woman as a perfect residence for death. In the very throes of erotic love, the woman appears to experience the agony of her last seconds on earth, death rattle and all, as is clear from the following voyeuristic description, "Souvenirs d'Elisabeth V.":

Quand elle jouissait, sa tête pâle se renversait les yeux clos, avec la raideur d'une statue; elle râlait, elle sanglotait, elle claquait des dents; complètement absente du

The woman on whose glance "Le néant est pendu" ("Nothingness is hung") ("Tempo di Mozart," *O*, 1:302) may nevertheless participate in what Jouve calls "la matière céleste." By following the path that descends toward nothingness, "le 'Nada,'" the woman can discover "le 'Todo'" (*O*, 2:1140), the sublime, spiritual road of divine resurrection:

> Les innombrables ombres d'Hélène voyagent
> Sur ce pays poussées par le souffle de Dieu
> Tout est profond tout est sans faute et cristallin
> Tout est vert bleu tout est joyeux et azurin.

> [The countless shadows of Hélène driven by
> The breath of God journey across this land
> Everything is profound everything is without sin and crystalline
> Everything is green blue everything joyous and like azure.]
> ("Adieu," *O*, 1:439).

What is therefore absent—be it the woman lost to death, the distant homeland under the oppressive power of Nazi invaders, or God exiled from a fallen world—rises up against the very forces that have destroyed it. "Le 'Souffle,' ou l'Absence," Jouve writes, "en face de la ruine, a pour moyen: 'Nier le non dans la présence'" ("'Breath,' or Absence confronting destruction has the means 'to negate nothingness within presence'"; *O*, 2:1140). Nothingness, *le nada*, is creative. It brings into existence an emptiness that may one day become plen-

---

monde où je la regardais, un corps, vaste et nu, la bouche d'en bas béante.
　Elle était l'inconscient même, et l'inconscient de la mort. Je suis sûr que dans sa jouissance elle entrait au tombeau. Six mois après cette scène elle était morte.

[When she came, her pale face was thrown back, eyes closed, with the rigidity of a statue; a rattling sound came from her throat, she sobbed, her teeth chattered; totally absent from the world where I watched her, a body, vast and naked, its other mouth agape.
　She was the unconscious itself, and the unconscious of death. I am sure that through her ecstasy she descended into the tomb. Six months after this scene she was dead.] (*Les Beaux Masques*, in *O*, 2:1627–28)

In love, possession and loss exist side by side, as do bliss and pain. Passion is a kind of dying for Jouve. But because death is also life—"nous n'avons que mort pour véritable azur" ("We have only death as our true sky"; "Ténèbres," in *O*, 1:323)—the death love embodies is a form of living. Similarly, for Bataille, eros is a force both of life and of death: "Anguish, which opens us to destruction and death, is always bound up with eroticism; our sexual activity ends up by attaching us to the agonizing image of death, and the knowledge of death deepens the abyss of eroticism . . . : there is in sexual anguish a deathlike sadness, a vague apprehension of death from which we can never free ourselves" (*L'Histoire de l'érotisme*, p. 72).

itudinous. This is "le Rien qui ouvre / Et porte le Tout à son sein," the "Rien sombre [qui] est le Tout de la Vie" ("the Nothing that opens / And carries the All at its breast," the "dark Nothing that is the All of Life"; *O,* 1:524, 528). It is possible, therefore, that the confrontation with the irreversible nothingness and suffering of human existence may be undone by the mystery of divine grace. "The experience of Death," Jouve writes in his study of Mozart's *Don Giovanni,* "is the experience of sin, as it is that of salvation."[5]

Every word for Jouve is necessarily founded on absence, because the only true word, and the one upon which all life and being are uniquely established—namely, the word of God—remains beyond reach, is perpetually lacking.[6] Loss flows into language with such intensity that language can no longer signify anything but the lack and absence that no word is ever able to compensate or reverse. The poem is marked by holes, which have also pierced the substance of reality. These punctures, holes, lacks—all signs of absence—are endowed with a concrete and material presence at the moment of their enunciation. They become syllables of loss, signifiers of lack. Loss occupies a space, a *topos,* in which it expresses the nothingness to which cries or whispers of grief alone give form. There is a definite *spatialization of loss* in Jouve's work. Within a landscape marked by absence and lack, a melancholic air or threnody—its notes emerging from a damaged instrument, from "Une harpe ayant plusieurs cordes brisées" ("A harp with many broken strings") ("Orphée," *O,* 1:342)—causes what has been lost to resonate. The Jouvean poem is a place of presence, an *ici,* where the pain of death bursts forth, where the melancholic light of loss quivers, where absence, suddenly made present, suddenly embodied, announces itself and becomes song. And the Jouvean woman, enshrouded by loss, has a singular, physical presence, uniquely coincident with that space of lack, with that *here and now* of night, with that landscape of nothingness in which she makes her appearance:

Qu'il fait noir aux limites de ton rouge sang
C'est ici qu'on entre dans la vierge nuit
C'est ici qu'elle déchaîne ses lumières

---

5. *Le Don Juan de Mozart* (Paris: Egloff, 1942), p. 267.
6. It is the *absence* of the true word that language designates, that it renders present, as Jouve remarks in the prose poem "Allégorie": "Jamais parole n'est en toute certitude la véritable parole, mais toute parole ouvre le sein en éternité et y plonge, ouvre l'Espérance de la parole" ("Never is a word in all certainty the true word, but every word opens the heart within eternity and plunges in; it opens the Hope of the word"; *O,* 2:1229).

Fourmillante d'espace et d'espace et de nuit
C'est ici qu'elle fait tomber ses fracas
Manteaux et nudités profondes

C'est ici que tout naît et se lève et adore
En néant dans le Rien et le Non de la nuit

[How dark it is at the bounds of your red blood
It is here that one enters the virgin night
It is here that it unleashes its lights
Teaming with space, with space and with night
It is here that its din abates
Cloaks and profound nakedness

It is here that everything is born and arises and loves
While being nothingness in the Nothing and the No of the night]
("Noir retour à la vie," *O,* 1:293)

Within the landscape where nothingness is born (*naît* / *né*ant) and is active (as if it were also a verb, a present participle: "En *néant*"), within this nocturnal place of death, which is also the *ici* of the poem, absence inaugurates a presence: that of melancholy, of sadness put into words. "De ce qui passe sur la douleur de tes yeux / Tout s'effondre en des fontaines nues de larmes" ("From what passes through the pain of your eyes / Everything collapses in naked fountains of tears"), Jouve observes in "Tempo di Mozart" (*O,* 1:303). As the place of suffering and deprivation, the poem is a black fountain, an inexhaustible spring, of dark words. The signifiers of loss and pain multiply in somber concert with the lack that, having initiated the flow of language, will never deplete itself. Despite everything, absence writes itself, creating in the poem what Jouve calls "une beauté pleurante" ("a weeping beauty"; "Fugue," *O,* 1:314). But it is out of such absence and emptiness that grace may one day make possible the union with divine presence:

Compte seulement le poids des larmes
Non pour elles mais pour le vide qu'elles font
Et roulant sur la noire paroi de vertige
De ce monde aboli: tu approches de l'Un.

[Count only the weight of tears
Not for themselves but for the emptiness they create

And rolling down the black vertiginous wall
Of this destroyed world: you approach the One]
("Poème," *O*, 1:315)

In the world of Jouve's poems, therefore, one finds the incarnation of loss. It is curious that the poet, this "Diseur de mots" ("Reciter of words"; *O*, 2:1080) who never wants for words, can only speak of want. This chapter studies the nature of that want, analyzes the figuration of loss in Jouve's poetry insofar as such figuration gives birth to the beauty of lack, to the sublimity of nothingness, to the presence of absence, and to what Mallarmé called "the 'sumptuous Allegories of Nothingness.' "[7] The chapter demonstrates three things: first, how by means of the materiality of form, which all writing produces, Jouve confronts the void left behind by the disappearance of the object of his love; second, how the poem, in attempting to represent loss, is transformed into a funereal space, a tomb, especially in those poems in which the "myth" of Hélène plays a role; and third, how the melancholy of loss—insofar as it is expressed in a writing that paradoxically makes present what is perpetually absent—suggests the possibility that a lost woman may be recuperated and preserved in some miraculous or illusory way.

The Substance of Loss

In Jouve's prose poem "Coffre de fer" (*O*, 2:1209), the narrator opens a chest containing dead women laid out, as he says, "for all eternity." The chest, however, is filled not with the women themselves, but rather with cherished vestiges of their past existences: photographs, letters, papers, dried flowers: in sum, "fragments of silk and parts of bodies, something so heartrending and natural that all regret seemed abolished." The chest is the burying place of mementos, of souvenirs, of all that remains of these lost beings; it is therefore not stretching the imagination to say, as the narrator of Jouve's poem does, that the chest is "filled with dead women." The very fullness of what the box contains points all the more to the emptiness upon which it rests.

The vestiges of the past preserved in the chest lead the narrator to the following conclusion:

Abolies, les créatures vivaient une seconde fois avec un peu d'ironie peut-être. Aboli, le parfum qui montait n'était plus celui de la mort.

7. Letter of 24 September 1867 to Villiers de L'Isle-Adam, in *Correspondance, 1862–1871*, ed. Henri Mondor (Paris: Gallimard, 1959), p. 259.

Sur *les abolies devenues substance,* je fermai le coffre de fer. [my emphasis]

[Destroyed, the creatures lived a second time with a little irony, perhaps. Destroyed, the fragrance that arose was no longer that of death. Upon *these destroyed women now materialized,* I closed the iron chest.]

Destroyed, lost, and dead, the women in the chest regain life as fragrances, as traces, as images. They are endowed with a new existence, but it is that of death, of the *aboli.* In opening the chest, the narrator experiences the physical presence, the substance, of loss itself; he feels the remains, touches the fragments, inhales the aroma of absences; loss is palpable: "le manque est *dans* les choses tristes" ("lack is *in* sad things"; *O,* 1:527; my emphasis). While the fragrances emanating from the women's remains have no association with the smells of decomposing flesh, these "creatures" are no less dead, no less "abolies." They live again, but with an ironic consciousness of their new condition as fragmented and lost beings. The fact of death—the reality of having been destroyed, canceled, and abolished—adheres to these women, endowing them with a different identity; they are *other.*[8] It is not the women who are preserved in the chest, but their absence. The work of art, the "coffre de fer," is thus marked with loss, for it is an artifact, a form, a space, a container in which lack materializes and in which *l'aboli* becomes substance. The work of art completes the transformation of loss into flesh, into *memento mori,* into "matérielle présence" (*O,* 1:1076). Jouve's poem, his "coffre de fer," literally embodies and *in*-corporates the lost object of love.

Loss and absence in Jouve's work have a definite form. Out of nothing, something remains, and this "something," this remainder, is nothingness itself:

Rien ne s'accomplira sinon dans une absence
Dans une nuit un congédiement de clarté
Une beauté confuse en laquelle rien n'est.

8. On the woman as "l'*autre,* par excellence," see Yves Bonnefoy, "Pierre Jean Jouve," in *Le Nuage rouge* (Paris: Mercure de France, 1977), p. 262; and on the woman as that primordial *you* with which every poem of Jouve's is in dramatic relation, see Jean Starobinski, "Situation de Pierre Jean Jouve," in *Pierre Jean Jouve: Poète et Romancier* (Neuchâtel: La Baconnière, 1946), p. 43. In addition, for a discussion of Jouvean desire as a movement toward an "essential alterity," which both valorizes and annuls the other, see Jérôme Thélot, "Hélène, Lisbé," in *Jouve, poète de la rupture,* ed. Daniel Leuwers, in *La Revue des lettres modernes: Pierre Jean Jouve,* no. 2 (Paris: Minard, 1985), pp. 75–91.

[Nothing occurs if not in an absence
In a night a dismissal of light
An obscure beauty in which nothing is.]

(*O*, 1:309)

The beauty of form is established for Jouve on nothingness, which, paradoxically, creates and destroys it. Beauty is built on death, because death alone achieves the perfection of all form: "Death is at the origin of a marvelously perfect form, of a 'limit' marked in an exquisite manner and always precisely and fully achieved."[9] The death Jouve imagines does not conjure up the Baudelairean image of a rotting corpse. Death, he writes, "n'est pas tant l'image cadavre que l'image 'sens de la fin'" ("is not so much the image of a corpse than the image of an ending"; *O*, 2:1124).[10] Death has a particular life of its own. What disappears into nothingness continues to exist, almost untouched, in a realm of purity which is fundamentally other:

Tu es morte et depuis longtemps mais ton visage
Ton visage ou l'albâtre rose de ton corps
N'ont pas été touchés par le voile du vide
Tant qu'ils n'existeraient plus même au monde sans mort
De l'image; et je vois, ton adorable forme
De jeune fille nue et droite par amour
M'apparaît, d'autant matérielle présence
Que tout objet encor saisi par mes vieux yeux:
O sourire léger ô seins ô buisson d'or.

[You have been dead and for a long time but your face
Your face or the pink alabaster of your body
Have not been touched by the veil of emptiness
And could not exist even in the world if not for the death
Of the image; and as I watch, the lovely form
Of a young girl naked and candid through love
Appears to me, as material a presence

9. *Le Don Juan de Mozart*, p. 20.
10. Poetry, Jouve argues in "Inconscient, spiritualité et catastrophe," his preface to the collection of poems *Sueur de sang* (1933–35), need not become obsessed with the image of death as a putrefying corpse: "In the corpse there is neither revolution nor action. God is life; and if death must finally become one with the world or with God, this must never be by the 'way of the corpse,' which, extraordinary as it may be, man carries with him from the moment he is born—like a diabolical power generating sin" (*O*, 1:199).

As any object my aged eyes still can seize:
O gentle smile, o breasts, o golden tuft.]

(*O*, 1:1076)

The presentation, or more literally the *mise-en-scène*, of the lost woman in Jouve's poetry is nowhere more striking than in the twenty-seven poems of 1936 that compose the collection *Hélène* (*O*, 1:279–303). The representation of the dead woman as landscape, her *mise-en-paysage*, enables the poet to preserve the form that absence and loss have given her. United with stones and rocks, dissolved into the water of lakes, flowing underground like a hidden stream, incorporated into the landscape, her breath lightly touching the quivering leaves, her eyes "wide open in the earth" ("Juin ou Lisbé," *O*, 1:285), her breast giving sustenance to the natural world, her kiss making the forests stir—Hélène, after death, lives on in a "land of wounds" ("Ma Beauté," *O*, 1:296), which is also a land of pastoral beauty. Jouve imagines a woman who is both alive and dead, present and absent: a creature of flesh and of landscape, whose body has dissipated to form a countryside and a world of universal loss. Nature resembles the "coffre de fer," the iron chest, for it, too, contains and preserves the remains of a fragmented, scattered body. The presence-absence of the woman and the pantheistic integration of her decomposed body into a feminized landscape transform the natural world: "Le fantôme faisait le pays entier autrement vrai que la nature" ("The spectre made the entire land true in a different way from nature"; "Retour chez Hélène," *O*, 2:1195). Through the loss that death initiates, the woman is re-created. She enters the domain of divine otherness that Jouve calls "la matière céleste": "Ici mon ami s'est recomposée / Hélène, après qu'elle est morte" ("Here my friend regenerated herself / Hélène, after she had died"; "Matière céleste dans Hélène," *O*, 1:281).

Lost and destroyed, the woman reconstitutes herself through the fulfillment of form which death gives her. "I am," says the voice of death in the prose poem "Allégorie,"

> l'aboutissement, la limite, et par conséquent le calme. Je suis le but. C'est moi qui donnerai à la voix son accent, au sexe son objet véritable. . . . Je suis le froid, l'horrible, le mauvais parfum, l'ennemi adoré; je décompose l'homme mais je l'accomplis. Respecte tout d'abord cette ouvrière interminable, la mort.

> [the culmination, the limit, and consequently the calm. I am the goal. It is I who give the voice its accent and the sexual organs their true

object. . . . I am the cold, the horrible, the unpleasant scent, the admired enemy; I decompose man but I also perfect him. Respect from the start this indefatigable worker, death.] (*O*, 2:1230)

United with the void through a union that the eros of death alone sustains, the woman finds a second life.[11] She is transformed by the poet's work—by "the effort to chisel form and the desire to go beyond mind"—into a state of language (*O*, 2:1129) from which thoughts of neither sin nor salvation are absent: "The erotic figure becomes a feminine myth, for the body is envisaged as nature, element, a living country, the solid expression of a reverie of universal power and guilt" (*O*, 2:1130).

In death, the woman is more beautiful than she had been in life. Superlatives mix with negatives in Jouve's "rhetoric of nada."[12] That which is *more* intensifies on contact with that which is *no more*. Beauty imparts a radiance to experiences of deprivation, lack, and destitution. Overflowing with signs of the absent woman, the landscape becomes simultaneously erotic and melancholic; it is animated by the *eros of loss*.

11. The "erotic," as Jouve defines it, is "that which refers to an amorous encounter aimed at unity—and not (its lesser meaning) that which translates an obsession with sexual activity." It is this kind of eros, constituting erotic knowledge, the desire to "connaître par le mode érotique" (*O*, 2:1126), which all poetic language expresses. Poetry is the vehicle of love as it is of loss because it produces, Jouve remarks at the conclusion of "Inconscient, spiritualité, et catastrophe," "this 'sweat of blood,' this ascension to a profound or sublime corporeality springing from the wretched and beautiful power of human eros" (*O*, 1:200). But eros is also for Jouve an experience of sin, even though, as he sometimes admits, such transgression may facilitate humanity's emancipation: "Eroticism, the very center of the soul, is attacked from within, surrounded from without, by the sentiment of *being* a sin, of bearing guilt. A good part of its pleasure, always new, comes from that" (*O*, 2:1127). For Bataille, as well, eros expresses a desire for fusion and works to achieve a totality of being: "Eroticism responds to man's will to merge with the universe" (*L'Histoire de l'érotisme*, p. 145). But such experiences of erotic fusion and totality are not without their dark sides; they are linked to transgression, disgust, horror, and emptiness—experiences provoked by the lover's awareness of the always-imminent mortality of the beloved: "If the being I embrace has come to signify totality, through the fusion that takes place between object and subject, beloved and lover, I experience horror, without which I could not perceive the movement of totality. There is horror in being: this horror is the repugnant animality whose presence I discover at the very point where totality of being takes form" (*L'Histoire de l'érotisme*, p. 102).

Erotic transgression—which is not a sin for Bataille as it is for Jouve, but rather the breaking of certain social, moral, and religious interdictions, the overstepping of those codes that society has designated as proper—can lead to a totality that is also a void, a fusion so intense that nothing remains but nothingness itself: "Only eroticism has the power, in the silence of transgression, to make lovers enter that void where stammering itself is suspended, where no word is conceivable, where an embrace no longer only points to the other but to the bottomlessness and limitlessness of the universe" (*L'Histoire de l'érotisme*, p. 145).

12. Martine Broda, *Jouve*, Collection Cistre-Essais, no. 11 (Lausanne: L'Age d'Homme, 1981), p. 111.

Over and beyond the woman's participation in forests, fields, streams, and valleys, the landscape remains a tomb, a place of emptiness and lack, whose beauty can be conceived only in terms of the woman's true absence, as the following lines from "Hélène" reveal:

Que tu es belle maintenant que tu n'es plus
La poussière de la mort t'a déshabillée même de l'âme
Que tu es convoitée depuis que nous avons disparu
Les ondes les ondes remplissent le coeur du désert
La plus pâle des femmes
Il fait beau sur les crêtes d'eau de cette terre
Du paysage mort de faim
Qui borde la ville d'hier les malentendus
Il fait beau sur les cirques verts inattendus
Transformés en églises
Il fait beau sur le plateau désastreux nu et retourné
Parce que tu es si morte
Répandant des soleils par les traces de tes yeux
Et les ombres des grands arbres enracinés
Dans ta terrible Chevelure celle qui me faisait délirer.

[How beautiful you are now that you no longer exist
Death's dust has disrobed you, even of your soul
How coveted you are since we disappeared
Waves waves fill the desert's heart
The palest of women
The weather is fine on the watery crests of this earth
Of the countryside starved to death
That borders yesterday's city and misunderstandings
The weather is fine on the unexpected green circuses
Transformed into churches
The weather is fine on the devastated plateau barren and ploughed
Because you are so very dead
Scattering suns by the traces of your eyes
And the shadows of large trees rooted
In your terrifying Hair that makes me rant and rave.]

(*O*, 1:282)

In this landscape, signs of plenitude and lack mingle. This is a wasteland, a desert, a denuded and devastated land; yet, here in this starved countryside ("paysage mort de faim"), suns, shadows, and waves proliferate, great trees grow, fine weather prevails. Although robbed of her charms and reduced to the barren nudity of death, Hélène possesses the power to animate the diverse elements of the landscape. Because she is not simply dead but "*si* morte," Hélène, by the very intensity of her annihilation, gains a certain power over the world. Death endows her with a beauty that is consequently all the more creative and powerful. The transformation of Hélène's hair—an image of great erotic fascination for Jouve—into a "terrible Chevelure," the sinful essence of corporeal sensuality, reveals to what extent her loss has produced a nothingness, which, in its turn, participates in the creation of a plenitude.[13] In the Jouvean landscape, therefore, everything simultaneously signifies absence and presence, lack and fulfillment, vacancy and plenitude, *nada* and *todo*, sin and grace, melancholy and joy, death and life. This dialectical oscillation between contraries brings the poet to the threshold of absolute being: "Such is the effect of despair, coming on the heels of the most dazzling hope: it places you before your own absolute" ("Gribouille," *O*, 2:873–74).

The Tomb of Representation

The poem, for Jouve, is the tomb where the woman, although dead, continues to live. It is the afterlife in which the beloved takes refuge.

13. An indication of Jouve's fascination with hair is found particularly in the opening pages of *Dans les années profondes*. Léonide, the sixteen-year-old narrator, describes the alpine landscape that surrounds the village of Sogno: the towering mountain peaks, the vast meadows, the wildflowers, the rushing torrents, the deep valley, the grasslike tufts of hair, all of which in the heat of the summer afternoon he experiences as "a splendid land of the dead" (*O*, 2:962). And through this landscape comes Hélène de Sannis, whose hair Léonide finds utterly captivating: "What was extraordinary was what crowned her head; she possessed a mass, an edifice of hair; hair at once teeming like a nest of snakes and sparkling or dazzling like sunlight; its color, with glints of purple, blood, and dull red, was for the most part of an indefinable shade as warm as embers. I knew nothing about such hair, identical to the Wonder to come [*toute pareille au Phénomène Futur*]; I had never seen it; I never imagined such hair could exist" (p. 964). The mortal beauty of the landscape joins forces with the fatal and dangerous beauty of the woman to create an erotic ambiance, whose source Léonide identifies with Hélène's hair: "The beauty, the harmony, the creation of the world ended in an illumination, which revealed to me that at the center of all this—shining, like the halo of a saint, through the wind and heat—was a silver or black or purple substance: her Hair" (p. 966). The hair is a place of mystery, where one experiences "the delight of the pleasure of death" (p. 974); in it, disorder and confusion reign. It has a magic presence and a magnetic power capable of drawing one toward bliss (p. 979). It can perform miracles (p. 1041); it is a world unto itself, a "place more vast than the land of these mountains" (p. 974). Léonide dreams of inhaling this world and, conversely, of being erotically consumed by it: "I saw myself surrounded everywhere by these immense and sinister hairs, which on her body were more immense, more sinister than on any other body of a woman, and which, with their whorls, their

By means of writing, a crypt is formed, where the woman lives a radically other life. In the here-and-now of mortality, coincident with the here and now of the poem, the woman dwells; she also exists in what might be called *la sur-vie*, a life that transcends life. As the iron chest guards the remains of the dead women, so the poem, like a reliquary, contains remnants and traces of a lost presence. By means of the relic, of a corporeal fragment saved from an irreversible annihilation, the poet preserves the enigmatic essence of an absent body. A shroud of absence-presence and of death-life envelops the dead woman. The relic, according to Pierre Fédida, "derives its meaning from the desire to preserve *some thing* from what one is separated from, without, however, having to give up being separated from it."[14] The relic designates absence even as it denies the power of such absence. By means of a fragmentary vestige, the devastating lack of the beloved is made present. The poem harbors "a possible remnant, inalterable et indestructible, that is preserved beyond all separation."[15]

Because Jouve refuses to imagine the dead woman's body as being under attack from what Baudelaire in "Une Charogne" graphically described as the "noirs bataillons / De larves, qui coulaient comme un épais liquide / Le long de ces vivants haillons" ("black armies / Of maggots, flowing like a thick liquid, / Along this tattered flesh"), his figuration of Hélène as poetic relic suppresses an awareness of death as a natural though repugnant process of putrefaction.[16] Jouve does not refer to the body's decomposition, because death is for him fundamentally creative; it is the "'Rien créateur'" (*O*, 2:1139). But this does not imply that the essential truth of death as a force of total annihilation is completely forgotten. Jouve sees death in a double and ambivalent light. It is at once the presence of an absence and the absence of a presence. As Fédida notes, "the total visibility of the relic ensures that one will no longer believe in the anguish of destruction."[17] But, the melancholic poet, by his very desire to turn the lost body into a relic, unconsciously acknowledges the reality of an irreversible loss. He places the corpse, and its progressive decomposition, beyond representation; he persuades himself that, because the bodily traces of the dead

knots, their iron hairpins, revealed the force of her secret and her being!" (p. 975). The hair is thus "erotic" in the sense Jouve gives to that word: a force leading to the fusion of subject and object, self and other; as Léonide affirms, "la Chevelure, mystère d'Hélène, était *moi*" ("*I* was Hélène's Hair, her very mystery"; p. 1011).

14. "La Relique et le travail du deuil," *Nouvelle Revue de psychanalyse* 2 (Fall 1970): 249; reprinted in his *L'Absence*, pp. 53–59.

15. Ibid.

16. *Oeuvres complètes,* 2 vols., Bibliothèque de la Pléiade (Paris: Gallimard, 1975), 1:31.

17. "La Relique et le travail du deuil," 252.

woman have not disappeared, she must still exist *somewhere*. The relic is
thus "a *remnant* whose preservation challenges all appearances."[18] This
is a phantasmatic preservation accomplished only through the work of
repression.

Confronted by a loss that has burdened him with melancholy, if not
mourning, Jouve feels the need to envision the woman as a relic, as the
preserved image of what has disappeared. He must imagine her as the
re-presentation of an absence. He strives to put the woman in some
scene, to locate her spatially, and this scene is always one of writing.
The lost woman must be framed by a visible form or enveloped by an
audible word so that her existence in the afterlife, in the *sur-vie* of
death, will be assured. Recounting the details of his second breakup
with Lisbé, a separation he initiated, Jouve writes in *En Miroir:* "I had
to flee from her once again, I had to make her suffer, I had *to encounter
her as an image* without ever being able to leave her" (*O*, 2:1099; my
emphasis). It is important to note how the woman, once lost, becomes
still more beautiful and attractive through the image, the relic, that
now embodies her. Although destroyed in reality, the intensity of her
presence is preserved in imagination. If there were not a frame to
encircle the women, to hold her being within the confines of a representation, to fix her in an immobile image, it is possible, Jouve suggests,
that she would become a dangerous and maleficent force, as we shall
now see.

Overstepping the limits of a representation or a form designed to
contain her, the dead woman, like an evil specter, can fatally haunt the
poet's life. This occurs in "Le Tableau" (*O*, 2:1223–25), a remarkable
prose poem describing Balthus's painting of a young woman combing
her hair (*Alice,* 1933), which at one time hung in Jouve's bedroom.
Insofar as she remains comfortably ensconced within the confines of
the canvas, Alice—this "jeune femme aux yeux blancs, vêtue d'une
courte chemise, qui peigne sa chevelure d'une main ferme, tandis que
levant haut une de ses jambes sur une chaise vulgaire, elle démontre
bien ostensiblement son sexe de femme" ("young woman with blank
eyes, in a short slip, who combs her hair with a firm hand while, placing
her raised leg on an ordinary chair, she candidly reveals her puden-
dum") (p. 1223)—is the faithful and taciturn companion of the poet.
She watches over his restless nights and is witness to the unconscious
movements of his sleep. What so fascinates the poet about the painting
is its precise *mise-en-scène* of the erotic, of "an intense sensuality" (p.

18. Ibid.

1223). The image is more seductive than reality, because it has been sublimated and mediated by art. One morning, however, with sudden terror the poet notices that the seductive figure of Alice has disappeared; all that remains is an enframed emptiness, a "general yellow tone" surrounded by "a thick grey molding" (p. 1224).

The disappearance of Alice, who, like Dorothée in "La Victime," has become a "fausse morte-fausse vivante" (a "woman neither-dead-nor-alive"), results in an explosion of sexual aggression. The woman is no longer an image; she is no longer encrypted in the closed space of a representation. Having overstepped the bounds erected by a masculine hand (the painter's) to contain her, Alice abandons the region of the imaginary and now roams the world of everyday life as the living incarnation of eros and sin. Like a phantom, she intervenes in the daily life of the poet, making it impossible for him to write, to live, or to engage in sexual relations. Haunted by Alice, pursued by her at every turn, powerless to free himself from her constant presence, the poet is on the edge of insanity; but he is rescued at the last moment by his wife, symbol of the normality of a love authorized by social convention. In the allegory of erotic sin that "Le Tableau" dramatizes, Jouve is nearly deprived of his reason by a woman who, abandoning her place of figuration, revolts against her status as an immobile and sublimated image. Free of mediation, and able for the first time to express the purity and power of her erotic presence, Alice pushes the poet toward the insanity and death he associates with sin. Outside the confines of her representation, the woman is dangerous. But it is only when she is restored to her safe and "customary" place that the poet can once again feel at ease: "Je revins à moi et souris, on me souriait: tout était en place, et Alice avait repris sa figure dans le cadre" ("I became myself again and smiled, and the world smiled at me: everything was in its place, and Alice had resumed her position within the frame"; p. 1225).

It is thus evident that the representation, the literal *mise-en-scène,* of the woman, is essential to Jouve's vision of the world and of the relationship between the sexes. He feels the need to imagine the woman as a being who is truly absent, lost, and dead. The sin she incarnates, and "the disaster of bedrooms" ("A Balthus," *O,* 1:1270) in which she participates, lead fatally to her loss. In life she is too present, too true, too erotic. And it is this force of eros which condemns her to death. But artistic figuration is, for Jouve, a way to abolish the woman, to place her in a tomb, to master her erotic power. One discovers, in place of a flesh-and-blood woman, a figure, a trope. Transformed into an image, the woman is made to inhabit a crypt, which the representation constructs.

The Jouvean poem, like the feminized landscape where the woman's body is laid to rest, is, therefore, a tomb.

Writing is a burial of sorts. It is the creation of a crypt, where what has died can be preserved in a "living" state.[19] The most striking example of such entombment is found at the conclusion of Jouve's novella *Dans les années profondes*. After Hélène de Sannis's death, Léonide realizes that, more than his mistress, Hélène was a nourishing and protective mother, a muse. She was placed on earth to give birth to the writer he will one day become. Hélène's death, therefore, signifies a writing that is soon to begin; it has provoked a desire and a need for figuration on the part of a writer not yet fully born. And this writing will in its turn become the memorial, the tombal monument, to the one who had originally engendered it: "Je fis le voeu de consacrer à l'image de la Femme Noire, en mémoire d'Hélène," asserts Léonide, "le trésor des forces que je sentais presque naître" ("I vowed to dedicate to the image of the Dark Lady, and in memory of Hélène, the wealth of forces that I felt beginning to well up in me"; *O*, 2:1049).[20] In expressing through words and names different "states of melancholy, joy, annunciation, and despair," Léonide will find the way to repossess Hélène, to communicate once again with her:

> Je voulus fixer les états qui me faisaient tant de bien, les écrire sur du papier. Hélas, j'ignorais les signes, et ce qu'il fallait fixer. Je n'y parvenais pas. Mais une patience, nouvelle et profonde, se formait aussi.

19. For a discussion of the poetics of the crypt and of cryptic incorporation, see Jacques Derrida, "Fors," in Nicolas Abraham and Maria Torok, *Cryptonymie: Le Verbier de l'homme aux loups* (Paris: Aubier-Flammarion, 1976), pp. 7–73 ["Fors," trans. Barbara Johnson, *Georgia Review* 31 (Spring 1977): 64–116]. Derrida observes that "the inhabitant of a crypt is always a living-dead, a dead entity we are perfectly willing to keep alive, but *as* dead, one we are willing to keep, as long as we keep it, within us, intact in any way save as living" (p. 25/78). Moreover, according to Blanchot, all language is linked to the grave; it is epitaphic, for the word, because it takes the place of the thing it designates, announces the emptiness on which it is founded: "When we speak, we lean on a tomb, and the void of that tomb is what makes language true, but at the same time void is reality and death becomes being" ("La Littérature et le droit à la mort," p. 51/55).

20. The "Femme Noire," who in Jouve's imagination stands as a symbolic incarnation of the sensuality and sin of all women ("she stirred slowly, more sinuous than a snake, and her teeth illuminated the night"), figures in one of Léonide's dreams (*Dans les années profondes*, in *O*, 2:986–87). As a bride dressed completely in black and destined to both an unhappy marriage and an untimely death, she is a premonitory vision of Hélène, and thus of "everywoman," as Léonide will later realize: "I believed I spied or discovered in Hélène several women, seeing them detach themselves from her and then return to her, women who formed different layers, one more ancient than the other. All these women, who were deeper than Hélène and yet Hélène, came together in the Dark Lady [*la Femme Noire*]. I felt that for me, essentially, Hélène had always been identical to the Dark Lady and that the Dark Lady had always been idolized as Hélène" (p. 1048).

[I wanted to capture the states that were making me feel so good, to write them down on paper. Alas, I was blind to the signs and what was important to capture. I could not manage it. But a new and profound patience was also being formed.] (P. 1050)

Léonide is not sufficiently developed as a writer to be able yet to drink from that inexhaustible fount of writing that Hélène's death has created. Because the word is itself an annunciation of death and because writing digs a sepulcher in the loam of the real, Léonide does not feel the need to visit Hélène's tomb in order to pay his last respects. His writing will do that for him:

Je quittai le château de Ponte sans tourner la tête. Là—je le sus plus tard—s'était ouverte pour moi une source parfaite, c'est-à-dire iné-puisable.
Je partis sans avoir visité la tombe.

[I left the castle of Ponte without turning around. There, I later realized, a perfect and inexhaustible source had opened for me.
I went away without visiting the tomb.] (P. 1050)

The young writer-to-be turns his back, therefore, on the death of a decaying, buried corpse in order to embrace a death of a different kind: the resurrectional death that gives birth to writing. Poetry, asserts Jouve "is the very life of sublime Eros, dead and for that reason surviving" (*O*, 1:199). Léonide does not have to visit Hélène's tomb; he will himself erect another one, even more monumental and memorable. All his works to come, all the future creations of his imagination, will constitute, like Jouve's *oeuvre,* the tomb of a beloved woman. Having arisen from death, writing labors to give it form. Death is, for Jouve, incessantly creative. In destroying a body of flesh, it produces a body of works; in place of *le corps,* there is now the *corpus.* The absence of Lisbé, for example, from whom Jouve was separated in 1934 while writing *Dans les années profondes* (in which he uncannily prefigures her death two years hence), also inspires the Hélène poems of *Matière céleste,* written in May 1936. The poems are a direct result of the story, as Jouve explains: "Hélène, of *Matière céleste,* triumphantly emerges from the last sentence of the story: 'I went away without visiting the tomb'" (*O*, 2:1102). Atop the tomb of one woman—Hélène de Sannis—is erected another, that of Lisbé, of Madame E.V. One text accomplishes the resurrection of another. Within the sepulcher that writing hollows out, the absent woman continues to exist, for death is "the unnameable zone where a creature of God cannot help but still exist" (p. 1102). The comings and goings of a dead woman with innumerable names are what Jouve's work records: "In all periods of my work to this day, there is the passing of a dead Woman—only one, but under different names: for example, Aurora, who masks at once Lisbé and Hélène. Hélène overwhelms all her images, with different meanings and always the same fundamental meaning" (p. 1102).[21]

The laying to rest of the woman in the tomb of the poem ensures her continued presence, even though she is enveloped in the shroud of absence. In "Vie de la tombe d'Hélène," Jouve reveals the extent to which he dreams of the vigor, force, and energetic presence of the dead woman:

> Des glaïeuls (sur elle la plus belle) se balancent
> Il fait beau sur sa pierre à mourir de ciel bleu
> C'est le resplendissant automne sans alarme
> Le cri du marbre veiné
> Où elle noire est robuste enterrée
> Ensevelie nue sous le poids de mes songes
>
> . . . . .
>
> Les larmes brillent, ô ma pierre
> Les larmes coulent, ô mon sang
> Les larmes sont la rosée de ce théâtre
> Et la verdure veut ressusciter ton pied des montagnes
> Et nous attire
> Vers le bloc adouci de terre de ton coeur.

> [The gladiola (on her the most beautiful) sway
> It is so lovely by her stone one could die from the sky's blueness
> It is autumn resplendent and unmenacing
> The cry of veined marble
> Where dark and robust she is buried
> Entombed naked under the weight of my dreams
>
> . . . . .

21. Jouve's embodiment of Lisbé in fictive personages (such as Hélène) before her death in 1936 continues after her passing as well. As Jean Starobinski remarks, "an excess of experience calls out for an excess of writing." Death unleashes a flood of words and images: in particular, the sheaf of over one hundred pages of unpublished poetic fragments, erotic reveries, and notes for a future *récit* titled *Les Beaux Masques* ("La Douce visiteuse: Pages retrouvées et textes inédits de Pierre Jean Jouve," *Nouvelle Revue française* 417 [1 October 1987]: 75; see also 76–86, and René Micha, "Présentation," in *O*, 2:1595–1600).

Tears shine, o my stone
Tears flow, o my blood
Tears are the dew of this theatre
And from the mountains the verdant landscape wishes to awaken
    your foot
And draws us
Toward the softened lump of earth that is your heart.]

                        (*O*, 1:292–93)

The woman's presence is pure, clear, and vibrant, all the more so because this presence provokes melancholy and is enveloped by a veil of memories, words, dreams, and writing. Hélène is sustained by the radiant and flowing sadness she engenders. The entire landscape is inundated by melancholy. Through the poet's tears, Hélène regains life. No longer able to embrace the woman, the poet can now possess her through the tears of grief, the heaviness of dreams, which have taken her place, through, that is, the melancholic figuration he has given to his loss. Never has she been so pure, so present, or so beautiful as she is in death. Through emptiness, the woman regains plenitude: "Tu dors / Jamais plus nue jamais plus pâle jamais plus belle" ("You sleep / Never more naked never more pale never more lovely") ("E.V. dans le tombeau," *O*, 1:361). Through the tomb that is also the poem, Lisbé attains the summit of artistic expression. She is, as Martine Broda remarks, "the central void who by her aspiration summons and animates the poem's movement."[22] Inscribing the initials of her absent being on the stone under which she lies, Lisbé causes marble to resonate with the music (and the poetry) of her presence:

Jamais plus graves les pensées et grasses les tourterelles
Plus mystiques les pas sans traces
Autour de la tombe inspirée
Ni plus étrange la musique
Que tu fais dans la pierre E.V.

[Never more serious were the thoughts and plump the turtledoves
Nor more mystical the traceless steps
Around the inspired tomb

---

22. *Jouve*, p. 66. For a detailed discussion of the symbolic and psychoanalytic qualities of "la Morte" and her relation to the Hélène myth, see pp. 33–93. For an analysis of the interrelations of death, eros, and writing, see pp. 111–18.

Nor more strange the music
That you make in the stone E.V.]

(*O*, 1:362)

The Melancholy of Loss

The music that emerges from the tomb is that of melancholy. The poet responds to the beloved's loss by seeking an attachment that will keep her alive as a dead being, that will maintain a "douce communication / Entre toi et moi qui t'ai perdue" ("gentle bond / Between you and me, the one who has lost you"; "Le Même à la même," *O*, 1:298). To the void that loss has opened in his life, the poet responds with melancholy; he unflinchingly confronts the irreversible reality of what no longer exists. It is a nothingness inherent as much to reality as to love:

Le miracle de l'amour est de n'aimer rien
Par les trous d'étoiles de ne rien connaître
De ne rien savoir ni vivre ni paraître
D'être la flamme de n'exister en rien.

[The miracle of love is to love nothing
Through the gaps in stars to be aware of nothing
To know or live or show nothing
To be the flame that exists in nothing.]

("Nada," *O*, 1:291)

The melancholiac, as Roger Munier writes, "sees the Nothing of what is. He sees it in what is."[23] This "rien" is the only vestige, the only possession so to speak, that the melancholic poet salvages from the catastrophe of his loss. Lack is transformed into a substance, a form, a matter, often brilliant and dazzling, for melancholy has a light of its own; its rays penetrate to the bottom of a dark abyss.

Loss is expressed through melancholy in such a manner that it comes to take the place of the lost object of love. Thus, the discourse or the speaking of melancholy has its own particular and unique beauty. As nothing becomes everything, in accordance with Jouve's poetics of *nada*, so beauty is the underside of melancholy. To the yellow sun of presence corresponds the ashen sun—"l'autre plus cendreux soleil"

23. *Mélancolie* (Amiens: Le Nyctalope, 1987), p. 56.

("La Femme et la terre," *O,* 1:294)—of absence. Loss encircles the dead woman with a dazzling halo; it invests her with a unique beauty, that of a "Larme, cette goutte en désespoir qui brille" ("Tear, this desperate droplet that shines"; "Larmes," *O,* 1:183). And if melancholy has its own beauty, beauty also has its own melancholy. At the heart of the sublime lie loss, absence, lack, and vacancy, no less than at the heart of light moves a mortal and menacing shadow, ponderous and implacable in its domination of the world. Materialized, melancholy takes on a density and an oppressiveness, beautiful in themselves, which transform everyday reality:

> On voit une seule journée implacablement belle et chaude
> Un implacable déroulement de belle journée
> Et les terres frappées en hurlant font de l'ombre
> Et les oiseaux s'enfuient leurs ailes rabattues
> Et l'espace avec des mains d'azur se presse lui-même
> Sa poitrine gémit sous ses mains azurées.[24]

> [One sees a single day relentlessly hot and beautiful
> A beautiful day's relentless unfolding
> And the beaten earth howling makes shadows
> And the birds flee their wings folded back
> And space with hands of azure compresses itself
> Its chest groaning beneath its azured hands.]
> ("La Mélancolie d'une belle journée," *O,* 1:147)

Jouve's melancholy could be said to express itself through two fundamental desires: the *desire for incorporation* and the *desire for overnaming.* In the prose poem "L'Héroïne," the narrator confides to his lover that

> Je ne doutais pas de t'avoir aimée, aimée et possédée,—et pourtant de te contenir comme la partie éteinte de mon propre désir. Je tremblais donc de tes mouvements féminins secrets, je vivais tes déchirements, je pressentais tes folies, j'avais tes forces masculines; j'armais ton revolver, je tirais à ta place, et comme toi je suicidais la meurtrière abandonnée de Dieu. Le véritable artiste doit être incorporé à la créature, et je l'étais à ce point que ma voix chevrotait,

---

24. For a penetrating interpretation of this poem and a discussion of Jouve's melancholic imagination, see Jean Starobinski, "La Mélancolie d'une belle journée," *Nouvelle Revue française* 183 (March 1968): 387–402.

perclue par les larmes, dans ton état final de dépouillement, de renoncement et de pardon.

[I did not doubt having loved you and possessed you—internalizing you as the deadened part of my own desire. I trembled therefore from your secret, feminine movements, I experienced your agonies, I foresaw your extravagances, I had your masculine strength; I cocked your revolver, I fired in your place, and like you I caused the suicide of the murderess abandoned by God. The true artist must become one with another being, which I was, to the point that my voice quivered, paralyzed by sorrow, in your final state of deprivation, renunciation, and repentance.] (*O,* 2:1254)

The desire to unite with the lost beloved, especially in that cold, dark place where, following her death, she has taken up residence, is very strong in Jouve. It testifies to the poet's need to identify with the being he has lost: "Etions-nous du même sang quand je rencontrai ta blondeur / Avions-nous pleuré les mêmes larmes dans les cages," he asks in "Lisbé" ("Were we of the same blood when I came upon your golden hair / Did we shed the same tears in cages"; *O,* 1:298). And in the poem "Le Même à la même," the title of which is itself revealing, the desire for fusion with the other is expressed in a manner rendered all the more longingly (and candidly) erotic for being associated with distance, loss, and bodily fragmentation:

Si près, si loin, ma courbe féminine ou nue
Que mes regards sont toujours tendus vers tes trous d'ombre
Ces yeux que je n'ai plus qui sont mes yeux
Ce corps, que je veux pénétrer pour être l'ombre.

[So near, so far, my feminine my naked curve
How perpetually fixed are my glances on your openings of shadow
These eyes I no longer have which are my eyes
This body, which I desire to penetrate so as to become its shadow.]

(*O,* 1:299)

Melancholic incorporation translates the need to keep the dead woman alive by means of a profound dream of intimacy. This perhaps explains, beyond the obvious religious reasons, why Jouve refuses to conceive of death as a phenomenon of decay. It is essential for him to imagine the woman as enveloped by presence and immediacy: "Etrange! O je suis encore une vraie fois / Contre ton sein ton globe mystique au parfum / Plus suave que la rondeur du printemps' ("Strange! O, I am once more truly / Against your breast, your mystic globe with its fragrance / More sweet than the spring's fullness"; *O,* 1:294). Although conscious of the strangeness of his perception, he can, nevertheless, experience the woman as if she had never disappeared. Resurrectional desire creates the illusion of possession: "Elle monte! enveloppée de mémoires fidèles / Etouffante de douceur d'ancienneté" ("She arises! enveloped by faithful memories / Choked by the sweetness of longevity"; "Le Corps de l'inceste," *O,* 1:299). Jouve's desire to reexperience the profound intimacy of love, to incorporate in himself the being of the dead beloved, and to introject the lost object of love in such a way that, as Freud writes, "the shadow of the object [falls] upon the ego, so that the latter [can] henceforth be criticized by a special mental faculty like an object, like the forsaken object," leads to a phantasmatic need for devoration:[25]

> O toi mon bien-aimé! je mange tes jardins
> Je dévore les miens te souviens-tu des miens
> Leur chaleur défendue nous est plus triste encore
> Te souviens-tu des ris et des bois de parfums
> Coquetteries vêtues et nudités des morts
> Te souviens-tu de nos répétitions
> De vignes de faons et de roses
> Quand nous penchions sur la montagne dans ce sang
> Unique, et dans cet air tout tendrement
> Unique respiré par nos deux grandes bouches
> Enfances?

> [Oh you, my beloved! I eat your gardens
> I devour mine do you remember mine
> Their forbidden heat saddens us even more
> Do you remember the rice and the fragrant woods
> Coquettishness of dress and nakedness of the dead
> Do you remember our repetitions
> Of vines fawns and roses
> When we leaned on the mountain in this
> Unique blood, and in this delicately
> Unique air inhaled by our avid mouths
> Our childhoods?]

("Le Corps de l'inceste," *O,* 1:300)

25. "Mourning and Melancholia," in *General Psychological Theory: Papers on Metapsychology,* ed. Philip Rieff (New York: Macmillan, 1963), p. 170.

The desire to devour the woman, to keep her alive inside the self, as she is preserved within a poem, derives its strength from the phenomenon of cannibalistic incorporation characteristic of melancholic bereavement. Such cannibalism, notes Pierre Fédida, represents "the imaginary satisfaction that [melancholic] suffering achieves in consuming the lost object—an object whose 'loss' was in some way necessary, so that it would remain alive and present in its phantasmatically preserved primal reality."[26] The melancholic poet finds his own identity and forges his own being by means of the living void that has now opened in his life. He succeeds in knowing himself precisely through what he lacks. Melancholy, as we saw in our discussion of Baudelaire in chapter 2, is, according to Fédida, "less the regressive reaction to the loss of the object than the phantasmatic (or hallucinatory) capacity to *keep it alive as lost object.*"[27] More than remembering the beloved in poetry or preserving her memory intact, Jouve keeps alive—through the life of the poem, the life of the tomb—the very loss of the absent woman. "Beauty," writes Julia Kristeva (and one would assume the same for poetry as well), "reveals itself as the admirable face of loss; it transforms loss in order to make it live."[28] The loss, which Jouve's writing sustains and continuously embodies in the here and now (the *ici*) of the poem, manifests itself in the dark beauty and somber immediacy of melancholic mourning:

—Ici dans le pli deuil de notre inconnaissance
Ici dans l'instinct même, et le chagrin
Je regarde une très lumineuse misère

26. "Le Cannibale mélancolique," *Nouvelle Revue de psychanalyse* 6 (Fall 1972): 126, reprinted in his *L'Absence*, Collection Connaissance de l'inconscient (Paris: Gallimard, 1978), pp. 61–67.
27. Ibid. Similarly, Nicolas Abraham and Maria Torok observe that the melancholiac carefully preserves the memory of the lost object of love "as his or her most cherished belonging and at the cost of building a crypt for it out of stones of hate and aggression." But endless mourning sets in when the walls of the crypt give way and the self, in an effort to protect the lost object, unites with it. This melancholic identification with the lost other entails a certain theatricalization of mourning; the self makes a show of "its sadness, its gaping wound, its universal guilt." Loss becomes open display: "Staging [*mettre en scène*] the grief, which the subject lends to the object he has lost, is this not the only way remaining for him to relive, unknown to everyone, the secret paradise that has been wrenched from him? . . . When I am melancholic, I stage—all the more to emphasize its intensity—the object's grief at having lost me ("Introjecter-Incorporer: Deuil *ou* mélancolie," *Nouvelle Revue de psychanalyse* 6 [Fall 1972]: 121).
28. *Soleil noir: Dépression et mélancolie* (Paris: Gallimard, 1987), p. 111. For a different psychoanalytic approach to the relationship of loss and literature and to the role of bereavement in literary creativity, see David Aberbach, *Surviving Trauma: Loss, Literature, and Psychoanalysis* (New Haven: Yale University Press, 1989).

Je retourne le soleil jaune en soleil noir
Pour ton bien.

[—Here in the dress's fold, mourning of our ignorance
Here in instinct even and sorrow
I watch a luminous misery
I turn the yellow sun into a black sun
For your good.]

("Dialogue," *O*, 1:481)

The dream of melancholic incorporation, by means of which the poet longs to recapture the immediate presence of the lost woman, coincides with his desire not only to name her but also to *overname* her. In excess lies the hope of repossession, as if so many proliferating names, all designating the same creature, could endow her with the substance or the flesh she no longer has. In the tomb several languages are spoken. In the wake of loss, a multitude of naming words are enunciated, each searching vainly to fill the bottomless hole that death has opened in the real. In Jouve's extensive work there is only one dominant woman: the mythic, unseizable, forever absent Hélène. "In short," he writes, "Lisbé had given me the myth of Hélène, without knowing it. Nevertheless, she incarnated the myth fully: the inner myth of the woman that few women dare copy. The myth of Hélène is the union in a single act of passive eros and death" (*O*, 2:1100). But this mythic woman makes herself known by a host of names: la Capitaine H., Suzanne H., la Capitaine Humbert, la Commandante, Hélène de Sannis, la Femme Noire, Lisbé, Lisbeth, Elisabeth, E.V., "la douce visiteuse," Emily, Zabie, Léa, Claire, Aurora, and others still. She is simultaneously singular and plural, a mixture of pure similarity and pure alterity. The myth of Hélène, with its proliferating incarnations and its unchanging meaning—its endless signifiers and its immobile signified—is indeed, as Jouve affirms, a myth that will never stop haunting him.

Overnaming derives its power from the reality of melancholy. The origin of language can be traced to an immemorial loss, for, as Walter Benjamin writes, "to be named . . . perhaps always remains an intimation of mourning." Because man, since the Fall, has been separated from the pure, paradisiac language that God had used to name the things of Creation, he is condemned to speak an imperfect language in which things, by virtue of their distance from the source of divine essence, are overnamed. "There is, in the relation of human languages to that of things," remarks Benjamin, "something that can be approximately described as 'over-naming': over-naming as the deepest linguistic reason for all melancholy and (from the point of view of the thing) of all deliberate muteness."[29] The state of exile in which man lives obliges him to use imprecise words; because these words fail to give full meaning to their objects, they proliferate endlessly. The loss of paradise and of divine presence, which once gave language its infrangible density, condemns man, Benjamin argues, to the use of a language of fragments. As a language that has lost its moorings, it lends itself easily to allegorization, for any word can potentially signify anything else. Overnaming thus becomes the rule, not the exception. Mourning for what he has lost, man must make use of a language that, like himself, is adrift and in exile. Nevertheless, for a poet such as Jouve, there is always the possibility, if not the hope, enveloped as much by uncertainty as by faith, that the incessant nomination initiated by loss and the overnaming that sustains the linguistic being of melancholy will suddenly cease and that the multitude of names will finally coalesce in the one that underwrites all others: the Name of God.

Conclusion

Loss, for Jouve, is "Une hémorragie [qui] met en doute ma vie" ("A hemorrhaging that places my life in doubt"; *O*, 1:292). In the wake of death, the experiences of life, eros, and poetry have no real, permanent meaning:

> Qu'importent ce vit, et le chant
> Retiré de l'admirable abîme? Hélène est morte.

> Séparé comme je suis de moi et d'Hélène
> Je sais à peine que je vis et qu'elle est morte.

> [What do they matter, this virile organ, and the song
> Delivered from the admirable abyss? Hélène is dead.

> Separated as I am from myself and from Hélène
> I barely know that I am alive and she is dead.]

> (*O*, 1:292)

29. "On Language as Such and on the Language of Man," in *Reflections: Essays, Aphorisms, Autobiographical Writings*, trans. Edmund Jephcott (New York: Harcourt Brace Jovanovich, 1978), p. 330. See chapter 2 above.

All imagination is established on the absence that loss hollows out in the ground of the real. But when all is said and done, the experience of loss leaves the poet with a singular possession, the only one he has been able to salvage from the catastrophe of death. From the remains of a lost and abolished woman, from the "passage de la Morte," the poet has succeeded in creating a song of melancholy: a crystallization of names, forms, figures, signs, reflections, and words which, in giving voice to the dead woman in her very absence, makes her the plaintive and haunting object of the eros of loss:

> O mon amie je t'ai perdue depuis l'aurore
> Je n'ai que tes reflets à mon coeur encombré
> De ces formes de ces urnes qui m'approchent
> Je n'ai plus que ces mots que me donnent ces bouches.

> [Oh my beloved friend I have lost you since dawn's light
> I have only your reflection in a heart oppressed
> By these forms by these urns that draw near to me
> I no longer have but the words imparted by these mouths.]

("Je suis en deuil de toi," O, 1:374)

CHAPTER 5

"The Cry That Pierces Music": Yves Bonnefoy

Il n'y a expérience au sens strict que là où quelque chose de radicalement *autre* est en jeu.

[There is no such thing as experience in the strict sense except where something radically *other* is in play.]
—Maurice Blanchot, *L'Entretien infini*

"The poem," wrote Wallace Stevens in "An Ordinary Evening in New Haven," "is the cry of its occasion, / Part of the res itself and not about it."[1] In its mortalness, the world speaks, sings, screams, and laments through the verses of the poem. The cry of the real pierces the poem's forms—its syntax, its images, its music—making them express the finitude of being. The poem, or its cry, fuses with the world; it coincides with the here and now of temporal existence. It is with such a cry—"ce cri / Qui a fait naître" ("this cry / That gives birth"),[2] ce "plus

1. *The Collected Poems* (New York: Alfred A. Knopf, 1964), p. 473.
2. Yves Bonnefoy, *Poèmes* (Paris: Mercure de France, 1978), p. 282; cited in the text as *P*. Further references to Bonnefoy's works are cited in the text according to the following abbreviations:
  AP   *L'Arrière-pays*, Collection Les Sentiers de la création (Geneva: Albert Skira, 1972).
  CQFSL *Ce qui fut sans lumière* (Paris: Mercure de France, 1987).
  DH   "Du Haïku," in *Haïku*, ed. Roger Munier (Paris: Fayard, 1978).
  E   *Entretiens sur la poésie*, Collection Langages (Neuchâtel: La Baconnière, 1981).
  HRD   *Hier régnant désert*, in *Du mouvement et de l'immobilité de Douve*, Collection Poésie (Paris: Gallimard, 1970).
  I   *L'Improbable*, followed by *Un rêve fait à Mantoue*, new ed., corrected and augmented (Paris: Mercure de France, 1980).
  NR   *Le Nuage rouge* (Paris: Mercure de France, 1977).
  O   *L'Ordalie* (Paris: Maeght, 1975).
  PI   *La Présence et l'image: Leçon inaugurale de la Chaire d'Etudes Comparées de la Fonction Poétique au Collège de France, 1981* (Paris: Mercure de France, 1983).

grand cri qu'être ait jamais tenté" (this "greatest cry a man ever attempted"; *Poèmes*, 60/*On the Motion and Immobility of Douve*, 77), "ce cri
brûlant, / Comme une épée / Dans la paroi rocheuse" ("this seering cry /
Like a sword / In the rock wall"; *Hier régnant désert*, 168), ce "cri aux
confins de la nuit" (this "cry at the limits of night"),[3] this startled voice
of incoherent sound which awakens us to the presence of death, this
scream so anguished it could not possibly have meaning—that Yves
Bonnefoy opens his long poem *Dans le leurre du seuil* (1975):

Mais non, toujours
D'un déploiement de l'aile de l'impossible
Tu t'éveilles, avec un cri,
Du lieu, qui n'est qu'un rêve. Ta voix, soudain,
Est rauque comme un torrent.

[But no, once again
Unfolding the wing of the impossible
You awaken, with a cry,
From the place which is only a dream.]

(*P*, 231/*Poems*, 63)

At the threshold of the poem, the reader is greeted by a cry resounding
with the sounds of the mortal world. A harsh, raucous, booming voice
awakens the poem's sleeper from a dream world, plunging him or her
into the torrential flow of life. From the outset, both reader and sleeper

RR   *Récits en rêve* (Paris: Mercure de France, 1987).
RT   *Rue Traversière* (Paris: Mercure de France, 1977).
VP   *La Vérité de parole* (Paris: Mercure de France, 1988).
Translations of Bonnefoy's work are cited according to the following abbreviations:
A   *The Act and the Place of Poetry: Selected Essays*, ed. John T. Naughton (Chicago:
University of Chicago Press, 1989).
D   *On the Motion and Immobility of Douve*, trans. Galway Kinnell (Athens: Ohio
University Press, 1968).
PO   *Poems, 1959–1975*, trans. Richard Pevear (New York: Random House, 1985).
SP   *Selected Poems*, trans. Anthony Rudolf (London: Jonathan Cape, 1968).
All other translations are my own.
   3. "Raymond Mason," in *Raymond Mason* (New York: Pierre Matisse Gallery, 1969),
unfolioed. (This essay is reprinted in Bonnefoy's *Sur un sculpteur et des peintres*, Collection
Carnets [Paris: Plon, 1989], pp. 21–27. As revised, the essay no longer contains the
allusion to the "cri aux confins de la nuit," but it does suggest a link between poetry and
"the oldest voices of the earth, in particular the 'cry' of an owl on a summer night"
[p. 217].) See also Bonnefoy's "La Liberté de l'esprit," in *Raymond Mason*, Collection
Contemporains (Paris: Centre Georges Pompidou, 1985), pp. 9–33. For an enlightening
study of the cry and its reverberations in Bonnefoy's poems, see Georges Formentelli,
"La Poésie d'Yves Bonnefoy: Cri, Bruit, Sacrifice," *Critique* 457–58 (June–July 1985):
686–718.

learn that poetry and dream are pierced by the cry of time and mortality, of being and nothingness.[4]

This rude awakening to reality calls to mind an earlier moment in the history of poetry when a strident cry shakes a man of creative talents from his reverie, pierces the music of his sublime performance, wrenches him cruelly from the summits of artistic representation—the ideal, transcendental world of his creation—and installs him once again among the sordid and mortal realities of life. Condemned to death for having plotted against his prince, who, despite this treachery, gives him one more chance to perform, the jester Fancioulle, hero of Baudelaire's prose poem "Une Mort héroique," proves by his ethereal performance that

> l'ivresse de l'Art est plus apte que toute autre à voiler les terreurs du gouffre; que le génie peut jouer la comédie au bord de la tombe avec une joie qui l'empêche de voir la tombe, perdu, comme il est, dans un paradis excluant toute idée de tombe et de destruction.[5]

> [the intoxication of Art is more apt than any other to veil the terrors of the eternal abyss; and that genius can play a part, even on the edge of the grave, with such joy that it does not see the grave, lost, as it is, in a paradise that shuts out all thought of the grave and of death.]

But the narrator's concern with the grave—he repeats the word three times in the short space of the sentence—gives the lie to his confidence in "the intoxication of Art." Fancioulle's ecstatic and sublime representation causes a thin gossamer veil to hang over the world, blocking

4. Concerning Bonnefoy's preoccupation with mortality and finitude, see the following important studies: Mary Ann Caws, *Yves Bonnefoy* (Boston: Twayne, 1984); Michèle Finck, *Yves Bonnefoy: Le Simple et le sens* (Paris: José Corti, 1989); Gérard Gasarian, *Yves Bonnefoy: La Poésie, la présence* (Seyssel: Champ Vallon, 1986); Ronald Gérard Giguère, *Le Concept de la réalité dans la poésie d'Yves Bonnefoy* (Paris: Nizet, 1985); John E. Jackson, *La Question du moi: Un Aspect de la modernité poétique européenne: T. S. Eliot—Paul Celan—Yves Bonnefoy* (Neuchâtel: La Baconnière, 1978); John T. Naughton, *The Poetics of Yves Bonnefoy* (Chicago: University of Chicago Press, 1984); Jérôme Thélot, *Poétique d'Yves Bonnefoy*, Histoire des idées et critique littéraire, no. 214 (Geneva: Droz, 1983); and Richard Vernier, *Yves Bonnefoy ou les mots comme le ciel* (Tübingen: Gunter Narr and Paris: Jean-Michel Place, 1985). See also James Gaylord McAllister, "*Poèmes* d'Yves Bonnefoy: Le Dialogue tenté: Les Chemins du retour," Ph.D. diss., University of Wisconsin, 1981; and the following journals, which have devoted special issues to Bonnefoy's work: *L'Arc* 66 (1976); *World Literature Today* 53 (Summer 1979); *Cahiers de l'Université de Pau et des pays de l'Adour (Poétique et Poésie d'Yves Bonnefoy)*, no. 18 (1983), and (*Yves Bonnefoy: Poésie, Art, et Pensée*), n.s., no. 7 (1986); *Sud* 15 (1985); and *Poetry World* 3 (Fall 1990).

5. *Le Spleen de Paris*, in *OC*, 1:321 [*Paris Spleen*, trans. Louise Varèse (New York: New Directions, 1970), p. 56].

one's vision of the real and masking its fragmented mortal aspects. But the secure calm of Fancioulle's solipsistic, perfect, timeless universe is broken suddenly by "un coup de sifflet aigu," a shrill hiss, a catcall, coming from an enemy in the wings, which, like air rushing to fill a vacuum, overwhelms the artist with more painful reality and temporality than his sensitive soul can withstand:

> Fancioulle, secoué, réveillé dans son rêve, ferma d'abord les yeux, puis les rouvrit presque aussitôt, démesurément agrandis, ouvrit ensuite la bouche comme pour respirer convulsivement, chancela un peu en avant, un peu en arrière, et puis tomba roide morte sur les planches.[6]

> [Fancioulle, awakened from his dream, closed his eyes, and when almost at once he opened them again, they seemed to have grown inordinately large, then he opened his mouth as though struggling for breath, staggered forward a step, then backward, and fell dead upon the stage.]

Here, a cry has again pierced the music. A sound of otherness emerging from the temporal world has disrupted the illusory dream world of art, opening the closed spaces of this paradise to temporal being. The elegant mask of art and of image, placed over the contorted face of existence, is ripped away by Baudelaire and Bonnefoy, demystifying poets who, because they know that the cry of otherness echoing relentlessly in a temporal world of constant movement and change cannot be stifled, refuse to believe in the transfiguring power of art, as Bonnefoy asserts in *Dans le leurre du seuil:*

> Mais toujours et distinctement je vois aussi
> La tache noire dans l'image, j'entends le cri
> Qui perce la musique, je sais en moi
> La misère du sens. Non, ce n'est pas
> Aux transfigurations que peut prétendre
> Notre lieu, en son mal.

> [But always and distinctly I also see
> The black stain in the image, I hear
> The cry that pierces the music, and know

6. Ibid., p. 322/57.

In myself the poverty of meaning. No,
Our place, in its darkness, can make no claim
To transfigurations.]

(*P*, 295/*PO*, 135–37)

Image, metaphor, rhetoric, syntax, form, color, line, perspective, proportion, measure, rhythm, tone, note, chord, meaning—all the strategies of mimetic representation in poetry, painting, and music are veils
easily pierced by the cry of otherness coming from the world, from
"Notre lieu, en son mal." One tends to forget that the skeleton lies close
to the surface of the skin, that a skull grins beneath a joyful face, that
within every *écrit* echoes the *cri* that may be its source. There is no
repressing what is other, no dressing up the nothing that is ultimately
human existence, no stopping the passage of time, no vaunting the
meaning of things. As the historian in Bonnefoy's intriguing story "Les
Découvertes de Prague" explains:

> Ah, toute évidence est énigme! Toute plénitude est barrée d'une
> ligne pâle, resserrée sur soi, qu'on ne voit plus, mais qui, à des
> moments, zigzague dans le blé de l'image—oui, dans les montagnes,
> les corps—et décolore tout, mon amie, comme la foudre. Nous rap-
> prochons ces lambeaux, ces couleurs, ces signes, nous recousons . . .
> Mais par-dessous, dans l'abîme . . .
> —Le ciel? Les pierres?
> —J'appelais cela de la nuit.

> [Ah, all reality is engima. All plenitude is transversed by a pale line,
> closed in on itself, no longer visible, but that at times zigzags through
> the wheat of the image—yes, through mountains, bodies—and dis-
> colors everything, my friend, like lightning. We bring together these
> shreds, these colors, these signs . . . But underneath in the abyss . . .
> —You mean the sky? Stone?
> —I called them night.] (*Rue Traversière*, 72)

Structures of Otherness

The "presence of the other," writes Bonnefoy, "never stops haunting Baudelaire's poems" (*Entretiens sur la poésie*, 86). It is perhaps one of
the several influences of Baudelaire's poetry on Bonnefoy's that this
sense of the other, this consciousness of otherness, continues to fasci-

nate and to haunt the latter's work. There is in Bonnefoy's poetry and criticism always the possibility of the surging forth of otherness, which could be defined as a phenomenon of sudden appearance, or as a dialectical experience in which what is both the same and other struggle, or as a disquieting encounter opening things of the familiar world to a radical and alienating difference that questions, contests, and negates them. By means of the eruption in the world of what is other, three possible disorienting events occur: first, the apparition of a completely unforeseen reality; second, the sudden appearance of what Bonnefoy calls "une dérive," a swerving or turning away from the familiar toward the unknown, the improbable; and third, the decentering of perception and experience, as, for example, when the narrator of one of Bonnefoy's stories, who is carefully trying to study the bizarre perspective of certain Italian Renaissance paintings, notices with surprise that

> au moment où l'oeil appelé là-bas, au point de fuite, va s'apaiser dans la convergence des lignes, qui a mûri la cohérence du sens, une force irrésistible l'appelle ailleurs, vers un autre centre.

> [at the moment when the eye, attracted to the distant vanishing point, is about to find calm in the convergence of lines, which has brought to fruition the coherence of meaning, an irresistible force summons it elsewhere, towards another center.] (*RT,* 32)

Otherness is this irresistible force, this magnetic field, that deflects perception, turning it toward other unknown possibilities, other centers. Imagining that he stands in a mountain village at sunset, passionately watching "a red cloud setting the sky ablaze with its light, while I continually wonder if it is not the reflection of yet another light" ("Du Haïku," xxxvi); or walking through a far-off landscape believing that he hugs the shore of an unseen *arrière-pays;* or reminding himself as he sets pen to paper that he wishes to "write from the starting point of, on the subject of, with the eye of someone in me who is not a writer, someone who existed before I wrote and would continue to exist, if I were to stop" (*E,* 55); or contemplating a painting in order to put himself face to face with the other living being, its creator, who speaks to him across the centuries from within its depths; or addressing friends or loved ones in whom he recognizes and accepts an essential difference and existence, knowing that we lead "Des vies qui se séparent dans l'énigme" ("lives parted / In the enigma"; *P,* 294/*PO,* 135)—at each of these moments, in each of these experiences, Bonnefoy listens to the murmurs of otherness whispering beneath the surface of the real; he regards the light of alterity as it escapes from the cracks in a closed door; he looks everywhere for the signs of what is other in the world, in the work, and in the self. In his poetic vision, all reality vibrates with otherness, and all the phenomena of the physical world—trees, stars, rivers, stones, clouds, the beings who live among them, and the words, colors, forms by which they give them representation and meaning— all, that is to say, that dwells within what Bonnefoy calls, in homage to Rilke, "l'ouvert du monde" (the "Open"), all this vibrates *autrement*. Being and writing turn toward otherness and toward the other (*autrui*) the way the sunflower follows the arc of a sun advancing toward night. Existence is "allotropic"; that is, it is a turning toward and into the open of alterity, a swerving toward what is *allos*, "other." "What is a writing," asks Bonnefoy, "that does not foreshadow, does not postulate an outside [*un dehors*]?" (*E*, 55) and, one might add, "an alterity?" What is a representation that does not, "in the blurred mirror of the last hour," reveal, "comme une main / Essuie la vitre où a brillé la pluie, / Quelques figures simples, quelques signes / Qui brillent au-delà des mots" ("like a hand / Wiping the glass where rain once glistened, / A few simple figures, a few signs / That shine beyond words"; *Ce qui fut sans lumière*, 68–69)?

Otherness in Bonnefoy's poetry and criticism takes several forms and expresses itself through several different modes. In general, it falls into three categories: the alterity of place, the alterity of writing or representation, and the alterity of person. It is worth examining each in some detail, for together they "represent"—if such representation is at all truly possible through writing or any other means—the alterity of being as Bonnefoy feels it, lives it, and strives poetically to articulate it.

It is in remote and rugged terrains, in distant villages lost from sight, in enclosed valleys, in hidden landscapes, on uninhabited mountain slopes, within ancient subterranean cities—topographies that the work *L'Arrière-pays* poetically evokes—that Bonnefoy searches for the *otherness of place*. He is attracted by "the wonder and appeal of some completely other region of the earth" (*L'Arrière-pays*, 35). But this other land is no transcendent paradise "anywhere out of this world" (to quote Baudelaire), no second Byzantium constructed with what Yeats called "the artifice of eternity" ("ce haut artifice, l'éternel," as Bonnefoy renders it in his translation of Yeats's poem).[7] Rather, it is a place "of flesh

7. "Byzance, l'autre rive," in *Quarante-cinq poèmes de W. B. Yeats*, followed by *La Résurrection* (Paris: Hermann, 1989), p. 63.

and time, like our own, and such that we can live there, grow older there, die there" (*AP*, 62). The hidden interior spaces he seeks are marked by signs of otherness, imparted by events of loss and temporal disintegration. These lands are radically and fundamentally *other*. All that is known or can be said about them is that there, a different mode of being, one belonging to what Bonnefoy calls "le vrai lieu" ("the true place"), prevails. These places belong to a temporal zone that from our perspective is purely conditional, as if, alongside the road on which our lives advance, there existed a parallel, invisible, *other* road that followed it for a while, only to veer off suddenly in an unforeseen direction. This is the hypothetical, yet-to-be discovered, shadow land, the *arrière-pays*, or back country, which Bonnefoy describes as "a land beyond the horizon: place of life that one could have regained . . . if at the cross-roads one had taken *the other road*" (*E*, 15). In addition to being conditional and part of an uncertain future, the *autre pays* can sometimes be a place out of the past, a locale of former intimacy, once possessed but now lost; it is a mysterious, almost mythical, site, like the "rue Traversière" of Bonnefoy's childhood in Tours, which despite wanderings through the city and the study of maps, he can not locate, except in his memory and through imagination. Indeed, all of childhood, and especially those years predating a child's brutal encounter with, and sudden awareness of, the reality of death, can be designated a "moment" of otherness, a time of ephemeral presence, of immediacy with being itself, when the child, according to Bonnefoy, finds his place "at the center of the world, in the transparence of things" (*L'Improbable*, 318). At the moment of looking back at a past that has become enveloped with an irreversible otherness, we suddenly recognize that we have become outsiders to our own history:

> Remonter à ses origines, n'est-ce pas se faire le visiteur, qui vient de loin, de ce qu'on avait jadis éprouvé comme une intériorité, une présence à soi-même, une certitude?

> [To return to our origins is this not to come from afar to visit what we had once experienced as an interiority, a presence unto itself, a certainty?] (*E*, 104)

The *autre terre*, the *vrai lieu*, the *arrière-pays*, the remembered sites of a joyful childhood still ignorant of death—these are all places favoring the possible revelation of presence (*la présence*), that much-desired, mysterious, Edenic, yet nontranscendental experience of "non-mediated unity" (*La Vérité de parole*, 235) which Bonnefoy never ceases to search for and that his poetry and prose continually describe and celebrate as the real ("le réel") itself. Presence is the ephemeral apparition of an experience of oneness, wholeness, and identity—of a furtive plenitude and intimacy—suddenly announcing itself in the chaotic, fluxing, disjointed world of mortal existence: "This presence of everything to everything," as he writes. It is thus the most intense, the most absolute, and therefore the most evanescent, of all possible experiences of otherness in Bonnefoy's world.[8]

In the middle of certain places or landscapes, Bonnefoy thinks of "l'insitué qui les nie" ("the unsituated that negates them"; *AP*, 46) and recognizes the different reality that the otherness of space establishes. Similarly, in the very midst of writing, he becomes aware of an alterity that his discourse is omitting, repressing, leaving to the side; this is an "insitué" in the space of his language. It is the unwritten, invisible "arrière-texte," which, if called into existence, would challenge, if not negate, by the power of its otherness the text that the poet has already written. This is, then, the second kind of alterity which Bonnefoy's work expresses: the *alterity of language and representation*. Writing is also a crossroads, where different roads converge for a moment before advancing in various directions. Many are the paths that writers see to the side or in the distance, but that they cannot possibly follow as they write, having already chosen the one that will take them along a different way. The ideas, images, thoughts, reflections, and associations, constituting a kind of intellectual or mental *arrière-pays*, fly so quickly in and out of the imagination of poets intensely concentrating on writing that they can find no means to translate or to capture them in language. How infinite are the memories and feelings locked in the unconscious, which remain covered by an enigmatic alterity that is beyond representation except for the surrogate and displaced forms— the "écriture première," as Bonnefoy calls it—that incompletely and inadequately articulate it! Traces of otherness are evident everywhere in a written text: in the blanks between lines, in the gaps between words, and in the empty white margins, whose muteness speaks volumes. Every sentence, Bonnefoy observes, is a labyrinth of infinite

8. For a study of the evolution of *la presence* in Bonnefoy's *oeuvre*, in particular the subtle ways in which Bonnefoy's understanding of it has changed, see John T. Naughton, "The Notion of *Presence* in the Poetics of Yves Bonnefoy," *Studies in Twentieth-Century Literature (Contemporary French Poetry)* 13 (Winter 1989): 43–60. Regarding the allegory of presence and the presence of allegory in Bonnefoy's work, see my "The Allegory of Loss and Exile in the Poetry of Yves Bonnefoy," *World Literature Today* 53 (Summer 1979): 421–29.

otherness, with hidden tunnels and secret corridors, which await discovery: "Many of these words," he writes, "within the figure of the whole, are so many rustlings where other figures are already foreshadowed" (*RT,* 73). What is absent, invisible, embryonic, repressed, displaced, and unseizable in a poetic work produces an alterity that makes exploration and interpretation of the textual labyrinth necessary; otherness could thus be said to be the raison d'être and the point of departure for hermeneutics.

The reality of textual otherness is most evident and insistent when the poet begins to rewrite his texts or when he decides that, given the inadequacy of what he has created, he has to destroy his manuscripts. In Bonnefoy's work, an aesthetics of revision founded on destruction functions to bring otherness to its fullest potential, to reveal its creatively revisionary power. In tearing up a story or a poem, Bonnefoy makes it possible for another to come into being. *Du mouvement et de l'immobilité de Douve*—Bonnefoy's first poetic work (1953)—owes its existence to the poet's destruction of the story "Rapport d'un agent secret," from the textual ruins of which only one word and one image, that of "Douve"—the linguistic seed from which the new poetic text would ultimately grow—survived. Upon the ruins of "Rapport d'un agent secret," and upon those also of *L'Ordalie* (written and destroyed in 1950), the image of Douve constructs what Bonnefoy calls an "entirely other space" (*L'Ordalie,* 40; *Récits en rêve,* 251); it brings to life a new and completely other work of art. By crossing out words that seem inexact, by rewriting the first sentence of a work only to realize immediately afterward that the second, the third, the fourth, and so on will have to be changed as well, Bonnefoy illustrates strikingly the operation of alterity; in particular, how it literally comes to express, to embody, to write itself. Through the destruction of earlier texts—and the list is long of the works that Bonnefoy has not let enjoy the light of day ("Le Voyageur," "Un Sentiment inconnu," "L'Ordalie," "Rapport d'un agent secret," the original version of *L'Arrière pays*)—or through erasures that permit otherness to speak, or through a conscious attempt to revise manuscripts, or through the use of one text to put a second in question (for example, "Les Découvertes de Prague" and "Nouvelle suite de découvertes" in *Rue Traversière*), Bonnefoy searches for what he calls "cet *autre* de ma parole" ("this *other* of my word"; *E,* 26). He uses a poetics of decentering, of drift, of "la dérive," to make the omnipresence of alterity visible in his writing and also to avoid the coherence, closure, and finality all poetic forms create. Each text swerves away from the one that preceded it, moving in a centrifugal and errant pattern. At any moment, the text can unwrite itself, for the most completed, finished work, according to Bonnefoy, is at once a "new text and a new disavowal of the new text" (*E*, 148). In the midst of one form of "écriture," another surges into being to interrupt and undo it. Writing, thus, is a matter of shifts and swerves: "a sudden and soon rapid drifting through a writing already underway" (*E*, 15). It is as if writing were to hollow itself out, to reveal a secret calligraphy hidden within its interior, an *écriture autre*, which, because of its very alterity— an otherness embodying the openness and impermanence of mortal existence—negates the closure that all representations, poetic and artistic, pretend to achieve.[9]

For Bonnefoy, the act of writing is an act of destruction, involving the marking, tearing, piercing, cutting, and (his word) "decrystallizing" of the poetic text underway. It involves the undoing of what has already been inscribed on paper, initiating "in the very heart of writing . . . a questioning of writing" (*La Présence et l'image*, 40/*The Act and the Place of Poetry*, 167). Within the work of art lies an endless anteriority, a *mise-en-abyme* of alterity. Otherness is the unconscious of all representations, because, as Bonnefoy writes, "toute représentation n'est qu'un voile, qui cache un autre réel" ("every representation is only a veil which hides another reality").[10] As the painter struggles to put on the canvas what he perceives in the world—like Alberto Giacometti, in agony, chastising himself for not being able to capture, to copy in all its elusive

9. For Bonnefoy, it is essential that works of literature open themselves to the loss, death, and deterioration that constitute the otherness of the world. The act of reading, Bonnefoy writes, "is compassion, shared existence" (*E*, 97). He argues that what has been lost in some forms of contemporary criticism, especially those dogmatic critical systems that look to the sciences for their model, is "the relationship of a human being, be he author or reader, to the lived moment, to his existence and destiny" (*La Poésie et l'univer-sité* [lecture delivered 15 November 1983], Discours universitaires, n.s., 36 [Fribourg: Editions Universitaires Fribourg, 1984], p. 19). Reading and criticism have no meaning if they do not connect with life and temporal being, with events of passage and death which readers experience in their daily lives. Thus, the critic, even as he or she tunnels through the dense substance of the literary text, cannot forget the world and its otherness, out of which the work has emerged and to which it never ceases to refer. The light of otherness cannot be blocked by "the shutters of a text." Priority must continually be given to the "open word of daily existence over and above the closed letter of the text" ("Quelque chose comme une lettre," in *Pour un temps/Jean Starobinski*, Collection Cahiers pour un temps [Paris: Centre Georges Pompidou, 1985], p. 278; reprinted in *VP*, 321–28). On the subject of reading, see also Bonnefoy's "Lever les yeux de son livre," *Nouvelle Revue de Psychanalyse* 37 (Spring 1988): 9–19, and my essay "The World beyond the Word: Yves Bonnefoy's Poetics of Reading," *Poetry World* 3 (Fall 1990): 44–51.

10. *Leçon inaugurale* [delivered 4 December 1981], no. 88 (Paris: Collège de France, 1982), p. 21. In the definitive version, published as *La Présence et l'image*, the sentence is in a slightly different form: "Toute représentation n'est qu'un voile, qui cache le vrai réel" ("Every representation is only a veil which hides the true reality"; *PI*, 41/*A*, 167).

truth, the face he sees before him—so Bonnefoy is sensitive to the impossible problem of trying to represent in art and in language what in the world is absent, fleeting, lost, and other.

How does the painter or the poet copy a blankness, a hollow, an absence? How does he or she show an otherness hidden beneath the surface of the real? Discovering a badly eroded inscription in stone, the writer in Bonnefoy's story "L'Indéchiffrable" decides to copy the worn, almost indecipherable letters—"these enigmatic figures, this presence perhaps absence" (*RR*, 183)—onto the white sheet of his notebook, hoping, literally, to carry the words away with him, "like a memory" (p. 182). But time and the elements have made the inscription, in particular certain eroded letters, unreadable, and thus totally "other." The copyist's problem—and it is that of all those who wish to *re*-present (whether poet, painter, historian, archaeologist)—is how to find words to express that which is no longer visible in the inscription; that which the years have removed; that which, because of being so different from what the inscription formerly was, thwarts the recuperating power of representation. How to bring lack, absence, and death *into* a representation in such a way that a mimesis acknowledging and embracing nothingness is accomplished? How to copy a lacuna? How to give form to death, the decomposition of all form? How, finally, can the writer in "L'Indéchiffrable" introduce into the moment of *his* own writing the presence of that once living, but now dead being, who had composed these effaced words, whose shaking hand—"la main qui fut la parole" ("the hand that once was word"; *RR*, 183)—had ages ago painstakingly engraved these letters? The writer fails to represent what he sees because the signs of an effaced writing convey no meaning beyond their own, indecipherable otherness, for, as Bonnefoy writes in *Dans le leurre du seuil* of the "pierres écrites," the "written stones," he discovers in a landscape:

> Ici, c'est un tracé, de l'écriture,
> Ici vibra le cri sur le gond du sens,
> Ici . . . Mais non, cela ne parle pas, l'entaille
> Devie. . . .

> [There is a line here, some kind of script,
> Here a cry trembled on the hinge of meaning,
> Here . . . But no, it says nothing, the mark
> Swerves off. . . .]

> (*P,* 307/*PO,* 151)

Such silence and nonmeaning do not characterize the third of the categories of alterity that Bonnefoy presents in his work: namely, the *alterity of person*. Each of his five poetic works—*Du mouvement et de l'immobilité de Douve* (1953), *Hier régnant désert* (1958), *Pierre écrite* (1965), *Dans le leurre du seuil* (1975), and *Ce qui fut sans lumière* (1987)—is oriented toward, addressed to, and moves in the direction of an elusive, errant *you* (a *toi*), whose qualities, although always concrete and sentient, are universal. For this reason, the poetry of Bonnefoy, as the critic Jean Starobinski has remarked, is "one of the least narcissistic that is."[11] The existence of the self depends on the distant, unseizable other, this "toi," as Bonnefoy writes in *Pierre écrite*, "Qui a bu ma vie" ("That has drunk my life"; *P*, 214/*PO*, 45), which the poet's self looks at, pursues in a landscape, tenderly leans over, and touches. A word uttered by the self has no meaning, no substance, unless it can pass through the other, its raison d'être. In this way, an intimacy is announced, like that between the narrator and Douve, the allegorical female presence who is land, river, place, word, and person in Bonnefoy's first poem, *Du mouvement et de l'immobilité de Douve:*

Et si grand soit le froid qui monte de ton être,
Si brûlant soit le gel de notre intimité,
Douve, je parle en toi; et je t'enserre
Dans l'acte de connaître et de nommer.

[And however great the coldness rising from you,
However searing the ice of our embrace,
Douve, I do speak in you; and I clasp you
In the act of knowing and of naming.]

(*P*, 55/*D*, 67)

It is in the *you* that the self finds sustenance, comes to life, for, as the narrator tells Douve,

Je saurai vivre en toi, j'arracherai
En toi toute lumière,

Toute incarnation, tout récif, toute loi.

[I will know how to live in you, I will
Tear every light from you,

11. "Yves Bonnefoy: La Poésie, entre deux mondes," *Critique* 35 (June–July 1979): 509.

Every incarnation, every reef, every law.]

$$(P, 59/D, 77)$$

A *poetics of allocution*, therefore, dominates Bonnefoy's poetry. The knowledge of otherness compels the poet, the *moi*, to move in a centrifugal motion away from the self and out into the world. Alterity draws him away, for, as the philosopher Emmanuel Levinas has observed, "the relationship with the Other calls me into question, empties me of myself, and continues to empty me."[12] The poet moves away from himself in order to engage in the world, place of the other and of otherness. The *you* reveals itself in a landscape, which, because it is traversed and marked by the presence of the other, is transformed into a subjectified and human dwelling. The *toi* roaming through the world opens the landscape to its otherness, initiates an "Ouverture tentée dans l'épaisseur du monde" ("Attempted rift in the thickness of the world"; *P*, 41/*D*, 39). Thus, the universe becomes a space that the summoning, searching poetic self names "tu." The *toi* is perceived and experienced as a place, a world, a landscape, as, for example, in these lines from Bonnefoy's poems, in which the *you* is valley, water, earth, dawn, and branch: "Je me penchais sur toi, vallée de tant de pierres" ("I bent above you, valley full of stones"; *P*, 177/*PO*, 15); or "Donne-moi ta main sans retour, eau incertaine" ("Give me your unreturning hand, fitful water"; *P*, 264/*PO*, 99); or "Parfois je te savais la terre" ("I knew you sometimes as the earth"; *P*, 203/*PO*, 37); or "Je me penche sur toi, aube, je prends / Dans mes mains ton visage" ("I bend over you, dawn, I take / Your face in my hands"; *P*, 274/*PO*, 109–11); or, finally, "Branche, je pense à toi maintenant qu'il neige" ("Branch, I think of you, now that it is snowing"; *CQFSL*, 43). This universal place named "tu," which the poet has brought to the threshold of speech and from which a response is awaited, signals the beginning of a reciprocal exchange between a human being and what Bonnefoy calls the "Open" of the world. In designating as "tu" the earth, cloud, tree, water, river, star, stone, light, fire, dawn, and the salamander among many realities, Bonnefoy presents the things of the world as the incarnation of the other, as its "espace charnel" ("fleshy space"; *P*, 32/*D*, 21). "Tu" is the pronoun of the Open, the sign of the finite world, of the "Ici sans fin" ("Here without end"; *CQFSL*, 23), by means of which a darkening sky, a flowing stream, a clap of thunder, an almond tree in blossom, a setting sun speak and are personified. For there where the world is named "tu," the place of human presence and habitation is found.

12. "La Trace de l'autre," *Tijdschrift voor Filosofie* 25 (September 1963): 612.

In sum, then, the *arrière-pays* that lies hidden behind the landscape, the writing that shifts toward forgotten, hidden subjects, and the presence of a human being, a *toi*, belonging to the world, are the three states of being *"other"* which Bonnefoy's poetry and criticism express: the alterity of place, of representation, and of person. In the pages that follow, I shall study in depth the problem of alterity in Bonnefoy's work by concentrating on two of its aspects: first, the way poetry can be perceived as a speech or a speaking directed always toward an *other;* and second, the way human beings create relations of otherness in which the *I* and the *you* establish reciprocal, compassionate ties of love or friendship. I shall discuss these poetic and ontological phenomena in order to describe the sudden revelation and surging forth of otherness in our lives and to understand how poetry, the language of lyric allocution, initiates an ephemeral, tenuous dialogue, a "desperate conversation," according to the poet Paul Celan, through which the word of the other is born.[13] This is a dialogue between self and other, poem and world, word and being, which, like the ferryman probing the river bottom with his pole in Bonnefoy's *Dans le leurre du seuil*, seeks the reality of otherness and the presence of the other:

Perche
De chimères, de paix,
Qui trouve
Et touche doucement, dans le flux qui va,

A une épaule.

[Pole
Of chimeras, of peace,
That finds
In the quick of the flow and gently touches

A shoulder.]

(*P*, 288/*PO*, 127)

The ferryman's searching, probing pole, like the poet's hesitant, searching language (and pen), discovers in the flux of what is other—and in the precariousness and human finiteness that the other's shoulder represents—the reality of a relation, of a sharing, and, above all, of a love.

13. "The Meridian," in *Collected Prose*, trans. Rosmarie Waldrop (Manchester: Carcanet, 1986), p. 50.

The Poetics of Otherness

"Life," the Russian critic Mikhail Bakhtin wrote, "by its very nature is dialogic. To live means to participate in dialogue: to ask questions, to heed, to respond, to agree, and so forth."[14] Being in the world is an experience of communication, the feeling of a need for another with whom to talk, to exchange words, and thus to define one's identity: "I am conscious of myself and become myself only while revealing myself for another, through another, and with the help of another. . . . I cannot manage without another, I cannot become myself without another; I must find myself in another by finding another in myself."[15] The other represents the exterior world, *le dehors*, with which it is consubstantial and which the self wishes to embrace. It is the other that shows me, as if in a mirror, what it is in myself that I lack, that I *am* not. The other is an incarnation of my fundamental difference, become visible and tangible, the revelation of the essential lack that defines me. The other represents the limits of my own subjectivity, the frontier separating the "me" from the "not-me." The encounter, the "face-à-face" with the other, therefore, offers a lesson in the lack, absence, and difference that characterize mortal existence.

For Bonnefoy, poetry creates a relation with the other: "To write poetically, in my opinion, is to speak, more or less, the language of the other" (*E*, 36). The poem moves out toward the other because there one finds the changing center of the experience of being: "To say 'I' remains for [poets] the substance of reality and a precise task, the task of reorienting words, once beyond the confines of dream, towards our relationship to others, which is the origin of being" (*PI*, 49/*A*, 169). The fundamental subject of a poem is perhaps this effort to move into the world, to be always tentatively en route toward the other. Poetry is the centrifugal movement away from the narcissistic ego and from the imaginary—the blinding, world-denying dream ("le rêve")—which, Bonnefoy explains, "protects us from the other, that is to say, from time truly lived, from finitude" (*Le Nuage rouge*, 64–65). To lose oneself in dream or in the self deforms poetry, for the poet is inhabited by "a word that, establishing *the other*, moves from the *I* towards the *you*" (*NR*, 307). The presence of an other whose being is nourished by love, for example, of a child, whose birth and existence are celebrated in *Dans le leurre du seuil* and *Ce qui fut sans lumière*—"l'enfant / Qui porte le monde" ("The child who bears the world"; *P*, 258/*PO*, 93), "l'enfant,

14. Ed. and trans. Caryl Emerson, *Problems of Dostoevsky's Poetics*, Theory and History of Literature, no. 8 (Minneapolis: University of Minnesota Press, 1984), p. 293.
15. Ibid., p. 287.

qui est le signe" ("the child, who is the sign"; *P,* 306/*PO,* 149), "[l'enfant qui] était le chant même" ("the child who was song itself"; *CQFSL,* 92)—announces the paradigmatic experience of a radical decentering, of a shift from the preoccupation with self to the love and care of an other; as Bonnefoy explains in a commentary on his story "Les Découvertes de Prague,"

> c'est bien vite un décentrement, où le doute et ses mirages s'effacent, si une autre vie paraît au sein de la nôtre, présence encore fragile qu'il va falloir aider à sa maturation inconnue. Qui peut penser longtemps qu'il n'est pas, s'il lui est donné de faire être? . . . On est le fils de son enfant, c'est tout le mystère.

> [a decentering very quickly occurs, where doubt and its mirages are dissipated, if another life appears at the center of our own, a still fragile presence that we must help in its unpredictable growth. Who can imagine for long that he does not exist, if he has had the chance to create being? . . . One is the son of one's child, therein lies all the mystery.] (*RT,* 90)

The fundamental reality of a poem is that it is a speaking [*un dire*] directed toward another, which is, as Emile Benveniste has shown, the essential reality of all speech acts and the primary means through which subjectivity is created: "c'est dans et par le langage que l'homme se constitue comme *sujet.* . . . Est 'ego' qui *dit* 'ego'" ("It is in and through language that man constitutes himself as *subject.* . . . 'Ego' is he who *says* 'ego'").[16] What counts above all, however, is the direction of

---

16. *Problèmes de linguistique générale,* 2 vols., Bibliothèque des sciences humaines (Paris: Gallimard, 1966, 1974), 1:259–60 [*Problems in General Linguistics,* trans. Mary Elizabeth Meek, Miami Linguistics Series, no. 8 (Coral Gables: University of Miami Press, 1971), pp. 224–25]. Benveniste observes that dialogical discourse with the other establishes the identity of the self:

> Je n'emploie *je* qu'en m'adressant à quelqu'un, qui sera dans mon allocution un *tu.* C'est cette condition de dialogue qui est constitutive de la *personne,* car elle implique en réciprocité que je deviens *tu* dans l'allocution de celui qui à son tour se désigne par *je.* . . . C'est dans une réalité dialectique englobant les deux termes et les définissant par relation mutuelle qu'on découvre le fondement linguistique de la subjectivité.

> [I use—*I* only when I am speaking to someone who will be a *you* in my address. It is this condition of dialogue that is constitutive of *person,* for it implies that reciprocally I become *you* in the address of the one who in his turn designates himself as *I.* . . . It is in a dialectic reality that will incorporate the two terms and define them by mutual relationship that the linguistic basis of subjectivity is discovered.] (P. 260/224–25)

the communication. The poem is turned to, pointed in the direction of, oriented toward, addressed to someone or something other (a *you*) destined to receive the message—be it a person, an object of desire, or an aspect, conscious or unconscious, of the speaker's self; the poem is, as René Char observed, "toujours marié à quelqu'un" ("always married to someone").[17] The poem's point of origin and its most fundamental meaning—what defines it above all other attributes—is this directed speech, this thrusting language that moves out toward the other and that expresses the speaking subject's desire to reach the path leading to the other's difference: "The fact of speaking to the other—the poem— precedes all thematisation," Emmanuel Levinas writes.[18] The poem calls the other into the domain of speech; it initiates a dialogue, inviting the other to take up the word and to respond. Speaking is felt as a necessity, a condition of life, as Celan asserts: "I had to talk, maybe, to myself or to you, had to talk with my mouth and tongue."[19] Thus, the poem opens itself to the world, venturing into a space of being which is beyond itself, in the hope of coming face to face with the reality of otherness. The poem, Celan writes,

> intends another, needs this other, needs an opposite. It goes toward it, bespeaks it.
>
> For the poem, everything and everybody is a figure of this other toward which it is heading.[20]

Poems are movements, approaches, steps, made in the direction of what is open; they are, Celan suggests, "*en route:* they are headed toward. Toward what? Toward something open, inhabitable, an ap- proachable you, perhaps, an approachable reality." A poem, because it is language and thus dialogue, "may be a letter in a bottle thrown out to sea with the—surely not always strong—hope that it may somehow wash up somewhere, perhaps on a shoreline of the heart."[21]

Poetry is a calling out to what is other in order to lure it into the visibility and presence of a relation. When one has the power of speech, of *la parole*, one is, Bonnefoy writes, "able to venture out to the

---

17. "Partage formel," in *Fureur et mystère*, Collection Poésie (Paris: Gallimard, 1962), p. 69.
18. "Paul Celan: De l'être à l'autre," in *Noms propres*, Collection Le Livre de poche (Montpellier: Fata Morgana, 1976), p. 53.
19. "Conversation in the Mountains," in *Collected Prose*, p. 20.
20. "The Meridian," p. 49.
21. "Speech on the Occasion of Receiving the Literature Prize of the Free Hanseatic City of Bremen," in *Collected Prose*, p. 35.

other and carry him or her towards a destiny" (*NR*, 175).[22] Bonnefoy achieves this in a poem as fascinated by, and centered on, the other as *Dans le leurre du seuil.* By its innumerable questions, communications, invocations, and imperatives—for example, the litany or refrain, "Je crie, Regarde" ("I cry, Look"; *P,* 271–88/*PO,* 107–27)—the poem forces the other into a possible response, calling it by a word of command ("Regarde," "Dors," "Vois," "Ecoute," "Passe," "Heurte," "Accueille," "Bois," "Penche-toi" ["Look," "Sleep," "See," "Listen," "Pass," "Knock," "Welcome," "Drink," "Bend down"]) to respond, to participate in an experience the self wishes to share. The poetic word seems to have the power to "develop," in a photographic sense, the hidden reality of otherness, to bring it to the surface of the real. As Bonnefoy at a crossroads causes what is clearly other (for example, the road he decides not to follow) to take on reality and to adopt the visibility and tangibility of what is possible—a scene that opens *L'Arrière-pays*—so he ensures that the other in the world will take on form and flesh. No longer a conceptual abstraction, otherness becomes the very force of incarnation.

In addition, otherness can be internalized in the poetic text and given a presence marked by typographical signs. In *Dans le leurre du seuil,* for example, ellipsis (arranged in single, sometimes double lines of nineteen periods) literally designates gaps and interruptions in the

22. Indeed, alterity is at the very heart of poetic desire and of poetry for Bonnefoy; it is the truth of poetry's being and the precondition for the advent of presence:

> Voici l'essentiel, qu'il importe de souligner. Sous le signe de l'unité . . . le rapport à autrui renaît, que la pensée conceptuelle brouille, et permet trop aisément de détruire. Et c'est dans cette dimension de l'altérité, aussi bien, que la pensée proprement poétique se développe. Sachant qu'il n'est d'expérience de la présence que si autrui aussi est rencontre pleine, il lui faut par nécessité rechercher les désirs, les biens, les impressions, les valeurs que les habitants de la terre peuvent chacun accepter sans avoir pour autant à se démettre. Pour dire la présence, la poésie doit élaborer un lieu qui vaudra pour tous. Voilà la sorte d'universel que sa vérité recherche.

> [Here is the essential that is important to emphasize. Under the sign of unity . . . the relation to the other is reborn, a relation that conceptual thought confuses and allows all too easily to be destroyed. And it is within this dimension of alterity, as well, that truly poetic thought develops. Knowing that there is no experience of presence unless the other, also, participates in the fullness of an encounter, poetic thought must necessarily find the desires, possessions, impressions, and values that the inhabitants of the earth can each accept without being obliged, however, to give up their own sense of themselves. In order to invoke presence, poetry must elaborate a place that has value for everyone. This is the kind of universality that its truth seeks.] ("Y a-t-il une vérité poétique?" in *Vérité poétique et vérité scientifique* [Paris: Presses Universitaires de France, 1988], p. 53)

poetic discourse, where other words, other ideas, other images from the poet's memory or unconscious could have been written but were not. In this "interstitial space" (*E*, 66), many things remain virtual and unexplored. The "dots of ellipsis" are signs, Bonnefoy explains, "of explorations that I did not make, but whose obscure presence I wished to suggest" (*E*, 66). The ellipsis signifies the presence of an absence, the memory-trace of an unrepresentable image, idea, or event and thus brings into the poetic work the reality of lack and nonbeing. The text reveals its own deficiency, its own failure to capture something in the world for representation. Thus, it self-consciously "represents" through these typographical markings the failure of its own artistic form and the insufficiency of mimesis. The poet has not succeeded in grabbing hold of what is hidden, silent, and scattered in the world in order to bring it into the poem, to render it in words. The closed forms of art, thus, are broken and opened up by this failure of representation, which the appearance of alterity has provoked.[23]

The goal of art and poetry, according to Bonnefoy, is the openness of a self to an other, of an *I* to a *you*, who, although remaining individual and different, exchange and share their feelings, ideas, and concerns through the one possession they have in common: the word, which in us, Bonnefoy writes, is "older than any language, a force that is our origin" (*E*, 34). This copresence of beings—whether in the world, where men and women love, or in art, where the voice of a poet or painter hidden for centuries inside the work can suddenly speak to us and provoke a dialogue—grows out of an intimacy, a *rapprochement*. Art and existence, writes Bonnefoy, must be established upon

la coprésence d'êtres d'autant plus avertis de leur finitude qu'ils ont tenté . . . de la vaincre. Ils sont toujours vivants, ils sont là. Et ce qu'attend de nous leur effort mais ce qu'aussi il prépare, c'est cette

23. For a study of Bonnefoy's attempt to subvert representation through a poetics of alterity which is motivated by a fascination with color and light, phenomena existing beyond representation, see my essay "The Crack in the Mirror: The Subversion of Image and Representation in the Poetry of Yves Bonnefoy," *French Forum* 13 (January 1988): 69–81. Bonnefoy's desire for an art and language freed from mimesis is lyrically expressed in a series of short poetic *récits*: see, for example, "Deux et d'autres couleurs," "Le Vautour," "La Mort du peintre d'icônes," "L'Artiste du dernier jour" (*RR*, 143–48, 168–69, 170–73, and 174–78, respectively); *Les Raisins de Zeuxis et autres fables/The Grapes of Zeuxis and Other Fables*, trans. Richard Stamelman (New York: Monument Press, 1987); *Encore Les Raisins de Zeuxis/Once More the Grapes of Zeuxis*, trans. Richard Stamelman (New York: Monument Press, 1990); and the longer *récit Une autre époque de l'écriture* (Paris: Mercure de France, 1988).

intimité du moi et de l'autre qui recrée l'horizon de la présence du
tout, arbres, pierres, montagnes—cette immanence où veut et peut
se dissoudre l'oeuvre qui fut personnelle.

[the copresence of beings all the more aware of their finitude for
having tried . . . to overcome it. They are still alive, they are there.
And what their effort expects from us, and what it also prepares for,
is this intimacy of self and other that re-creates the horizon of the
presence of all things—trees, stones, mountains—that immanence
in which the subjective work seeks and finds fusion.] (*E*, 58)

In art and poetry, it is vital that the presence of what is other
preserve its fundamental independence, that it not be eclipsed by the
poetic self expressing it, that it not be swept away by the self-interested
discourse of the *I* that articulates it. It is this egocentric self, this
" 'second' or dreamt self, this self of the book"[24] and of writing which,
according to Bonnefoy, tends to move away from the "incarnated being
that carries it," as "la fleur semble opposer sa beauté, qui est une forme,
à la précarité de la plante obscure" ("the flower appears to oppose its
beauty, its form, to the precarious life of the dark plant").[25] Bonnefoy is
suspicious of the pretensions of personality, of the private, closed world
that he calls the "moi construit" (*E*, 58). Thus, he refuses to "say 'me' at
the very moment when the 'I' is asserting itself" (*PI*, 50/*A*, 170). There
is always the unfortunate possibility that the other will be absorbed into
the authoritarian, imperial *I*, presented only through its "eyes" and in
terms of its desires alone. The result is, Bonnefoy explains, the death of
the other. For the poet, who has succeeded in assimilating the voice of
the other into his, will have deformed the truth of this other, will have
taken away its difference, will have, Bonnefoy writes, "made *use* of what
this existence appears to be." And, he continues,

J'en aurai fait un mot de ma langue, un symbole dans mon théâtre, je
ne l'aurai pas du tout préservée en ce qui assure son être et constitue
sa présence, et qui est sa liberté de demeurer autre que ce que veut
mon désir. Autre est *aboli*, eût dit Mallarmé, au moment même où
une oeuvre semble le révéler, et l'aimer.

24. "Un Champ de solitude," in *Gaëtan Picon*, exhibition catalogue (Paris: Centre
Georges Pompidou, 1979), p. 30; reprinted as "Gaëtan Picon allait parler, ce soir-là," in
VP, 279–90.
25. "Boris de Schloezer," in *Pour un temps/Boris de Schloezer* (Paris: Centre Georges
Pompidou/Pandora Editions, 1981), p. 53.

[I will have made of it a word in my vocabulary, a symbol in my theatre, I will certainly not have preserved it in a way that affirms its being and constitutes its presence, and that is its freedom to remain other than what I desire for it. *Destroyed* is the other, Mallarmé might have said, at the very moment a work seems to reveal it, and to love it.] (*E*, 35)

The key to the writing of otherness is to maintain the breath of the voice which the other speaks, to preserve the orality of the word—above all, its open, changing, bodily quality—within the written discourse itself. The spoken word must avoid becoming appropriated by the *I*, distorted by the "optique déformante" (*O*, 43, *RR*, 252), which seals written discourse within closed, unliving forms. A writing able to preserve the vivid presence of the word, *la parole*, without forcing it to become part of the "system" of written language, thus weakening it, would remain open to otherness and would succeed, although imperfectly, in representing it. There where the other resides can be uncovered both the world and *la parole* that breathes, for, as Bonnefoy writes:

On ne peut rejoindre la finitude, c'est-à-dire se pénétrer de la relativité de notre être propre, de l'illusoire de notre "moi," qu'en s'ouvrant au fait difficile de la différence d'autrui, point de vue qui dénie le nôtre: ce qui signifie d'ailleurs lui parler—j'insiste sur ce mot—dans notre écriture même, lui parler ne serait-ce qu'en silence, devant nous-mêmes, dans cet instant où notre écriture est au carrefour. Le vrai commencement de la poésie, c'est quand ce n'est plus une langue qui décide de l'écriture, une langue arrêtée, dogmatisée, et qui laisse agir ses structures propres; mais quand s'affirme au travers de celles-ci, relativisées, littéralement démystifiées, une force en nous plus ancienne que toute langue, une force notre origine, que j'aime appeler la parole.

[We can encounter finitude—assimilate the relativity of our own being, the illusiveness of our own "self"—only by opening ourselves to the difficult fact of the other's difference, a point-of-view that negates our own: which means, moreover, to speak—I emphasize this word—to him or her in our very writing, to speak to the other, even if it be silently, in our own presence, in this instant when our writing is at a crossroads. The true beginning of poetry comes when it is no longer a language that determines writing, an arrested, dogmatic language that allows its own structures to act, but when, through these structures, relativized and literally demystified, a force older than any language affirms itself in us, a force, which is our origin, that I like to call the word.] (*E*, 33–34)

The communion between beings that Bonnefoy desires can be initiated by certain words, which, because endowed with considerable ontological power, are more than mere signifiers, mere verbal representations; they possess the creative force of being. They are like points of condensation within the poem itself, in which drops of the real, the mortal, and *le dehors* form. These words are accustomed to dwelling in the Open of the world; they are already filled with otherness, which they bring into the closed world of the text. As the expression of being and of the presence of things within the temporal instant, they speak and signify *autrement* ("otherwise"). Such a language, vibrating with the rhythms of the here and now and sensitive to "nos grands besoins d'existants" ("our great needs as living beings"), inspires communion and communality, creating fundamental relations between human beings and their world:

> Que je dise: *le pain, le vin,* ces deux mots seulement, et l'on aura tout de suite à l'esprit, je pense, un certain type de relations essentielles entre les êtres, on va penser à leur solidarité, sous le signe des grands besoins de la vie et de ses grandes contraintes, ce sont là des mots pour la communion, des mots qui font souvenir que la langue n'est pas vouée seulement à décrire des apparences, mais à nous tourner vers autrui pour fonder avec lui un lieu et décider de son sens.

> [If I were to say, "bread," "wine," only these two words, there will suddenly come to mind, I think, the image of a certain kind of fundamental relationship between beings; we will think of their solidarity, as dominated by the great needs of life and its great constraints; here are words for communion, words that remind us that language is dedicated not only to describing appearances but to turning us toward the other, in order, with his or her help, to establish a place and determine its meaning.] (*E*, 21)

It is language that edges human beings into the world and there joins them one to the other. Consequently, existence is shown to be less an affair of self than of other, than of community, founded in and by *la parole*. The alterity of being touches all aspects of a human life lived, as Shakespeare wrote, in "this wide gap of time" (*The Winter's Tale*, 5.3.154), this temporal gulf in which human beings, sharing the mortality of existence, seek to come together and to live in an exchange that only friendship and love can establish.

The Love of the Other

In the *récit* "Les Découvertes de Prague," a historian, who earlier in the day destroyed a recently uncovered cache of valuable paintings, which, until he had been lowered into the hidden, secret room housing the works, no one had seen for centuries, hesitantly and reluctantly speaks to his wife about the reasons for his violent act, reasons about which even he is uncertain. There was, he explains, something mysteriously terrifying about the hidden paintings, a terror residing not in their style, subject matter, theological meaning (many depicted the Annunciation), or artistic form, but in their otherness. "The past," he observes, "is *other*" (*RT*, 71). A frightening halo surrounds the enigma of otherness when perceived in its pure, concentrated form. These hidden paintings, because they express a difference so striking and total, negate anything outside of themselves. This negation is the mute and inaccessible otherness associated with death or nothingness. No word can be addressed to such an alterity because, like death—that ultimate experience that makes of a person, according to Blanchot, "l'Autre à jamais" ("the forever Other")[26]—there is no speech or gesture that can soften or humanize its reality. Yet, what is most interesting and paradoxical about the conversation between the historian and his wife is that they discuss the terror of otherness, in particular its strangeness and alienating power, at the very moment that they participate in an intimate dialogue, an exchange of words which depends on otherness and which emphasizes its necessity. Bonnefoy shows us a painful, tender dialogue between a man and woman who, because of the void that has been revealed to them, try desperately (and imploringly, in the case of the woman) to reach out to each other, to exchange meaningful words, to dissolve differences and misunderstandings, and to nourish the intimacy of love. Even though the link between them remains fragile and precarious, their dialogue—and, above all, the desperate questions, intense interpellations, and uncertain answers they exchange—continues to unite them.

26. *L'Entretien infini* (Paris: Gallimard, 1969), p. 103.

It is *la parole*, the keystone to every dialogic encounter, that holds this man and this woman together, as they lie in bed talking near an open window, through which they see a dark night lit only by the stars and feel the coldness of a wind coming from the indifferent world. It seems that only the woman's intensely posed questions keep the man from sinking into total silence and despair; she keeps the dialogue going out of fear that "contact might be lost" (*RT*, 69) and that their exchange of words, their love, will die. At the end of this sad and moving encounter, through which the man has come to accept the omnipresence of *le néant* and tries to persuade the woman, who now weeps, of the need to face this ineluctable reality, a weak and mysterious light begins to glimmer:

> Et par la fenêtre qui est ouverte,... toutes ces étoiles déjà, ces vapeurs de la voie lactée qui les enveloppent,—et quelque chose comme une forme dans cette brume, qui respire. L'aube va bien paraître pourtant, comme la dispersion des images.

> [And through the open window,... already all these stars, the mists of the Milky Way enveloping them—and something like a form in the haze, that breathes. Dawn is truly, however, going to appear, like the dispersion of images.] (*RT*, 73)

This form, barely breathing in the predawn mist, announces the birth of a child, sign of hope in the world:

> C'est une naissance, à venir, une naissance au degré du ciel étoilé, de la terre, une naissance qui soit divine,—sauf que toute naissance est divine, toute vie qui prend forme une terre et un ciel qui recommencent.

> [It is a birth, to come, a birth at the level of the starry sky, of the earth, a birth that may be divine—except that every birth is divine, every life that takes shape an earth and sky beginning anew.] (*RT*, 89)

Into the precarious relationship between the man and woman surges the other who is truly redemptive, the child, this "other life appearing at the heart of our own" (*RT*, 90). The child is the principle and the force of Incarnation, who, in his relation with the world, has no need of mediation or representation, because his knowledge of the world is direct and intimate; he is the light of the world (*CQFSL*, 92). The child contests the exile of our lives, turns us away from egocentric desires, decenters our existence, and reinvigorates our engagement with the world. It is this other, so close to us and so dependent on us, that paradoxically gives birth to us: "One is the son of one's child, therein lies all the mystery" (*RT*, 90), Bonnefoy remarks. This mystery comes from the fact that the child embodies an alterity that is unique and different. As Levinas has asserted, paternity or maternity involves "la relation avec un étranger qui, tout en étant autrui, est moi; la relation du moi avec un moi-même, qui est cependant étranger à moi" ("the relationship with a stranger who, while being other, is me; the relationship of the I with a myself that is, however, a stranger to me").[27] Because of the child—this being that is simultaneously self and other, me and not-me, this "still fragile presence that we must help in its unpredictable growth" (*RT*, 90)—the *je* and the *tu* are drawn together into the *nous*. They become the couple, leading a life together and drawing from their relation to the child, the other, a communion, a love, and a hope:

L'enfant redescendit plus tard, de branche en branche
Dans ce qui nous parut un ciel étoilé.
Rien ne distinguait plus dans ce silence
La cime bleue des arbres et des mondes.

Il chantait, il riait, il était nu,
Son corps était d'avant que l'homme, la femme
Ne se fassent distincts pour retrouver
Criant, dans une joie, une espérance.

Il était le chant même.[28]

27. *Le Temps et l'autre* (1948), Collection Quadrige (Paris: Presses Universitaires de France, 1983), p. 85.
28. The child, like the poetic sign, is a force of "rassemblement" ("gathering") for Bonnefoy. Child and word bring beings and things together; they both provoke an exchange. In many ways, poet and child are similar. Bonnefoy explains that just as a child of fifteen months will pick up a twig (or stone or any other small object) and offer it in silence to another child—not by this gift to placate a possible adversary, but rather "to proclaim, by an intuitive understanding of the sign, that between them a strange mediation will occur, one of potential solidarity, one that constitutes our humanity"—so the poet offers a small token, an unassuming gift, a "rien," to the reader. So much the better, Bonnefoy writes, if the twig turns green and blossoms with "some meaning that can be shared." The poet tenders his or her gift to the reader primarily to express confidence in the world and a sense of hope. Reading, Bonnefoy asserts, is an activity undertaken not to "move again along the winding paths of language, of thought—but to regain faith in the world" (*La Poésie et l'université*, p. 28; see also "Y a-t-il une vérité poétique?" pp. 45–46).

[The child climbed down again later, from branch to branch
In what seemed to us a starry sky.
Nothing separated in the silence
The blue summit of trees and worlds.

He sang, he laughed, he was naked,
His body was from a time before man and woman
Became distinct to recapture
Hope, with cries of joy.

He was song itself.]

(*CQFSL*, 92)

For Bonnefoy, the child represents an otherness that is both liberating and life-enhancing: "the only important reality is the child who,
born hands without strength, is still entrusted with the future of humanity" (*E*, 165). But for the self and other to reach that precarious
conjunction from which the child is born a difficult movement away
from self and egoism is necessary. Bonnefoy's poem *Dans le leurre du
seuil* explores the centrifugal movements the *I* and the *you* take in their
efforts to free themselves from the closed world of egocentrism and to
struggle against the forces of separation and distance, which work to
oppose their union and their coexistence as a couple. The poem goes
from *desire,* the quest for the other undertaken by the poetic self, to
love, the ephemeral realization of a momentary union and coalescence.
But because all events and phenomena in *Dans le leurre du seuil* are
affected, as they are in the world, by a dialectics of gathering and
dispersion, by a struggle between growth and depletion—as things
advance toward fulfillment, plenitude, and the experience of oneness,
they never fully escape their original condition of emptiness, separation, and difference—so love always reverts to desire. It never escapes
the gravitational force of finitude, continuously pulling it back to the
world of mortal time, in which distance, division, and incompleteness
prevail, as Bonnefoy makes clear in a question from *Ce qui fut sans
lumière:*

    L'homme, la femme
Quand savent-ils, à temps,
Que leur ardeur se noue ou se dénoue?
Quelle sagesse en eux peut pressentir
Dans une hésitation de la lumière
Que le cri de bonheur se fait cri d'angoisse?

[Man, woman,
When do they know, in time,
That their passion waxes or wanes?
What wisdom in them can foresee
In the light's vacillation
That the cry of happiness becomes a cry of pain?]

(Pp. 33–34)

The *je* and the *tu* live a fluid, threatened existence; they are like the passing clouds Bonnefoy often refers to in *Dans le leurre du seuil*, sometimes joined together in a large mass, sometimes solitary and pushed errantly in different directions by a destructive, hollow wind.

Yet, such precariousness and ephemerality do not nullify love. Although, as Bonnefoy writes in *Dans le leurre du seuil*, "le vide, clair, / Soit notre couche" ("the bright void / Is our bed"; *P*, 282/*PO*, 121), the self and the other persist in their desire: "se trouvant, / Nos mains consentent / D'autres éternités / Au désir encor" ("having found / Each other, our hands consent / To yield to desire's / Eternities again"; *P*, 282/*PO*, 119). They know that their love, because it is of the world, will always be darkened by death and finitude:

Retrouvons-nous, prenons
A poignées notre pure présence nue
Sur le lit du matin et le lit du soir,
Partout où le temps creuse son ornière,
Partout où l'eau précieuse s'évapore.

[Let us meet again, let us take
Our pure naked presence in our hands
On the bed of morning and the bed of evening,
Wherever time digs its rut,
Wherever the precious water evaporates.]

(*P*, 279/*PO*, 117)

Between the *I* and the *you*, desire weaves a union, which, although brief, is creative and dazzling; it is like an ephemeral flash of lightning disappearing into the nothingness of the surrounding air, but not before shaking the landscape for a few seconds with the rumblings of its passage; or, as Bonnefoy expresses it:

Et soyons l'un pour l'autre comme la flamme
Quand elle se détache du flambeau,

La phrase de fumée un instant lisible
Avant de s'effacer dans l'air souverain.

. . . . .

Et tout attachement
Une fumée,
Mais vibrant clair, comme un
Airain qui sonne.

[And we shall be for each other like the flame
When it leaves the torch,
A phrase of smoke briefly legible
Before it vanishes in the sovereign air.

. . . . .

And all attachment
Smoke,
But vibrating brightly
Like a sounding brass.]

                              (*P*, 278–79/*PO*, 115–17)

In love, as in the world, possession is not possible; one cannot seize what is, after all, nothing. From love and from being, one can gain only what Bonnefoy calls "Or de ne pas durer, de ne pas avoir," "or sans matière" ("Gold of impermanence, of non-possession," "immaterial gold"; *P*, 280/*PO*, 117), a treasure that paradoxically has no substance, no body, and is ephemeral. It is a sensuous nothingness, for to live in mortal time is to become dispossessed of everything, to "move away from having toward being" (*I*, 323). Nevertheless, from the expanding vibrations of light within the nothingness of finite existence, from "la douleur / Qui se fait lumière" ("a suffering / That turns to light"; *P*, 283/*PO*, 121), comes the child, sign of hope and the future. The couple's cry of despair is transformed: "au-dessus de la vallée de toi, de moi / Demeure le cri de joie dans sa forme pure" ("above the valley of you, of me / The cry of joy remains in its pure form"; *P*, 286/*PO*, 123). The child possesses the key to a new threshold, to a rediscovered paradise of plenitude and presence: "Il offre / Dans la touffe des mots, qui a fleuri, / Une seconde fois du fruit de l'arbre" ("He offers / In the tuft of words, which has flowered, / The fruit of the tree for a second time"; *P, 284/PO,* 123). Where the *I* and the *you* live in separation far from each other, it is there, in the open and in harmony with the reality of things, that the child finds his place of habitation:

L'enfant a pris la main du temps vieilli,
La main de l'eau, la main des fruits dans le feuillage,
Il les guide muets dans le mystère.

[The child has taken aged time by the hand,
And the water, and the fruit among the leaves,
He leads them silently into the mystery.]

(*P,* 305/*PO,* 149)

The child connects the *I* and the *you* to the world and affirms the possibility of a *nous,* a couple, as well as the hope of a plenitude. Out of nothingness, something uncertain and precarious—"une forme dans la brume" ("a form in the haze")—has surged into existence to illuminate the night of the world and to bring a smile of peace and joy to the lips of those who watch the child playing, like that subtle smile that crosses the radiant, maternal face of pharaoh's daughter in Poussin's painting *Moïse sauvé des eaux* (*The Finding of Moses*), which plays so important a role in *Dans le leurre du seuil.* Through the child, *la présence* speaks; it becomes flesh in the triumph of Incarnation.

In *Dans le leurre du seuil,* Bonnefoy represents, thus, the tentative and always reversible movement that advances from desire to love and back to desire again:

Désir se fit Amour par ses voies nocturnes
Dans le chagrin des siècles; et par beauté
Comprise, par limite acceptée, par mémoire
Amour, le temps, porte l'enfant, qui est le signe.

[Desire became Love on its nocturnal ways
Through the grief of the ages; and through beauty
Understood, through limits accepted, through memory
Love, time, has brought the child, who is the sign.]

(*P,* 306/*PO,* 149)

Bonnefoy makes a distinction between the self-centeredness of desire and the altruism (the other-directedness) of love. In desire, the self contemplates the object of its longing in a possessive and egocentric manner. It imagines a oneness with the object not possible in reality, but for that reason all the more realizable in fantasy and by imagination. The other is for the self only an instrument, a means for realizing its own desires. Because the reality of the other is distant and thus unseizable, the self invents images, fantasies, and representations, which, dedicated to a long-lasting fictive intimacy, serve to mediate the self's relationship to the desired object. But love lacks such egocentricity; it is truly selfless: "aimer, c'est-à-dire sortir de soi" ("to love is to leave the self behind"; *E*, 59). It encourages the other to remain free of the self, to declare its unique difference and independence, and to live in a state of distant otherness, which the self cannot appropriate and which no image or representation can seize completely. Love is a human relation requiring no mediation. Sufficient unto itself, it lacks nothing. It does not need representation to exist. Love is never subordinate to the image, to the figure of speech, or to knowledge, as Bonnefoy remarks:

> N'est-ce pas, cette libération de l'objet par un acte de connaissance, la définition de l'amour par opposition à l'idolâtrie, ou pour mieux dire peut-être celle de l'*agapé* . . . par opposition à l'*éros:* La poésie qui vainc l'image dans l'écriture est amour, et en cela même.

> [The freeing of the object by an act of knowledge, is this not the definition of love in contrast to idolatry, or put a better way perhaps, that of *agape* . . . in contrast to *eros*. Poetry, which masters the image in writing, is love, and for that very reason.] (*E*, 149)

The path, which narcissistic desire, as well as poetry and painting, follows, is characterized by the adoration of an invented, fetishized image of the other, which exists only through the illusory magic of art. Idolatry transforms the living, changing other into a work of art, an icon, an unbreathing form, like the statue of the dead Hermione in the recognition scene of Shakespeare's *The Winter's Tale*, which Bonnefoy reinterprets and recasts in *Dans le leurre du seuil*. Of an unchanging beauty, which appears perfect, the statue of Hermione comes to life only because Leontes's love—newly rekindled from the ashes of a long-smoldering grief—fractures the sculpted image of stone, thus bringing her back to a world of time and death. Love, or *agape*, looks upon the other not as an image, an icon, or an idol, but as a person, a living, changing being in the world whose incompleteness and imperfectness are accepted and not idealized: "A face, not an essence" (*E*, 141). While desire (eros) seeks to satisfy the interests of the self by fantasizing an intimacy with the other, which does not in truth exist, love (agape) accepts the other as it is in the world, in its own unique otherness and particular difference; that is to say, as "the *other,* there in its relation to itself, its freedom."[29]

At the end of *Dans le leurre du seuil,* a couple is formed, as are all things in the world, by the dialectical relationship of "l'épars" ("the scattered") and "l'indivisible" ("the indivisible"), the title words of the last section of the poem. Of all the events, realities, and phenomena that the poet affirms in the many litanies of *Dans le leurre du seuil*—such as those refrains beginning "Je consens" ("I consent") or those repeated words of absolute affirmation (the series of "Oui") by which many verses begin—it is the simple act of saying yes ("this profoundly shareable word"; *E,* 23) to the other, of saying "Oui, par la main que je prends / Sur cette terre" ("Yes, by the hand I take / On this earth"; *P,* 325/*PO,* 173), which stands out for Bonnefoy as essential. As Hermione and Leontes, whose union and separation are recounted in *Dans le leurre du seuil* through the language, imagery, and the stanzaic configuration of massing and dispersing clouds (*P,* 291–94/*PO,* 130–34), reveal, and as the historian and his wife also show as they talk intimately among signs of menacing finitude in "Les Découvertes de Prague," the couple exists in a precarious state of being. It is only hesitantly and gropingly that one person approaches another. To take the hand of the other, to tell him or her yes, is to move away from the self and to direct one's steps toward an other that one wishes to embrace by means of an ephemeral word, which joyously affirms only its own tentative act of groping, of reaching out. Thus comes to be established a relation of sharing, from which will emerge the precarious, never final form of the word and of the child:

Et en nous et de nous, qui demeurons
Si obscurs l'un à l'autre, ce qui est
La faute mais fatale, la parole
Etant inachevée comme l'être encor,

Que sa joie prenne forme: pour retenir
L'eau dans sa coupe fugitive; pour refléter
Le feu, qui est le rien; pour faire don
D'au moins l'idée du sens—à la lumière.

29. Bonnefoy, "Gilbert Lely," in *Gilbert Lely* (Losne: Thierry Bouchard, 1979), p. 6.

[And in us and of us, who remain
So dark to each other, which is the one sin
But inescapable, our human speech
As yet unfinished, like being itself,

May its joy take form: to hold
The water in its fleeting cup; to reflect
The fire, which is nothingness; to offer
At least the idea of meaning—to the light.]

(*P*, 306/*PO*, 149)

Word, couple, being, they are all witnesses to the advent of a form—not one that captures and holds onto meaning, for, as the passage indicates, water, even though contained in a cup, is always evaporating; fire, even though reflected, still remains nothing; meaning, although evoked, is but an abstract idea. Yet, word, couple, and being in their incompleteness ("Etant inachevée") participate in an incarnation: "Que sa joie prenne forme: pour retenir/ . . . pour refléter/ . . . pour faire don." Through love, the imperfect world is accepted as it is in its fundamental difference and obscurity. To love the other in the world is to "accept what is given" (*E*, 90), to "étreindre la réalité rugueuse" ("to embrace rough reality"), as Rimbaud wrote. It is to descend into the matter of mortal existence, for there dwells

l'*autre* exigé dans sa différence profonde, sa liberté, afin que notre forme puisse accéder à son sens. La conscience de l'autre est la voie de l'incarnation, le déchiffrement du réel.

[the other called on in its profound difference, its freedom, so that our form can arrive at its meaning. The consciousness of the other is the way of incarnation, the deciphering of the real.] (*E*, 90)

"Dire 'Je' . . . de façon autre"—Bonnefoy

"Le prédateur" (the bird of prey), at the pinnacle of its upward flight, writes Bonnefoy in *Dans le leurre du seuil* in a subtle allusion to the rhapsodic poet lost, like Baudelaire's Fancioulle, in the ethereal heavens of art and of the self, suddenly cries out and

Se recourbe sur soi et se déchire.
De son sein divisé par le bec obscur

Jaillit le vide.
Au faîte de la parole encore le bruit,
Dans l'oeuvre
La houle d'un bruit second.

[Bends back and tears itself.
From the breast cleft by the dark beak
The void spills out.
At the peak of speech there is still noise,
In the work
The swell of a second noise.]

(*P*, 250/*PO*, 83–85)

Emerging from the self-inflicted wound in the bird's body—and by analogy from the hole in the word, from the imperfections of the self, from the blemish in the formal coherence of a work—otherness in the form of void, noise, and nonbeing surges into existence. The chaos of the inarticulate, the formless, and the unrepresentable (what the poem calls "le vide," "le bruit") inhabits the center or pinnacle of a work of art (the "faîte de la parole"), like the hidden death's head that leaps into a spectator's view from the foreground of Holbein's anamorphic painting *The Ambassadors*, obliterating the images of wealth, wisdom, and achievement represented there.[30] At the crest of a sublime experience of plenitude, the poet or the painter, who "se recourbe sur soi et se déchire" ("bends back and tears [him]self"), opens his work and remembers the reality of alterity: "La tache noire dans l'image" ("The black stain in the image"; *P*, 295/*PO*, 135), le "cauchemar dans le plus beau rêve" (the "nightmare in the most beautiful dream"; *E*, 33), the tear in the weave of a fabric, la "ronce dans les bouquets" (the "thorn among the flowers"; *RT*, 52), and "le cri / Qui perce la musique" ("The cry that pierces the music"; *P*, 295/*PO*, 135). The lightning flash of otherness, zigzagging through the space of writing, produces a text as broken, cut, pounded, deflected, rough, transitory, errant, and refracted as the world of finitude that at every second traverses it. The cry of otherness thus gives birth to "cette poétique de l'écart, de la goutte

30. For a discussion of the representation of death, finitude, and loss in the art of Holbein, Mondrian, Giacometti, and Garache, as well as its relationship to Bonnefoy's search for signs of imperfection and otherness in works of art—his poetics of rift and wound—see my essays "Transfigurings of Red: Color, Representation, and Being in Yves Bonnefoy and Claude Garache," in *The Comparatist: Journal of the Southern Comparative Literature Association* 10 (May 1986): 89–107, and "The Incarnation of Red," in *Claude Garache: Prints 1965–1985*, exhibition catalogue (Middletown, Conn.: Ezra and Cecile Zilkha Gallery, Wesleyan University, 1985).

noire à jamais dans l'encrier de cristal" ("this poetics of divergence, of the black drop forever in the crystal inkwell"; *NR*, 208). It enables "L'amande de l'absence" ("The almond of absence"), in all its density and compactness, to open within the word (*CQFSL*, 42).

Bonnefoy's poetry is haunted, therefore, by the enigmatic presence of the other, who breathes, loves, speaks, and responds in "this wide gap of time." It opens itself to the otherness of mortal existence or celebrates "au delà de toute forme pure / . . . un autre chant et le seul absolu" ("way beyond any pure form / . . . another song, the only Absolute"; *P*, 137/*Selected Poems*, 65); it designates the other places, other lands, other countries, other thresholds where presence, the most perfectly realized form of alterity, may appear; it hurls against the shore of its own verse the crashing waves of an eroding, distinguishing otherness; it reveals the hollow spaces within artistic representations where the alterity of death and nothingness lies trapped; it reverses the magnetic field of egocentrism so that the totalizing, egoistic self, lost in dream and fantasy, will connect with the real world of finitude; it shows the otherness that zigzags through existence, causing it to become refracted, decentered, and dialectical; and finally, it signifies *autrement* ("otherwise") in a way so completely different and unexpected that meaning becomes problematic and elusive. Therefore, to write poetically "is to speak, at the very least, the language of the other" (*E*, 36). It is to listen attentively with all one's being to the word of the other and to the otherness of the word.

Poetic language, because it is turned toward what is other and therefore world, follows the path of incarnation; it is "the residue of a word inscribing man in being" (*E*, 91). In Bonnefoy's poetry and criticism, *l'être, c'est l'autre;* inscribing someone in being is to inscribe him or her in otherness. In those elsewhere places, far and near, where the other resides—in a hidden landscape, or in the eroded letters of a stone inscription, or in a vibrant red cloud scudding across a blue summer sky, or in a puddle of oil, or in the red dress at the center of a Poussin painting, or in an isolated, solitary tree, or in the cry of an owl, or in the chirp of a cricket, or, finally, in a form breathing softly in the morning mist—there appear the possibility and promise of human warmth, sympathy, and friendship: what Bonnefoy calls "a true fire, a true face" (*I*, 127–28/*A*, 115). The poetry of the future, he assures us, will open itself to the possible apparition of this true face, for such a poetry will deliver writing from the egocentricity of self. It will pierce the closure of signs and forms, and it will allow the temporal world to speak directly and freely from within the poem of its unapproachable and unrepresentable alterity. As Bonnefoy writes, ce qui doit caractériser la poésie à venir, ce n'est pas le renoncement à dire "Je," c'est qu'elle cherche à le faire de façon autre, par effraction de ce "moi" qui ne dispose d'un monde que parce que celui-ci, qui est l'image, n'est rien. . . . Dire "Je," que ce ne soit plus se prêter à la démesure du "moi" mais simplement l'acte de la connaissance en son lieu le plus naturel, celui où illusion et lucidité ont l'une et l'autre leur origine. Que ce soit le tâtonnement qui va vers le "nous," sous l'étoile, même si le chemin qui ne pourrait manquer de conduire loin, dans la nuit encore première, au plein sens du mot naturelle, est incessamment obstrué par des éboulements, des piétinements, des clameurs que la poésie ne maîtrise pas.

[what must characterize the poetry to come is not the refusal to say "I," but that it try to say it in another way, by the breaking open of the "self" which makes use of a world only because, as an image, such a world is nothing. . . . To say "I" should no longer be a conforming to the excesses of the self, but should be simply the act of knowledge in its most natural place, where illusion and lucidity, each, have their origin. It should be a groping that moves toward the "we," underneath the stars, even if the road, which is bound to lead us faraway in the night that is still fresh and, in the fullest sense of the word, natural, is constantly obstructed by falling rocks, trampled earth, uproars, which poetry cannot control.] (*E*, 158)

"Dire 'Je' . . . de façon autre" ("To say 'I' . . . in another way"), so that it may become "un tâtonnement vers le 'nous,' " a difficult and uncertain groping toward communality, a step toward the reciprocity of the couple, and a movement toward the selflessness of a love extending into the precarious, fearful night of existence, where we—"real beings . . . who make signs, who cry, who move forward gropingly, who hope!"[31]—must make our way, is, then, the lesson that a consciousness of alterity and an openness to the other teach. A poetry such as Bonnefoy's, able to interiorize this consciousness and to express this openness, advances from absence and abstraction—"for all meaning, all writing, are absence"—to presence and incarnation: "the presence of something or some being, it makes little difference, suddenly looming before us, within us, in the here and now of an instant of our existence" (*E*, 141). Bonnefoy's work teaches us to probe the world for signs of this alterity that reveals presence and to seek traces of its passage. It encourages us to listen for "le cri qui perce la musique," the piercing cry that

31. "Un Champ de solitude," p. 33.

rips through the paralyzing perfections of art, the imaginary fantasies of dream, the immobilizing stasis of image, the blinding delusions of self to surge into the Open, into the world. But, above all, as Bonnefoy's ardent and hopeful words affirm:

> En art comme dans la vie apprenons la parole de l'autre, et la terre adviendra, figure intense parce que lieu partagé. Tel me paraît le dessein de la poésie.

> [In art as in life, let us learn the word of the other, and the earth will come forth, as much a figure of intensity as a place of shared being. Such is, it seems to me, the goal of poetry.] (*E*, 59)

CHAPTER 6

Traces, Fragments, and Empty Spaces: The Poetry of the Ephemeral

Nos traces prennent langue.

[Our traces become language.]

—René Char, *La Nuit talismanique*

"On Sand Dunes of Wandering Words": The Syntax of the Ephemeral

Poets are perhaps not the ones to ask about the nature of syntax. Paul Valéry informs us in two of his essays that syntax is a kind of algebra, an operation of mathematical logic, and yet in another essay he refers to it as a "faculty of the soul."[1] Stéphane Mallarmé associates syntax with intelligibility, as if it were a warranty protecting the reader against the breaking down of the poetic line.[2] But then Wallace Stevens asserts that "the poem must resist the intelligence / Almost successfully;"[3] and Roland Barthes writes that "words are never crazed (at most perverse), but . . . syntax is."[4] If, on the subject of syntax, the thoughts of poets and critics are evidently as diverse as this, then perhaps we should turn to another possible source of elucidation: to the painter and sculptor Alberto Giacometti.

1. "La syntaxe était à ce poète [Mallarmé] une algèbre qu'il cultivait pour elle-même." "La Syntaxe, qui est calcul, reprenait rang de Muse," and "La syntaxe est une faculté de l'âme" (*Oeuvres*, Bibliothèque de la Pléiade, 2 vols. [Paris: Gallimard, 1957, 1960], 1:685, 646; 2:481, respectively).
2. "Quel pivot, j'entends, dans ces contrastes, à l'intelligibilité? il faut une garantie—La Syntaxe" (*Oeuvres complètes*, Bibliothèque de la Pléiade [Paris: Gallimard, 1945], p. 385).
3. "Man Carrying Thing," in *The Collected Poems* (New York: Alfred A. Knopf, 1964), p. 350.
4. *Fragments d'un discours amoureux*, (Paris: Seuil, 1977) [*A Lover's Discourse: Fragments*, trans. Richard Howard (New York: Hill and Wang, 1978), p. 10/6].

159

The painting of a face was for Giacometti an agonizing task, an existential situation in which he squarely came up against the sheer impossibility of artistic representation. A Giacometti portrait carries traces of a tortured, agonized battle between the painter and his medium. The face is a network of overlapping, intertwining, crisscrossing, swirling, conflicting, incomplete, and battling lines, none of which completely fixes the head in its space. The lines do not add up to a finished portrait, but rather to a highly mobile form in a state of becoming. The signs of a labored creation are inscribed on the canvas, reinforcing the ephemeral, incomplete, and uncertain character of the portrait. The head imposes its presence, but by its precariousness only. It exists a hair's-breadth away from chaos. Menaced by an ever-present nothingness, the face could return suddenly to the void with which it is practically cognate. It stands at a threshold between being and nonbeing. By multiplying lines, observes Jacques Dupin, Giacometti refuses meaning and certainty to any one line. "We find here contestation as the principle of creation. To draw a second line is to call into question the first without effacing it; it is to have second thoughts and to bring a correction to bear; it is to open between the two lines a contradictory debate, a dispute, which a third line will come to arbitrate and to continue in a new direction."[5] From the perpetual making and unmaking of the head comes a portrait at once present and absent. Giacometti's adding of line after line, according to an aesthetics of correction by contestation, does not affirm the system of relations under construction; rather, it helps to undermine those relations, if not eventually to destroy them. "'You have to do something by undoing it,'" Giacometti remarks. "'You have to dare to give the final brush stroke that makes everything disappear.'"[6] For Giacometti, the creation of a work of art can proceed in no other way but a dialectical one. By the process of construction and disintegration, Giacometti keeps his work open to the world and to the impossible reality he agonizingly struggles to represent.

In painting or sculpting a face, Giacometti uses gestures that ask the question so poignantly posed by Leontes in *The Winter's Tale:* "What fine chisel / Could ever yet cut breath?" (5.3). To find the chisel or the pen with the power to embody mortal breath, to accord desire with representation, and to create a work at once of art and life, this is the dream of Giacometti and the impossible goal recognized as such by

5. "Textes pour une approche," in *Alberto Giacometti* (Paris: Maeght, 1962), p. 32.
6. James Lord, *A Giacometti Portrait* (New York: Farrar, Straus and Giroux, 1965, 1980), p. 79.

Yves Bonnefoy in his poetry. Bonnefoy, who seeks to write a poetry open to the world and in harmony with its contradictory rhythms of being—life and death, plenitude and emptiness, possession and loss, absence and presence—yearns for a poetry that will unite "la longue phrase et . . . un peu de l'être qu'elle n'est pas" ("the long sentence and a little of the being it is not").[7] As Giacometti proceeds artistically by assembling and then effacing forms, Bonnefoy and the poets Jacques Dupin and André du Bouchet—all of whom collaborated on the journal *L'Ephémère* from 1967 to 1972—write poetry that acts in a similarly dialectical and contestative manner; it is a poetry capable of being written and unwritten. It gives voice and form to the struggle between written language (the formal, ordered arrangement of words and lines) and being (the finite life, which is ultimately resistant to efforts of representation). The structural principles of and the motivating forces for this creatively dialectical act of contestation are *syntax*—the ordered and disordered arrangement of words in constantly shifting relations and patterns—and the *mise-en-page*—the arrangement of words and lines in varying configurations of compression and dispersion. In the works of these three poets, syntax and the *mise-en-page* constitute a new kind of writing, what Dupin calls an "écriture ajourée de vide" ("writing pierced by emptiness").[8] A line added to another line or an adjective affixed to a noun whose meaning it negates (particularly in the poetry of Dupin and du Bouchet) throws earlier words and their syntactic relations into confusion. Syntax connects and disconnects; it both establishes and undermines relations between signs. The poetic line in Dupin's telling expression becomes a "ligne de rupture" (*Dehors*, 7). By

---

7. *Le Nuage rouge* (Paris: Mercure de France, 1977), p. 304; cited as *NR*. Other works by Bonnefoy and their translations will be referred to according to the following abbreviations: *CQFSL: Ce qui fut sans lumière* (Paris: Mercure de France, 1987); *I: L'Improbable*, followed by *Un rêve fait à Mantoue*, new ed., corrected and augmented (Paris: Mercure de France, 1980); *P: Poèmes* (Paris: Mercure de France, 1978); *PO: Poems, 1959–1975*, trans. Richard Pevear (New York: Random House, 1985); and *TD: Things Dying, Things Newborn: Selected Poems*, trans. Anthony Rudolf (London: Menard Press, 1985). See above, chapter 5, n.2.

8. "La Difficulté du soleil," in Georges Raillard, *Jacques Dupin*, Collection Poètes d'aujourd'hui, no. 219 (Paris: Seghers, 1974), p. 135; hereafter cited as *JD*. For Dupin, artistic creation invariably involves a confrontation with the void; the object that Giacometti draws, for example, cannot be "separated from the void that bathes and protects it" ("La Réalité impossible," in Jacques Dupin and Michel Leiris, *Alberto Giacometti* [Paris: Maeght, 1978], p. 42; reprinted in Dupin's *L'Espace autrement dit* [Paris: Galilée, 1982], pp. 53–62; cited as *EAD*). Other works by Dupin are cited in the text according to the following abbreviations: *AS: Une apparence de soupirail* (Paris: Gallimard, 1982); *C: Contumace* (Paris: P.O.L., 1986); *CT: Chansons troglodytes* (Montpellier: Fata Morgana, 1989); *D: Dehors* (Paris: Gallimard, 1975); and *E: L'Embrasure*, preceded by *Gravir*, Collection Poésie (Paris: Gallimard, 1971).

means of a syntax of contestation and rupture, these poets practice a dialectical aesthetics, which in a fundamental way reflects the metaphysics of contradiction and negativity they share. There is a will-to-negation in the poetry of Bonnefoy, Dupin, and du Bouchet; it is apparent in the way that the syntactic organization of their poems destroys continuity, encourages the mobility of errant words, organizes verse fragments into tenuous and provisional configurations, creates a fugal interplay between words and their surrounding white space, suppresses predication, subverts meaning, disrupts conventional syntactic order, refuses closure, affirms becoming, and, finally, encourages a necessary hermeticism by which the difficulty of being and the uncertainty of existence are reenacted in the unreadability of the poetic text.

Thus, the contestative syntax and the elliptical, discontinuous *mise-en-page* permit these poets to avoid the formal, finished beauty of traditional poetry. They create imperfect poems, in keeping with Bonnefoy's belief that only "L'imperfection est la cime" ("Imperfection is the summit"; *Poèmes*, 117/*Things Dying, Things Newborn*, 50). In these fractured poems, syntax does even more than serve a semantic function. For in the affirmation and nullification of syntactic relations, in the contestation of one word by another, and in the obliteration of linguistic signs by the white space of the page, the poems of Dupin and du Bouchet in particular represent graphically and illustrate typographically the struggle between dialectical forces of being. Syntactically, these poems present a mimesis of contradiction and of *la rupture*. Syntax thus becomes an instrument of dialectical contradiction: orderly arrangements of words following rules of syntactical combination are contested by passages in which traditional grammatical and syntactical operations have been suspended.

This chapter describes the tactics of a dialectical syntactics in the poetry of Bonnefoy, Dupin, and du Bouchet. It analyzes the manner by which phenomena such as the void, nothingness, and absence penetrate the poetic text and there assume a figurative and mimetic form, disturbing the order and continuity of the poem. It is necessary to examine the different kinds of syntactical relations which each of the three poets creates, because these everchanging, self-negating relations express the coexistence of dialectical movements or forces: namely, in Bonnefoy's long poem *Dans le leurre du seuil* (1975), the struggle between dispersion and gathering; in Dupin's work *Dehors* (1975), the tense encounter (mediated by a "vide actif") between violent destruction and creation; and finally, in du Bouchet's *Laisses* (1979)—a radical example of dialectical syntax—the confrontation between a dispersed language and its annihilating opposite, silence. In this dialectical way, the poems of Bonnefoy, Dupin, and du Bouchet open poetic language to the world of finitude, join the "longue phrase" to the being it can never fully become, and, in the words of Paul Celan, turn poetic space into "sand dunes / of wandering words."[9]

Yves Bonnefoy: Words and Syntax like the Sky

Standing before an unfinished portrait, Giacometti complains bitterly that the painting is going poorly, that he does not have the talent to capture the face as he sees it, and that he will have to start anew.[10] Similarly, Bonnefoy tells the story of sitting down to recopy a manuscript and of beginning to change so many words that he completely unravels the work; "I am always in the process of destroying," he remarks" (*Le Nuage rouge*, 274). For Bonnefoy, as for Giacometti, creation involves destruction; for the poet, the act of writing is an act of violence. Recopying the manuscript, Bonnefoy breaks the forms of his text. Suddenly made aware of *other* words and *other* images that could, and then eventually do, replace the initial writing, he comes under the spell of an "otherness" at once destructive and creative. The fact that a poem can open itself to other possible words, that its structure and network of relations can suddenly rip apart and reveal "something open, perforated, in the substance of language" (*NR*, 274), represents Bonnefoy's desire to undermine the formally structured, world-denying nature of poetic discourse. The loosening of syntactical bonds and the opening of the poem to the world beyond it favor the discovery of an "autre chant" hidden underneath, behind, and within the apparent order of the words. Otherness delivers words from a language that seals them shut. Bonnefoy searches for the syntax capable of liberating

---

9. "Speak, You Also" ["Sprich auch du"], in *Paul Celan: Poems*, trans and ed. Michael Hamburger (New York: Persea Books, 1980), p. 85. Compare Celan's image to Dupin's conception of a poetry perpetually in movement and in transit: "Migrations incessantes des mots jusqu'au dernier à travers l'écriture, tentative pour rendre un seul instant visible à leur crête celui qui disparaît déjà" ("Incessant migrations of words to the very last word through writing, an attempt to make visible, for only an instant of their cresting, the word that already disappears"; *E*, 144). Celan himself could be called a poet of *L'Ephémère*, if for no other reason than for his participation on the editorial board that founded and directed the review. For perceptive studies or lyrical evocations of the poetry and poetics of Celan by his collaborators on *L'Ephémère*, see Bonnefoy's essay "Paul Celan," in *NR*, 303–9; Dupin's poem "Paul Celan," in *JD*, 136–38; and du Bouchet's poetic homage, "Tübingen, le 22 mai 1986," in . . . *désaccordée comme par de la neige et Tübingen, le 22 mai 1986* (Paris: Mercure de France, 1989), pp. 51–93; hereafter cited as *Désaccordée*.

10. *A Giacometti Portrait*, pp. 9, 10, and passim.

words from the crypt in which artistic perfection has placed them, from "le néant de quelque forme" ("the nullity of some form"; *P*, 324/*Poems*, 171): a syntax not only of words but also of being. He dreams of "un écrire qui serait d'abord une voie" ("a writing that would first be a path") and hopes to "retrouver au profond de la parole le vocabulaire et la syntaxe premiers du naître, du vivre et du mourir" ("discover in the depths of the word the primal vocabulary and syntax of birth, life, and death"; *NR*, 280). This syntax of being can enter the poem by means of the incomplete and imperfect relations existing between words. The poetic word, which Bonnefoy often describes as wounded, broken, torn, or filled with holes, generates, in combination with other words, a syntax equally dissevered.

In *Dans le leurre du seuil*, a poem of one hundred pages (*P*, 229–329/*PO*, 61–177), Bonnefoy uses a syntax whose purpose is to achieve and represent "une dialectique de l'exister et du livre" ("a dialectics of existing and of the book"; *NR*, 280). Its free-verse form is matched by irregular stanzas composed of lines of differing lengths. Short stanzas of a haikulike compression alternate in a random manner with more monolithic blocks of verse, some continuing for several pages. Stanzas are separated by blank spaces and in some instances by single, sometimes double, rows of ellipses. The poem has the appearance of a changing cluster of irregularly shaped clouds of different magnitudes and thicknesses. Some are ample and ponderous; others, wispy and dispersed. The poem moves so swiftly, the short and long verses alternate so unexpectedly, and the stanzaic configurations contract and expand so suddenly that one senses the poet's desire to make his poem as finite and transitory as the world, thus demonstrating how "le vent / Dispersait à grandes lueurs la phrase vaine" ("the wind / In great flashes scattered the useless phrase"; *P*, 290/*PO*, 129).

It is the movement of *Dans le leurre du seuil* that is most striking. Bonnefoy is reluctant to suspend the poem's momentum for fear that in the pause a crystallized meaning may form. In an effort to "porter du réel dans ce dire" ("to bring some of the real into this speaking"; *NR*, 304), he employs several syntactical structures that reproduce a mobility and an ephemerality of relationship in accord with the finitude of existence. These structures can be briefly described as follows: first, the continuous change in the length of lines and stanzas; second, the assembling of long enumerations and catalogues; third, the use of periodic sentences that compose several verses, drawing into their orbit different and often contradictory elements; fourth, the deliberate creation of long, ramified, sometimes parenthetical digressions; these have their point of origin and attachment in a simple sentence, whose presence is reiterated over many lines by the mere repetition of a connecting preposition, as in the following example, in which the infinitive clauses, introduced by the preposition "de" ("to"), echo the subject-predicate phrase "je suis tenté" ("I am tempted"), on which they are dependent:

Et je sais même dire; et *je suis tenté*
De vous dire parfois, signes fiévreux,
Criants, les salles peintes,
Les cours intérieures ombragées,
La suffisance de l'été sur les dalles fraîches,
Le murmure de l'eau comme absente, le sein
Qui est semblable à l'eau, une, infinie,
Gonflée d'argile rouge. *De* vous donner
L'anneau des ciels de palmes, mais aussi
Celui, lourd, de cette cheville, qu'une main
De tiédeur et d'indifférence fait glisser
Contre l'arc du pied maigre, cependant
Que la bouche entrouverte ne cherche que
La mémoire d'une autre.

[And I can even speak, and *am sometimes tempted*
To speak to you, feverish signs,
Crying out, of great painted halls,
Shaded inner courtyards, summer's fullness
On the cool flagstones, the murmur
As of absent water, the breast
That is like water, one, infinite,
Swollen with red clay. *To* give you
A ring of palm-tree skies, but also
This heavy ring at the ankle, that a warm
And indifferent hand slips over the arch
Of a lean foot, even though
The half-opened mouth seeks only
The memory of another.]

(*P*, 295–96/*PO*, 137; my emphasis)

Another kind of syntactical structure animating the poem is the use, though infrequent, of agrammatical constructions that momentarily stop the thrust of a line in midsentence: "Oui, par la voix / Violente contre le silence de, / Par le heurt de l'épaule / Violemment contre la distance de" ("Yes, by the violent / Voice against the silence of, / Through the violent lunge / Of the shoulder against the distance of"; *P*, 313/*PO*, 157). Finally, there is the crescendo effect created by anaphora, phrasal recurrence, and syntactical parallelism, especially in those instances when the repeated word, relentlessly driving the passage forward, is a preposition—either like "par" in the reiterated expression "Oui, par . . ." ("Yes, by . . ."; *P*, 311–27/*PO*, 155–75) or like "dans" ("in") in the opening verses of the second part of *Dans le leurre du seuil:*

Heurte,
Heurte à jamais.

Dans le leurre du seuil.

A la porte, scellée,
A la phrase, vide.
Dans le fer, n'éveillant
Que ces mots, le fer.

Dans le langage, noir.

. . . .

Dans le rassemblement, où a manqué
Le célébrable.

Dans le blé déformé
Et le vin qui sèche.

Dans la main qui retient
Une main absente.

Dans l'inutilité
De se souvenir.

Dans l'écriture, en hâte
Engrangée de nuit

Et dans les mots éteints
Avant même l'aube.

[Knock,
Knock forever.

In the lure of the threshold.

At the sealed door,
At the empty phrase.
In iron, awakening
Only the word, iron.

In speech, blackness.

. . . .

In the gathering, that failed
Of celebration.

In the deformed wheat,
The parching vine.

In the hand that holds on
To an absent hand.

In the uselessness
Of recollection.

In writing, hastily
Garnered at night

And in words that die out
Before dawn.]

(*P*, 237–39/*PO*, 69–71)

Dans le leurre du seuil is composed of what Bonnefoy calls an "écriture comme nuée" ("a cloudlike writing"; *NR*, 327). The most striking example of this dispersion and assembling of words, of "Les mots comme le ciel" ("Words like the sky"; *P*, 329/*PO*, 177), is found in the poem's final pages, in a section appropriately entitled "L'Epars, L'Indivisible" ("The Scattered, the Indivisible"), which up until the very end is written as all one sentence. The section begins with the word "Oui" (*P*, 311/*PO*, 155). Then in a crescendo of yeses that builds over the next eighteen pages, it breathlessly affirms a host of diverse realities, until ending in a final image of a swelling, rising, foaming, and crashing wave, in whose crescendo movement to fullness and in whose subsequent descent and depletion are reiterated the dialectical movements of gathering and dispersion and of plenitude and emptiness, which have characterized many of the poem's metaphors and several of the textual interactions existing between the lines and the stanzas. The poem concludes:

S'enfle (oui rassemblé, brûlé,
Dispersé,

Sel
Des orages qui montent, des éclaircies,
Cendre
Des mondes imaginaires dissipés,

Aube, pourtant,
Où des mondes s'attardent près des cimes.
Ils respirent, pressés
L'un contre l'autre, ainsi
Des bêtes silencieuses.
Ils bougent, dans le froid.
La terre est comme un feu de branches mouillées,
Le feu, comme une terre aperçue en rêve),

Et brûle, oui, blanchisse puis déferle
(Vivre, nuées
Poussées mystérieusement, étinceler,
Finir,
Aile de l'impossible reployée)
La vague sans limite sans réserve.

. . . .

Les mots comme le ciel
Aujourd'hui,
Quelque chose qui s'assemble, qui se disperse.

Les mots comme le ciel,
Infini
Mais tout entier soudain dans la flaque brève.

[Swells (yes gathered, burnt,
Scattered,

Salt
Of mounting storms, of clearings,
Ash
Of imaginary worlds dispelled,

Dawn, even so,
Where worlds linger near the summits,
Breathing, huddled
Against each other
Like silent beasts,
Stirring, in the cold.
The earth is like a fire of damp sticks,
The fire, like a land seen in dream),

And burns, yes, whitens and breaks
(Live, clouds
Mysteriously moved, flash
And end, wing
Of the impossible, folded back again)
The unlimited, unstinting wave.

. . . .

Words like the sky
Today,
Something that gathers, and scatters.

Words like the sky,
Infinite
But all here suddenly in the brief pool.]

(*P,* 328–29/*PO,* 175–77)

The development of the wave image is accomplished by means of a
kernel sentence, which is inverted: "S'enfle . . . // . . . // Et brûle, oui,
blanchisse puis déferle/ . . . /La vague sans limite sans réserve" ("Swells
. . . // . . . // And burns, yes, whitens and breaks/ . . . /The unlimited,
unstinting wave"). The elements of this sentence are dispersed over
twenty lines; its syntactical continuity is broken (in a way that recalls

Mallarmé) by two long parenthetical digressions, each of which develops a second image, that of a cloud. But through the nearly simultaneous elaboration of the metaphors, wave and cloud share the same predicates; the verbs used to describe the rising momentum of the former are perfectly expressive of the gathering motion of the latter, as the crashing, depleting movement of the wave rushing toward extinction accords perfectly with the dispersing, dissipating action of the cloud disappearing into thin air. What we have, formally and syntactically speaking, at the end of *Dans le leurre du seuil* is, on the one hand, a strictly syntactical, extremely compact kernel sentence, which has been interrupted and dispersed, and, on the other, two digressive, literally parenthetical passages, whose interruption of the *phrase matrice* is the precondition for the formation and coalescence of a cloud image. Compression leads to dispersion and fragmentation to fusion in a perpetually circular reversal of opposites. The final passage of the poem is engineered so that it not only expresses semantically the formation of wave and cloud and their depletion but also reproduces syntactically (in the interplay of linguistic elements and the construction and deconstruction of relations) a mimesis of the dialectical relationship between dispersion and gathering: what the penultimate stanza identifies as the "Quelque chose qui s'assemble, qui se disperse" ("Something that gathers, and scatters").

The intelligibility that is substituted for the world in every artistic representation, taking its place and blocking it—the same all-too-perfect intelligibility that syntax forms and guarantees—is eroded in *Dans le leurre du seuil* by the poem's openness to the forces of mortal existence. In the poem, words are like the sky and syntax recapitulates "The main drift of the cloud" (*P*, 324/*PO*, 171). Thus the words of the poem, contested and corrected by the otherness of being that comes from beyond it, reveal a syntax that is not only linguistic but also ontological.

Jacques Dupin: Syntax and Fragments

As in Bonnefoy's poetry, Dupin's verse has a form that reproduces the existential contradictions that he experiences in the world. Poetry, he writes, "does not satiate, but on the contrary deepens even more the lack and anguish that occasion it" (*L'Embrasure*, 135). His poetry is one of destructuration; it is a potentially explosive confrontation of words, in which "the slightest word is loaded with violence" (*E*, 147).[11] Rela-

11. For a discussion of the poetics of rupture in Dupin's work, see Mary Ann Caws, "Jacques Dupin: Inscription on the Rise," in her *A Metapoetics of the Passage: Architextures in Surrealism and After* (Hanover: University Press of New England, 1981), pp. 148–77,

tions created between signs do not complement or complete one another; they do the opposite. Dupin's arrangement of sharp, "jagged words" (*E*, 82) favors the contestation and subversion of relations. The linguistic sign can be active only if "it is neither finished nor fixed" (*L'Espace autrement dit*, 151). One of the poems in "Trait pour trait," for example, begins:

> Le corps
>> cache-t-il ce qu'il cache
>
> —ou le feu?

>> Crise de l'espacement
> dispersion, passage   —théorie
> d'un corps   expatrié bouleversé transparent

> afin qu'il, par degrés   regagne
>> la verticale
>>> du point   dehors exclu

> non sans gaucherie

>> [The body
>>> does it hide what it hides
>
> —or the fire?

>> Crisis of spacing
> scattering, passage   —theory
> of a body   expatriated upset transparent

> so that, by degrees   it regains
>> the vertical
>>> of the point   outside excluded

> not without clumsiness]

(D, 90)

---

and her "Jacques Dupin: Access, or Speaking It Through," *Poesis* 5 (1984): 39–47. In addition, for a study of Dupin's poetic encounter with the closure and discontinuity of space and its relation to his fragmented writing, his "écriture seconde," see Dominique Viart, *L'Ecriture seconde: La Pratique poétique de Jacques Dupin* (Paris: Galilée, 1982). Finally, on Dupin's lyric confrontation with landscape space, see Maryann De Julio, "Jacques Dupin and the Rhetoric of Landscape Poetry," *Symposium* 41 (Winter 1987–88): 257–66, and her "Jacques Dupin and a New Kind of Lyricism," *French Forum* 14 (May 1989): 209–17.

Dupin's poems, as this passage shows, are composed of what he calls innumerable "unintelligible fragment[s]" (*E,* 50), gathered together and placed at different distances from one another on the line and page. But the syntactic ordering and the *mise-en-page* are not designed to compensate for the lack of intelligibility; they reinforce it. The question beginning the poem invokes a plurality of meanings and creates a strong aura of poetic ambiguity. It achieves this by expressing an interrogative tautology, which has two possible subjects ("le corps," "le feu"), each capable of an act of hiding, as well as two possible direct objects ("ce qu'il cache," "le feu"), each capable of being hidden. Moreover, even Dupin's use of simple conjunctions (*et, mais, ou*) here and in other poems only serves to organize his verse fragments into a provisional, soon-to-be-destroyed order.

Whereas Bonnefoy's syntax favors arrangements of subordination, Dupin's tends to establish relations of coordination. The reason is obvious. In Dupin's later poems, there are very few principal clauses to which the fragments could be subordinated. Each fragment is of equal importance; none is privileged by a fuller development or by a favored position in the poem. While a poem by Mallarmé (his influence on the spacing of verses in Dupin and du Bouchet is undeniable) may be constructed around a kernel sentence—the constituent elements of which are dispersed and ramified over a series of lines, with the result that the poem's élan is momentarily halted so as to permit the development of further digressions—a poem by Dupin does not possess similar syntactic trunks to which the branching verse fragments can be attached; there is no kernel, or central, sentence. The poem is composed of a series of linked digressions with no return to a point of origin: "Le poème / n'a de cesse / ni le livre n'a de fin" ("The poem / has no rest / nor the book an end"), he writes in "Paul Celan" (*Jacques Dupin,* 138). One series of fragments is followed by another, whose relation to the first, because it is contentious, oppositional, and negative, prevents the poem from following a fixed trajectory. Syntactical relations are created by a form of textual *clinamen*. Words have a dynamism of their own, coursing and swerving through a resistant space, generating new forms of themselves in ever-renewed but hardwon configurations:

> Que les mots fassent souche dans l'air,
> à la surface et dans la profondeur de l'air,
> qu'ils s'écrivent
> > qu'ils relancent, qu'ils réactivent

une énergie disloquante
et, contre la blancheur qui les récuse, les aiguise,
contre la douleur dont ils se gorgent,

qu'ils s'écrivent, là encore, obstinément.

    [Let words sire in the air,
on the surface and in the depths of the air,
let them write themselves
              let them revive, let them reactivate
a dislocating energy
and, against the whiteness that rejects them, accentuates them,
against the suffering they feed on,

let them write themselves, there still, tenaciously.]
                                        (*Contumace*, 103)

    For Dupin, writing is an unending struggle, an act of fracturing and shattering, which never lets up; it is "a necessary succession of ruptures, drifts, conflagrations. . . . To break, to seize again, and thus to reassemble" (*E*, 146). He favors a lacerating syntax, which creates new and alternative relations by turning against and annulling old ones in an act of linguistic suicide:

L'exception   qu'ici
  en ce non-lieu   j'aime
                 —ou le lieu d'une dérive

            d'un désastre méticuleux

selon des nourritures de surface

           favorise l'affilé de tout tranchant
           contre soi

[The exception   that here
in this non-place   I love
               —or the place of a drifting

      of a meticulous disaster

in accordance with surface sustenance

> encourages the sharpening of any blade
> against itself]

(*D*, 81)

This passage raises many questions, each creating the possibility of new and different relations. To what, for example, does the image of "the exception" refer? Does the appearance of the conjunction "or" preceded by a dash announce yet another break or divergence, what might be interpreted as an exception to "the exception"? Does the establishing of a "here" in the opening line conflict with the later image of "a drifting"? What relation exists between the "non-lieu" and "le lieu"? How can the "non-place," which is the absence or negation of place, be established in the physical, present domain of the "ici," while "place" itself is founded on drift, the very absence or negation of an "ici"? And, finally, what subject determines the action of the verb "favorise"? Is it "the exception" that "encourages" the sharpening of the blade, or is it "the place"—of drifting, of disaster—that does so? In many ways, this passage from "Trait pour trait" illustrates iconically how language can turn its own sharpened blade against itself and, through an act of syntactic self-laceration, create new relations; the mystery and obscurity of these relations prevent closure and promote the opening of the poem to an endless succession of broken fragments, momentarily taken in hand and reassembled before being broken apart again, so that the cycle can begin anew. Dupin's poetry in general as well as his syntax in particular are examples of what he calls "a fecond divorce" (*E*, 135). The severing of connections is still productive of relations, but they are no more than incomplete traces, and ephemeral ones at that, because "every word disappears at the moment of its utterance" (*Une apparence de soupirail*, 84).

There is little doubt that Dupin's poetry is, in the words of an early poem, "Le chant qui est à soi-même sa faux" ("The song that is its own scythe"; *E*, 48) and, in the words of a later poem, "a node of negative articulation" (*AS*, 88). Words are turned against other words in the belief that negation and division will lead to affirmation. Dupin seeks to express "le pour du contre" ("the pros of the cons"; *D*, 88). Negation, destruction, fragmentation, division—these are the acts that the poems describe and the realities that they incarnate. The poem is host to the "free circulation of the void among the fragments" (*EAD*, 129). Emptiness is given a textual presence. It exists, not as nothingness ("le néant") but as "the womb of space," for "space only exists through form, and form emanates from the void, which gives it its consistency and power" (*EAD*, 260). The void is like a wind blowing in and out of the interstices between words, moving around "the white spaces of an open and serrated typography," circulating through "the gaps of a fragmented, wavering, disjoined text of which, like a beneficent, silent energy, it is the unifying principle" (*JD*, 134). The "corrosive power of emptiness" and of white space (*JD*, 141) eats away at the syntactic connectives of the poem, making every relation ephemeral or, in Dupin's expression, "fuyante" (*D*, 85). The result is a text that, in its rejection of fixed meanings, in its making and unmaking of relations, in its dynamic contestation, and in its avoidance of closure, approaches a provisional, sporadic unreadability: an "illisibilité clignotante" (*E*, 190). Poetic obscurity reproduces ontological difficulty. Syntax in Dupin's poetry only provisionally orders the bits and pieces—the "metal shavings" (E, 95)—of words, perpetually migrating across the page, for "les gerbes refusent mes liens" ("the sheafs resist my rope"; *E*, 54). Dupin's disordering of syntactical relationships, aiming as it does to negate logic, to reveal the anonymity of poetic creation, and to sever and disarticulate the text, reflects the presence of the "vide actif" (*JD*, 135) in all things and thus the fundamental precariousness of being itself. To write is indeed to die: "écrire c'est trépasser" (*Chansons troglodytes*, 81).

André du Bouchet: Syntax and Silence

If, in Dupin's poetry, writing is "perforated by emptiness," then in du Bouchet's more explosive poetry, especially the poems in *Laisses*, poetic language is burst open by the void. Whereas Dupin's poems allow small openings to appear between words and verses—cracks of invisibility, mere fissures of blank space—du Bouchet's poetry reveals gaping, yawning chasms between highly fragmented word-hordes, spread over and down the page, as in the following passage:

Soif

à la hauteur des lèvres,

ce qui se dit glacier, ou le ciel — et plus haut,

éclaire,

le glacier.[12]

[Thirst

reaching to the lips,

what calls itself glacier, or sky — and higher,

illuminates,

the glacier.]

The intervals occupy as much space as the words. Consequently, one is no longer certain whether the poet wishes to express silence or language. The poem is as vocal as it is mute. And the disjointed, errant, and aleatory typography of du Bouchet's poems accomplishes the disintegration of syntactic linearity. Words, isolated or grouped together, seem to float on an air of whiteness; they are composed of "Lettres aérées. Lettres à flot" ("Airy letters. Floating letters").[13] They inhabit a space whose vacancy is expressive: "là, ce que j'ai voulu dire, / le papier, mieux que moi—et avant moi, l'éclaire" ("there, what I wanted to say, / the paper, better than I, and before me, clarifies it").[14] They are words not only dispersed but also close to disappearance, on the verge of invisibility; they are soon to pass into air. Contiguous with the white space above, below, around, between, and in the margins, the word enters into relation with its beyond, with what exists in the realm of absence and silence. "In the word," du Bouchet writes, "must . . . sometimes be heard the undulating air that carries the word away" (*Désaccordée*, 23). At the threshold separating sign from blankness, the word encounters the "hors-parole," that "other-side" of itself which only its disappearance can restore. Of the three poets, du Bouchet is the one who gives the greatest importance to the poetic function of white space.[15] In the confrontation between word and page, the sign

12. "Laisses," in *Laisses* (Paris: Hachette, 1979), unfolioed.
13. "Dans un livre que je n'ai pas sous la main," in Pierre Chappuis, *André du Bouchet*, Collection Poètes d'aujourd'hui, no. 239 (Paris: Seghers, 1979), p. 102; cited as *AB*.
14. *Une Tache* (Montpellier: Fata Morgana, 1988), unfolioed; hereafter cited as *T*.
15. This space is a place of habitation, "un point d'habitation" (*T*). It leaves a *white* mark: "opened momentarily, space itself / will make a mark" (*T*). And the white "mark" of the page makes reading possible; it illuminates the dark signs inscribed on its surface; it is "the still unoccupied space / illuminating the word that must be left behind" (*T*). And yet,

encounters once again the silence and invisibility of breath, the mutism and the vacuity from which it has emerged and to which it will return; it is the "voice of nothingness become / word again" (*Désaccordée,* 16). Blank space has another function for du Bouchet: it effaces. No word can be written, he remarks, except on the ashes of an earlier word, already obliterated and consumed. Fire, "c'est cela, le blanc" (*André du Bouchet,* 86). Thus, the searing white spaces of the poem appear to impede the operations of syntax. The momentum of the poetic line is interrupted by the blank space, which consumes it. The white space is a tabula rasa. After the interval a new verse fragment, forgetful of its antecedent, appears; "a word," writes du Bouchet, "at the moment I utter it I no longer possess it" (*AB,* 89). In his poems, the *mise-en-page* and syntax are in extreme tension. In their confrontation and in the undoing of syntactic continuity through the spacing of words—"la cassure réitérée de la langue" ("the repeated fracturing of language"; *Désaccordée,* 70)—they represent the conjunction of being and nonbeing, of language and silence. "From syntax to *mise-en-page,* there is an accord between the order of the word and what is outside the word" (*AB,* 87). The substitution of space and language, the interruption of speech and the subsequent surge of silence, the swallowing up of words by the white spaces, and the accelerated displacement of signs reproduce mimetically the dialectical interactions of the forces of being. Moreover, within the passages themselves, syntax is continuously short-circuited by the accumulation of fragments placed in apposition, by the substitution of dashes for words of coordination, by the omission of verbs (a suppression inherited from Mallarmé), by the assigning of predicative function to past participles, prepositions, and infinitives, and, finally, by parentheses and other marks of interruption and ellipsis.

    Du Bouchet also makes frequent use of a nonreferential simile, in

---

even though it sustains the word, even though it "advances silently in the word" (*T*), the paper is elusive; it is "the support that illuminates and never allows itself to be represented" (*T*). "Les blancs" in du Bouchet's poetry, as Henri Maldiney has written, are "the very *means* of his speaking [*son dire*]" (p. 203). White space makes the poetic word "not a spoken [*un dit*], inscribed black on white, but a speaking [*un dire*], always instantaneous" ("Les 'Blancs' d'André du Bouchet," *L'Ire des vents* [*Espaces pour André du Bouchet*] 6–8 [1983]: 195–215). For a detailed discussion of the grammatical and typographical elements that separate white from printed space in du Bouchet's discourse, see Jacques Depreux, *André du Bouchet, ou La Parole traversée* (Seyssel: Champ Vallon, 1988), esp. pp. 103–32. On the relation of space to time in du Bouchet's work, see Yves Peyré, "La Coïncidence des temps," in *Autour d'André du Bouchet,* ed. Michel Collot (Paris: Presses de l'Ecole Normale Supérieure, 1986), pp. 41–54. Michel Collot explores the horizons of du Bouchet's different spatial worlds (those formed by the word and page and those formed by air, fire, ice, earth, and light) in "André du Bouchet et le 'pouvoir du fond,'" in his *L'Horizon fabuleux,* 2 vols. (Paris: José Corti, 1988), 2:179–211.

which one of the terms of the comparison remains undesignated. The
analogic power is dissipated by the ambiguity of the comparison and by
the absence of a referential antecedent. In du Bouchet's hands, the
simile promises an association that it cannot deliver; it is a bridge between two shores, one of which is forever beclouded in mist. In the section of *Laisses* entitled "L'Intonation," for example, a simile is printed at
the top of a page, preceded by a blank space and a black dot:

.

Comme
élargi au-delà de sa langue
respirer

perdu.

[•

As
extended beyond its language
to breathe

lost.]

("Luzerne")

The link to an antecedent context is lost. Consequently, the word
fragments composing the simile float free and unattached; each has a
curious autonomy and independence. The preposition ("au-delà de"),
past participles ("élargi," "perdu") and the infinitive ("respirer") become surrogate predicates, making up for the absent principal verb.
The notational quality of the simile intensifies the mystery and the
indeterminate quality of the actions of expansion, breathing, and loss.
The absence of a subject (a referent to which the disembodied acts
could be assigned) and the absence of an articulated antecedent in
which to ground the simile produce an intense poetic obscurity. But
such obscurity is, for du Bouchet, also "la clarté," for the poem's
hermeticism derives only from the reader's having been briefly dis-

possessed of a certain "will to elucidation." Although we may fail to comprehend the obscurity of the poem, it, at least, "appears to understand us" (*Désaccordée*, 89–90).

The result is a text in perpetual metamorphosis, in which a relation can never last for long because it is never firmly anchored in any given context. Every meaning leads to a chasm of nonmeaning as words are engulfed by indeterminacy and silence. The poem is composed of a proliferation of competing and unprivileged significations, but no one meaning crystallizes from their various interactions. The syntax of ephemeral reality becomes an ephemeral syntax. Du Bouchet's poems are texts without memories. A verse does not necessarily refer back to, or "remember," its antecedent, even though it may be connected by a conjunction or by some other form of syntactic linking. "Here," writes du Bouchet, "no birth is memorable," and

nous sommes, pour le dire, sans langue natale, la surface qui contient une parole passe par-dessus et au travers, et l'emporte.[16]

[we are, to state it clearly, without a native language; the surface that contains a word passes over and through, and carries it away.]

The amnesia is practically complete because the blank space that surrounds words and lines weakens the power of retrospective coordination customarily found in poetry. The unreadability of this difficult poetry derives from its obscure discontinuity and from the poet's reluctance to build patterns or to develop systems of images which would make possible a coherent retrospective reading. The poems in *Laisses* are just what their title implies, "leavings": signs or traces, which, having been left behind in the sand, will soon be blown away by the wind or covered by the sea.

Du Bouchet wishes to represent the precariousness of the spoken word, of the poem read aloud. Speech is closer to being than writing; it takes place in a finite world of change, where words quite literally disappear into thin air. He calls on the word to address its own silence, to give voice to its very muteness (*Désaccordée*, 12). To restore being to writing, du Bouchet invents a written, poetic language with the evasiveness, ephemerality, tenuousness, fragmentariness, and abruptness of spoken language. He wishes to lighten his words, to reinfuse them with mortal breath, to transform them into air. Like Bonnefoy, he seeks

16. "Hölderlin aujourd'hui," in *L'Incohérence* (Paris: Hachette, 1979), unfolioed; hereafter cited in the text as "Hölderlin."

"words like the sky," words that "comprising silence, become song"
(*Désaccordée*, 64).

"Speak—/But keep yes and no unsplit."—Celan

The poet, wrote Mallarmé, "yields the power of initiative to words"
and disappears. Similarly, in the poetry of Bonnefoy, Dupin, and du
Bouchet, the poet's presence is tenuous, if not nonexistent. But if he
surrenders his will to the power of words, it is only because he knows
that those words are already controlled by a force greater than that of
the poem and of language: namely, the force of being, the paradoxical
coincidence of life and death, of the yes and the no.[17] The syntax of
words aspires to a perfection that is false and must be corrected or
contested by a dialectical syntax emerging from beyond the poem,
from the region of the "hors-parole." When the syntax of a poem
motivates words to be like the sky (as in Bonnefoy), or to become traces
of ephemeral relations (as in Dupin), or to be engulfed and consumed
by silence (as in du Bouchet), then it compels them to represent mimetically the syntax of being, of "Whatever," in Yeats's expression, "is
begotten, born, and dies."[18]

The Art of the Void: Alberto Giacometti and the Ephemerality of Perception

When Giacometti decided in or around 1935 to stop making works
of art uniquely inspired by dreams and to return to working *d'après*

17. Paul Ricoeur suggests that it is the very function of syntax to turn language
toward the world ("La Structure, le mot, l'événement," *Esprit* 360 [May 1967]: 801–21).
Nouns and verbs, for example, are forms of discourse which, because they work to
represent reality in its spatial and temporal aspects, permit our signs to be, in the words
of the linguist Gustave Guillaume, " 'transferred to the universe' " (815). By giving a
word either a nominal or a predicative function, and thus placing it in a fixed position
within a sentence, syntax moves to "seize the real" (815), thus avoiding the closure of a
finite system of signs. Syntax activates the words it positions, turning them away from an
abstract, intransitive ideality of meaning and toward the reality of things-in-the-world;
"what is essential in language," Ricoeur writes, "begins beyond the closure of signs"
(821). Through the patterns syntax arranges, the sentence realizes the potentiality of the
words constituting it, and thus there surges into being a speaking that Ricoeur defines as
"the very mystery of language; speaking [*le dire*] is what I call the opening, or better yet,
the aperture of language" (821). In some respects, Bonnefoy echoes Ricoeur's thoughts
in asserting that "the writing of poetry is the reciprocal intensification of the reality one
lives and of the language that questions it" ("Gilbert Lely," in *Gilbert Lely* [Losne: Thierry
Bouchard, 1979], p. 4).
18. "Sailing to Byzantium," in *The Poems: A New Edition*, ed. Richard J. Finneran (New
York: Macmillan, 1983), p. 193.

nature in front of a live model, he committed his creative energies to the task of copying the human head. As a result of his heretical return to mundane reality, he was expelled from the surrealist movement. André Breton was not amused, remarking ironically, "Une tête, on sait bien ce que c'est qu'une tête!" ("A head, everyone knows what a head is!"). But Breton was wrong, because after thousands of years of representation little was still known, even in 1935, about copying the human figure. Each day, amidst the rubble of destroyed statues littering his studio floor and in front of sculptures or paintings abandoned with dissatisfaction the night before, Giacometti was reminded of how little indeed he and other artists knew about representation. "A head," he once stated—and it is an appropriate response to Breton's remark— "became for me an object completely unknown and without dimensions."[19]

To model a head, to paint a face, to draw an eye—to represent reality as he saw it at the moment of perception—was Giacometti's lifelong, unrealized ambition. And for most of the half-century he worked as an artist (he was sixty-four at his death in 1966) that impossible mission was fraught with self-doubt, frustration, anguish, anxiety, and failure, feelings he was frank in admitting: " 'If only I could accomplish something in drawing or painting or sculpture . . . it wouldn't be so bad. If I could just do a head, one head, just once. . . . But it's impossible.' 'I simply can't seem to reproduce what I see. To be able to do that, one would have to die of it.' "[20]

Reality perpetually eluded Giacometti's grasp; it was the absolute for which he was continuously in search. His being was oriented, James Lord remarks, toward "the ideal void where reality, untouched and unknown, is always waiting to be discovered."[21] But part of Giacometti's problem in capturing the real was his belief that merely representing figures alone, without copying the density and materiality of their circumambient space or without representing the distance between himself and the object of his perception, offered an incomplete and inauthentic picture of reality. Giacometti's eye was profoundly sensitive to different kinds of empty, so-called negative, space: to the vacant, airy space surrounding or passing through his statues; to the white, sometimes gray space that, like a halo, encircled the heads of his painted portraits; and to the corrosive space of paper eating into the

19. "A Letter from Alberto Giacometti to Pierre Matisse, 1947," in *Alberto Giacometti* (New York: Museum of Modern Art, 1965), p. 26.
20. *A Giacometti Portrait*, pp. 9–10 and 23, respectively.
21. Ibid., p. 113.

unbounded network of lines which precariously shaped a head in his drawings. Wherever possible, Giacometti represented and gave form to space, opening his figures from within to its presence or surrounding them from the outside with its ambiance.[22] Particularly in his drawings, he turned the white paper surface into a substance to be molded, shaped, even chiseled. The dark lines that are drawn in pencil or ink make the white areas they touch stand out in relief; the space of the picture surface acquires a third dimension. "The lines are only there," Jean Genet writes, "in order to give form and solidity to the white spaces. . . . It's not the line that is full, it's the white."[23] Giacometti gives form and density to absence itself. This creates an art in which volume and space, figure and ground, form and field, the opaque and the transparent exist in a tense, sometimes dialectical relationship, which dissolves the boundaries normally separating them; one is often not able to determine where the figure ends and its space begins.

The work that inaugurated Giacometti's attempt to give form and presence to space and to transform emptiness into a palpable, almost measurable, substance was the early sculpture *L'Objet invisible* (1934). Subtitled *Mains tenant le vide*, it has attracted considerable critical attention over the years from those writers, poets, and philosophers who have been fascinated by Giacometti's work in general. In particular, Bonnefoy, Dupin, and du Bouchet have, since the early days of their careers, been drawn to, and influenced by, the work of Giacometti. They have discovered in the artist's paintings, sculptures, and drawings similar attitudes toward the human condition and analogous concerns about the place of artistic representation in the world. For them, Giacometti's figures are, as Bonnefoy affirms, "icons, totally preoccupied, through the object, with the experience of being" (*NR,* 314). They are figures that not only represent the presence of death and disintegration in the world but also, by their profound loneliness, their isolation in vast, open, and distant spaces, their scarred, pitted surfaces, and their resemblance to barely formed matter, testify to having been touched directly by the finitude of being.

22. As Marcelin Pleynet writes, "each sculpture, each statue, each sign, each standing being appears and disappears (vision, illusion, phantasm) in the solid body of an air, a space that it stretches like a bow. . . . The statue is here the standing being that makes present the being of its space" ("Le Sujet invisible d'Alberto Giacometti," *Tel Quel* 93 [Fall 1982]: 47).
23. *L'Atelier d'Alberto Giacometti* (Décines: Marc Barbezat and L'Arbalète, 1958), p. 42. For an interesting study of negative space in poetry, see Lorraine Liscio, "The Role of Negative Space in the Works of Alberto Giacometti and Stéphane Mallarmé," *Revue du Pacifique* 3 (1977): 131–39.

Bonnefoy, Dupin, and du Bouchet share an aesthetic and ontological belief in the irrefutable primacy of mortal and temporal existence and in the preponderance of being over language, art, and other forms of representation. The windows of their poems are never closed to the breezes coming from the real world; as Bonnefoy writes. "Que la rosée / De la nuit se condense et coule, sur l'image" ("May the night's / Dew condense and flow, over the image"; *Ce qui fut sans lumière*, 79). The word, when severed from its traditional connotations and when opened to the presence of *le néant*, becomes as ephemeral, elusive, and incomplete as existence itself. Their poetry presents a mimesis, albeit a problematic one, of being. It dwells at that point of intersection where existence and language dialectically interpenetrate. Here, world and book unfold in a copresence, which transforms the poem into an object that, like a Giacometti statue, is fragmented, scarred, torn, hollowed, fissured, pulverized, and brought as close to a state of nothingness and silence as possible. Bonnefoy, Dupin, and du Bouchet reverse Mallarmé's assumption that "tout, au monde, existe pour aboutir à un livre" ("everything, in the world, exists to end up in a book"). Everything in a book or a poem, they suggest, leads to the ephemeral, mortal world. Therefore, it is not surprising that when, early in 1967, Bonnefoy and du Bouchet (Dupin was to join them later) collaborated on the founding of the journal of poetry *L'Ephémère*, the inaugural issue was devoted to the memory of Giacometti, who had died the year before.[24] During the five years of the review's existence (1967–72), the same drawing by Giacometti of a standing nude was printed on the cover of each issue, and several issues contained essays on his work and reproductions of his drawings.

Of the *Ephémère* poets, Bonnefoy and du Bouchet were especially taken with *L'Objet invisible*. The statue's title refers not to what the sculpture contains or represents, but rather to the reality it is literally incapable of making visible: namely, the immaterial and ubiquitous presence of the forces of death and nothingness, which exist in the world but have no precise, concrete formulation or reality that can be represented other than by an invisibility or an absence. The figure of a startled woman, stylized in a way reminiscent of the human shapes of Oceanic art, is depicted in an almost upright position, leaning against the seat of a chair or stool. Her knees are slightly bent, as if she were

---

24. For a history of *L'Ephémère* and a discussion of Dupin's and du Bouchet's involvement with it, see Robert W. Greene, *Six French Poets of Our Time: A Critical and Historical Study* (Princeton: Princeton University Press, 1979), pp. 11–15, 124–25, and 140–42. Greene also devotes two interesting chapters to Dupin's and du Bouchet's work.

suddenly getting to her feet; her arms are rigid. Her eyes and mouth, set in a masklike face, are wide open in a grimace of pain, surprise, or fright. The figure's open, outstretched hands are three to four inches apart. Between them is clasped what one imagines—and what the work's title says—is an invisible object, having the form of the empty space framed and shaped by the hands. The rigidity of the woman's body, the fear written on her face, and the movement toward flight suggested by her bent knees indirectly evoke what must be the terrifying nature of the unknown and unseen object. All visible signs point to a frightening invisibility. The sculpture seems to exist in order to give form to the enigma of absence, in order to serve as the "frame" or support for the negative space lying between the figure's hands. Everything about the statue gives value to that contained void, which, paradoxically, has acquired palpable and tangible form.

L'Objet invisible is fundamentally an enigma, for, as Bonnefoy, struck by the aura of paradox emanating from the work, remarks, the statue is "upright like a human being, articulated and rigid like an insect, blind despite its eyes, sexless despite its cold and heavy breasts, indecipherable in spite of its evident reality as an idol" (*L'Improbable*, 319). For Bonnefoy, the figure represents "L'Etranger . . . ou l'Absence," and this Stranger, "ce chevalier de ténèbre" ("this dark knight"; *I*, 318), is an incarnation of death; his appearance announces the end of the idyllic experience of openness and transparence which a child enjoys in his or her intimate and imaginative unity with the world. Where there had once been only the child's joy in the immediacy of an endless present, there now appears an anxious concern for a changing and unpredictable future. Faith in the world is replaced by a pervasive doubt and insecurity. Thus, *L'Objet invisible* represents the terror born from a sudden and swift awareness of death, the fear that follows a sudden homelessness.[25] Bonnefoy finds in it, as well as in other works by Giacometti, the "brutal signs of the triumph of being" (*I*, 323). The

25. Bonnefoy has noted a possible association between *L'Objet invisible* and the death of Giacometti's father: "His father died at the age he himself would one day die and less than a year before *The Invisible Object*, in which, beneath the feet of the mysterious creature, a tomb can be detected" ("Etudes comparées de la fonction poétique," in *Annuaire du Collège de France, 1982–1983*, Résumé des Cours et Travaux, no. 83, p. 649). In the invisible object, which the figure holds, death takes up residence, as François Gantheret observes. The empty space between the fingers represents "the void immobilized in its quivering," for Giacometti's aim is to assign "to death a space and to stand before it, alone. To cause an object to exist in its only state of truth: invisibility. . . . The invisible object derives at the same time from death and from life. From death, because it is a drawing finally finished, completed; from life, because it is a void that resists. Death, here, is positive negation, it serves as a limit" (*Incertitude d'Eros*, Collection Connaissance de l'inconscient [Paris: Gallimard, 1984], pp. 9, 10).

invisible object in this sculpture and the *page blanche* in Giacometti's drawings both mirror the cold, menacing radiance of the void, of what he calls "the familiar glare of the towering glacier of absence" (*I*, 327).[26]

Yet, the knowledge of the reality of death does not prevent Giacometti from fighting the power of the Stranger. He longs to rediscover the sensation of plenitude and the experience of centeredness which the child, in blissful ignorance of death, once had. This is the absolute, the unknown. It is the miracle of a pure and plenitudinous reality, perceived and copied in an instant, which Giacometti tries with every work of art to make appear. It is the dream, as Bonnefoy describes it, that "suddenly, the real has its center *here*, that present being suffices" (*I*, 325). This is the miracle of presence, what Bonnefoy calls "the mystery that at times transforms an instant into the eternal" (*NR*, 119). The impossible reality Giacometti and Bonnefoy both seek, therefore, is an instant of furtive and unpossessable plenitude.

Giacometti's figures are, according to du Bouchet, "mortal effigies,"[27] figures of an always-imminent death crossing the open streets and plazas of the living. His emaciated, filiform statues and his miniscule, pin-size figurines, perched precariously on tall bases, stand only a step away from obliteration. They are pared down to a minimal existence, beyond which they would turn to dust and nothingness. They stand only a hair's-breadth away from the void and thus express, according to Bonnefoy, "the terror . . . of having seen nothingness [*le néant*] appear, there where one sought to inscribe being."[28] They are, du Bouchet observes, "Poussières à face d'homme" ("Dust with a human face": *Qui*, 171). But their humanness is unable to hide or dissipate the fundamental nothingness that dwells within and around them. Giacometti's sculptures melt into nonbeing, into inanimate matter, before our eyes. As we approach them, the critic David Sylvester has observed, there is a point at which we see the standing figure whole; but a step closer and it loses its human resemblance:

26. Marcelin Pleynet offers another, more psychoanalytic interpretation of *L'Objet invisible*. Because the work had originally been titled *Personnage féminin*, before being rebaptized *L'Objet invisible*, the unseen object that the mysterious female figure lacks, Pleynet concludes, is in truth not missing at all. The lack is erased by the phallic statue itself: "In *The Invisible Object (Female Personage)*, the missing object is declared missing, and I would say that, consequently, it is not missing, because the entire sculptural erection aptly represents it for what it is" ("Le Sujet invisible d'Alberto Giacometti," p. 42).

27. *Qui n'est pas tourné vers nous* (Paris: Mercure de France, 1972), p. 24; hereafter cited in the text as *Qui*.

28. "Etudes comparées de la fonction poétique," in *Annuaire du Collège de France*, *1982–1983*, p. 652.

When I face one of [Giacometti's standing women] from the far side of a room and start moving towards her, for the first few paces she seems to come nearer, then she begins to recede from me as fast as I approach. She keeps, so it seems, her distance. It is as if she were detached from the physical space of the room and existed within a separate space of her own. As I get near, I do not, as one normally would, see only the part of the figure around the point I am focusing on; I can still see the figure entire. And when I get right up to her, to the point at which I expect to be seeing details in close-up, relishing the curve of a cheek, of a breast, I see hardly anything of a figure at all, but a piece of bronze and the light flickering over the imprints of the artist's fingers or knife—a hard, tangible object which has replaced a body become intangible at the moment it was near enough to be touched. Once the figure is no longer seen as if from far enough to be seen as a whole, she dissolves away.[29]

For Bonnefoy, the oscillation of Giacometti's figures between appearance and disappearance, tangibility and intangibility, near and far, possession and loss, *fort* and *da* (to recall the child's exclamations in Freud's game) is a result of the artist's encounter with an elusive presence—namely, "a presence engulfed by matter." And, Bonnefoy continues,

What [Giacometti] wanted in art was to give the impression of distance by somehow inscribing in the work the appearance of relative smallness that the human being seen from afar has but that our consciousness corrects. . . . The perception of the human being from a distance is in fact the same experience he had had earlier in front of some pieces of fruit in his father's studio. It is the experience of *ecceity* taking the place of *quiddity*, the experience resulting from the apprehension of a person *here and now*, in his or her moral and essential totality, there where yesterday the body alone still spoke in its proximate and, above all, suggestively sensual being: in a word, this is *presence* which manifests itself as the key to experiencing the world, but also as the aim of the work of art, which will assist the artist in understanding himself better or, in any event, in coming to know himself better.[30]

29. "The Residue of a Vision," in *Alberto Giacometti: Sculpture, Paintings, Drawings, 1913–65* (London: Arts Council of Great Britain, 1965), unfolioed.
30. "Etudes comparées de la fonction poétique," in *Annuaire du Collège de France, 1982–1983*, pp. 652 and 651, respectively. According to Bonnefoy, Giacometti loved

The void is a constant presence in Giacometti's work; it animates the sculpted figures standing in groups or in isolation; it gives energy to the heads whose painted and repainted lines swirl centripetally in chaotic disarray; it dissipates the faces whose edges, because they are drawn without contour lines, are swallowed up in the whiteness of the paper. Sartre remarks that Giacometti "sees the void everywhere"; it creeps in all places, for "every creature secretes its own void."[31] Giacometti's first encounter with emptiness was a frightening experience because it revealed the ubiquitous presence of death lying close to the surface of all things:

Je commençais à voir les têtes dans le vide, dans l'espace qui les entoure. Quand pour la première fois j'aperçus clairement la tête que je regardais se figer, s'immobiliser dans l'instant, définitivement, je tremblai de terreur comme jamais encore dans ma vie et une sueur froide courut dans mon dos. Ce n'était plus une tête vivante, mais un objet que je regardais comme n'importe quel autre objet, mais non, autrement, non pas comme n'importe quel objet, mais comme quelque chose de vif et mort simultanément. Je poussai un cri de terreur comme si je venais de franchir un seuil, comme si j'entrais dans un monde encore jamais vu. Tous les vivants étaient morts, et cette vision se répéta souvent, dans le métro, dans la rue, dans le restaurant, devant mes amis.[32]

---

works of art, ancient and modern, sacred and profane, in which "networks of elementary symbolisms are traversed by the sudden appearance of a presence that designates itself as such with authority and mystery." He was attracted by "a poetics of Presence" ("Etudes comparées de la fonction poétique," in *Annuaire du Collège de France 1981–1982*, Résumé des Cours et Travaux, no. 82, pp. 651 and 653, respectively). Bonnefoy also finds signs of presence in Giacometti's manner of representing the faces and gazes of his subjects. Giacometti's style, Bonnefoy observes, is based on a "questioning of the real," which remains open to the presence of other beings and, as a result, contests the hegemony of the mimetic tradition in Western art. Giacometti's work expresses the conviction that "the aim of the artist does not have to be the *image* of human beings but their *face*, and in particular their *glance* which expresses the relation of the individual to itself in its very relationship with its universe, which dereifies the world, and which is the source that ensures presence on earth" (*Annuaire du Collège de France, 1982–1983*, p. 657). For Bonnefoy, Giacometti's art, particularly his drawing, is an act of creation which "conveys sympathy, compassion; it collaborates on the possible actualization of being in a community beseiged by nonbeing; it is the search for meaning, the re-creating of the world" (ibid., p. 658). For a discussion of Giacometti's preoccupation with the gaze of the other, with what Ed Hill calls "the *epiphany of being* in the look, the glance of an 'other,'" provoking the artist to confront the "primordial strangeness—found at the heart of ordinary experience," see his "The Inherent Phenomenology of Alberto Giacometti's Drawing," *Drawing* 3 (January–February 1982): 97–102.
    31. "Les Peintures de Giacometti," *Les Temps modernes* 9 (June 1954): 2223.
    32. "Le Rêve, le sphinx, et la mort de T.," *Labyrinthe*, nos. 22–23 (December 1946): 12. On the genesis, symbolism, and biographical aspects of this *récit* and the dream that

[I began to see heads in the void, in the spaces surrounding them. When I first clearly noticed the head I was looking at become in an instant permanently frozen, immobilized, I shuddered with terror as I would never again in my life, and a cold sweat ran down my back. It was no longer a living head, but rather an object that I looked at like any other object, but no, differently, not like any object, but like something alive and dead simultaneously. I let out a cry of terror as if I had crossed a threshold, as if I had entered a world still unseen. All living beings were dead, and this vision recurred often, in the subway, in the street, in a restaurant, with my friends.]

The people and things of the world have fallen into a state of radical alienation, separated one from the other by a surrounding aura of emptiness, a halo of nonbeing, which makes each person and each object totally "other." On awakening one morning, Giacometti is terrified at the frightening autonomy and otherness of things:

> Je vis ma serviette pour la première fois, cette serviette sans poids dans une immobilité jamais aperçue, et comme en suspens dans un effroyable silence. Elle n'avait plus aucun rapport avec la chaise sans fond ni avec la table dont les pieds ne reposaient plus sur le plancher, le touchaient à peine, il n'y avait plus aucun rapport entre les objets séparés par des incommensurables gouffres de vide.[33]

[I saw my towel for the first time, this towel without weight in an immobility never before seen, and as if suspended in a terrifying silence. It no longer had any relationship to the chair without a seat or to the table whose legs no longer rested on the floor, or were barely touching it; there was no longer any relationship between things now separated by immeasurable gulfs of void.]

The void not only encloses things within an impenetrable distance but also carries them into oblivion. For example, returning to France by boat in October 1965 after a visit to New York, Giacometti finds it extremely difficult to concentrate on writing a preface for a collection of drawings he has made of works by great artists of the past. The ocean, that seemingly infinite expanse of emptiness, oppresses his consciousness:

inspired it, see James Lord, *Giacometti: A Biography* (New York: Farrar, Straus and Giroux, 1985), pp. 268–80.
33. "Le Rêve, le sphinx, et la mort de T.," p. 12.

La mer envahit tout, elle est pour moi sans nom bien qu'on l'appelle aujourd'hui l'Atlantique. Pendant des millions d'années elle n'avait pas de nom et un jour elle n'aura plus de nom, sans fin, aveugle, sauvage comme elle est pour moi aujourd'hui.[34]

[The sea invades everything; it is for me nameless, even though we today call it the Atlantic. For millions of years it had no name and one day it will no longer have a name, endless, blind, savage as it is for me today.]

The void cannot be named; no word has the syllabic range to express its infinite openness. And to give thought to the artworks of the past while the ocean howls around him reminds Giacometti again of the futility of human creativity, of the ever-present death no work of art can escape:

Comment parler ici de copies d'oeuvres d'art, d'oeuvres d'art éphémères et fragiles . . . qui se défont, qui s'étiolent, qui se délabrent jour après jour et dont beaucoup, et parmi celles que je préfère, étaient déjà ensevelies, enfoncées sous le sable, la terre et les pierres, et toutes suivent le même chemin.[35]

[How to speak here of copies of works of art, of ephemeral and fragile works of art . . . that come undone, that deteriorate, that fall into decay day after day, of which many, including those I prefer, were already buried, sunk under sand, earth, and stones, all following the same path.]

One can understand why Giacometti's sculptures look as if they had been lost or buried for centuries. They resemble pieces of hardened lava—relics, that is, of a distant disaster. From the moment of their creation and throughout an arduous and anxious process of construction, involving much destruction and effacement, Giacometti's works undergo a disintegration characteristic of mortal existence. These works not only represent finitude but also bear its scars. They have encountered what du Bouchet describes as the "dehors ennemi de la conservation" ("the outside, enemy of preservation"; *Qui*, 109).

"The object seen and drawn," Dupin observes, "whether it be woman, studio or flower, cannot be separated from the void that bathes and

34. "Notes sur les copies," *L'Ephémère*, no. 1 (1967): 106.
35. Ibid.

protects it."[36] In Giacometti's drawings, the heads are composed of multiple lines that fight one another for the space they occupy; one line following in the wake of another corrects and thus annuls it. As Dupin remarks, "we find here contestation as the principle of creation."[37] In the spaces between the lines lie apertures through which the white surface of the paper peers. As happens in the sculptures, the density of form is dissolved by what Dupin calls "un vide actif." A line is broken or interrupted by the surging forth of negative space, "a pulsation of the void against the crumbling walls that contain it" (*EAD*, 269). But this uprising of the void is subdued by the continuous multiplication and circulation of the dark lines. The coming and going of such lines, the hollowing out of form to reveal an underlying blankness, and the contestative relationship between figure and void—all qualities of Giacometti's drawings that Dupin describes in his various studies of the artist's work—also characterize Dupin's own poetry.[38] In his poems, a syntax of contestation operates to fragment the poetic line, to erase syntactical links between linguistic elements, to place words at a distance from each other and scattered over the page, and to open the poem to wide expanses of blank space. In the discontinuities of its form, the poem imitates the realities of loss, vacancy, and indeterminacy, which define mortal existence and modern consciousness. The void circulates around the edges and in the margins of his poem, as well as within the intervals between words and line fragments. Infused by silence, infiltrated by negativity, Dupin's poetry expresses the sounds and silences of nothingness.

If Bonnefoy and Dupin present in their poetry a mimesis of being, a representation that parallels Giacometti's in its insistence on the precariousness of the figure and of the human being, du Bouchet goes a step further in *Qui n'est pas tourné vers nous,* his long poem-commentary on Giacometti's drawings. In an attempt to represent the absence and presence of being, he offers not only a mimesis of that being but also an imitation through the interplay of word and space of the Giacomettian style. By describing how figure and space unfold in the drawings through distance or transparence, how the artist's lines hurtle like meteors across the surface of the paper, dissolving amorphously into the surrounding vacancy of space, and, finally, how the void bubbles up from wells, flooding everything in whiteness and condemning all

36. "La Réalité impossible," p. 42.
37. "Textes pour une approche," p. 32.
38. For a discussion of the influence of Giacometti's aesthetics on Dupin's poetic theory, see Michael Bishop, "Jacques Dupin," in his *The Contemporary Poetry of France: Eight Studies* (Amsterdam: Rodopi, 1985), pp. 35–53.

tracings to effacement—du Bouchet, through his notational style, disrupted syntax, and open *mise-en-page* (equivalents in poetry to Giacometti's fractured forms), illustrates the process of making and unmaking by which a poem surges in and out of existence. This follows an ontology, shared with the other *Ephémère* poets and with Giacometti, that asserts that (to quote du Bouchet's idiosyncratically elliptical and lacunary language) "être — et non . . . même tenant" ("to be — and not . . . all of a piece"; *Qui,* 156).

The problem Giacometti faced from the start of his career, Sartre observes, was "how to make a man out of stone without petrifying him?"[39] For du Bouchet, as for Giacometti, the answer lies in the disruption of the will-to-eternity characteristic of artistic form. As soon as it appears, the figure (in a Giacometti drawing) or the word (in a du Bouchet poem) is swallowed up by the whiteness of the paper it marks. Forms do not have the time to become permanent. Spoken words revert to the insubstantial breath they once were. Lines lead into the void. Space is where the word "inscribes itself in order to disappear." The word, whether written or spoken, becomes "a lacuna, a hole" ("Hölderlin"). A poem is the point of intersection between words in fugitive motion (similar to the self-correcting, self-canceling lines of Giacometti's drawings) and the white expanses of the paper surface (*les blancs*), where "a sound, in silence, is figured" (*AB,* 102). Here a word in its newly found absence and invisibility, having literally passed into thin air, attains the plenitude and presence of a realm beyond speech. The word or the figure is vitalized and at the same time shattered by the void. A drama of ontological and existential proportions is played out on the white paper. Words struck by nonbeing pass into the oblivion of a surrounding absence. The mimesis of being-in-the world, which du Bouchet presents both in his poetry and in these poem-essays on Giacometti, is intensified by stylistic and typographical innovations. Through textual interruptions, syntactic breaks, fragmented poetic lines, scattered words scudding across the page—all achieved by the use of dashes, ellipses, parentheses, commas, appositions, and a lyrically free *mise-en-page*—du Bouchet creates a representation of the discontinuity of existence, of the unpredictability with which it swerves and deviates into nothingness and death. What we experience in reading his poetry is the "ellipse de l'être inachevé en cours" ("ellipsis of uncompleted being in progress"; *Qui,* 33), the sudden breach or elision that disrupts the course of a life.

Du Bouchet's poetry, like Giacometti's painting, sculpture, and draw-

39. "La Recherche de l'absolu," *Les Temps modernes* 3 (January 1948): 1155.

ing, dramatically and mimetically enacts the failure of artistic representation to express and contain being, for it is not of the ontological nature of existence to be possessed by either word or figure. "The essential," he writes, "is unimaginable—cannot be *represented*."[40] Reality is always lost, always beyond representation; it is an impossibility, which any work of art will, by the imposition of form and structure, always deform. Giacometti used his work, as does du Bouchet his poetry, to question and probe this impossibility, to study reality's resistance to artistic capture. "I do not know," he remarked, "whether I work in order to make something or in order to know why I cannot make what I would like to make."[41]

To make breath, open space, and emptiness materially and formally present in a poem, so as to prevent it from coalescing into a petrified and "artistic" form, is du Bouchet's goal. He imagines that his word is as sharp as a scythe, that it is a "parole de la rupture" ("Hölderlin"), which will lacerate the meanings it has just established, so the surface of the paper will become scarred by the struggle of word effacing word. The result is a poem as miminal and as vulnerable to extinction as a Giacometti statue, a representation, Richard Wilbur observes, "shaved and scraped / Of all but being there, / Whose fullness is escaped / Like a burst balloon's: no nakedness so bare / As flesh gone in inquiring of the bone."[42]

The work of art is unfinishable and the poem endless because the artist and poet meet "with things dying, . . . with things new born" (*The Winter's Tale*, 3.3.112–13). The irregular and ceaseless rhythms of birth and death and of presence and absence are articulated by the works of Giacometti and the *Ephémère* poets. In the force of a written word soon to be effaced by the white page and in the projection into emptiness of a tiny, sculpted human figure, surging from its base like a far-away mountain peak that pierces the clear and vacant sky, are joined the tenacity and the precariousness of an existence lived close to the edge of nothingness: "Cette terre," du Bouchet writes, "qui surgit dans la dénégation du vide,—niée par le vide, niant le vide" ("This earth arising in the denial of the void—denied by the void, denying the void").[43] An art of the void like that of Giacometti and the *Ephémère*

40. "Baudelaire irrémédiable," *Courrier du Centre international d'études poétiques* 9 (May 1956): 17.
41. Quoted in Peter Selz, *New Images of Man* (New York: Museum of Modern Art, 1959), p. 68.
42. "Giacometti," in *New and Collected Poems* (New York: Harcourt Brace Jovanovich, 1988), p. 331.
43. "Baudelaire irrémédiable," p. 11.

poets identifies the work of art as the place of interruption where life flows into and disrupts form: in other words, where the void arises to destroy its own figuration. Such an art reflects the infinite emptiness and the frightening indeterminacy of a reality in which the simple act of copying a nose can sever the fragile ties that hold the world together, for, as Giacometti writes: "One could have spent a lifetime without achieving a result. The form dissolved, it was little more than granules moving over a deep black void, the distance between one wing of the nose and the other is like the Sahara, without end, nothing to fix one's gaze upon, everything escapes."[44] Thus, art for Giacometti is a mirror held up not to reality but to the deep, black void: it is a mirror shattered by the encounter—and voided.

44. "A Letter from Alberto Giacometti to Pierre Matisse," p. 18.

CHAPTER 7

The Unseizable Landscape of the Real: Philippe Jaccottet

Le réel se creuse à l'infini, jusqu'à l'invisible.

[The real opens itself infinitely, unto invisibility.]
—Philippe Jaccottet, *Une Transaction secrète*

Since the end of World War II, French poets have been fascinated by the intensity and beauty of the natural world. Turning away
from a symbolist and surrealist heritage, which emphasized the hegemony of the imaginary and of experiences of dream and the unconscious, they have returned to natural reality, to the elemental, earthly,
material things of the world that they call *le Dehors (the Outside)*.[1] They
have been drawn to the simplicity as well as to the radiance of different
landscapes and terrains, celebrating the expressive joy of a meadow, as
does Francis Ponge, or the simple beauty of a garden, as do Jean Tortel
and Pierre-Albert Jourdan, or the intense presence of a hidden, un-
discovered hinterland, an *arrière-pays*, as does Yves Bonnefoy, or the
elemental barrenness of the desert, as do Edmond Jabès and Lorand
Gaspar.[2] Fascinated by the ephemerality and transparence of the real

1. In an interview Yves Bonnefoy states that one of the major tendencies of contemporary French poetry since the fifties has been to focus "incisive attention on natural
reality, or on what I would call the earthly [*le terrestre*]: paths, distant mountain peaks,
bare stones, but also gardens; that is nature as our life encounters it and recovers or loses
itself in it. This kind of poetry is new to us, because since the end of the Middle Ages our
great poets have only been witnesses to the city: think of Villon, Du Bellay, Racine, Hugo
(for whom nature is a jail of suffering souls), Baudelaire, surrealism" ("La Poésie, c'est ce
qui nous délivre du rêve," *Le Nouvel Observateur*, no. 1192 [11–17 September 1987]: 61).
And writing, as well, occupies the "outside;" it is "le dehors à jamais" (*La Vérité de parole*
[Paris: Mercure de France, 1988], p. 214; cited as *VP*).
2. See, for instance, Francis Ponge, *La Fabrique du pré* (Geneva: Albert Skira, 1971);
Jean Tortel, "Critique d'un jardin," in his *Relations* (Paris: Gallimard, 1968); Pierre-
Albert Jourdan, *Les Sandales de paille* (Paris: Mercure de France, 1987); Yves Bonnefoy,

world, by its openness to light and wind and its responsiveness to the probings of a poetic consciousness seeking to represent it through the manipulations of word and image, these poets search for what Bonnefoy calls "cet absolu / Qui vibre dans le pré parmi les ombres" ("this absolute / That in the meadow trembles among the shadows"; *Ce qui fut sans lumière*, 66). To see the absolute concealed within the folds of the real, to experience the presence surging momentarily into being from a torn leaf or the cry of a distant bird, to feel the trembling, short-lived radiance of almond trees in bloom, to watch billowing clouds enshroud the sun—in other words, to perceive the flash of the real against the night of death and pain, which characterizes the human condition, and at the moment it encounters a language powerless to seize it, this is the goal of a modern poetry of immanent being like that of Philippe Jaccottet.

The Alterity of the Real

Jaccottet is a poet who seeks to look into "le visage insoutenable du réel" ("the unbearable face of the real"), a face all the more striking because it is unadorned, elemental, and of the utmost simplicity.[3] The real is the force of life itself, as Jaccottet observes:

> Pour nous qui vivons de plus en plus entourés de masques et de schémas intellectuels, et qui étouffons dans la prison qu'ils élèvent

L'Arrière-pays, Collection Les Sentiers de la création (Geneva: Albert Skira, 1972); Edmond Jabès, *Le Livre des questions* and *Le Livre des ressemblances* (Paris: Gallimard, 1963–73 and 1976–80, respectively); Lorand Gaspar, *Sol absolu* (1972), in *Sol absolu et autres textes* (Paris: Collection Poésie, Gallimard, 1982).

3. *Une Transaction secrète: Lectures de poésie* (Paris: Gallimard 1987), p. 306, cited in the text as *TS*. Other works by Jaccottet are cited according to the following abbreviations; unless otherwise stated, these works were published in Paris by Gallimard:

ALH   *A la lumière d'hiver*, preceded by *Leçons* and *Chants d'en bas* (1977).
ATV   *A travers un verger* (Montpellier: Fata Morgana, 1975; reprint, Paris: Gallimard, 1984).
EM   *L'Entretien des muses: Chroniques de poésie* (1968).
ES   *Eléments d'un songe* (1961).
O   *L'Obscurité* (1961).
P   *Poésie, 1946–1967*, Collection Poésie (1971).
PA   *La Promenade sous les arbres* (Lausanne: Mermod, 1957).
PFA   *Paysages avec figures absentes* (1970).
PN   *Pensées sous les nuages* (1983).
S   *La Semaison: Carnets, 1954–1979* (1984).
Translations of Jaccottet's verse are my own, unless noted by the following abbreviations: *B: Breathings: The Poems of Philippe Jaccottet*, trans. Cid Corman (New York: Grossman, 1974), and *SP: Selected Poems*, trans. Derek Mahon (Winston-Salem, N.C.: Wake Forest University Press, 1988).

autour de nous, le regard du poète est le bélier qui renverse ces murs et nous rend, ne serait-ce qu'un instant, le réel; et, avec le réel, une *chance de vie.*

[For us who live surrounded more and more by masks and intellectual schemes and who stiffle in the prison that such things erect, the poet's gaze is a battering ram that topples these ramparts, giving us the real, if only for an instant; and with the real a *chance at life.*] (*L'Entretien des muses,* 301)

Poetry, turned as it is toward the real in all its visible forms, is committed to capturing "a fullness, a diversity, an intensity, a depth . . . of *reality*" (*EM,* 300). The profound and essential realism of poetry is not merely an attempt to catalogue the features of the visible world; it is

une attention si profonde au visible qu'elle finit nécessairement par se heurter à ses limites; à l'illimité que le visible semble tantôt contenir, tantôt cacher, refuser ou révéler.

[an attentiveness to the visible that is so deep that it necessarily runs up against its limits, against the unlimited that the visible seems sometimes to contain or to hide, to refuse or to reveal.] (*EM,* 304)

Jaccottet writes that the real, while open to the poet's gaze, while an intense experience of the instant in all its immediacy—"we are real only in the encounter with the present, there where the prow slices through the water" (*La Semaison,* 110)—can never, however, be completely possessed. Poetry offers no knowledge or mastery of the world.[4] Poetry is only a rapid, fleeting perception, made all the more ephemeral by the mimetic imprecision of language. The poem is

une manière de parler du monde qui n'explique pas le monde, car ce serait le figer et l'anéantir, mais qui le montre tout nourri de son refus de répondre.

[a way of speaking about the world that does not explain the world— for this would be to immobilize and destroy it—but that reveals it as fully sustained by its own refusal to respond.] (*Eléments d'un songe,* 153)

4. "A book of poems," Jaccottet writes, "will for me never be an object of pure knowledge; rather an open, or half-opened, door—sometimes all too quickly closed— onto *more reality*" (*EM,* 7).

Because the real is ultimately limitless, unseizable, and unknowable for a poet who, by his own admission, is without knowledge, living in a state of "ignorance," of *non-savoir*, and because it is an enigmatic plenitude beyond the power of words or images to fix meanings or represent events, Jaccottet refers to the real by means of abstract or universal terms, such as *l'illimité* ("the limitless"), *le centre* ("the center"), *l'invisible* ("the invisible"), *l'insaisissable* ("the unseizable"), and "[l']insituable partout présent" (the "unlocatable that is everywhere present"; *ES*, 136). While the *illimité* is only vaguely perceptible—for it is

le pressentiment de quelque chose d'essentiel qui n'était autre que notre rapport avec ce qui est en dehors de tout rapport, notre lien avec ce qui ne se peut lier.

[the presentiment of something essential that is other than our relation to what is beyond all relation—our link to that which cannot be linked.] (*L'Obscurité*, 95)

—the *insaisissable* is a phenomenon of absence; it is

ce chant que l'on ne saisit pas, cet espace où l'on ne peut demeurer, cette clef qu'il faut toujours reperdre. Cessant d'être insaisissable, cessant d'être douteuse, cessant d'être ailleurs (faut-il dire: cessant de n'être pas?), elle s'abîme, elle n'est plus.

[this song that we cannot possess, this space in which we cannot dwell, this key that we must continuously lose. Ceasing to be unseizable, ceasing to be doubtful, ceasing to be elsewhere (should one even say: ceasing to not be?), it is engulfed; it no longer exists.] (*La Promenade sous les arbres*, 148)

We are never more real, more alive, and more certain of reality than in those moments when we encounter the "impossible place" (*ES*, 147), the incomprehensible, enigmatic opening that the *insaisissable* announces. The most one can say about the real is that it is "something" ("quelque chose") always other than what one has just perceived or written about it: "Une beauté lointaine, imprenable, une lumière inconnue. Portant toujours un autre nom que celui qu'on s'apprêtait à lui donner" ("A distant, impregnable beauty, an unknown light. Continuously carrying another name than the one we were ready to give it"; *A travers un verger*, 13). What defines the unseizability and the elusiveness of the real is its fundamental otherness. The poem is a space through which this otherness passes, a necessary space, for without it the *alterity* of the real could never be expressed. Poetry is not the reconstruction or re-presentation of reality; it does not give voice to something that has been perceived, but rather to something that has *not* been perceived and that needs the poem in order to manifest its otherness:

> Je me dis que le travail consistait beaucoup moins à "bâtir," à "forg-er," à "ériger" une oeuvre qu'à permettre à un courant de passer, qu'à enlever des obstacles, à effacer des traces; comme si, en fin de compte, le poème idéal devait se faire oublier au profit *d'autre chose* qui, toutefois, ne saurait se manifester qu'*à travers* lui.

> [I told myself that the effort consisted less in "building," in "forging," in "erecting" a work than in allowing a current to pass, in removing obstacles, in effacing traces; as if, after all, the ideal poem must consign itself to oblivion on behalf of *another thing* that could only come into existence *through* it.] (*Une Transaction secrète,* 322; my emphasis)

Jaccottet is a poet remarkably sensitive to the elusiveness of all things, and it is this quality of elusiveness, above all, which fascinates him, even while it frustrates him. It presents him with a problem and a challenge; "comment dire," he asks in a poem, "cette chose qui est trop pure pour la voix?" ("how to say / this thing that is too pure for the voice?"; *Poésie,* 57). The great limitation of poetic language is that it exacerbates the natural elusiveness of things in the world. The time it takes to find the words to describe an event or a scene is enough to allow them to disappear: "l'objet évoqué efface l'objet à saisir" ("the object spoken effaces the object to be seized"; *ES,* 76). He searches, thus, for words that will have the immediacy and the transparency of a countryside bathed in morning light: words that might have half a chance at expressing what it means to hear the cries of invisible birds in the evening air. Language deforms experience, distorting reality in strange ways, which can be blamed on the demands of rhetoric, the rules of syntax, the laws of grammar, the self-indulgence of metaphor, and the tyranny of meaning. For this reason, Jaccottet modestly at-tempts to fashion a minimal poetic language and to use images of great simplicity. He seeks the unnarcissistic metaphor, which will not murder significance, and a poetic line without ornaments and adjectives, hop-ing by means of such immediate language to approach "what is completely simple and yet impossible to say" (*Paysages avec figures absentes*, 48).

There is an interesting paradox here. In order to approximate the immediacy of experience, Jaccottet wishes to find a language of almost unmediated perceptiveness. But in order to deal with the elusiveness of experience he must be indirect. The language has to be direct and simple; the approach, oblique and elusive. The only way to express the fleeting reality of the *insaisissable* is by accident, by describing something else, something "other." Because language tends to deviate from the object in whose direction the poet, figuratively speaking, points it, then this propensity for swerving away from the "target" can be exploited. Since enigma cannot be approached by a frontal attack, a strategy of indirection may have greater success. Perhaps, one day, without consciously trying to explain it, Jaccottet will "cause this river, these leaves, these birds to spring up in a poem intent on speaking of something else" (*PA*, 93). Confronted with enigma, the poet turns away, hoping by this detour to capture a part of the enigma. A poetry of indirection, reducing itself to a simple, bare mode of expression, is also a poetry of self-effacement. Together, both poetic strategies (indirection and effacement) hold the promise of returning the poet, for a moment at least, to the source of life itself: the unseizable center.

Jaccottet depends on a laconic and elliptical style of writing, which has internalized loss. By omitting details, he attains a fuller expression. Alluding in the simplest ways to a subject, which he has thereby eluded, Jaccottet finally and obliquely reaches his subject. Through a stylistics of effacement, he reproduces in his poems the elusiveness and tenuousness of life. As the slightest wind can upset the arrangement of the elements in a landscape, so the movement from one line to the next in the poem, or the replacement of one image by a new image, or the change from one perspective to another, can signal a breaking off of continuity, an irreversible displacement. Even his verses become discontinuous, adopting the form of brief haikulike notations or of a catalogue of fragmentary perceptions. In their simple and bare way, his verses tremble with uncertainty. The instability of the landscape is matched by a hesitancy of style, as in these lines from the poem "La Semaison":

Tout ce vert ne s'amasse pas, mais tremble et brille,
comme on voit le rideau ruisselant des fontaines
sensible au moindre courant d'air; et tout en haut
de l'arbre, il semble qu'un essaim se soit posé

d'abeilles bourdonnant; paysage léger
où des oiseaux jamais visibles nous appellent,
des voix, déracinées comme des graines, et toi,
avec tes mèches retombant sur des yeux clairs.

[All this green does not accumulate, but trembles and shines,
like the streaming curtain of fountains one sees
responsive to the least stir of air; and up on top
of the tree, it seems that a swarm has settled
of buzzing bees; easy countryside
where always invisible birds call to us,
voices, uprooted like seeds, and you,
with your curls tumbling over clear eyes.]

(P, 43/Breathings, 17)

No image, no perception, no impression in the poem is allowed to compose a pattern for very long or to coagulate into an enduring meaning. The symmetry of falling water is disturbed by the passing wind. The swarm of bees, even in a moment of repose, remains an active, buzzing congregation of incipient movement. Words are like seeds, removed by the wind from a point of origin and scattered far and wide. The origin is lost, but each word in its exile and uprootedness recalls its source. Words speak of a distant event, such as the cries of invisible birds. Already separated from their source, these cries exist only as traces of the past.

In Jaccottet's landscape, signs, events, and natural forms cohere in a vast hesitation. This is a countryside rich with ephemera. If any ordering of landscape elements occurs, it lasts only the briefest moment:

L'air tissait de ces riens
une toile tremblante. Et je la déchirais,
à force d'être seul et de chercher des traces.

[The air wove of these nothings
a trembling web. And I ripped it apart,
by dint of being alone and looking for traces.]

(P, 44/B, 18)

These lines from "La Semaison" emphasize the poet's desire for loss. By necessity, he must undermine any formation of meaning, any "trembling web," that begins to appear, even if it is the most precarious of constructions. Jaccottet is aware that at the moment one meaning affirms itself other possible webs of meaning are annulled. When traces begin to combine into a meaningful pattern, they have excluded other possible patterns. So the web must be undone. Possession must be refused, understanding denied, instability reaffirmed, because in a meaningless world, lying perpetually in the shadow of death, all patterns of meaning are ultimately false and distorting: "Seule demeure l'ignorance" ("Only ignorance remains"; *P,* 90), he remarks. The poet seeks dispersed signs of loss, even encourages them as in his tearing of the web, because loss generates that state of continual disappearance and absence which Jaccottet calls "le passage," the fundamental, irrefutable reality of existence, for

> même sédentaires, même casaniers, nous ne sommes jamais que des nomades. Le monde ne nous est que prêté. Il faudrait apprendre à perdre.

> [even sedentary, even homebound, we are never anything but nomads. The world is only loaned to us. We will have to learn to lose.]
> (*ATV,* 46–47)

The poetics of passage, of passing through, of *à travers,* is essential to Jaccottet's vision of the world. The *insaisissable* is an enigma that the poet's consciousness traverses without grasping or representing. It resists figuration. Through (*à travers*) the poet's sensibility and through the space of the poem moves something real—that is to say, something instantaneous, enigmatic, and *other,* which the poet tries to understand and explain, but which his images only deform or lose: "The image hides the real, distracts our gaze, all the more sometimes if it is precise and is attractive to one or other of our senses and to our daydreams" (*PFA,* 68). And yet this indefinite something, this "quelque chose— which may even be too precise a description, because it is "quelque chose, à peine quelque chose" ("something, barely something"), as Jaccottet writes of the orchard in *A travers un verger* (p. 11)—is the "insaisissable réel" (*TS,* 289) which alone makes language possible. For it is precisely what cannot be spoken that makes us speak. We can only talk about what we cannot say. Absence provokes and sustains discourse: "Je dévore comme nourriture souhaitable ce qui n'est peut-être qu'absence" ("I consume as desirable sustenance what is perhaps only absence"; *S,* 65). Through (*à travers*) the encounter with what is unseizable and unrepresentable, we come into language. It is not being that

dwells in language, but the *lack* of being: that absence, that inexpressibility, that unseizability which alone constitute the real and thus
inform our expression of it. As Roger Munier observes, it is precisely
that which makes us speak that is ultimately effaced and abolished by
our act of speaking, for the being of the real is ultimately *insaisissable:*

> L'Etre n'est rien, hors les choses qui sont. On voit bien—on sent, on
> touche, on entend—les choses qui sont, mais on ne voit pas *qu*'elles
> sont. Leur être, qui fait qu'elles sont, reste caché, s'abolit au profit
> d'elles qui sont, de leur parution pour nous. . . . L'Etre qui fait
> qu'elles nous apparaissent comme étant aussitôt s'abolit, s'efface de-
> vant elles qui sont, qui seules occupent le champ de la vision. Je ne
> verrai jamais l'être de la rose, mais seulement la rose qui est. Son être
> n'est rien d'elle, qui est. Telle est l'absence opérante, l'insistance
> abîmée, de l'Etre. C'est elle sans doute, avant toute autre invite, qui
> déjà nous fait parler.[5]

> [Being is nothing outside of the things that exist. Indeed, we see—we
> feel, we touch, we hear—things that exist, but we do not see *that* they
> exist. Their being, which makes them be, remains hidden, abolishing
> itself on behalf of their existence, their appearance for us. . . . Being,
> which makes these things appear to us as being, immediately disap-
> pears and vanishes in face of these things that are, that alone occupy
> the field of vision. I will never see the being of the rose, but only the
> rose that is. Its being has nothing to do with it, with what it is. Such is
> the enabling absence, the overwhelming insistence, of Being. It is
> an absence, undoubtedly, that, prior to any other invitation, already
> makes us speak.]

The appearance of a thing eclipses and effaces the being which that
appearance was supposed to embody. The unseizable absence of being,
resistant to any effort to speak it or give it figurative form, remains
outside the limits of our words. We cannot speak it; we can only express
the impossibility of its being spoken. The nature of the *insaisissable*, of
that which initiates language but is not transported into expression by
the language act, reveals that the perceived plenitude of a landscape,

---

5. "Ce qui nous fait parler," *Nouvelle Revue française* 416 (1 September 1987): 60–
61; hereafter cited in the text. To speak is to efface, to lie, as Jaccottet affirms—"Parler
alors semble mensonge" ("To speak is to lie"; *ALH*, 42/*SP*, 121)—and as Munier writes:
"When I say, 'The world is *real*,' when I indeed *say* it, it is no longer true, for the *real*
cannot be spoken" (*Le Visiteur qui jamais ne vient* [Paris: Lettres vives, 1983], p. 34).

like that of an orchard of blossoming almond trees, or of a summer meadow in flower, or of a snow-covered mountain peak enveloped in mist and clouds, is nothing, after all, but an irretrievable absence. It is a reality that, because we have no way to speak it, to figure it, to re-create or relive it, except by pointing to our very powerlessness to do so, can only be experienced as a lack. There is nothing to grasp, and yet this nothing is all there is. For without this absence, which no image can describe, the real would not be what it is: namely, the otherness that our language brings forth into being. What makes us speak, Munier observes, is the elemental absence that language discloses at the heart of reality, an absence of which we are unaware until language, through its failure to make it present, reveals it to us. Words continuously circle a place of emptiness:

> Absent du monde, ce qui nous fait parler l'est par force aussi bien de ce que nous disons. Il ne se "dit" que lorsque nous parlons, mais non dans ce que nous disons. Aussitôt biffé par ce que nous disons et dès que nous disons, mis à l'écart et sans voix par le mouvement même de dire. . . . Comme on ne dit jamais que la chose qu'il signale, on ne dit aussi que sa perte, à lui. Le dire est sa perte, son écart. Il n'est dire qu'en cet écart—qu'il suscite, qu'il anime tant qu'il dure, qu'il soutient de sa perte.

> [Absent from the world, what makes us speak is absent as well by force of what we say. It "expresses" itself only when we speak, but not in what we say. Immediately erased by what we say, as soon as we say it, it is banished and silenced by the very movement of speaking. . . . Because we express only the thing it designates, we express only its loss. Speaking *is* its loss, its deviation. Speaking exists only insofar as it is deviation—which it brings into being, which it enlivens for as long as possible, which it sustains by its loss.] (Munier, "Ce qui nous fait parler," p. 64)

The real that calls on us to speak is effaced by the discourse it brings into being. The real can only be spoken by that which fails to speak it.

Similarly, for Jaccottet the essence of what is real—because it is always other and different—is never present; it is this otherness of the real that provokes poetic language. Poems are "small lanterns in which the reflection of *another* light still burns"; *S*, 263; my emphasis). The poetry of the unseizable real, is, for Jaccottet, a poetry of alterity and absence:

C'est le Tout-autre que l'on cherche à saisir. Comment expliquer qu'on le cherche et ne le trouve pas, mais qu'on le cherche encore? L'illimité est le *souffle* qui nous anime.

[It is the Completely Other that one wishes to capture. How to explain that one searches for it and does not find it, but that one continues to search? The unlimited is the *breath* that gives us life.] (*S*, 39)

Alterity is the breath that animates the poet and the poem, as well as the world. If anything passes through the body of the poem, it is the otherness of the real, the fact that what the words and images of the poem speak are *not* the thing that has called out for expression, but rather the absence of the thing, the *no-thing:* "A partir du rien," Jaccottet writes, "Là est ma loi" ("To start from nothing. That is my law"; *S*, 56).[6] Thus, images are always leading the poet far from the real that he wishes to represent. Although forced to embrace images, he is exceedingly ambivalent about their role in poetic discourse:

Méfie-toi des images. Méfie-toi des fleurs. Légères comme les paroles. Peut-on jamais savoir si elles mentent, égarent, ou si elles guident? Moi qui suis de loin ramené à elles, moi qui n'ai qu'elles ou à peu près, je me mets en garde contre elles.

[Beware of images. Beware of flowers. Light as words. Can we ever know if they lie, or mislead, or guide? I, who from faraway return to them, who depend only on them, or nearly so, I am wary of them.] (*ATV*, 23)

The ideal would be to speak without images, to enjoy an unmediated

---

6. Rilke, whose writings Jaccottet has translated and whose fascination with the beauty of the orchard and the suggestiveness of its name in French inspired the series of short poems "Verger" (1926), also sees landscape as a place of otherness: "Men only began to understand Nature when they no longer understood it; when they felt that it was the Other, indifferent towards men, without senses by which to apprehend us" ("Concerning Landscape," in *Selected Works, I: Prose*, trans. G. Craig Houston [London: Hogarth Press, 1954], p. 4). Similarly, Bonnefoy associates the beginning of landscape painting with the moment when nature, no longer perceived as the seamless incarnation of God's eternal and ubiquitous presence, reveals unsettling signs of ephemerality, strangeness, and difference: "Landscape begins in art with the first sufferings of metaphysical consciousness, which is suddenly troubled by the shade that moves beneath things" ("Le Peintre dont l'ombre est le voyageur," in *Récits en rêve* [Paris: Mercure de France, 1987], p. 216).

relationship with the real; but to do so would be to renounce one's imperfect humanness:

J'aurais voulu parler sans images, simplement
pousser la porte . . .
                            J'ai trop de crainte
pour cela, d'incertitude, parfois de pitié:
on ne vit pas longtemps comme les oiseaux
dans l'évidence du ciel,
                            et retombé à terre,
on ne voit plus en eux précisément que des images
ou des rêves.

[I would have wished to speak without images, simply
To open the door . . .
                            I have too much fear
for that, too much uncertainty or, sometimes, pity:
we do not, like the birds, live long
in the clear presence of the sky,
                            and once returned to earth,
we see in them only images
or dreams.]
                            (*A la lumière d'hiver,* 49)

The intensity of pure unmediated reality throws Jaccottet back, *faute de mieux,* to images; "I have trouble," he admits, "renouncing images" (*P,* 137/*B,* 85). The poet, whose ambivalence toward images prevents him from being completely seduced by their beauty, their eloquence, and, in contrast to the simplicity of the real, their excessiveness, recognizes, however, that they can indicate the directions things in the world may take. While images can never replace things, they indeed show "how things open themselves to us and how we enter into them" (*PFA,* 17). Nevertheless, in Jaccottet's poems the mimetic power of the image is greatly diminished. All that the image can say about the thing it describes is simply "c'est cela, et c'est toujours autre chose encore" ("it's that, and it's always something else as well"; *PFA,* 18). The most successful image, therefore, is the one that refers to the otherness it cannot figure, to the unknown, whether distant or proximate, that it does not know how to recognize or master. Words, asks Jaccottet in one of his poems,

devraient-ils donc faire sentir
ce qu'ils n'atteignent pas, qui leur échappe,
dont ils ne sont pas maîtres, leur envers?

[should they give the sensation
of what they cannot reach, of what escapes them,
of what they cannot master, of their other side?]

(ALH, 82)

If landscape, as Joachim Ritter observes, is "nature made aesthetically present," an untouched space, sometimes foreign, sometimes hostile, which because it is made into something "beautiful, grand, sublime . . . becomes an aesthetic object," then the image that has been opened to the otherness of the real and forced self-consciously to confront its own metaphoricity is freed from the aestheticizing impulse that transforms nature into landscape.[7] Jaccottet's experience of the *insaisissable*, therefore, works against the aesthetic presence that language and art seek to establish. By presenting the *insaisissable* as a phenomenon of radical difference, unknowable and unrepresentable except by abstract or deictic signifiers of minimal meaning, such as *quelque chose*, or *cela*, or *l'illimité*, Jaccottet tries to ensure that the images he uses to describe the natural landscape will not produce an aesthetic presence; his images, therefore, are "distant, threatened, precarious, placed within a whole that is made coarse and opaque so as not to 'show them off,' so as not to immobilize and distort them" *(ATV, 36)*.[8]

Through the Orchard of the Real

Walking through the countryside, ever vigilant to the myriad events that transpire there, Jaccottet seeks to "seize the evasive language of

7. "Le Paysage," *Argile* 16 (Summer 1978): 36. For a more general discussion of the poetics of landscape representation, see my "Landscape and Loss in Yves Bonnefoy and Philippe Jaccottet," *French Forum* 5 (January 1980): 30–47.
8. For further discussion of Jaccottet's notion of *l'insaisissable* and his insistence on "ignorance," effacement, and passage, see Michael Bishop, "Philippe Jaccottet," in his *The Contemporary Poetry of France: Eight Studies* (Amsterdam: Rodopi, 1985), pp. 54–67; Jacques Borel, *Poésie et nostalgie* (Paris: Berger-Levrault, 1979), pp. 125–64; Anne-Marie Hammer, *Philippe Jaccottet ou l'approche de l'insaisissable* (Geneva: Eliane Vernay, 1982); Jean Onimus, *Philippe Jaccottet: Une Poétique de l'insaisissable* (Seyssel: Champ Vallon, 1982); and Jean-Luc Seylaz, *Philippe Jaccottet: Une Poésie et ses enjeux* (Lausanne: L'Aire, 1982). In addition, see the special issues that have been devoted to Jaccottet by *La Revue de Belles-Lettres* 3–4 (1975); *Versants* 11 (1987); and *Faire Part* 10–11 (Fall 1987); and the

the landscape where I live" (*TS*, 321). To this end, he strives to find words that will not betray what the countryside is communicating to him. But what calls out to be spoken, thus causing the poet to speak, is never carried over into the discourse he creates. The call of the real is abolished by the language that expresses it.[9] Things translated into words are easy to manipulate and to substitute one for the other, because they have lost their being-in-the-world, as Jaccottet affirms: "facile à dire! et trop facile de jongler / avec le poids des choses une fois changées en mots!" ("easy to say, and easy too to play / with weighty matters when transformed to words"; *ALH*, 77/*Selected Poems*, 133).

The prose poem and the self-conscious meditation that compose Jaccottet's *A travers un verger* (1975) are an effort to resuscitate the memory of a vibrant and radiant experience of landscape: first, the orchard of flowering almond trees near his home in Grignan in the Drôme, through which the poet had walked one gray April day; second, the poetic text, abandoned several times between May 1971 and January 1974, through which Jaccottet, struggling with the inadequacy of word and image, tries in a different manner to find his way.[10] In both instances, the poet passes through a space, either of quivering blossoms or of trembling words. It is the passage *through* the orchard, *à travers le verger*—both physically and mentally, in reality and in memory, on foot and with pen in hand—which brings Jaccottet to understand the opposition between the limits of writing and the limitlessness of the real. Concerning the object of his perception—namely, the trembling petals of the almond blossoms—Jaccottet has no illusions, for, as he writes in one of his poems: "je passe, je m'étonne, et je ne peux en dire plus" ("I pass, I am filled with wonder, and I can say no more"; *Pensées sous les nuages*, 22).[11]

---

two volumes of *Sud* titled *Jaccottet* 32–33 (1980), and *Alentour de Philippe Jaccottet* 80–81 (1989). Finally, see the proceedings of the colloquium "Philippe Jaccottet, poète et traducteur," held at the Université de Pau in 1984 and published by the Centre de Recherches sur la poésie contemporaine in *Cahiers de l'Université* (Pau), no. 3 (1985).

9. "The unspoken call, which by definition is absent from speech," Munier writes, "is precisely the lack that excavates writing, that points to its insufficiency" ("Ce qui nous fait parler," p. 65).

10. *A travers un verger* has not yet received the full critical attention it deserves. However, for an excellent discussion of one aspect of the work, see Marie-Claire Dumas, "'Ne Te Retourne Pas': Sur le paragraphe liminaire de la seconde partie d'*A travers un verger*," in *La Poésie de Philippe Jaccottet*, ed. Marie-Claire Dumas (Paris: Champion, 1986), pp. 73–82. And for a brief, yet insightful, discussion of *A travers un verger* in the context of Jaccottet's general poetic concerns, see Mark Treharne, "Postface à l'édition anglaise d'*A travers un verger*," *Sud* 80–81 (1989): 215–22.

11. Many contemporary French poets have been attracted by the shimmering beauty of almond trees in bloom during the first days of spring. Jaccottet describes their

Several times in *A travers un verger* Jaccottet tries to reconstruct his experience of that cloudy April day. In retrospect, he knows that two things are true: first, that the splendor of the orchard filled him with wonder; second, that, unable to comprehend its enigma, he has failed to find the "right image" for it (pp. 23–24). Wonder and failure are mixed, as they are in so many of Jaccottet's landscapes. The problem may lie in the poet's dependence on a memory that resonates with nostalgic longing. His landscape description is not done *sur le motif;* it lacks immediacy from the outset. Year after year, at the beginning of each spring, Jaccottet had intended, he tells us, to describe the almond trees at their fugitive moment of flowering so as to remember what he calls their "lesson" (p. 9). But always some other thing or event has distracted him. When he does finally put paper to pen, the blossoms have long dropped from the branches. It is no surprise, then, that the trees have now become "a different kind of almond tree," whose flowers seem more confused, more "insaisissable," more akin to "un brouillard à peine blanc" ("a barely white mist"; p. 10).

Through the tentative intertwinings of word and image in the first part of *A travers un verger,* Jaccottet attempts to capture the essence of the vibrant, luminous orchard he has experienced. It is a difficult task, because the words do not always seem right; they are off-target, hesitant, misleading, wrong. Jaccottet offers a word, a thought, then qualifies and modifies it before moving on, with a sense of resigned failure, to some other subject: "I do not want to affirm anything here, in this moment. I venture a word, an image, a thought, I withdraw or abandon them, that's it; then I leave" (pp. 17–18). An example of this "poetics of rectification" is evident in Jaccottet's continual effort to capture the trembling whiteness of the almond blossoms. He struggles to evoke the delicate, shimmering multiplicity of their petals in the most tentative, halting, and questioning manner, and with the lightest possible touch, as if too rich a vocabulary, too intricate a syntax, too "poetic" or "painterly" a description would make the perception disappear. The flowering of the trees, Jaccottet writes, is "above all of a white less pure and less dazzling than that of a single flower, seen from close up" (p. 10). It is "un brouillard à peine blanc, en suspension au-dessus

blossoming in his notebook entries for 1960, 1966, and 1967 (*S*, 31–32, 95, and 124, respectively). Pierre-Albert Jourdan compares flowering almond trees to falling snow, a cathedral, a constellation of stars, a winged fire, an "explosion of Life," and the movements of the absolute (*Les Sandales de Paille* [Paris: Mercure de France, 1987], pp. 161, 162–63, 267, and 336). For Bonnefoy, the almond tree, whose flowers last only an instant but contain "the imperishable part of life," is an image of the copresence of life and death, of light and darkness (*Dans le leurre du seuil*, in *PO*, 268–69 and 272–73).

de la terre encore terreuse" ("a barely white mist hanging over the dull
earth"; p. 10); it is a "bourdonnement blanc" ("white buzzing"). Not
only is the landscape in a state of blurred suspension; so is the language
describing it. Even the adjective "white" is called into question:

> "Blanc" est déjà trop dire, qui évoque une surface nette, renvoyant
> un éclat blanc. Là, c'était sans aucun éclat (et pas transparent pour
> autant). Timide, gris, terne? Pas davantage. Quelque chose de multi-
> ple, cela oui, un essaim, de multiplié: des milliers de petites choses,
> ou présences, ou taches, ou ailes, légères—en suspens, de nouveau,
> comme à chaque printemps—; une sorte d'ébullition fraîche; un
> brouillard, s'il existait un brouillard sans humidité, sans mélancolie,
> où l'on ne risque pas de se perdre; quelque chose, à peine quelque
> chose . . .
>
> Essaim, écume, neige: les vieilles images reviennent, elles sont
> pour le moment les moins disparates. Rien de mieux.

["White" is already saying too much; it suggests a clean surface giving
off a white radiance. But things, there, are without any radiance (and
not at all transparent). Reserved, gray, dull? Nothing more. Something multiple, myriad, yes, a swarm: thousands of small things, or
presences, or spots, or wings, weightless—in suspension once again,
as is the case every springtime—a kind of fresh effervescence; a fog,
if there ever existed a fog without moisture, without melancholy, in
which we do not risk getting lost; something, barely something . . .

Swarm, froth, snow: old images return, being for the moment the
least incongruous. Nothing better.] (Pp. 10–11)

The passage moves notationally from subject to subject, affirming a
perception and then qualifying it in an effort to make it more precise,
more exact. Parenthetical expressions, questions, sentence fragments,
dashes, qualifying prepositions or adverbs (*sans, à peine*), ellipses, all
work to undo the tendency of words to say too much. But in the
movement toward greater precision and exactness, the image of the
landscape becomes more indistinct and unfocused. Mentally walking
in circles around the almond trees, trying poetically to seize the luminous simplicity of what in another time and another language might
have been called the "epiphany of the real," Jaccottet wends his way
from image to image, passing from noun to noun—"quelque chose,"
"essaim," "présences," "taches," "ailes," "ébullition," "brouillard," "éc-
ume," "neige"—with little or no further elaboration. When all is said

and done, the best description of the shimmering orchard is the most vague, the most tentative, the most imprecise and immediate: namely, the one that, like a breeze lightly touching the almond blossoms, says in the most tentative and quivering way that they are "quelque chose, *à peine* quelque chose . . ." ("something, *barely* something . . ."; p. 11; my emphasis).

This description is only a first attempt. A few paragraphs later, Jaccottet returns to his experience of the orchard. This time, however, adding a new image to the representation, which forces the other elements of the landscape to rearrange themselves, he creates a different descriptive configuration:

> Peut-être était-ce tout de même assez pareil à de la neige, à un nuage de neige en suspens, arrêté un instant dans sa chute, au-dessus du sol—à cause de ce blanc pas éclatant et encore un peu froid, frileux, et de la multiplicité des fleurs. Un murmure de neige?

> [Perhaps, it was somewhat akin to snow, a cloud of snow in suspension above the earth, immobilized an instant in its fall—all because of this whiteness, undazzling and still a little cold or chilly, all because of the myriads of blossoms. A murmur of snow?] (P. 12)

With haikulike intensity, subsequent paragraphs briefly evoke other images, which are then quickly abandoned. The almond trees first resemble a flock of birds preparing to fly away, then a hovering presence that has been momentarily immobilized, and, finally, a nebula, a milky cloud, of stars (pp. 13–14). And behind this chain of images lies the poet's awareness that the landscape of the real, which he is trying vainly to represent—through a poetic discourse whose errancy and tentativeness are mimetic of the fragile nature of reality—is too light, too airy, too immaterial to be seized:

> Sans poids, presque sans forme, et surprenant, émerveillant chaque fois. Passé presque inaperçu. Quelque chose qui se poserait là, précaire, une brève rumeur.

> [Weightless, almost formless, and each time surprising, wondrous. Passing almost unnoticed. Something that tentatively settles there, an ephemeral din.] (P. 13)

The orchard is an enigma; it is a *cela*, a *quelque chose*, a *rien*, so ephemeral that it defies memory and representation. Only these neutral pronouns, these signifiers of minimal and laconic assertion spoken in an instant as it were, can possibly express the flash of the real as it bursts forth from the orchard.[12] The whiteness of the almond petals seems to emerge from nothingness itself (p. 15) and to be sustained by the insubstantiality of the air. The orchard exists on the threshold of nonbeing, that space of absence, lack, and unseizability into which the landscape event recedes after its brief appearance and without which the orchard would not be what it is. Through (*à travers*) its very disappearance into the realm of the *insaisissable,* the orchard comes to express itself. The real is precisely that which it cannot say it is and which is therefore articulated by the expressiveness of this nonsaying. It is the surging light of being which the shutter of language is too slow to capture, but whose presence is contained in the trace it leaves behind. The impossible task Jaccottet has set for himself is the translation into words of a perception that has occurred in the blink of an eye (*ATV,* 18). In his chance encounter with the radiance of the real, as it explodes in the snowy cloud of the almond trees, the poet experiences "ce qui scintille et va s'éteindre" ("what sparkles and grows dim"; *P,* 65), a plenitude that in an instant will be transformed into emptiness, a presence that is only real because it is an absence.

The beginning of the second part of *A travers un verger,* with its indictment of images—"Méfie-toi des images. Méfie-toi des fleurs. Légères comme les paroles" ("Beware of images. Beware of flowers. Light as words"; p. 23)—calls into question the landscape description of the work's first part. In the realm of discourse and in the domain of memory, everything is by necessity mediated; everything is either image or word. Nothing exists without the assistance of intermediaries, without a poetics of the *à travers:*

> Qu'ils disent légereté ou qu'ils disent douleur, les mots ne sont jamais que des mots. Faciles. A de certains moments, devant certaines réalités, ils m'irritent, ou ils me font horreur; et moi *à travers* eux, qui continue à m'en servir: cette façon d'être assis à une table, le dos tourné aux autres et au monde, et de n'être plus capable, à la fin, que de cela.

> [Whether they express levity or pain, words are only words. Easy. At certain moments, before certain realities, they annoy or disgust me; and I, *through* them, who continue to use them: this way of sitting at a

---

12. According to Jaccottet, a word such as *cela* signifies "the thing we continuously pursue but that cannot be spoken" (*PFA,* 153 n.1).

table, keeping one's back turned to others and the world, and being in the end only able to do that.] (P. 28; my emphasis)

Words turn the poet away from the real, the particular, the immediate, from "l'intimement vécu" ("the intimately lived"; *S,* 156). They drive him into another world distant from the real one; here, he is forced to work not with sensual or immediate forms of expression but with "the dust or soot of words" (*ATV,* 46), with crumbling traces or blackened residues of absent things:

> Comme on est vite entraîné, en écrivant, en rêvant, en "pensant," loin des choses, loin du réel! Comme se dissout vite une saveur qui est la seule chose essentielle!

> [By writing, dreaming, "thinking," how quickly we are drawn far-away from things, from the real! How quickly dissipates their savor, the only essential thing!] (*ATV,* 46)

The Face in the Orchard

Throughout *A travers un verger,* and particularly in the second part, Jaccottet's vision of the real is consistently ambivalent. He oscillates between one pole and another, lamenting, for example, the loss of the real which words provoke, but then cautiously asserting that certain "true" words can protect us, can help us to live (p. 31), can leave "a very weak residue of hope" (p. 29). He criticizes the facticity of images, but then lets his text proliferate with several highly imaginative metaphors: images that show the impact of death on writing (it is like a stick pushed into an ant hill); images that represent the role of words (they resemble crisscrossing ferries, tugboats, and barges, whose intersecting paths create "a network"); and images that represent the nature of life (it is like a work of music in which the dissonances outnumber the harmonies). Jaccottet admits that there is indeed a place for images in writing, as long as they are articulated with the same precarity, finitude, and mortality that menace the real, in which they participate. But the most striking and repeated image of *A travers un verger*—the one that perhaps best explains Jaccottet's ambivalence and vacillation—is an affirmation of the fundamental duality of being:

> J'ai toujours eu dans l'esprit, sans bien m'en rendre compte, une sorte de balance. Sur un plateau il y avait la douleur, la mort, sur

l'autre la beauté de la vie. Le premier portait toujours un poids beaucoup plus lourd, le second, presque rien que d'impondérable. Mais il m'arrivait de croire que l'impondérable pût l'emporter, par moments. Je vois à présent que la plupart des pages que j'ai écrites sont sous le signe de cette pesée, de cette oscillation.

[I have always had in mind, without being fully aware of it, the image of a scale. On one pan were pain and death, on the other the beauty of life. The former always held a much heavier weight; on the latter rested almost nothing but lightness itself. But I came to believe that lightness may at times triumph. I see now that most of the pages I have written are under the sign of this balancing, of this oscillation.] (Pp. 25–26)

Ideally, Jaccottet would like to bring the two scales together, even fuse them, if such a synthesis of the forces of beauty and death were possible. He seeks a vision of the real which will simultaneously sing the world's beauty and mourn its loss. Death and beauty constitute the real, but they are beyond the limits of figurative language. The poetic work, the prose text, and even the description of the orchard are insipid and irritating because they enclose themselves in an hermetically sealed world of artificial light, while outside, in the world of the real, sickness and time "work to extract screams, to flay" (p. 35). Death undoes writing, melts the glue of sentences, rips the page into shreds:

C'est comme si un corps réel, ignoblement maltraité par les années, rien que par les années . . . , déchirait la page où sans peine, sans risque, les mots voudraient continuer à s'écrire; et tout à coup, comme sous le bâton dans la fourmilière, ils se troublent, ils se débandent—et il n'est pas sûr qu'ils recommencent ailleurs leur travail peut-être vain.

[It's as if a real body, disgracefully mistreated by the years and only the years . . . , tore up the page where, without difficulty or danger, words wanted to continue being written; and suddenly, as when a stick is pushed into an ant hill, they become confused and are routed—without any certainty that they can begin their possibly futile work somewhere else.] (P. 28)

Confronted with the nothingness of death, speech is meaningless, as Jaccottet eloquently affirms in his long poem "Parler." Speaking involves no risk. One can use words at will without being physically touched by them. The word, "blood," for example, leaves no stain on the page. Death and pain are, therefore, radical experiences of inexpressible otherness:

C'est autre chose, et pire, ce qui fait un être
se recroqueviller sur lui-même, reculer
tout au fond de la chambre, appeler à l'aide
n'importe qui, n'importe comment:
c'est ce qui n'a ni forme, ni visage, ni aucun nom,
ce qu'on ne peut apprivoiser dans les images
heureuses, ni soumettre aux lois des mots,
ce qui déchire la page
comme cela déchire la peau,
ce qui empêche de parler en autre langue que de bête.

[It is something else, and worse, that makes a human being
shrivel up in himself, cringe
in the corner of the bedroom, call to anyone,
in anyway, for help:
it is what has neither form, nor face, nor any name,
what we cannot tame through felicitous images,
nor submit to the laws of words,
what tears the page
as it rips the flesh,
what prevents speaking any other language but the animal's.]

                                                              (*ALH*, 44)

Jaccottet's recognition that, as Bonnefoy has written, "*what is* transcends all fiction"[13] leads to a vision of the real which is always double and which, like light, involves both brightness and shadow. The poet discovers that within the radiant orchard lies a somber reflection:

A travers l'heureux brouillard des amandiers, il n'est plus tout à fait sûr que ce soit la lumière que je vois s'épanouir, mais un vieux visage

13. "Hommage à Jorge Luis Borges," *Le Débat*, no. 46 (September–November 1987): 182; reprinted as "Jorge Luis Borges," in *VP*, 305–17. Bonnefoy goes on to explain that

écrire nie la réalité qu'ont les êtres là devant nous, en leur instant et leur lieu, nous détruisons cet absolu même que nous devrions respecter, aimer—cette seule réalité qui soit fondement pour l'amour. En bref, la fiction trahit la présence.

[writing negates the reality human beings have in their time and place, as they stand before us; we destroy this absolute that we should respect: namely the act of loving—the only reality that is the foundation of love. Fiction, therefore, betrays presence.] (P. 183)

angoissé qu'il m'arrive de surprendre sous le mien, dans le miroir, avec étonnement.

[Through the blissful mist of the almond trees it is no longer entirely certain that it is the light I see appear, but an old, anguished face that, with amazement, I happen to surprise under my own in the mirror.] (Pp. 26–27)

Jaccottet's descriptions of the sublime beauty of a landscape always contain intimations of mortality, which acknowledge the imminent disappearance of the precarious scene or of the aging observer who witnesses it. The poet forces himself to see both sides of the real and to make his words vibrate with the mortal rhythms of existence, as he does at the end of *A travers un verger:*

Voici ce que j'ai vu tel jour d'avril, comme j'errais sans savoir, comme ma vie s'écoulait lentement de moi sans que j'y pense; on aurait dit qu'un nuage de neige flottait au-dessus du sol sous le ciel gris—et si moi, à cet instant précis de ma vie, je n'avais à me plaindre d'aucune douleur précise, je sais que je ne perds rien pour attendre, que j'arriverai un jour dans les régions où l'on n'a plus aucune force pour lutter, alors même que cela contre quoi il faudrait lutter gagne en force d'heure en heure; moi, future loque, avant de basculer dans la terreur ou l'abrutissement, j'aurai écrit que mes yeux ont vu *quelque chose* qui, un instant, les a niés.

[This is what I saw on such a day in April, as I unconsciously wandered and as my life slowly ebbed from me without a thought on my part; one would have said that a cloud of snow floated above the earth under the gray sky—and if, at this exact moment of my life, I had no particular pain about which to complain, I also knew that I had nothing to lose by waiting, that I would arrive one day at the place where one no longer has the strength to struggle, and where what one must struggle with gains force even by the hour; I, future pile of rags, before sinking into terror and exhaustion, shall write that my eyes have seen *something* that in an instant has blinded them.] (Pp. 48–49; my emphasis)

Once again, the most that can be said about the landscape, the most that can be learned from one's uncertain experience of it, is that "something"—it is not clear exactly what—has been perceived. But this is a "something" (a "quelque chose") that cannot be stated or described. Only the fact that something was there and that it was experienced can be attested to. For the gaze of the poet is negated by whatever it has seen. The word "something" is the sign and trace of what was annulled in an instant, in an unrepresentable flash of light and being. The undeniable reality of the real—be it the radiance of beauty or the darkness of death—is that as the *insaisissable* it dwells in the "beyond" of representation.

Surrounded by the flowering almond trees, the poet, torn between visions of beauty and intimations of death, between the brilliant orchard and the anguished face he sees within its light, feels both at home and in exile; this is a place of security and vulnerability. And yet, he cannot help being drawn to the warm, enveloping intimacy that dreams, reveries and other such illusions create to hide the horror of death or soften its brutal reality. He harbors an old belief in the power of magic to transport him into the Unknown:

> Une fois de plus, il doit s'agir du désir profond, craintif, de passer sans peine un seuil, d'être emporté dans la mort comme par une magicienne. Un tourbillon de neige, qui aveugle, mais qui serait aussi une multiplicité de caresses, un étoilement de bouches fraîches, tout autour de vous—et dans cette enveloppe, grâce à ce sortilège, on est ravi dans l'inconnu, on aborde à une Terre promise.

> [Once again, it has to be a question of the profound and frightening desire to cross effortlessly over a threshold, to be carried away unto death as if by a sorceress. A whirlwind of snow that is blinding but is also a multitude of caresses, the filling of the night sky with cool mouths surrounding you—and in this mantle, through this spell, one is carried off into the unknown, one arrives at a Promised Land.]
> (Pp. 24–25)

Even though he acknowledges that this is a "profoundly interior reverie" and struggles against its seductive power, aware that he must destroy it "as one angrily tears up a page" (p. 25), nevertheless the attraction is great. He knows that "no magic lasts when the body is attacked" (p. 32); yet, this magic has the power to transport him effortlessly into another world. It appeals to a hidden desire for transcendence, so deeply entrenched in him that even the awareness that it is an illusion, a mirage, cannot fully suppress its spell:

> J'ai toujours su que cette métamorphose n'avait rien de "réel," que ce n'était qu'un jeu ou, si on veut, un mensonge de la lumière. J'ai

compris aussi depuis longtemps que, si ce jeu me touchait, c'est qu'il
correspond à un désir caché, qu'il le figure hors de moi, qu'il le mime
devant moi: celui de l'effacement magique de tout obstacle.

[I always knew that there was nothing "real" about this metamorphosis, that it was only a game, or, if you like, an illusion of light. I have
also known for a long time that, if this game affected me, it is because
it corresponds to a hidden desire, which it represents outside of me,
which it imitates before my eyes: the desire for the magical obliteration of all obstacles.] (Pp. 33–34)

The knowledge that a magical transcendence is impossible does not
prevent the desire for such transcendence from often appearing in *A
travers un verger,* although it is always enveloped by the poet's self-
critical consciousness. Jaccottet bows before the supreme power of
death and yet in the same breath wishes fervently that "something"
unknown, or absolute, or other—"something" beyond language and
thought—will appear suddenly in the here and now of temporal being
and that in a burst of light it will give him an experience of *l'insaisissable.*
The moving and eloquent final paragraph of *A travers un verger* tries to
resolve the ambivalence that the dialectical relationship of beauty and
death and of joy and horror has posed for the poet, who vacillates
hopelessly between the poles of the real. It proposes a way out of the
orchard, and of Jaccottet's struggle to write about the orchard, so the
poet—now able to pass through this radiant space, which magic or
unconscious desire has transformed into a place of light and imma-
teriality, but which the opaque shadow of death has marked with the
image of a tormented face—can declare in word as well as deed, in
writing as well as in life, that he has moved "à travers un verger":

Peut-être y a-t-il une espèce d'issue. Car ce qui m'a arrêté dans mon
élan—quand j'allais franchir le verger comme un réfugié la frontière
qui le sauve—est si dur, si massif, si opaque, cela échappe si définitivement à la compréhension, à l'acceptation que, ou bien il faut lui
concéder la victoire absolue, après quoi il ne sera plus possible de
survivre qu'hébété, ou bien il faut imaginer *quelque chose* d'aussi
totalement inimaginable et improbable qui fasse sauter ce mur, *quelque chose* dont ces vues seraient des éclats épars, venus comme d'un
autre espace, étrangers à l'espace, en tous cas différents du monde
extérieur non moins que du monde intérieur à la rencontre desquels
ils surgissent—sans qu'on puisse jamais les saisir, ni s'en assurer la
possession.

[Perhaps, there is some kind of resolution. Because what stopped my momentum, as I was going to cross the orchard like a refugee the frontier that saves him, is so hard, so massive, so opaque, and it so definitely escapes comprehension and acceptance, that either we must concede it absolute victory—after which we can only survive in a state of bewilderment—or we must imagine *something* so totally unimaginable and improbable that it would bring down this wall: *something* of which these vistas would be scattered flashes that— seeming to come from another space or unbounded by any space or just different from the exterior as well as the interior world, out of whose encounter they arise—we could never possibly grasp or possess.] (P. 50; my emphasis)

Conclusion

The landscape of the real is unpossessable. What one carries away from the sight of a river meandering through a valley, of mountains bathed in the red light of a setting sun, of birds gliding on invisible currents of air, and of almond trees amurmur with bees and shimmering in the heat of their blossoms is no more than an imprecise image blurred by the feelings, desires, and longings it has stirred. The landscape, as Jaccottet observes, is only given to us on loan. We do not inhabit it but, like nomads, wander errantly and in error (*ATV*, 46). Our transactions with the natural world are informed by loss and absence, experiences of deprivation which are the pretext for writing. For we only speak that which cannot be spoken, we only imagine that which no image can fully convey, we only experience that which no word can completely express.

What emerges from language is the unrepresentable radiance of an absence. Poetry points continuously to the promised land it cannot enter, to the threshold it cannot cross, to the landscape that is always distant. But there is always *something* that poetry points to, even if that something, that "quelque chose," be an absence or a lack that cannot be rescued from nothingness. The orchard of the real, where beauty and death, light and shadow, joy and horror coexist, may ultimately be the place of *l'insaisissable;* but a spark, a glimmer, an echo, a trace, a "presque rien" (*S*, 57) remain. Perhaps we can now understand why Jaccottet gives so much meaning to the insignificant, unremarkable, minimal words—the adverbs, conjunctions, impersonal pronouns—he uses. The distinction between being and nothingness, memory and oblivion, presence and absence, and therefore the only hope we can possibly find in this precarious and uncertain world, may lie at the very edge of an adverb, for, as Jaccottet writes: "l'image du verger, *à peine* la retenir" ("the image of the orchard, hold onto it, but *barely*"; *ATV*, 47; my emphasis).

PART THREE

The Poetic Narrative of Loss

Je cherche et je trouve presque, et je perds.

[I search, I nearly find, and I lose.]
                    —André Frénaud, "Où est mon pays?"

In this emptiness only the
singing sometimes almost fills.
                    —Galway Kinnell, "Brother of My Heart"

Only one thing remained reachable, close and secure amid all losses: language. Yes, language. In spite of everything, it remained secure against loss. But it had to go through its own lack of answers, through terrifying silence, through the thousand darknesses of murderous speech. It went through. It gave me no words for what was happening, but went through it. Went through and could resurface, "enriched" by it all.
                    —Paul Celan, "Speech on the Occasion of Receiving
                    the Literature Prize of the
                    Free Hanseatic City of Bremen"

CHAPTER 8

THE NOMAdic WRITING of
Exile: Edmond Jabès

La vie ne fait jamais qu'imiter le livre, et ce livre lui-même n'est qu'un
tissu de signes, imitation perdue, infiniment reculée.

[Life never does more than imitate the book, and the book itself is
only a tissue of signs, an imitation that is lost, infinitely deferred.]
   —Roland Barthes, "La Mort de l'auteur"

Le premier mot est mot de deuil.

[The first word is a word in mourning.]
   —Edmond Jabès, *Un étranger avec, sous
le bras, un livre de petit format.*

  There was once a time when to put thoughts or feelings into
words, to write them on paper, to make them present and visible in the
distinct shapes and dark lines of letters, assured their future. To write
black on white was to give reality, if not immortality, to the shadowy,
imprecise experiences of subjective life. Writing was a means of preservation, of halting the erosion of thought, feeling, and memory caused
by the passing of time. By inscribing words on a page, a writer was able
to grasp permanently an elusive idea, to transfix a fleeting impression,
and to seize an ephemeral perception before it disappeared.
  In the last century, however, confidence in the indelibility of the
written word has waned. Modern poets no longer look at the poem as
an unchanging, ineffaceable monument of feeling and perception; it
has lost the presence it was once able to articulate. No longer is the
poetic word a place of stability and rootedness; no longer is the white
page a haven for permanent, centered speech. Rather, they have become places of mobility and dispersion. Writing, like the life it tries to

represent, is perceived as being perpetually in movement. It is a language fragmented by absent, inexpressible realities; torn apart by lacks and lacunae, which defer its completion; and fractured by flaws, which weaken its expressive power. The poem is, in John Ashbery's metaphor, "only a vast unravelling."[1] The meanings words convey disappear or are altered at the moment of their inscription; they are displaced, if not effaced, by other words destined to suffer in turn a similar depletion. Words roam the open white spaces of the page searching for the permanence, fullness, and certainty of meaning they once possessed. Poetic language has become, in Mallarmé's expression, a "centre de suspens vibratoire" ("center of vibratory suspension").[2] Words, he once explained (commenting on his experimentally modernist poem "Un Coup de dés jamais n'abolira le hasard"), sail across an opened book like a pitching vessel tossing to and fro on a whitecapped, endless sea. The words in a poem are mobile, errant forms, which either congregate to create new configurations or move apart in order to initiate other patterns and relationships. "Writing," Roland Barthes argues, "ceaselessly posits meaning ceaselessly to evaporate it, carrying out a systematic exemption of meaning."[3] The poem is a shifting, unstable terrain, filled with traces of lost correspondences. Poetic writing has its own particular kind of mobility, an impermanence that belongs to the "extra-vagant" nature of meaning itself. Nomadic in form and intention, this is a poetry that presents a mimesis of the world's errancy. "The music / in poems," writes A. R. Ammons, "is different, / points to nothing, / traps no / realities, takes / no game, but / by the motion of / its motion / resembles / what, moving, is."[4]

Decentered and discontinuous, its meanings effaced by the perpetual mobility of the writing, the poem is the tenuous expression by a poet compelled, in the words of Edmond Jabès, "to roam nomadically

1. "Pyrography," in *Houseboat Days* (Harmondsworth, Eng.: Penguin, 1977), p. 10.

2. "Le Mystère dans les lettres," in *Oeuvres complètes*, Bibliothèque de la Pléiade (Paris: Gallimard, 1945), p. 386. For an examination of Mallarmé's and Jabès differing conceptions of the Book, see Serge Meitinger, "Mallarmé et Jabès devant le livre: Analyse d'une divergence culturelle," in *Ecrire le livre: Autour d'Edmond Jabès*, ed. Richard Stamelman and Mary Ann Caws (Seyssel: Champ Vallon, 1989), pp. 133–45, and Walter A. Strauss, "*Le Livre des questions* de Jabès et la question du livre," in *Ecrire le livre*, pp. 295–98.

3. "La Mort de l'auteur," in *Essais critiques*, 4: *Le Bruissement de la langue* (Paris: Seuil, 1984), p. 66 ["The Death of the Author," in *Image, Music, Text*, trans. and ed. Stephen Heath (New York: Hill and Wang, 1977), p. 147; hereafter cited in the text].

4. "Motion," in *Collected Poems, 1951–1971* (New York: W. W. Norton, 1972), pp. 146–47.

in the infinite expanse of the word" (*Le Livre des ressemblances*, 120).[5] Diaspora is the condition of all writing. Because the past can never be recovered in its full intensity, because the immediacy of experience can never be translated into words, because the objects of longing are forever eluding the grasp of desire, because the self is so plural and protean as to be always different from the definition or expression words may give it, and because the notion of a beginning or an origin is a construction of human invention—a fiction bespeaking the longing for an idealized, perfectly complete but nonexistent source—language is therefore in a state of profound and irreversible exile: a rootlessness that reflects the essential separation and distance at the center of being.

Writing and Distance

Few poets have made the errancy of language and being as central to their work as Jabès. For him, to live in exile means to write in exile; he

5. References to Jabès's works are cited in the text according to the following abbreviations; all texts were published in Paris by Gallimard, unless otherwise noted.

A	*Aely* (1972).
CSC	*Le Livre des marges, 1: Ça suit son cours* (Montpellier: Fata Morgana, 1975).
DDD	*Le Livre des marges, 2: Dans la double dépendance du dit* (Montpellier: Fata Morgana, 1984).
DL	*Du désert au livre: Entretiens avec Marcel Cohen* (Paris: Pierre Belfond, 1980).
E	*Elya* (1969).
El	*El, ou le dernier livre* (1973).
ESB	*Un étranger avec, sous le bras, un livre de petit format* (1989).
II	*Le Livre des ressemblances, 3: L'Ineffaçable, l'inaperçu* (1980).
"Interview"	"Book of the Dead: An Interview with Edmond Jabès," by Paul Auster, in *The Sin of the Book: Edmond Jabès*, ed. Eric Gould (Lincoln: University of Nebraska Press, 1985), pp. 3–25.
LD	*Le Livre du dialogue* (1984).
LP	*Le Livre du partage* (1987).
LQ	*Le Livre des questions* (1963).
LR	*Le Livre des ressemblances* (1976).
LY	*Le Livre des questions, 2: Le Livre de Yukel* (1964).
MM	*La Mémoire et la main* (Montpellier: Fata Morgana, 1987).
P	*Le Parcours* (1985).
PLS	*Le Petit Livre de la subversion hors de soupçon* (1982).
RL	*Le Livre des questions, 3: Le Retour au livre* (1965).
SD	*Le Livre des ressemblances, 2: Le Soupçon, le désert* (1978).
Y	*Yaël* (1967).

Translations of Jabès are taken from the following sources, all translated by Rosmarie Waldrop and published in Middletown, Conn., by Wesleyan University Press: *The Book of Questions*, 1: *The Book of Questions* (1976); *The Book of Questions*, 2 and 3: *The Book of Yukel, Return to the Book* (1977); *The Book of Questions*, 4, 5, and 6: *Yaël, Elya, Aely* (1983); *The Book of Questions*, 7: *El, or the Last Book* (1984); *The Book of Dialogue* (1987). All other translations of Jabès are my own.

perceives existence and writing as corresponding situations, as facing mirrors, which reflect each other's errant, circling, hesitant motions. The writer, like the exiled Jew, entrusts his being to written language until that being becomes a language in its own right. Writer and Jew share a similar fate, because "every writer in some way experiences the Jewish condition, because every writer, every creator, lives in a kind of exile" ("Interview," 12). Both are tormented by an "ancient word" (*Le Retour au livre*, 60/195), whose source lies in a catastrophic event of loss and separation: namely, the breaking of the tablets of Law, which initiated the Jew's exile from divine language and which is a metaphor for the writer's perpetual separation from the power of pure and total expression. As Jabès asserts, "every word is, primarily, the echo of a lost word" (*Le Livre du partage*, 65); "the place of the book is forever a lost place" (*Ça suit son cours*, 53).

Because writing accomplishes an expansion of being and is "an opening by which life will become text" (*Le Soupçon, le désert*, 81), the errant nature of existence is translated into an unending book with unfixed pages and ephemeral words: "The book of errancy could only be the errancy of the book" (*L'Ineffaçable, l'inaperçu*, 85). The text exists in a state of vacancy and *déracinement* profoundly different from the state of plenitude which once prevailed in the preexilic, prelapsarian homeland of the divine word: "Writing alone is movement" (*Dans la double dépendance du dit*, 25). It is intimately joined to a temporal world, whose precariousness and discontinuity it echoes:

> La parole doit sa force, moins à la certitude qu'elle marque, en s'articulant, qu'au manque, à l'abîme, à l'incertitude inventive de son dit. . . . —Ce manque fut mon lieu.
>
> [Words owe their strength less to the certainty of their articulation than to the lack, the abyss, the inventive uncertainty in what they say. . . . "This lack was my place."] (*Le Livre du dialogue*, 45, 60/27, 37)

For Jabès, there is no distance between world and text; both are identical in their instability. They share the same pangs of separation, the same despair of loss, and the same existence founded on the errancy of meaning. The book *is* the world, for it is writing that calls the universe into existence:

> Nous n'existons que dans et par le nom; . . . nommer c'est donner existence à l'être, à l'objet nommés; . . . l'on reconnaît que rien n'ex-

iste hors du livre, que l'univers est dans le livre, c'est-à-dire qu'il est, lui-même, le livre par lequel il se fait univers à travers chacun de ses feuillets.

[We exist only in and by the name; . . . naming gives existence to the being and object named; . . . one realizes that nothing exists outside of the book, that the universe is in the book; that is to say, it is, itself, the book by which it becomes the universe through each of its pages.] (*SD*, 92)

Like the world, Jabès's books are in exile.[6] His poetry of aphorisms, questions, quotations, prayers, dialogues, meditations, commentaries, enigmas, riddles, fragments, parables, erasures—an encyclopedia of the diverse forms of expression in the history of writing—is achieved by a rhetoric of discontinuity, which mirrors the decenteredness of nomadic existence. "I write," he observes, "in order to maintain words in their separation" (*LR*, 96); this is because "on ne parle vraiment que dans la distance. Il n'y a de parole que séparée" ("one only speaks truly at a distance. There is no word but separated"; *DDD*, 83). Jabès's language of separation transports the absences and losses of Jewish history into the diaspora of the book. The white spaces between words, the margins that surround the writing, the open-ended quality of the discourse, the infinite *mise-en-abyme* of questions (to which no answers, but instead more questions, are given), the fragmentary quotations of imaginary rabbis, the absence of narrative continuity, and the progression of self-displacing books circling around one another like an infinitely extensible spiral—these are the hallmarks of Jabès's *oeuvre*, which presents more than just a monumental mimesis of exile. His books do not only re-create the experience of exile; they *are* the experience. The void of exilic existence is buried deep within the ephemeral meanings and fragmented forms of Jabès's words. History is transformed into text, world into book, and the traces of footprints on the desert sand into the evanescent signs of words on a page.

Readers experience Jabès's writing as an unending digression in twenty books of poetic prose and two works of verse. Reading becomes an experience of exile. In their journey across the homogeneous sands

6. Jew and word are, according to Jabès, united in exile: "Perhaps the ultimate affirmation of the Jew is, paradoxically, that there is no such person as the Jew. There is only the exile of a word, which he came to take on himself, not to try and save it, or himself, but to guide it from dawn to dusk of the longest day, from the point catching fire to its grandiose conflagration" (*EI*, 105/91).

of this desert, readers encounter few oases of permanent meaning where they can stop to rest and ponder this errant experience; few markers of narrative consistency by which they can judge the extent or distance of the wandering; few signs in the textual landscape by which they can fix in memory the innumerable caravans of words marching from page to page and book to book. Forgetfulness effaces Jabès's pages the way the wind blows away footprints in the sand. Each new quotation erases words just quoted; each new paragraph or page or book effaces an earlier text. From one end of Jabès's textual universe to the other—from the invisible wound that writing opens at the threshold of *Le Livre des questions* (p. 11/15), to the already "wounded wound" that continues to bleed at the conclusion of *Le Petit Livre de la subversion hors du soupçon* (p. 90), to the "inguérissable blessure" ("incurable wound") that a silent dialogue opens in *Le Livre du dialogue* (p. 36/20), to "the blood of the word" in *La Mémoire et la main*—Jabès re-creates the endlessness of exilic movement. At every moment, his work expresses "an action caught in its hesitations and turns" (*Elya*, 50/149). Errancy is the fundamental condition of being-in-the-world, which is, for Jabès, a being-in-the-book.[7] It sustains the existence of a people for whom the only permanent, unchanging reality, the only home, is exile itself, and the writing coincident with it: "Qui jamais écrira l'errance?— Elle s'écrit avec nous. / Errant, *je suis son écriture*" ("Who will ever write wandering?—It writes itself with us. / Wandering, *I am its writing*"; *LP*, 30). It seeps into the deepest recesses of life to influence the fundamental gestures of human activity, to touch the most vital forces of existence, for it is the human lot "to wander, wander as one breathes or talks" (*E*, 76/167).

The Jew is the living incarnation of exile. "Being Jewish," affirms one of Jabès's narrators, " 'means only this for me. . . : to bear my exile as the camel bears its two humps' " (*Aely*, 153/320). As the being whose existence through history is tied inextricably to the book, the Jew embodies the diaspora of writing; he is the "figure of exile, wandering, strangeness, and separation, a condition that is that of the writer as well" (*SD*, 85). For Jabès, to write and to be a Jew means to live in a state of estrangement and difference. Writing, like exile, involves a constant awareness of otherness, because the words expressed by the poet are

7. Jacques Derrida writes that "one emerges from the book only within the book, because, for Jabès, the book is not in the world but the world is in the book" (*L'Ecriture et la différence* [Paris: Seuil, 1967], p. 113) [*Writing and Difference*, trans. Alan Bass (Chicago: University of Chicago Press, 1978), p. 76]; cited in the text as *ED*.

consistently different from the objects or realities to which they refer. Each of Jabès's books, having moved in an unforeseen direction dictated by the exilic, centrifugal force of the writing itself, is followed by another book, which, in trying to restore the original orientation, forces the trajectory of the work into still other digressive directions. Writing produces a digression and thus initiates alterity; it moves away from its source. And exile also is an experience of otherness and digression. The homeless person lives at a distance from a place that is the lost center of her existence, the homeland without which she is incomplete and profoundly, if not existentially, different. In exile from her own image of the past and estranged from her own sense of herself as a former inhabitant of that past, she is a stranger condemned to live at the margins of a desired place of existence. Her exile and loss become her identity:

> Perdre terre: se perdre. Sans pays, à nulle époque, le juif ne s'est perdu. Il a récupéré sa perte, en s'y enlisant, en s'y lisant.

> [To lose a land: to lose one's way. Without a country, at no time was the Jew lost. He made up for his loss by burying himself in it, by reading himself in it.] (*Le Parcours,* 17)

Thus, the writer who longs to seize in language the elusive object he perceives in the world, or to express in all its potent immediacy the image in his imagination, and the exile who yearns to return to a distant homeland whose vibrant life is ingrained in his memory, wander in search of a promised land they cannot enter; their torment lies in their alienation. What was once so proximate has become increasingly distant; what was once so familiar, so intimate, has become exceedingly different. The exile and the writer inhabit a distance that their actions and lives sustain. Both are, as Jabès writes of the Jew, figures whose faces have taken on "the features of farewell" (*A,* 125/298); their being is a being-in-distance. The exiled Jew is "he who distances himself in order to exist" (*LR,* 30), and this moving away and the errant existence it produces become a domicile. All relations or contacts with the Jew

> s'inscrivent dans cet éloignement, dans cette distance imposée où il se meut, parle et meurt, comme si son chemin engendrait sans cesse le chemin; comme si, seul, un rouleau de parchemin pouvait contenir sa loi, puisque image matérielle de son errance, en se déroulant

indéfiniment, il se donnerait comme représentation de cette incalculable distance, ponctuée de commandements, que le juif est appelé à
parcourir.

[are inscribed in this remoteness, in this distance imposed where he
moves about, speaks and dies, as if his road endlessly created the
road; as if, alone, a parchment scroll could contain his law, since it is
the concrete image of his errancy, unwinding indefinitely, and presenting itself as the representation of this incalculable distance, punctuated by commandments, which the Jew is summoned to traverse.]
(*LR*, 30)

Judaism reveals the identity between word and distance. Where
there is language, there is also the otherness that separates a word from
its referent, that forces apart a signifier from its signified, that keeps
writing in exile from the full meaning it seeks, that estranges intention
from expression, and that turns human utterance into nomadic language. Through wandering words, the Jew establishes a relationship
with distance itself; he finds a "home" within the very difference that
makes him eternally homeless. Judaism, which Jacques Derrida, following Levinas, calls an "experience of the infinitely other" (*L'Ecriture
et la différence*, 226/152), has given humanity, Maurice Blanchot observes,

the revelation of the spoken word as the place where men stand in
relation to what excludes all relation: the infinitely Distant, the absolutely Foreign. . . . If there is, indeed, an infinite separation, it falls to
the word to make it the place of understanding, and if there is an
insurmountable abyss, the word must traverse the abyss. Distance is
not abolished, it is not even diminished; to the contrary, it is kept
preserved and pure by the severity of the word which sustains the
absoluteness of difference.[8]

The word is the realm in which distance is signified; it is where the Jew
in exile confronts the reality of what Blanchot calls "le Dehors" ("the
Outside"), a place of marginality where writing and exile can only exist.
It is the desert and the page, places of whiteness and exteriority which
"conjugate the nothing" (*Le Livre des questions*, 57/55). Writing is the
tracing of signs on a field that will efface them as soon as they appear,

8. "Etre juif," in *L'Entretien infini* (Paris: Gallimard, 1969), p. 187.

for language, Jabès writes, "confronts nothingness, where it ceases to mean, no longer designating anything but the Nothing" (*Le Petit Livre de la subversion hors de soupçon*, 40). In the space of Blanchot's "Dehors" and Jabès's desert, nothingness appears as the only possession, difference as the only identity, writing as the only trace, wandering as the only activity, and suffering as the only inheritance. As the desert of writing affirms its existence in vacancy and distance, so the Jew establishes his being and his history in a vast space of emptiness and loss: "'White, like the page, is the Jewish soul,' said Reb Assayas; 'on it our remittent errancy is printed in characters of lost places'" (*LR*, 112).[9]

By their writing, wandering, and history, the Jewish people are continually in transit through a place that is in reality a nonplace, a realm of emptiness which the words "outside," "desert," and "book" describe. Here nothingness is a "means of being and of surviving"(*RL*,

9. On the desert as the primordial image of *le dehors*, see Maurice Blanchot, *Le Livre à venir*, Collection Idées (Paris: Gallimard, 1959), pp. 118–20; for a discussion of the poet as the eternal wanderer and of the poem as a place of exile, see his essay "L'Expérience originelle," in *L'Espace littéraire*, Collection Idées (Paris: Gallimard, 1955), esp. pp. 322–24 and 332–38. See also Julia Kristeva, *Etrangers à nous-mêmes* (Paris: Fayard, 1988), esp. pp. 9–60, for a discussion of the stranger as the being who, "continually elsewhere, is nowhere." Regarding the importance of the desert in Jabès's works and its relationship to the experiences of exile and writing (including the phenomenon of the white page), see the following essays: Gabriel Bounoure, "Edmond Jabès ou la guérison par le livre," *Les Lettres nouvelles* (July–September 1966): 98–114, and his "Edmond Jabès: La Demeure et le livre," *Mercure de France*, 353 (January 1965): 114–23, both reprinted in his *Edmond Jabès: La Demeure et le livre* (Montpellier: Fata Morgana, 1984); Joseph Guglielmi, "Edmond Jabès ou la fascination du désert," *Critique* 296 (January 1972): 32–52, and his "Le Dernier état des questions," *Change* 22 (February 1975): 177–92 (the entire issue is devoted to the subject of "l'écriture nomade"); Pierre Missac, "Marge pour deux regards," *Les Cahiers Obsidiane* (special issue on Jabès) 5 (February 1982): 44–53; Agnès Chalier, "Le Chant de l'absence," in ibid., pp. 54–59; Jean Starobinski's brief statement in Janine Gdalia et al., "Edmond Jabès aujourd'hui," *Les Nouveaux Cahiers* 31 (Winter 1972–73): 61–62; Elisabeth Gardaz, "Jabès: Poétique de l'exil et l'exil à l'oeuvre," in *Exil et Littérature*, ed. Jacques Mounier (Grenoble: Ellug, 1986), pp. 283–88; Rosy Pinhas-Delpuech, "Dans la double dépendance du désert," in *Ecrire le livre*, pp. 181–90; Agnès Chalier, "Le Désert jabésien et la notion de vide dans la philosophie classique chinoise," in *Ecrire le livre*, pp. 191–200; and David Mendelson, "La Science, l'exil et les sources du désert," in *Ecrire le livre*, pp. 233–52. See also general essays on Jabès's work published in *The Sin of the Book;* in *Ecrire le livre;* in *Studies in Twentieth-Century Literature (Special Issue on Edmond Jabès)* 12 (Fall 1987); and in *Instants (Pour Edmond Jabès)* 1 (1989). In addition, for an intriguing discussion of nomadism as integral to Jewish thought, history, and being, see Olivier Revault d'Allonnes, *Musiques: Variations sur la pensée juive* (Paris: Christian Bourgois, 1979). Important general studies of Jabès's work are: Adolfo Fernandez Zoïla, *Le Livre: Recherche autre d'Edmond Jabès* (Paris: Jean-Michel Place, 1978); Joseph Guglielmi, *La Ressemblance impossible: Edmond Jabès* (Paris: Editeurs Français Réunis, 1978); Miryam Laifer, *Edmond Jabès: Un Judaïsme après Dieu*, American University Studies, ser. 2, Romance Languages and Literatures, vol. 39 (New York: Peter Lang, 1986); and Warren F. Motte, Jr., *Questioning Edmond Jabès* (Lincoln: University of Nebraska Press, 1990).

96/232). This nonplace of exile is a region of negativity, the other side of existence defined by the dominance of absence, loss, and death. It has no center, lacking a sense of "hereness" and presence. It is a perpetually changing "elsewhere"—"an elsewhere which leaves us out" (*A*, 148/316) Jabès remarks—where the Jew wanders and the poet writes and into which the book is inserted. Inhabiting a region that is always distant from a desired place of existence defines Jewish Diaspora. Finding himself in an "elsewhere" of unrootedness and suffering, the Jew fervently desires to be transported to yet *another* place. " 'Being elsewhere,' " Charles Péguy wrote of the Jews, near the beginning of the century, is " 'the great vice of this race, the great secret virtue, the great vocation of this people.' "[10] And Jacques Derrida expresses a similar sentiment when he writes that "the Poet and the Jew are not born *here* but *elsewhere*. They wander, separated from their true birth. Autochthons only of speech and writing, of Law" (*ED*, 102/66). The place of writing is an "elsewhere," a marginal location far from a desired home; the desert, indeed, is "at the heart of every word" (*DDD*, 33). Writing is merely the passage of words moving toward a distant horizon. The book is a place words pass through en route to other books as yet still unwritten. "My books," states Jabès, "are, in fact, only places of passage" (*Du désert au livre*, 155), a statement corroborated by the series of volumes he has written, in which each new book is a continuation and an effacement of an earlier one. Writing, as Blanchot remarks, tends to "move toward the absence of the book,"[11] toward the passing away of the written work. Texts are only stations through which a nomadic writing passes. The journey is endless, for written language, which has no homeland, no resting place, no oasis, moves errantly among several tenuous and ephemeral meanings.[12]

10. Quoted by Gershom Scholem, in *On Jews and Judaism in Crisis: Selected Essays*, ed. Werner J. Dannhauser (New York: Schocken Books, 1976), p. 82.

11. *L'Entretien infini*, p. 623. For a comparison of Blanchot and Jabès, see Riccardo de Benedetti, "Dans l'incondition de l'écriture: Jabès et Blanchot," in *Écrire le livre*, pp. 171–79.

12. This desire to be always elsewhere, to search constantly for a renewing difference, is the source of poetry, which emerges from the absence in the world of a true place, a homeland, of being. As Harold Bloom writes, "*to be different, to be elsewhere*, is a superb definition of the motive for metaphor, for the life-affirming deep motive of all poetry" (*Kabbalah and Criticism* [New York: Seabury Press, 1975], p. 52). Signification is on the move, wandering in search of the "elsewhere," the *other* place, that would end its exile. "Meaning wanders, like human tribulation, or like error, from text to text, and within a text, from figure to figure" (p. 82). Texts and meanings are born in exile. "Increasingly," Bloom states, "a poem must be an error about poetry, and every poem begins by misreading itself. Every poetic trope is an exile from literal meaning, but the only homecoming would be the death of figuration and so the death of poetry, or the triumph of literal meaning, whatever that is. . . . Meaning, whether in modern poetry or in

The Breaking of the Word

The writing of the Torah unrolls in keeping with the circular, repeatable, and endless nature of Jewish exile, because writing and errancy come into being at the same time. They are born from the same experience of banishment and from the same need to overcome the void caused by God's withdrawal. The birth of human language coincides with the moment of exile, for when God, in his anger at the Hebrew people for their unfaithful worship of the golden calf, withdrew his word and interrupted his communication of Law, he created a distance and an absence that provoked the appearance of a compensating, entirely human word. The first tablets Moses brought down from Sinai were broken. The tablets that replaced them were inscribed with a "fallen" writing, a script expressing loss and marked by the distance God had placed between himself and humanity. "No one," writes Gershom Scholem, "has yet read the Torah of the Tree of Life which was inscribed on the first tablets. Israel was entrusted only with that second set of tablets, and they render the Torah as it is read under the dominion of the Tree of Knowledge and Differentiation, which is also called the Tree of Death."[13]

The language with which the Law finally comes down to humanity is separated and distant from the pure, original writing of God found in the "primordial" or "spiritual" Torah, as the first tablets are called. The human word is a fragment, a vestige, in exile from a sacred, unreadable text—the lost homeland of the divine Word—which all "fallen" writing remembers and desires to repossess. Everything that is written after the breaking of the first tablets refers to that originary catastrophe; it is, to use the title of a book by Blanchot, "l'écriture du désastre." This is an exiled writing that thinks of nothing but what it has been separated from, that can only speak and comment, no matter whatever else it may express, about the event of its exile. This writing returns again and again, almost obsessively, to interpret and question the origin from which it is eternally separated. As Derrida remarks, "the necessity of commentary, like poetic necessity, is the very form of exiled speech. In the beginning is hermeneutics" (*ED*, 102/67). For Jabès, writing is the

---

Kabbalah, wanders wherever anteriority threatens to take over the whole map of misreading, or the verbal universe, if that phrase be preferred. Meaning swerves, enlarges oppositely, vacates, drives down so as to rise up again, goes outside in the wan hope of getting itself more on the inside, and at last attempts to reverse anteriority by forsaking the evasions of mental space for those of mental time" (p. 89).

13. *The Messianic Idea in Judaism and Other Essays on Jewish Spirituality* (New York: Schocken Books, 1971), p. 71; hereafter cited in the text.

endless commentary on an absent word—namely, the invisible language and page of God's unreadable book: "every commentary is first the commentary of a silence," he asserts (*DL*, 142). Writing emerges from a lack; it comments unceasingly upon an absence that it ends by making present, for "every book is the written space of a missing word" (*II*, 30). But no such "presencing," no such writing, ever overcomes absence because "absence is the persistence of a lack" (*Un étranger avec, sous le bras, un livre de petit format*, 63).

Writing is postlapsarian; it is born from an irreversible loss of plenitude and unity. According to Walter Benjamin, the expulsion from Eden created the human word, "in which name no longer lives intact, and which has stepped out of name language, the language of knowledge," to become a word fallen into "the abyss of . . . mediateness."[14] However, Blanchot links the loss of language's perfect expressibility to a second "Fall"—namely, the exile from the Word initiated by the breaking of the tablets. The original Law and Word are shattered, and with them is destroyed the purity of an unmediated origin. Blanchot, like Benjamin, identifies the loss of the undifferentiated language of God with a fall into mediateness, difference, and repetition. "It is from an already destroyed word," he writes, "that man learns the demand that must speak to him: there is no real first understanding, no initial and unbroken word, as if one could never speak except the second time, after having refused to listen and having taken a distance in regard to the origin. . . . The first text (which is never the first), the written word, the scripture . . . is also at the same time a commented text that not only must be re-uttered in its identity, but learned in its inexhaustible difference."[15]

All books henceforth resemble the broken tablets, the model for future writing. According to one of Jabès's rabbis, "each line of writing is a break pledged to legibility" (*LR*, 99). The shattering of a text makes it readable by substituting a human word for a divine one, by making the writing imperfect and mortal, and by placing it within the flux and repeatability of time and history. Reading, like writing, did not exist—it was unnecessary—until language, which had been mystically commu-

14. *Reflections: Essays, Aphorisms, Autobiographical Writings*, trans. Edmund Jephcott (New York: Harcourt Brace Jovanovich, 1978), pp. 327 and 328, respectively.
15. "Le Livre des questions," in *L'Amitié*, p. 254 ["The Book of Questions," trans. Paul Auster, in "Interruptions," in *The Sin of the Book*, p. 49]. On the breaking of the tablets and on the notion of two torahs, one written, one oral, see Blanchot, *L'Entretien infini*, pp. 630–33. In addition, see Moshe Idel, "Infinities of Torah in Kabbalah," in *Midrash and Literature*, ed. Geoffrey H. Hartman and Sanford Budick (New Haven: Yale University Press, 1986), pp. 141–57.

nicated, was broken: "One crack, and the building crumbles and initiates the endless reading of its ruins," Jabès writes (*El*, 122/104). The shattered writing used by humanity is a broken language of interpretation yearning to repossess the wholeness of an original, divine language, which at one time had required no exegeses or commentary, because it was understood without mediation. Thus, to write is, as Jabès suggests, to have "a passion for origins" (*RL*, 22/159), to seek through words to return to an original discourse; it is to wander on the periphery of a sacred text searching for the entrance that has been concealed by the very commentaries to which this text has given rise and to attempt thus to answer the question that every origin is (*ESB*, 149).

Writing enables human beings to express the dark, other side of Creation: a place in exile from the pure Word of God, in which written words are fragmented, meanings multiplied, and men and women wander in a desert wilderness. Writing expresses man's proximity to nothingness; it "traces his devotion to the void, it becomes the record of his negativity" (*A*, 43/235). The need to break apart language derives from the original shattering of God's writing on the tablets, an event that opens "l'abîme de la blessure" ("the abyss of the wound"; *LR*, 87). Every act of writing from this moment forth becomes an act of mimetic violence; every text now emerges from a wound, and this is evident in the textual destruction that Jabès's books reenact. Contexts are torn apart, letters erased, words surrounded by a corrosive blankness. One book deconstructs another, unwrites it by rewriting it. The destruction of an anterior work creates a new one, as the effacement or annulment of one word creates a second; "it is upon the ruins of a book one has turned away from that the book is built," affirms Jabès (*PLS*, 39). The book that survives is the one that "destroys itself in favor of another book that will prolong it" ("Interview," 22). Destruction is necessary if a word is to exist in all its humanness, if a book is to be the repetition of the original shattering of language by which a human writing came into being. The Hebrew people, Jabès remarks, provoked Moses to break the tablets, because "they were not able to accept a word without origins, the word of God. It was necessary for Moses to break the book in order for the book to become human. . . . This gesture on the part of the Hebrew people was necessary before they could accept the book. This is exactly what we do as well. We destroy the book when we read it in order to make it into another book. The book is always born from a broken book. And the word, too, is born from a broken word" ("Interview," 23). Each of Jabès's books continues the exile of an earlier text and the fragmentation of an earlier word. At every moment of its precarious existence, the "Book" enigmatically is and is not, for Jabès sees it "as the impossibility of the book, or rather, as the place, as well as the non-place, for any possibility of creating the book" (*SD*, 85).

The Exile of Creation

If it is true that the book is in exile, that writing expresses and relives exile, and that all acts of expression and creativity embody exile, then it follows that everything that is born or that appears in the world has exilic being. All Creation is in exile, including the Creator himself, as Jabès often asserts:

> "Mon exil est l'exil antérieur de Dieu.
> "Mon exil, de syllabe en syllabe, m'a conduit à Dieu, le plus exilé des vocables. . . .
> "La parole de Dieu est l'erratique parole."

> ["My exile is anticipated in the exile of God.
> "My exile has led me, syllable by syllable, to God, the most exiled of words. . . .
> "The word of God is the erratic word."] (*Le Livre de Yukel*, 92–93/86)

> "Dieu est absence de Dieu. L'exil dans l'exil."

> ["God is absence of God. Exile within exile."] (*LY*, 110/104)

Errante est la parole de Dieu. Elle a, pour écho, la parole du peuple errant. Point d'oasis pour elle, nulle ombre, nulle paix; mais l'immensité du desert assoiffé; mais le livre de cette soif, le feu dévastateur de ce feu qui réduit en cendres tous les livres, au seuil de l'obsédante illisibilité du Livre légué.

[The word of God wanders. It has, as echo, the word of a wandering people. No oasis for this word, no shade, no peace; but the immensity of the thirsting desert; but the book of this thirst, the devastating fire of this fire, which reduces all books to ashes at the threshold of the haunting illegibility of the bequeathed Book.] (*SD*, 124–25)

Jabès's image of the *deus absconditus*, the "God who is hidden in His own self" and whose invisibility implies an absence from the world, bears a striking resemblance to the ideas of the sixteenth-century Cabalist Rabbi Isaac Luria, whom Gershom Scholem has studied in great historical detail.[16] Lurianic Cabala interpreted "Galut" (the Hebrew term for exile) not only as "a terrible and pitiless state permeating and embittering all of Jewish life" but also as "the condition of the universe as a whole, even of the deity" (*Messianic Idea*, p. 43). God, according to Luria, created the universe in two seemingly contradictory, although in reality complementary, stages: first, by concealing himself; second, by manifesting his divine being in two circles of light, emanations or *sefirot*, from which all Creation eventually descended. What was most radical about Luria's interpretation of Creation was his explanation of the first stage, to which he gave the name *tsimtsum*, a word originally meaning "concentration" or "contraction," and which the Cabalists used in the sense of "withdrawal" or "retreat" (*Major Trends*, p. 260).

Through the notion of *tsimtsum*, Luria attempted to resolve the question of how God, the "all in all," could have created things that were not divine; how, in other words, a world could have been created out of nothing if there was no such "thing" as nothing, because the idea of God excluded such a notion. The image of God withdrawing into himself and leaving behind a place emptied of his presence offers an ingenious solution to this problem of Creation. Scholem describes the concentration and concealment of God as an act of self-exile: "There is voluntary restraint and limitation, something related to the quality of harshness and rigidity in God, for all concentration and limitation imply the functioning of this quality. There is ruthlessness toward Himself, for He exiled Himself from boundless infinity to a more concentrated infinity. There is a profound inward Galut, not the Galut of one of the creatures but of God Himself, who limited Himself and thereby made place for the universe" (*Messianic Idea*, p. 44). God's concentration into himself leaves a vacancy, which is the point of initiation for Creation, for the appearance of the nondivine. Where God is absent, there Creation can being. "*Tsimtsum*," writes Scholem, "does not mean the concentration of God *at* a point, but his retreat *away* from a point" (*Major Trends*, p. 260). The Infinite Being takes a step inside, contracts into himself, withdraws into the recesses of his own presence. Scholem perceives the recoil of God, his self-banishment into

16. Gershom G. Scholem, *Major Trends in Jewish Mysticism* (New York: Schocken Books, 1954), p. 12; hereafter cited in the text. See also his essay "Galut," in *Encyclopaedia Judaica* (Jerusalem: Keter Publishing House; New York: Macmillan, 1971).

profound seclusion, as a fundamental paradigm of exilic movement; *tsimtsum* is "the deepest symbol of Exile that could be thought of" (*Major Trends,* p. 261).

The process of *tsimtsum* is followed by a second stage of Creation, in which God, ending his self-imposed exile, returns to the universe. God creates the worlds through the ten concentric circles of radiating light, the *sefirot,* which emanate from him. Placed in each of the ten circles is a "vessel," which functions to contain the light of Divine Being as it flows into the *sefirot.* But the light entering the vessels is too strong, especially in the lower *sefirot,* and some of the vessels shatter. Divine light escapes from the containers and is dispersed in the impure world. Although much of it is recaptured and returned to its source, some "sparks" remain fallen and scattered.[17] The "breaking of the vessels," therefore, presents a cosmological interpretation of the exile that is human existence and history. From this moment forth, "nothing is perfect. The divine light which should have subsisted in specific forms and in places appointed for it from the beginning is no longer in its proper place because the vessels were broken, and thereafter all things went awry. There is nothing that was not damaged by the breaking. Nothing is in the place appointed for it; everything is either below or above, but not where it should be. In other words, all being is in Galut" (*Messianic Idea,* p. 45).

In the Lurianic system, the stages of limitation (*tsimtsum*) and of destruction (the shattering of the vessels) are followed by a third process: reparation (*tikkun*). Because it is out of kilter, the world must be restored to its former oneness: "The primal flaw must be mended so that all things can return to their proper place, to their original posture," Scholem remarks (*Messianic Idea,* p. 46). Even the unity of God's name, YHWH, destroyed by the original defect—the first two letters of the tetragrammaton having been torn away from the last two—must be restored (*Major Trends,* p. 275). God begins the process but leaves its completion to humanity. Just at the moment when redemption of the broken world seems certain and the Messianic state seems near, Adam's sin interrupts the reparation, causing the world to plummet back into exile. Thus, the self-exile of God before Creation (*tsimtsum*), the exile of his radiant light during Creation (the breaking of the vessels), and the

17. In his study of Lurianic Cabala as a theory of writing, Bloom suggests that the force of the light which shatters the vessels can be interpreted as "too strong a force of *writing,* stronger than the 'texts' of the lower *Sefirot* could sustain. Paradoxically God's Name was too strong for his Words" (*Kabbalah and Criticism,* pp. 40–41).

continued unredeemed exile of all being after Creation (the interruption of *tikkun*) indicate the inescapable and universal burden of Galut for all humanity.[18] Creation appears as a form of eternal exile, which only a future redemption—creating what Scholem describes as "the perfect state, a flawless and harmonious world in which everything occupies its proper place" (*Messianic Idea*, p. 47)—will reverse.

The Lurianic concept of *tsimtsum*, which explains the withdrawal of God as the precondition for Creation, informs several of Jabès's images of exile. Throughout Jabès's several works, the absence of God from the world is expressed in so reiterative and dialectical a manner that it comes to constitute a tentative form of presence; God "is the blank present" (*E*, 48/148). As the presence of an ultimate absence, or, as Jabès prefers to describe it, "an immeasurable absence in presence" (*ESB*, 88), God communicates himself through the white spaces around words and by means of a hidden, white writing. He is heard, but only through his silence; present, but only through his invisibility; named, but only through an unknowable, unpronounceable word; perceived, but only through the void his withdrawal has created; felt, but only through the whiteness and the nothingness that stand in his place. He is "faceless, completely Other" (*DDD*, 72). The book is not where "God asserts Himself, but where he withdraws into a Word struck deaf and blind" (*A*, 117/292). The language of God is the language of absence, the expression of his retreat from the world and from the book, because, according to Jabès, "God died in creating, in creating Himself" (*Yaël*, 49/35). In him, death and distance proliferate. "What I mean by God in my work," Jabès explains, "is something we come up against, an abyss, a void, something against which we are powerless. It is a distance. . . . the distance that is always between things. . . . We get to where we are going, and then there is still this distance to cover" ("Interview," 19). This distance of God is taken over by the human word. His disappearance signals the advent of language: "God retreats from the world not to put man there but the word" (*II*, 90). Writing reenacts the separation, the tearing apart, of man and God; it represents the effacement by which God retreats into his own being, so that the creative processes engendering the world can begin to operate. Writing repeats the banishment and the distancing of the Divine Being, for, as Jabès suggests, it is

18. For Bloom, exile receives its most essential expression in the Cabala, which he describes as "a doctrine of Exile, a theory of influence made to explain Exile." "As a composite trope of limitation," *tsimtsum* "became the ultimate trope of Exile" (ibid., p. 83).

la tentative suicidaire d'assumer le vocable jusqu'à son ultime effacement, là où il cesse d'être vocable pour n'être plus que trace relevée—
blessure—d'une fatale et commune rupture: celle de Dieu avec
l'homme et celle de l'homme avec la Création.

[the suicidal attempt to take possession of the word up until its
ultimate effacement, there where it ceases to be word in order to be
no more than a heightened trace—a wound—of a fatal and shared
break: that of God with man and that of man with Creation.] (*PLS*,
57)

Writing is, therefore, a reenactment of *tsimtsum*, in which exile and
rupture predominate. In order to write a text, the writer-creator exiles
himself, like God, from his creation, and from his language which then
moves autonomously in its own direction until effaced and replaced by
other writings. The controlling, authorial presence disappears. Only
writing continues tenuously to exist, articulating the randomness and
errancy of the loss and exile that have given it existence. Words no
longer slavishly mime a writer's subjectivity. Had he really been the
author of his sentences, observes Jabès,

"elles auraient été le reflet et l'écho de ce que je voyais, de ce que
j'entendais ou de ce que j'avais sauvé d'autrefois. Au contraire, elles
s'acharnaient à m'éliminer dans le présent, à tout abolir autour
d'elles, au nom d'une mémoire, d'un passé, d'une existence qui n'ont
jamais été les miens, mais qui étaient devenus leur propre présent,
leur éphémère vie."

["they would have been reflection and echo of what I saw, heard, or
had saved up from other occasions. But, on the contrary, these
sentences were intent on getting me out of my present, on abolishing
everything around them in the name of a memory, a past, a life which
had never been mine, but had become their own present, their
ephemeral life."] (*A*, 66–67/255)

Without the presence of a creator, creation runs free; the mobility of
writing continues unchecked. The text whose author-god has disappeared, Barthes argues, becomes "a multi-dimensional space in which
a variety of writings, none of them original, blend and clash. The text is
a tissue of quotations drawn from the innumerable centres of culture"
("La Mort de l'auteur," 65/146). Meaning, in the sense of a final,

contained, arrested, and "true" signification, is unreachable and acknowledged as lost. "In the multiplicity of writing," Barthes asserts, "everything is to be *disentangled*, nothing *deciphered*" (p. 66/147). The errant movement of the various writings that compose the text empties it of meaning. The text not only achieves the exiling of the authorial presence but also causes the breaking of the "word-vessels" that once contained definitive significations. Thus, the Jabès text is fractured, and through its cracks flow the indeterminate meanings that a plurality of errant words evokes.

The Rhetoric of Exile

One of the roots of the word *exile* (to go out) is *salire* (to leap). An exile is compelled by circumstances to leave his or her homeland so abruptly that he or she almost leaps away from it; the exile jumps far into the distance. The movement of exile implies the sudden displacement, the abrupt dislocation, the rapid traversing of space, and the landing at a considerable distance from a starting point that the meaning of the word *leap* conveys. A nomadic writing such as Jabès's can also be described as a kind of leaping, because it produces a disruption in the continuity of meaning, a separation from familiar contexts, and a sudden dislocation between the textual elements inscribed on a page. The decentered movement of this writing—"the center, which is the node of truth, is always elsewhere" (*CSC*, 31)—creates interruptions and gaps, and thus the text, its continuity suspended, becomes a collection of autonomous and separated fragments. The leaping motion of exile generates broken souls and a writing that is in pieces. The fragment, Derrida writes, "is neither a determined style nor a failure but is the form writing takes" (*ED*, 108/71). It is a style that reproduces the distances, the sudden changes in direction, the ever-renewed departures, the centrifugal movement, and the wandering into open spaces that characterize exile and meaning. "Without interruption—between letters, words, sentences, books—no signification could be awakened," Derrida observes, for writing "proceeds by leaps alone" (ibid.).

There are many stylistic strategies of discontinuity, many rhetorical "leaps," that Jabès uses to make his writing both express and create the experience of exile. The errancy of his books and the nomadism his writing performs are achieved by a highly developed rhetoric of exile. Of the many forms, figures, and manipulations of language which create this textual nomadism (such as parataxis, anaphora, litany, ellipsis, paronomasia, oxymoron, the highlighting of white space, and the erasure or reversal of letters to form punning words), there are three in particular that Jabès uses more than any others to represent errancy and to install exile within the movement of the writing itself; they are quotation, aphorism, and question.

Most of Jabès's quotations are the words of imaginary rabbis (with names such as Reb Seni, Veil, Leha, Nas, Golim, Daber, Dérissa, Tadié, Arad) which appear in the first three volumes of *Le Livre des questions*, although in later books there are citations of passages by Kafka, Proust, Wittgenstein, Bataille, Leiris, Levinas, and several others. Jabès even quotes himself, reprinting, for example, at the beginning of *Le Livre des ressemblances* (pp. 19–27) and again in *Le Livre du partage* (pp. 77–81) the short summaries, or *prières d'insérer*, that had appeared on the back covers and jacket flaps of earlier books. For Jabès, the quotation is a textual fragment in exile. Although it has been torn from an earlier text and transported to a contemporary one, where it is installed in a new linguistic environment among new groupings of words, it still retains certain mnemic traces of its earlier textual milieu. It is a text that, having been cited and summoned, is literally "set in motion" (from the Latin *ciere*).

For Benjamin, who dreamed of creating a work consisting entirely of quotations, citation functions as an interruption. "To quote a text involves the interruption of its context," he wrote.[19] This interruption liberates the word from its prison in the already written, freeing it from the tyranny of context so that it can discover a new relationship in a contemporary text. The quotation, he observed, "summons the word by its name, wrenches it destructively from its context, but precisely thereby calls it back to its origin. . . . In quotation the two realms—of origin and destruction—justify themselves before language. And conversely, only where they interpenetrate—in quotation—is language consummated. In it is mirrored the angelic tongue in which all words, startled from the idyllic context of meaning, have become mottoes in the book of Creation."[20] The release from context frees the word to remember its source in an earlier and more sacred text. The quotation nostalgically recalls not only its most recent home but also the original homeland—the word of God—in which it and all words once dwelled. Having been made errant by the Fall, all words in a sense become quotations. Their wanderings through history compel them to adopt

19. *Illuminations*, trans. Harry Zohn (New York: Schocken Books, 1969), p. 151.
20. *Reflections*, p. 269.

new and always provisional places of textual residence. They are assimilated into contexts whose meaning they help to build. But when a new act of citation (of "interruption," in Benjamin's sense) tears them from that context, liberating them to move on to newer contextual homes, quotations reveal their exilic nature as nomadic fragments; they migrate from text to text, remembering the textual lands (all the way back to the original Book of Creation) they have inhabited. Quotation represents the survivorship of words in the postlapsarian diaspora of language. It points to the dispersive and decentered nature of writing, for there is always another, anterior text lying behind whatever is written. Quotation is the reinscription of the already written. There is no writing that is not quotation, with the exception, of course, of the original divine language of the primordial Torah.[21]

Fundamentally, Jabès's books of quotations, aphorisms, and questions are books of fragments. The fragment is a node of verbal energy, a concentrated mass of language, simultaneously broken and whole. In itself, it is complete and self-sufficient, but it is a piece broken off from a lost, nonexistent text to which it refers. In temporal terms, the fragment is a moment, an instant, a flash of time, and is never of continuous duration; it ends as quickly as it begins. It is a surge of power that lacks continuity and persistence. As Barthes suggests, it is "a method of sudden, separated, and broken openings."[22] Isolated from the other fragments with which it is assembled and motivated by a paratactical autonomy, it occupies a space that is an "in-between," an interstice. The fragment acts as an interruption because of the strong, initiating force of its beginning. Swerving away from the topic developed in a previous passage, the fragment announces a new subject, a new discourse, and a new textual adventure.

For Jabès, the aphorism (like the quotation and the question) is a fragment; it is a miniature text whose beginning and end are telescoped so that they happen almost within the same moment. A series of aphorisms is a series of new beginnings, of unrelated excursions of

21. For formalist and historical studies of the poetics of quotation, see Antoine Compagnon, *La Seconde main; ou, Le Travail de la citation* (Paris: Seuil, 1979), and Herman Meyer, *The Poetics of Quotation in the European Novel,* trans. Theodore Ziolkowski and Yetta Ziolkowski (Princeton: Princeton University Press, 1968). An interesting study of quotation as a form of criticism is Pierre Missac's "Eloge de la citation," *Change* 22 (February 1975): 133–50, which applies Benjamin's theory of quotation to certain texts by Jabès. For a study of the way quotation as a survivor-text subverts both past and present contexts, see my review essay "Edmond Jabès: *The Book of Questions," MLN* 94 (May 1979): 869–76.

22. *Roland Barthes par Roland Barthes,* Collection Ecrivains de toujours (Paris: Seuil, 1975), p. 98.

thought going their own way, what Barthes calls "a pure suite of interruptions."[23] Aphorisms are also a sequence of concentrations. As God through *tsimtsum* withdraws into himself in order to leave an empty space from which Creation will surge, so the aphorism is the retreat of writing into itself so as to leave a surrounding white space on the page from which another presence, another meaning may emerge. "The aphorism—what you might call the naked phrase—" Jabès observes, "comes from a need to surround the words with whiteness in order to let them breathe" ("Interview," 15). By contracting itself into a limited area of writing, the aphorism, like the sea retreating from a shore, exposes vacant areas of the page. It thus gives life to the invisible words, the white writing, the books-within-the-book, the "livre absolu, mythique" ("the absolute, mythic book"; *DDD*, 85) that are hidden in the open spaces of Jabès's pages.

The compactness of Jabès's aphorisms—so concise in some instances as to border on the tautological—is due to their strange, enigmatic autonomy. Such aphoristic statements as "The book survives the book" (*LY*, 23/23), " 'Origin is abyss' " (*SD*, 124), " 'God denies Himself [*se nie*] where He ties Himself [*se noue*]' " (*RL*, 46/182), "Illegibility is at the end of a losing legibility" (*LR*, 7), and "An absence held captive to a captivated absence" (*ESB*, 12) are expressions complete in themselves; they express a whole thought or idea. But the aura of enigma surrounding them cancels the sense of completeness. The reader understands the words and the relations between the words, but the concentration of so much signification in so small a space and through so few words explodes the classical form of the writing. In Jabès's aphorisms, writing is reduced to enigma. Behind the apparent fullness of the aphorism lies an abyss of indeterminacy. While the form suggests presence, its meaning expresses absence.

The aphorism's self-contained completeness and classical perfection are misleading. Jabès's aphorism is not an answer but a perpetually open and reopened question. Its concentrated essentialness demands further thought, provoking greater elaboration by the reading mind. But the reader, stimulated to deepen and widen his or her meditation, moves further and further away from the aphoristic center; he or she moves centrifugally in indeterminate directions, musing about ideas that, because they are expressed in a most laconic, abstract, and gnomic manner, remain incomplete. Paradoxically, the aphorism, which means etymologically to mark off a boundary or a horizon, goes beyond the very bounds it delineates; it encompasses a space that spills over its own

23. Ibid.

borders. The encompassing action is undone by the boundless enigmas that have been enclosed. The aphorism literally cannot contain itself. It is a fragment, complete in itself, and yet exploding into further fragments. So reduced is its meaning, at least in Jabès's hands, that the aphorism comes to signify a plurality of possible, sometimes contradictory meanings. There is no finality, therefore, to the interpretation of the aphorism in Jabès's writing; it stimulates endless thought. The reader moves into it as toward a center of meaning, only then to be thrust centrifugally away into a plurality of indeterminate meanings. In form, the aphorism is implosive; in meaning, explosive. It concentrates writing but only in order to scatter meaning. It is a force of dispersion, contributing to the nomadism of words and the diaspora of signification in Jabès's works.[24]

Jabès's books are involved in a perpetual self-fragmentation, because they are composed "as much of contradictions as of affirmations torn apart by contradictions" (*SD*, 59). The book is written through the destruction of the book. The signs of textual fragmentation are evident, for instance, in the open, interlinear spaces that interrupt the flow of the writing, or in the short, self-contained paragraphs that in a paratactic manner remain distant from and unconnected to what precedes or follows, or in the different typographies that express invisible texts hidden within the text. Jabès's writing is open-ended and naturally disruptive.[25] Sentences end in enigmas, which do not conclude but, to the contrary, initiate a host of further questions. Paragraphs end in a frustrating perplexity that the next entry tries unsuccessfully to

24. On the link between aphorism and the textual fragment, especially in Nietzsche's work, see Gilles Deleuze, "Nomad Thought," in *The New Nietzsche: Contemporary Styles of Interpretation*, ed. David B. Allison (New York: Dell, 1977), pp. 142–49. For a different interpretation of the centripetal and centrifugal aspects of aphorism (especially as they pertain to Wallace Stevens's aphoristic writings), see Beverly Coyle, "An Anchorage of Thought: Defining the Role of Aphorism in Wallace Stevens' Poetry," *PMLA* 91 (March 1976): 206–22. See also Pierre Missac's interesting observations on Jabès's aphorisms in his "Edmond Jabès apocryphe," *Les Nouveaux Cahiers*, no. 55 (Winter 1978–79): 48–57, and his more general study "Situation de l'aphorisme," *Critique* 323 (April 1974): 372–83. On the uniqueness of Jabès's use of rhetorical tropes, see the following essays published in *Ecrire le livre:* Helena Shillony, "Métaphores de la négation," pp. 23–30; Elisabeth Gardaz, "Rhétorique et figures du silence dans l'oeuvre de Jabès," pp. 31–43; Didier Cahen, "Les Réponses du livre," pp. 57–70; and Ronnie Scharfman, "Mort-né: Itinéraire d'un vocable," pp. 285–90.

25. The illusion of completeness which the book gives is antithetical to the nature of writing, which is fundamentally dispersive and perpetually incomplete and, thus, constitutive not of a book but of a text. As Derrida remarks, "the idea of the book, which always refers to a natural totality, is profoundly alien to the sense of writing. It is the encyclopedic protection of theology and of logocentrism against the disruption of writing, against its aphoristic energy, and . . . against difference in general" (*Of Grammatology*, trans. Gayatri Chakravorty Spivak [Baltimore: Johns Hopkins University Press, 1976], p. 18).

dissipate, thus further aggravating the discontinuity of the text. The result is a writing that seems always—whether it is in the form of an aphorism, a quotation, a prayer, an enigma, a poem, a *récit*, a fragment, an epigraph, a title—to raise a question. At the end of a line, in the margins or at the bottom of the page, in between books, an invisible question mark seems to exist, as if to confirm Jabès's belief that "there is no truth but interrogative; no reality, but interpretative" (*II*, 103). Thus, reading becomes a profoundly hermeneutical experience, a voyage along a road without end: "The question is a trail which, opening, blazes the trail" (*LD*, 42/25).

There are, moreover, hundreds of conventional questions throughout Jabès's books. That most of these interrogative statements receive no answers explains their multiplicity, for the silence following one question spawns another: "To every question the Jew answers with another question" (*LQ*, 125/116), because "the question settles in the solitude where any answer leaves us" (*LD*, 68/42), and because "Jewish, the question which does not stop questioning itself in the reply it calls forth" (*LD*, 66/41). Writing is the wandering of questions whose unanswerability makes their errancy infinite. The *mise-en-abyme* generated by the perpetual questioning mirrors the endless reflections of writing as it wanders in search of an unpossessable origin, and an unwritable Book.

Jabès's rhetorical figuration of exile thus depends on the genres of quotation, aphorism, and question, which are literary forms that not only represent mimetically the errancy of Jewish existence but also give an experience of errancy itself by being inserted as nomadic participants in a series of decentered, wandering books. The *quotation*, for example, is a fragment-text in exile from an earlier, original work, whose existence is recalled when the fragment is provisionally embedded in a new textual home. The *aphorism* is a miniature text whose meaning is so squeezed by the compression of language that it explodes into an enigmatic indeterminacy, an infinite plurality of signification. The *question* is a separated text, seeking the absent answer that would complete it, or becoming the chrysalis from which a new question will emerge. Each of these genres is forced to cope with absence, to signify a lack. Missing from the quotation is a distant, original text; from the aphorism, the presence of an immediate and unified meaning; and from the question, the fulfillment of an answer. Each form expresses a loss, and each desires a return to a complete state of being. These genres are figures of exile that relive, through their forms and functions in Jabès's texts, the experience of exile. Uprooted, as are all

forms of writing, from a homeland of language, from the undifferentiated word of Creation, where, to quote Octavio Paz, "Only one word
existed immense without opposite / A word like a sun,"[26] these fragments are compelled to leap and wander across the empty pages of a
universal book: the quotation moving out toward different contexts;
the question migrating toward responses that are only further questions; and the aphorism, despite its suggestion of closure and immobility, drifting toward scattered, dispersed meanings.

Jabès's books of questions, resemblances, dialogues, subversions,
shares, margins, and strangers are themselves pages in an unfinished
Book of Exile—in which words, mimetically reenacting the original
breaking of the tablets, are separated from the things they designate
and dispersed as discontinuous fragments; in which writing, recalling
the free play of Creation that God's withdrawal into himself initiated,
generates a multiplicity of indeterminate and provisional meanings; in
which written language, forever estranged from the undifferentiated
oneness of a uniquely meaningful language, expresses the difference
and alterity of exilic being; and, finally, in which words, because they
are no longer grounded in a pure, unmediated Word, repeat and
rewrite themselves in an unending dialogue of self-quotation and in-
tertextuality.[27] In Jabès's works a nomadic, decentered writing in mi-
gration across the desert whiteness of a page echoes the vast silence of
an unredeemed world of separation and distance. Like Creation and
like Being, the Book is in profound exile. Because writing is no longer
an act of personal or subjective communication, it has become the
articulation and repetition of the emptiness, absence, and loss at the
center of existence. This nomadic, exilic writing creates books that, to
quote Kafka, "affect us like some really grievous misfortune, like the
death of one whom we loved more than ourselves, as if we were
banished to distant forests, away from everybody, like a suicide."[28]
Thus, reading becomes the same sorrowful experience of homelessness that writing and living are. Everywhere in the world-that-is-the-
book, one reads, interprets, and questions signs of exile. The Jew (that

26. "Fable," in *Early Poems, 1935–1955*, trans. Muriel Rukeyser et al. (New York: New
Directions, 1973), p. 27.

27. For an interesting discussion of Jabès's poetics of dialogue as it relates to experi-
ences of exile, absence, and alterity and to "the essential desire for sharing" (*LP*, 140), see
"On Dialogue and the Other: An Interview with Edmond Jabès," *Studies in Twentieth-
Century Literature, (Special Issue on Edmond Jabès)*, 27–41, and my essays "The Dialogue of
Absence," in ibid., pp. 93–113, and "Le Miracle du 'tu,'" in *Instants (Pour Edmond Jabès)*,
pp. 27–32.

28. *I Am a Memory Come Alive: Autobiographical Writings*, ed. Nahum N. Glatzer (New
York: Schocken Books, 1974), p. 7.

is to say, everyman or everywoman, as he or she leads a life of nomadic being) is transformed into a sign, a word; and his or her writing, as Jabès represents and lives it within the shifting horizons of his spiraling books, becomes

> errance, méfiance, attente, confluence, blessure, exode,
>   exil, exil, exil.

> [wandering, suspicion, waiting, confluence, wound, exodus,
>   and exile, exile, exile.] (*A,* 114/290)

CHAPTER 9

The *Punctum* of Absence: Roland Barthes

Le moi ne discourt que blessé.

[The ego discourses only when it is hurt.]
—Roland Barthes, *Fragments d'un discours amoureux*

On 22 October 1977, Henriette Barthes dies. The following year, Roland Barthes delivers a lecture at the Collège de France, which, in the Proustian echoes of its title—the opening line of *A la recherche du temps perdu*—evokes the desire of a son to feel once again the radiant presence of his absent mother. Entitled " 'Longtemps, je me suis couché de bonne heure,' "[1] Barthes's lecture makes use of Proust's work to structure his own meditation on loss and to give expression to his own

1. *Essais critiques*, 4: *Le Bruissement de la langue* (Paris: Seuil, 1984), pp. 313–25 [*The Rustle of Language*, trans. Richard Howard (Berkeley: University of California Press, 1986), pp. 277–90]; hereafter cited as *BL*. Other important works by Barthes are hereafter cited in the text according to the following abbreviations:

CC   *La Chambre claire: Note sur la photographie* (Paris: Gallimard, Seuil, "Cahiers du cinéma," 1980) [*Camera Lucida: Reflections on Photography*, trans. Richard Howard (New York: Hill and Wang, 1981)].

ES   *L'Empire des signes* (Geneva: Albert Skira, 1970) [*Empire of Signs*, trans. Richard Howard (New York: Hill and Wang, 1982)].

FDA   *Fragments d'un discours amoureux* (Paris: Seuil, 1977) [*A Lover's Discourse: Fragments*, trans. Richard Howard (New York: Hill and Wang, 1978)].

GV   *Le Grain de la voix: Entretiens, 1962–1980* (Paris: Seuil, 1981) [*The Grain of the Voice: Interviews, 1962–1980*, trans. Linda Coverdale (New York: Hill and Wang, 1985)].

PT   *Le Plaisir du texte* (Paris: Seuil, 1973) [*The Pleasure of the Text*, trans. Richard Miller (New York: Hill and Wang, 1975)].

RB   *Roland Barthes par Roland Barthes*, Collection Ecrivains de toujours (Paris: Seuil, 1975) [*Roland Barthes by Roland Barthes*, trans. Richard Howard (New York: Hill and Wang, 1977)].

SE   *Sollers écrivain* (Paris: Seuil, 1979).

S/Z   *S/Z* (Paris: Seuil, 1970).

mourning. Proust's text serves as the intermediary through which Barthes talks, albeit obliquely, about his mother's death and about his own grief. By means of the strong identification that Barthes feels with Proust, the novelist becomes the spokesman for the critic, saying for him things that the private and tactful Barthes has no desire discussing in this public forum. The words of *A la recherche du temps perdu* and the events of Proust's life help Barthes to name things that he cannot put fully into words. Proust gives meaning to the silences in Barthes's lecture, as do Dante, Tolstoy, and Michelet, to whom Barthes also refers. The words of others embody that death, that radical alterity, of which he can not bring himself to speak directly. The commentaries, the interpretations, the literary allusions, the quotations, the allusions to an author's life—all the things that Barthes has chosen to put into his discussion of Proust's writing—circle around an event of loss, around an absence, for which all of his words, and those of others, are but mere signs.[2]

Having been attracted to Proust's work during most of his career, Barthes now finds yet another, more personal, more subjective reason for identifying with the writer. They have become brothers in loss. The death of Proust's mother in 1905, Barthes observes, begins a period in Proust's life when he searches for a literary form that would help him express, and perhaps even transcend, his mourning. Between 1905 and 1909, the year when he begins *A la recherche du temps perdu*, Proust is in a state of acute hesitation, unable to decide whether to write essays (the path of metaphor and criticism) or stories (the path of metonymy

2. It is interesting how Barthes keeps himself from directly addressing the fact of his mother's death. It is not that he is avoiding the subject; he may even be taking for granted that many in the audience who know him also know about her death. But it is curious that every time he begins to come close to speaking more openly about the reality of her loss, his interest is deflected to other subjects. He talks about something else, which then obliquely and through the "unconscious" of the discourse expresses what he had been on the threshold of saying. He proceeds indirectly, using surrogates to carry and express his grief. An interesting example of this usage is found in the concluding paragraph of the first part of the lecture, in which Barthes announces the subject to which he now plans to turn his attention. Explaining that he has discussed Proust's new logic in *A la recherche* because "this theme concerns me personally," Barthes then remarks that "hence I shall be speaking of 'myself'. . . . I shall be speaking of the one for whom no one else can be substituted, for better and for worse. It is the *intimate* which seeks utterance in me, seeks to make its cry heard, confronting generality, confronting science" (*BL*, 319–20/284). The new section, in which he himself is supposed to be the "subject," begins, however, with a discussion of Dante and the opening line of *The Divine Comedy*. Barthes then moves on to Michelet and Tolstoy before returning to Proust. This avoidance of the "void" that has changed his life and this channeling of mourning through the voices of others create a style of indirection. Barthes is practicing at the beginning of the lecture what he shall identify later as the form of the ideal novel that someday he would like to write: a new style of writing which would express feeling, but only indirectly (*BL*, 324/288).

and the novel). Caught between the writing of commentary, on the one hand, and the making of fiction, on the other, between criticism and affective expression, Proust experiences "a certain indecision of genres" (*Le Bruissement de la langue*, 315/279). Eventually, he resolves this indecisiveness by beginning *A la recherche du temps perdu*, which, being neither story nor essay, neither fiction nor criticism, is a new literary hybrid, which Barthes calls "une tierce forme" ("a third form"; *BL*, 316/280), whose structure is fundamentally "rhapsodic." In it, time literally pours out, the floodgates wide open. Pieces of a life, fragments of thoughts, the bric à brac of memories are arranged, repeated, overlapped, crisscrossed, and then, like a dress, sewn together. But they do not form a seamless whole, because there is something subversive about "la tierce forme;" it presents "the *disorganization* of Time" (*BL*, 317/281). Through the logic of this new form, Proust succeeds in abolishing the contradiction between novel and essay, an accomplishment Barthes finds particularly seductive because it suggests perhaps a way out of his own personal dilemma.

What, then, is the attraction of "la tierce form" for Barthes? Like Proust, Barthes, at the moment of his lecture at the Collège de France and in the wake of his own mother's death, experiences an "indecision of genres." For several years his critical writings had been veering further and further away from the structuralist and scientistic interpretations of such earlier studies as *Eléments de sémiologie* (1965), "Introduction à l'analyse structurale des récits" (1966), and *Système de la mode* (1967).[3] With his book about Japan, *L'Empire des signes* (1970), his analysis of the pleasure and bliss of reading, *Le Plaisir du texte* (1973), his third-person autobiography, *Roland Barthes par Roland Barthes* (1975), and his study of love as figurative discourse, *Fragments d'un discours amoureux* (1977), Barthes has been moving progressively in the direction of a more subjective and ludic style of writing. More and more avidly, he begins to practice what he calls an affective or "affectionate criticism" (*Sollers écrivain*, 78; *Le Grain de la voix*, 307–8/330). He comes to realize that feeling is the prime mover of criticism; it is the engine that powers the critical machine (*GV*, 308/331). The unique blend of criticism and fiction, of *essai* and *récit*, which he identifies as "the third form" of *A la recherche du temps perdu*, has already had its effect on his

3. For both a discussion of Barthes's radical break in the late sixties with the orthodoxy of structuralist analysis and an examination of the importance of *S/Z* in accomplishing the development of a different type of semiology, see Steven Ungar, *Roland Barthes: The Professor of Desire* (Lincoln: University of Nebraska Press, 1983), pp. 30–33 and 42–46.

own writing. The full flowering of this form will not occur, however, until *La Chambre claire: Note sur la photographie [Camera Lucida: Reflections on Photography]*, the book on photography and the loss of his mother that Barthes will write between April and June 1979, only nine months before his own tragic death.

As his lecture at the Collège de France continues, Barthes leaves Proust and turns to Dante, once again attracted by the opening line of a literary work—Dante's "Nel mezzo del camin di nostra vita"—and once again using the language of another to signify his own private loss. How and by what experience, Barthes asks, do we determine "the middle of our lives"? Because we cannot foresee the moment when death will arrive, how can we possibly know when our lives have been suddenly divided into two equal parts and the midpoint reached? It is a question that the death of his mother has made him ponder for the first time in his life. Suddenly, an event occurs in which mortality no longer seems an abstraction: "You *knew* you were mortal (everyone has told you so, ever since you had ears to hear); suddenly you *feel* mortal" (*BL*, 321/285). The world is no longer the same; the landscape has brutally changed. The comforting, though unquestioned, repetitions in a life—the work one performs, the friends one sees, the writing one does, the style and habits of living one follows—all come to a screeching halt. Death announces a radical difference. An ineffaceable fissure cuts through one's life like a fault opened by an earthquake. This is how one knows, Barthes suggests, that the middle of one's life has been reached:

> Pour Proust, le "chemin de la vie" fut certainement la mort de sa mère (1905), même si la mutation d'existence, l'inauguration de l'oeuvre nouvelle n'eut lieu que quelques années plus tard. Un deuil cruel, un deuil unique et comme irréductible, peut constituer pour moi cette "cime du particulier," dont parlait Proust; quoique tardif, ce deuil sera pour moi le milieu de ma vie; car le "milieu de la vie" n'est peut-être jamais rien d'autre que ce moment où l'on découvre que la mort est réelle, et non plus seulement redoutable.

> [For Proust, the "middle of life's journey" was certainly his mother's death (1905), even if the mutation of existence, the inauguration of the new work, occurred only a few years later. A cruel bereavement, a unique and somehow irreducible bereavement can constitute for me that "pinnacle of the particular" Proust spoke of; though belated, this bereavement will be for me the middle of my life; for the "middle of life" is perhaps never anything but the moment when you discover that death is real, and no longer merely dreadful.] (*BL*, 321–22/286).

Loss and grief shake the foundations of the life they disrupt. In their wake, we are compelled to decide on the new and final life that we shall now follow in the second "half" of our existence. For the writer, this means choosing a new life by finding a "new practice of writing" (*BL*, 322/286), by involving himself or herself in a new "making." Proust does this in the innovative style of novelistic production that *A la recherche du temps perdu* represents. And Barthes shall also do it by searching for the new form, the "utopian novel" (*BL*, 325/289), which *La Chambre claire* will attempt to approximate.

The new writing Barthes seeks will express pathos, something that criticism rarely acknowledges as being essential to the act of reading. His search for the new form, coinciding with his search for mastery over the loss that he has encountered at this midpoint of his life, leads Barthes to find consolation and instruction in two great literary works. Through the death of Prince Bolkonski in *War and Peace* and the death of Marcel's grandmother in *A la recherche du temps perdu*, episodes that are "'moments of truth'" for Barthes (*BL*, 323/287), he learns two lessons that shall assist him in creating the new writing of his new life: first, the coincidence of literary form and human suffering, of text and cry; and second, the necessity that the literary work be animated by love or such other experiences as kindness, generosity, affection, warmth, and compassion. If affect is the prime mover of criticism, then love becomes for Barthes the initiator of writing, in particular of the new novelistic form he seeks.

La Chambre claire may be the work that gave Barthes the opportunity to realize his desire for a new practice, a new erotics, of writing. In several respects, *La Chambre claire* seems to satisfy the requirements for what in his lecture he calls "l'oeuvre à faire" ("the work to be written"; *BL*, 323/288). Such a text would have to fulfill three essential missions. First, it must express love, but with a selflessness capable of transcending the narcissism of the lover. Second, it must allow for a full, though indirect, representation of feeling. Third, it must eschew the moral preaching and intellectual terrorism that subject a reader to the authority and often the tyranny of ideology, or what Barthes calls the "Doxa." The new writing would derive from "the truth of affects, not that of ideas" (*BL*, 325/289). In many ways, *La Chambre claire* fulfills these three conditions: first, it is a work that expresses a son's love for his mother but that does not overemphasize the role of the self in this love; second, it makes the complete yet indirect representation of feeling the center of an investigation into the nature of photography; and, finally, it rejects the hegemony of ideologically and socially coded images in favor of photographs giving an experience of the *punctum,* that concentration of affective energy beyond the doxa that pierces the viewer to the very core of his or her being. In sum, the narrative of loss in Barthes is the narrative of the *punctum*.

La Chambre claire brings together the subjective and the essayistic, the affective and the critical, hallmarks of Barthes's late style of writing. On the one hand, the writer, besieged by an errant, decentered, and protean subjectivity, writes about his feelings, desires, and private concerns; on the other hand, the objective, dispassionate critic analyzes photographic images in order to discover their essential nature. Although Barthes foregrounds the search for a suitable method by which to study the nature of photography, he recognizes that for this study to bear fruit it must be nourished by affectivity. This willingness to rely on affect, to accord it primacy, is prefigured in the final sentences of " 'Longtemps, je me suis couché de bonne heure' ":

> Peut-être est-ce finalement au coeur de cette subjectivité, de cette intimité même dont je vous ai entretenus, peut-être est-ce à la "cime de mon particulier" que je suis scientifique sans le savoir, tourné confusément vers cette *Scienza Nuova* dont parlait Vico: ne devra-t-elle pas exprimer à la fois la brillance et la souffrance du monde, ce qui, en lui, me séduit et m'indigne?

> [Perhaps it is finally at the heart of this subjectivity, of this very intimacy which I have invoked, perhaps it is at the "pinnacle of my particularity" that I am scientific without knowing it, vaguely oriented toward that *Scienza Nuova* Vico spoke of: should it not express at once the world's brilliance and the world's suffering, all that beguiles and offends me?] (*BL*, 325/290)

This new, as yet uncertain, form of writing will have its fullest embodiment in *La Chambre claire*. Paradoxically, the withdrawal into self provoked by mourning and loss shall enable Barthes to reach out to the world and find a unique knowledge, a *scienza*, deriving its power not from erudite ideas but from the painful awareness that in life there exists a fragile balance—between light and darkness, pleasure and pain, possession and loss—which the *punctum* of death continuously upsets.

Barthes concludes his lecture by asking if the time has indeed not come for him to begin writing a novel, something he has contemplated doing many times during his career. His answer is characteristically enigmatic:

Je n'en sais rien. Je ne sais s'il sera possible d'appeler encore "roman" l'oeuvre que je désire et dont j'attends qu'elle rompe avec la nature uniformément intellectuelle de mes écrits passés.

[How should I know? I don't know if it will be possible still to call a "novel" the work I desire and which I expect to break with the uniformly intellectual nature of my previous writings.] (*BL*, 325/289)

In keeping with a career noted for breaks and swerves in critical method and style, Barthes contemplates making yet another shift, one that would move his work closer to the "loving or amorous power" of the novel (*BL*, 323–24/288), of the Proustian "tierce forme," toward which much of his late writing seems directed. Thus, obsessed with the death of his mother, overwhelmed by an impossible mourning, worried about having reached the midpoint of his life, besieged by growing uncertainty over genres, attracted by the possibility of a new form and a new practice of writing, intrigued by the example of Proust's life and by Tolstoy's descriptions of death, distrustful of criticism and literary science, and convinced that discourses of every type must express subjectivity, affect, and love, Barthes in 1978, as he lectures at the Collège de France, contemplates writing a new text: the "uncertain Form," the "utopian Novel," the story without a story ("le romanesque sans le roman") (*S/Z*, 11), which eventually will become *La Chambre claire*.

Affective Criticism

La Chambre claire: Note sur la photographie [Camera Lucida: Reflections on Photography] is a book about mourning which also expresses mourning. Here, a *poetics of loss* approaches a *poetry of loss*. Barthes's meditation on his mother's death is as poignant, affective, and elegiac as that of many poets. His discourse aspires to be "lyrical," a term that for him means "homogeneous with pathos" (*RB*, 89/86). But Barthes's text also presents a critical and analytic side. The expression of grief and the meditation on his mother's absence are mediated through a study of the nature of photography. By means of a very private photographic image, Barthes seeks to say something universal about the aesthetics of photography. He wishes to reveal an image's relation to the referential reality it represents and to understand the role of representation in experiences of loss. From a more subjective point of view, he wishes also to discover why certain photographs move or fascinate him, whereas others have no effect whatsoever.[4]

La Chambre claire is really two books in one. It is divided into two parts, each containing twenty-four sections. The first part deals exclusively with the phenomenology of photography. Here Barthes distinguishes between what he calls, following his penchant for creative neologisms, the *punctum* (piercing detail) and the *studium* (commonplace element) of a photograph. The second part, considerably more subjective and autobiographical, concerns his mother and the photograph of her as a child standing in a *jardin d'hiver* (winter garden), an image that captures for Barthes the truth and essence of her being as a person. While there is little mention of his mother and no mention of the winter garden photograph in the first part of the book, there is hardly any reference to the *punctum* and *studium* in the second. As Barthes's study of the lover's discourse in *Fragments d'un discours amoureux* was constructed from notes and fragments, so the book on photography reveals a similar notational incompleteness with a similar insistence on writing as the play of discontinuous signifiers, as the place of endless textual production, as "the circulatory space of subtle, flexible desires" (*BL*, 370/333). Barthes admits that his is the approach not of an expert or a savant but of a passionate amateur:

4. For useful and illuminating studies dealing fully or partly with *La Chambre claire* and offering several different interpretations regarding the role of photography, death, mourning, the mother, the body, the Imaginary, and the evolution of Barthesian poetics, see the following important essays: Jean Arrouye, *"Mors alma mater:* De la photographie," *Revue des sciences humaines* 81 (April–June 1988): 151–61; Colette Assouly-Piquet, "Le Retour du mort," *Critique* 459–60 (August–September 1985): 812–24; Hubert Damisch, "L'Intraitable," *Critique* 423–24 (August–September 1982): 681–87; Jean Delord, *Roland Barthes et la photographie* (Paris: Créatis, 1980); Jacques Derrida, "Les Morts de Roland Barthes," *Poétique* 47 (September 1981): 269–92; Serge Doubrovsky, "Une Ecriture tragique," *Poétique* 47 (September 1981): 329–54; Daniel Grojnowski, "Le Mystère de *La Chambre claire*," *Textuel* 34/44 15 (1984): 91–96; Michael Halley, "Argo Sum," *Diacritics* 12 (Winter 1982): 69–78; J. Gerald Kennedy, "Roland Barthes, Autobiography, and the End of Writing," *Georgia Review* 35 (Summer 1981): 381–98; Lawrence D. Kritzman, "Roland Barthes: The Discourse of Desire and the Question of Gender," *MLN* 103 (September 1988): 848–64; Jacques Leenhardt, "La Photographie, miroir des sciences humaines," *Communications* 36 (1982): 107–18; Patrizia Lombardo, *The Three Paradoxes of Roland Barthes* (Athens: University of Georgia Press, 1989); Claude Reichler, "L'Ombre," *Critique* 423–24 (August–September 1982): 767–74; Ralph Sarkonak, "Roland Barthes and the Spectre of Photography," *L'Esprit créateur* 22 (Spring 1982): 48–68; Jean-Marie Schaeffer, *L'Image précaire: Du dispositif photographique* (Paris: Seuil, 1987); Domna C. Stanton, "The Mater of the Text: Barthesian Displacement and Its Limits," *L'Esprit créateur* 25 (Summer 1985): 57–72; Chantal Thomas, "La Photo du jardin d'hiver," *Critique* 423–24 (August–September 1982): 797–804; Steven Ungar, "Barthes via Proust: Circular Memories," *L'Esprit créateur* 22 (Spring 1982): 8–19, and Mary Bittner Wiseman, *The Ecstasies of Roland Barthes* (London: Routledge, 1989), pp. 152–62 and 181–89.

Un homme naïf, non culturel, un peu sauvage qui ne cesserait de s'étonner de la photographie. . . . J'ai pris pour guide mon *plaisir* ou mon *désir* à l'égard de certaines photographies. Et j'ai essayé d'analyser ce plaisir ou ce désir.

[A naïve man, outside culture, someone untutored who would be constantly astonished at photography. . . . I chose to be guided by my *pleasure* or my *desire* in regard to certain photographs. And I tried to analyze this pleasure or desire.] (*GV*, 332/357)

Barthes's discussion of photography is conducted, therefore, according to an affective phenomenology of his own invention. He seeks to discover by what mysterious power photography can arouse feeling and desire.

As he seeks to identify and name the essence of photography, to sketch "the movement of an eidetic science of the Photograph" (*CC*, 40/20), Barthes's text often digresses, thus subverting the knowledge and meaning his method might have established. The need to express feeling pushes him away from a systematic, rational, and objective treatment of his subject:

Au lieu de suivre la voie d'une ontologie formelle (d'une Logique), je m'arrêtais, gardant avec moi, comme un trésor, mon désir ou mon chagrin; l'essence prévue de la Photo ne pouvait, dans mon esprit, se séparer du "pathétique" dont elle est faite, dès le premier regard. . . . Comme *Spectator*, je ne m'intéressais à la Photographie que par "sentiment;" je voulais l'approfondir, non comme une question (un thème), mais comme une blessure: je vois, je sens, donc je remarque, je regarde et je pense.

[Instead of following of the path of a formal ontology (of a Logic), I stopped, keeping with me, like a treasure, my desire or my grief; the anticipated essence of the Photograph could not, in my mind, be separated from the "pathos" of which, from the first glance, it consists. . . . As *Spectator* I was interested in Photography only for "sentimental" reasons; I wanted to explore it not as a question (a theme) but as a wound: I see, I feel, hence I notice, I observe, and I think.] (*CC*, 41–42/21)

Barthes wishes above all to be stung, wounded, pierced, bitten and pricked by the photograph, or, more precisely, by one of its details.

This is the power of the *punctum,* "this prick, this mark made by a pointed instrument" (*CC,* 49/26). It is what in a photograph literally grabs hold of the spectator's glance, shattering the nonchalance or casual interest he or she shows toward what he or she sees. It is usually a small, almost insignificant detail—the collar of a woman's dress, a pair of strapped shoes, the bad teeth of a smiling child, wheel tracks on a dirt road, an outstretched hand—that suddenly, mobilized by a charge of emotional or psychic energy, invades our consciousness as spectators; it touches, moves, even wounds us. It is the locus of an intense feeling that may bring tears to our eyes without our really knowing precisely why, as if the diffuse loss that every photograph represents had suddenly crystallized into a diamondlike point cutting into the heart. The spectator does not consciously or studiously go looking for the *punctum;* it comes out of the photograph, hunting for him or her like an arrow homing in on a target.[5]

Barthes feels a certain dilemma in *La Chambre claire.* He wishes to

5. In contrast to the *punctum* is the *studium,* that element of a photograph which provokes only general, dispassionate, and uninvolved interest. The *studium* pleases but does not give pleasure. It never pierces the spectator or takes possession of his or her consciousness. It is the field of "le désir nonchalant," rather than that of passion or love. To understand the *studium* is to know the photographer's intentions in making the photograph. In addition, the *studium* is culturally determined and reconciles photography and society. It endows the photograph with functions of communication by which it informs, represents, signifies, and surprises. But, invariably, the *studium* keeps the spectator distant and disengaged from the photograph. It does not have the power to awaken strong feelings or affect; it is never, Barthes writes, "my delight or my pain" (*CC,* 51/28).

One of the intriguing aspects of the *punctum* is that in its brief and piercing appearance it resembles the haiku, keystone of Barthes's study of Japanese culture and semiology in *L'Empire des signes.* Like the haiku, the *punctum* gives an experience of satori, in which an ebbing or suspension of meaning and an emptying of the self take place: "il opère un *vide de parole*" ("it creates *an emptiness of language*"; *ES,* 10/4). The haiku evacuates meaning from things. It announces the moment when language stops; it is an "echoless breach" establishing a "form—brief and empty" (*ES,* 96/74). Language is stopped in its tracks; it reaches a dead end and can no longer be developed or prolonged. It can only be repeated endlessly. The game of symbolic substitutions which produces meaning is suspended. No longer do the construction, ordering, coagulating, and finalizing of meaning create a lasting wholeness or a permanent signified. The haiku is fragmented language. It does not express or describe; rather, it "simply *causes to exist*" (*ES,* 106/80). As an element of pure designation, the haiku merely points to things and declares "*C'est cela, c'est ainsi . . . c'est tel.* Ou mieux encore: *Tel!*" ("*It's that, it's thus . . . it's so.* Or better still: *so!*"; *ES,* 111/83). The copula is, finally, superfluous. Meaning is only a flash, illuminating and revealing nothing, except its own vanishing burst of light.

The haiku's manner of designation is like that of a child pointing to something and saying "*Ça!*" in a movement so quick, sudden, and brief that no mediation—no naming, no possession, no knowledge—is possible. Regarding the haiku, "il n'y a rien à *saisir,*" Barthes writes in the last sentence of *L'Empire des signes.* "There is nothing to *grasp*" (*ES,* 146/110), and yet this nothing is *all* there is to grasp. This is the void that Barthes locates at the heart of Japanese semiology and contrasts to the Western desire to capture, categorize, and possess meaning. The haiku presents signs that are either already empty, or in the process of emptying themselves, of meaning. Like the brush stroke of the Japanese calligrapher, the haiku is a representation begun and finished in one quick

understand the nature of photography, but he cannot allow himself to use an objective, logical system of analysis, which would reduce the object of study to a single, absolute meaning. In his search for a writing that can simultaneously express the complex meanings of a photograph and the profoundly emotional reaction of the spectator who looks at it, Barthes avoids the coded discourses belonging to disciplines such as sociology, semiology, and psychoanalysis. He finds himself torn between subjective experience and critical objectivity, "between two languages, one expressive, the other critical" (*CC*, 20/8). The decision to use an expressive language resolves the dilemma. From this point on, the self will be the guide, the standard, Barthes shall follow in saying something fundamental about photography: "I am myself therefore the measure of photographic 'knowledge'" (*CC*, 22/9).

From a photograph that has no importance except for himself alone, Barthes will derive the essential truth of photography. The winter garden photograph of the mother as child shall be the standard, the *image-mère*, against which everything shall be compared. Crystallized in this photo is a truth whose meaning for the life and being of Barthes is so great that it surpasses his ability to write. But, because, generally speaking, the photograph is "a certificate of presence" (*CC*, 135/87) experienced at the very moment that such presence is annulled by the reality of loss, it also initiates a search to repossess the truth of "Ce qui ne se retrouve / Jamais, jamais" ("What never can be found / again—never!"), as Baudelaire wrote.[6] At the crossroads of presence and absence, of possession and loss, and of intimacy and separation stands the photograph, which, through the lack it represents and the plenitude it recalls, strives to establish a utopian knowledge: "*la science impossible de l'être unique*" ("*the impossible science of the unique being*"; *CC*, 110/71).

The Mortification of the Imaginary

La Chambre claire, like the two books that preceded it—*Roland Barthes par Roland Barthes* and *Fragments d'un discours amoureux*—is a meditation on representation. Like them, it questions the relationship of self to

---

gesture, leaving behind only a trace of its passage. The haiku has the intensity and fulgurance of this brush stroke, as does the *punctum*. One must experience them at first glance, in the instant of their appearance, before mental association, memory, or thought intervenes to make meaning crystallize. The *punctum* is "un éclair qui flotte" (*CC*, 87/53); it is a piercing, floating flash of light unattached to the ground of meaning.

6. "Le Cygne," in *Les Fleurs du mal*, in *OC*, 1:87 ["The Swan," in *Les Fleurs du Mal/The Flowers of Evil*, trans. Richard Howard (Boston: David R. Godine, 1982), p. 91].

other. In his impersonal, third-person autobiography, Barthes had examined the plasticity, heterogeneity, and elusiveness of the self, allowing it to be expressed through different pronouns and voices—"I," "you," "he," "R.B."—each claiming to speak in the name of this man, "Roland Barthes." Next, in the study of the lover's discourse, Barthes turned his attention to the representation of the other, in particular to the strategies of rhetorical appropriation by which the lover figures or "writes" the loved object in a discourse that not only represents the love relationship but also invents it. In *La Chambre claire* Barthes again deals with the relationship of self to other, but this time the other is a unique and significant being whose relationship to the self has determined its amorous relation to all other human beings. This primal, originary other is the mother. She is the Other of others, the alpha and omega of alterity. She is the first being to teach the infant the painful but necessary truth of separation, which the effort of a lifetime will be dedicated (vainly) to overturning. Into the relationship of total unity between an infant and his mother—an experience of oneness beyond language—appear a tear and a wound. For the first time the infant feels separated from the person to whom he had always felt indissolubly united. This separation generates an experience of otherness, which, haunting the child for the rest of his life, gives birth to a restless, unfulfilled desire. But loss of maternal closeness also opens a space of creativity, imagination, and fantasy, in which the child fabricates new objects and representations designed to give the illusion that the absent mother is present. In many respects, Barthes in *La Chambre claire* is in a position similar to that of the child separated from his mother. By creating or appropriating what D. W. Winnicott called a "transitional object"—the corner of a blanket, the tail of a stuffed animal—the child succeeds in provisionally filling the emptiness that the mother's absence has generated. The child thus negotiates safe passage through the space of loss. For Barthes, the winter garden photograph is such an object of transition.[7]

7. In an essay on Stendhal's Italian journals, Barthes describes the transitional space in which the child, through play and imagination, creates the illusion of the mother's presence:

Cette dialectique de l'amour extrême et de l'expression difficile, c'est un peu celle que connaît le petit enfant—encore *infans*, privé de langage adulte—lorsqu'il joue avec ce que Winnicott appelle un objet transitionnel; l'espace qui sépare et lie en même temps la mère et son bébé est l'espace même du jeu de l'enfant et du contrejeu de la mère: c'est l'espace encore informe de la fantaisie, de l'imagination, de la création.

[Such a dialectic of extreme love and difficult expression resembles what the very young child experiences—still *infans*, deprived of adult speech—when he plays

The trilogy, at once critical and affective, that Barthes writes at the end of his life (*Roland Barthes par Roland Barthes, Fragments d'un discours amoureux, La Chambre claire*) deals repeatedly with the phenomenon of absence. These books attempt to understand the elusive identities of the self, the other, and the mother, who, at every turn, resist the images assigned to represent them. Barthes sees self and other as existing uniquely through language. But within the space of the discourse that constitutes them, self and other are constantly trapped by the image and the image-system (*l'Imaginaire*), without which they could not be represented. They pay a high price for such figuration, because the Imaginary immobilizes them, enveloping them in fixed, stereotyped representations, which distort their truth. The image participates in a closed, finite system of meaning, which, concealing what it represents behind ideological codes and immutable signifieds, creates a paralyzing meaning.[8] In the act of trying to re-create the presence of what they

with what Winnicott calls a *transitional object;* the space which separates and at the same time links the mother and her baby is the very space of the child's play and of the mother's counterplay: it is the still-shapeless space of fantasy, of the imagination, of creation.] (*BL*, 341/303)

In his essay "The Location of Cultural Experience," D. W. Winnicott defines the transitional object as "a symbol of the union of the baby and the mother (or part of the mother)," which has a very particular temporal and spatial location: "It is at the place in space and time where and when the mother is in transition from being (in the baby's mind) merged in with the infant and alternatively being experienced as an object to be perceived rather than conceived of. The use of an object symbolizes the union of two now separate things, baby and mother, *at the point in time and space of the initiation of their state of separateness*" (*Playing and Reality* [New York: Basic Books, 1971], pp. 96–97). The term "transitional object" indicates, Winnicott observes, the baby's new ability to perceive and, more significantly, to accept difference and similarity; it describes "the infant's journey from the purely subjective to objectivity" ("Transitional Objects and Transitional Phenomena" [1951], in *Collected Papers: Through Paediatrics to Psycho-Analysis* [London: Tavistock, 1958], p. 234). As the embodiment of that which must be lost, the transitional object belongs to "the realm of illusion which is at the basis of initiation of experience." The mother allows the infant the illusion that what he creates really exists, and throughout life this experience of embodied illusion is continued in the "intense experiencing that belongs to the arts and to religion and to imaginative living, and to creative scientific work" (ibid., p. 242).

8. Barthes gives an extraordinarily imaginative description of how systems of meaning, figuration, and representation (the *Imaginary*, in other words) create this petrification of self. In a parable that tries to explain how the self is transformed into a final, immutable product, he compares the work of the image-system to the frying of a potato. Into sizzling oil are dropped pieces of potato:

"C'est comme un appât lancé à des bêtes qui dormaient d'un oeil, guettaient. Toutes se précipitent, entourent, attaquent en bruissant; c'est un banquet vorace. La parcelle de pomme de terre est cernée—non détruite, mais durcie, rissolée, caramélisée; cela devient un objet; une frite." Ainsi, sur tout objet, le bon système langagier *fonctionne*, s'affaire, cerne, bruit, durcit et dore. Tous les langages sont des micro-systèmes d'ébullition, des fritures. . . . Le langage (des autres) me transforme en image, comme la pomme de terre brute est transformée en frite.

represent, images lose the very thing they are charged with making visible, and thus they engender absence. Because it is fundamentally a discourse in which the lover writes the other and is written by the other, love takes place through an unstable play of signifiers in which both the self and the other are elusive figures. The other is always absent, always different from what my discourse says about him or her, because, as Barthes remarks, "absence can exist only as a consequence of the other" (*FDA*, 19/13). Because writing transpires in the space between the speaking self and the elusive and distant other that it addresses, it can only represent, make present, the alterity of the other. The person we address as "you" is always elsewhere. In the here and now of a text, or a language, or a story, writing expresses an irremediable absence. Discourse as *dis-cursus* moves to and fro in the empty space once inhabited by the other (*FDA*, 7/103). It seeks to reverse this absence by replacing the other with a plethora of signifiers, an overwhelming polysemy, which tries in vain to signify and thus fill the void.

The problem Barthes confronts in *La Chambre claire* is the irreversible and unrepresentable loss of the other who was his mother. This loss is made all the more anguishing by his powerlessness to see, imagine, or remember her without the past events of their close relationship becoming hardened in the immobilized form of an image. The memories of his mother do not exist outside of the proliferating images that envelop them: mnemonic images, photographic images, the figures and tropes of writing. Death has turned the woman, the living person with whom Barthes spent and shared much of his life, into a representation from which he cannot free himself. In death, everything becomes image. Against the reality of the *mother as image*, Barthes places his impossible desire for the *mother as presence*, free from the mediations of memory, photography, and writing. This is the desire for "*la science impossible de l'être unique*" ("*the impossible science of the unique being*"; *CC*, 110/71), an affective, passionate, and unmediated knowledge beyond the mortifying power of the Imaginary.

Surrounded by inescapable images that do not restore anything as much as they constantly remind him of the irreversible absence of the

---

["It is like a morsel tossed to wild beasts only half asleep, waiting. They all fling themselves upon it, attack it noisily: a voracious banquet. The slice of potato is surrounded—not destroyed, but hardened, caramelized, made crisp; it becomes an object: a French-fried potato." This is how, on any object, a good language-system *functions*, attacks, surrounds, sizzles, hardens, and browns. All languages are micro-systems of ebullition, of frying. . . . The language (of others) transforms me into an image, as the raw slice of potato is transformed into a *pomme frite*.] (*BL*, 394/355)

mother, Barthes, while thumbing through a photo album, comes upon an old, faded, sepia photograph. Of all the images of his mother, this appears to be the one that is the most true and the least subject to mortification. Taken in 1898, it shows Barthes's mother at the age of five standing next to her older brother in the winter garden of their mother's family house at Chennevières-sur-Marne. The brother leans against the railing of a wooden bridge, and the sister, retiring and shy, stands farther back, holding the finger of one hand by the other in "an awkward gesture" (*CC*, 106/69). Standing side by side, brother and sister are united, Barthes imagines, by the imminent separation of their parents, who divorced not long after the photograph was taken. For Barthes, a presentiment of loss already hovers over the photographed scene. Yet, this photograph, more than any other image, comes closest to capturing the truth of the mother's being because she appears in a pose purified of the codes and signifieds of the Imaginary.

Barthes wrote *La Chambre claire* under the sign of the winter garden photograph and through the influence of its *punctum*. Given the failure of representation to reverse the ravages occasioned by loss and death, this photograph approaches, as closely as any representation possibly can, a state of presence: the "living resurrection of the beloved face" (*CC*, 100/64). Occupying the center of Barthes's melancholic imagination, the photograph lends itself to fetishistic identification. It is the perfect embodiment of a certain image of the mother, enabling Barthes at certain moments to accept her irreversible absence and at other times to hallucinate the return of her unifying presence. Yet his desire for maternal repossession is not so all-consuming as to blind him to the deceptions of his own unconscious. At certain lucid moments he recognizes that such presence is truly impossible, that such plenitude emerges from an image and not from a person. Barthes never forgets the reality of ineffable otherness that the photograph incarnates. Like the lover in *Fragments d'un discours amoureux*, Barthes, standing before the painful image of the other, is "someone who speaks within himself, *amorously*, confronting the other (the loved object), who does not speak" (*FDA*, 7/3).

The photograph, like a relic, is marked by tangible traces of the absent other. It is celluloid on which at one second in the past certain rays of light, having truly touched the object, came to rest forever. Photographic images, like things—a crystal flask, a powder box, a favorite chair—that survive in the afterlife of the mother's absence, testify to the phenomenon Barthes names the "*Ça-a-été*" ("*That-has-been*"; *CC*, 120/77). Insofar as these images and things preserve and signify the real presence of the absent person, they may be considered traces of an absence momentarily made present. Unfortunately, such presence does not mean that the loved one reappears. Recuperative desire stumbles against the impossibility of recuperation. Images and words strike the wall of the void. In death, the mother is enveloped for all time in the shroud of otherness. Sign of a lost plenitude, she becomes the perfect incarnation of loss, designating in the fullest way possible the hole in the real opened by her absence. Among the cruel ironies that the death of the other announces, there is one, perhaps, that is the most difficult for a mourner to bear. It is the irony by which Barthes, so fervently desiring the mother's return, so intensely expressing this longing in endlessly proliferating words, only drives her deeper and deeper into the nothingness of death, where she becomes ever more phantasmatic: "I appeal to and summon up the other, the Mother, but what comes is merely a shade" (*FDA,* 130/113).

The shade that returns is not, in truth, that of the mother but that of the image. The mother is its prisoner. She cannot escape its immobilizing power, which ironically constitutes the only form by which she can be known and signified in the present. Images stick to the person they represent. They contaminate her life through the codes they affix to her identity. We cannot prevent being defined by the Imaginary—the irreducible, essentialized Signified developed early in childhood and carried through life like baggage. This explains Barthes's conviction that "every Image is bad" (*BL,* 395/356). Throughout his career, he labors to resist its will-to-immobilization, its Medusalike spell. Recognizing that he cannot do without images, that they are indestructible, Barthes tries instead to distance and suspend them.

In life, as in death, there is no escaping the empire of the Imaginary. Indeed, we are assailed by several image-systems, each ready to take possession of our identity. The *Imaginaire,* Barthes observes, burns underground like an incompletely extinguished peat fire; it flares up again and again (*FDA,* 126/108–9). Although in infancy there is a brief period when, prior to the development of the image-repertoire and coincident with the union of child and mother, images do not exist, no such acme of fulfilled desire will ever occur again. Barthes knows in advance that all his efforts to escape the magnetic pull of the *Imaginaire*—the renewed attempts to change the subjects, styles, and methods of his writing, the use of discontinuous and fragmented discourses, the presentation of a decentered and divided self, the preoccupation with the adventures of the signifier, the death struggle with the signified, the distrust of analogy and adjectives—will all meet with failure.

"Believing, I could disperse myself, I end up merely returning, quite docilely, to the bed of the imaginary" (*RB*, 99/95), he writes. But even though the image-system finds ways of stealthily creeping back in, the knowledge of how it operates, how it exercises its power, can teach one how to keep it at a distance. Those things that are lackluster and flat ("matte," to use the word Barthes often employs) and that, deprived of éclat or meaning, are not easily appropriated for signification, stand the best chance of escaping the magnetic field of the Imaginary. Writing—because it is identified by Barthes with process, movement, dispersion, the endless play of signifiers, the "stereographic plurality" of meaning (*BL*, 73/60), and the production of the text—can slow down, without entirely stopping, the ascendancy of the image-repertoire. Writing allows Barthes, therefore, to move freely within the domain of the Imaginary, to breathe within the hermetically sealed confines of the suffocating image, and sometimes to break away momentarily from its magnetic field:

Dès que je produis, dès que j'écris, c'est le Texte lui-même qui me dépossède (heureusement) de ma durée narrative. Le Texte ne peut rien raconter; il emporte mon corps ailleurs, loin de ma personne imaginaire, vers une sorte de langue sans mémoire.

[Once I produce, once I write, it is the Text itself which (fortunately) dispossesses me of my narrative continuity. The Text can recount nothing; it takes my body elsewhere, far from my imaginary person, toward a kind of memoryless speech.] (*RB*, 6/4)

It is only through writing, through the production of the text with its infinite polysemy, that Barthes can contest the mortified image his mother has become, that he can temporarily mask the death's head leering from within the photograph. Barthes undoes the photographic image by rewriting it. He refuses to include the winter garden photograph, which represents the truth of his mother, among the twenty-five that are reproduced in *La Chambre claire*. It is too personal, too sacred, to share with strangers, he observes. But another, more important, reason accounts for its exclusion. The winter garden photograph must be read *as writing* and not seen *as image*. To escape the Imaginary, it has to become a text. This is precisely what *La Chambre claire* accomplishes. The winter garden photograph exists for the reader only insofar as Barthes puts it into signifiers and transforms it into a restless and fluid discourse. It has no reality other than the linguistic one Barthes gives it.

We do not see the photograph; we even have difficulty imagining what it looks like. But we do *read* it. Thus, the dispersiveness and decenteredness of the text offer the writer the means of provisionally undoing the mortification, the *mise-en-mort*, of the image. Although the tragic and melancholic truth is that, because of the paralyzing force of the Imaginary, "on échoue toujours à parler de ce qu'on aime" ("one always fails in speaking of what one loves"), as the title of Barthes's very last essay affirms,[9] writing can make an opening in the wall of the *Imaginaire:*

> L'Ecriture, c'est quoi? Une puissance, fruit probable d'une longue initiation, qui défait l'immobilité stérile de l'imaginaire amoureux et donne à son aventure une généralité symbolique.
>
> [What is writing? A power, probable fruit of a long initiation, which annuls the sterile immobility of the amorous image-repertoire and gives its adventure a symbolic generality.] (*BL,* 342/305)

La Chambre claire is, thus, not only a meditation on loss but also an attempt, through the act of writing, to divest that loss of immobility, mortification, and signification. The *punctum* disrupts and subverts the image of death which the photograph represents. It is a form of writing (it refers, among other things, to marks of punctuation) which, in piercing the surface of the photograph, escapes the confining limits of the representation and invades the being of the spectator. The *punctum*, like the haiku Barthes studies in *L'Empire des signes*, is a searing flash of writing which, arriving suddenly and enduring an instant, empties itself of meaning; for a brief moment it suspends the petrifying force, the mortifying power, of the Imaginary.

Photography as Thanatography

The photographic image, Barthes asserts throughout *La Chambre claire*, is the writing of death; whatever it represents, it mortifies, for it is fundamentally *thanatographic*, and, one might add, *thanatotropic*.[10] The

9. Barthes was preparing the essay—on the subject of Stendhal's Italian journals—for a colloquium in Milan. The manuscript was found beside his typewriter; the first page had been retyped; the second page was still in the machine (*BL,* 342).
10. On the notion of thanatography, see Christian Metz, "Photography and Fetish," *October* 34 (Fall 1985): 81–90; Philippe Dubois, *L'Acte photographique* (Paris: Nathan and Labor, 1983); and Jean Louis Schefer, *L'Espèce de chose mélancolie* (Paris: Flammarion, 1978), pp. 24–25 and 27–31.

irony of photography is that in its attempt to preserve life and the events of the living, it captures only the image of what no longer exists. It draws us toward death. Looking at a photograph, the spectator is reminded of "that rather terrible thing which is there in every photograph: the return of the dead" (*CC*, 23/9). Photography, Christian Metz remarks, "is the mirror, more faithful than any actual mirror, in which we witness at every age, our own aging."[11] Death is the great Signified of every image: "Each perception and reading of a photo is implicitly, in a repressed manner, a contact with what has ceased to exist, a contact with death" (*GV*, 331/356). To look at a photograph, then, is to read the wounded writing that death and loss have inscribed.

Death transcends not only symbolization but also representation. It exists beyond speech, language, analogy, and metaphor, none of which can redeem or find meaning in it. Death is a signified that no signifier can express, even though the sign may excessively and hysterically pursue it. This nullification of the signifying process constitutes death's most horrible, its most annihilating, dimension:

> L'horreur, c'est ceci: rien à dire de la mort de qui j'aime le plus, rien à dire de sa photo, que je contemple sans jamais pouvoir l'approfondir, la transformer. La seule "pensée" que je puisse avoir, c'est qu'au bout de cette première mort, ma propre mort est inscrite; entre les deux, plus rien, qu'attendre; je n'ai d'autre ressource que cette *ironie:* parler du "rien à dire."

> [The horror is this: nothing to say about the death of one whom I love most, nothing to say about her photograph, which I contemplate without ever being able to get to the heart of it, to transform it. The only "thought" I can have is that at the end of this first death, my own death is inscribed; between the two, nothing more than waiting; I have no other resource than this *irony:* to speak of the "nothing to say."] (*CC*, 145/92–93)

Conscious of the impotent means of expression available to him in the wake of his mother's death, Barthes confronts the flatness and the muteness of language. Words no longer signify; or, if they do, they give meaning only to nothing, to *the* nothing (*le rien*). Between the inexhaustible horror of death and the superficiality of the language expressing it opens a vacant space that only the speech of nothingness— the "rien à dire" (the "nothing to say"), the "rien à *saisir*" (the "nothing to *grasp*"; *ES*, 146/110)—can fill.

11. "Photography and Fetish," p. 84.

Barthes's own writing is subject to this linguistic void because it is a discourse that seeks to articulate nothing, "to speak the 'nothing to say.'" His mother's death, his textualization of that death, and the truth of the winter garden photograph have, along with the Japanese haiku, this power of expressing the nothing, of designating an emptiness. The "thisness" and "suchness" that Barthes refers to as the "*Ça*" or the "*tel*," and that he identifies with the concentrated flash of the haiku and with the piercing phenomenon of the *punctum*, are characteristic of death as well.[12] Before the terror of nothingness, discourses are reduced to monosyllables. The thanatographic image is a denotative sign emptied of meaning. Pointing to death and nothingness, the photograph utters the only word that can be spoken: "*Ça.*" Nothing more can be said, because that word is as complete a designation of the reality of death as the void allows.

The photograph thus embalms the subject, enveloping him in the nonbeing of death, where he is neither subject nor object:

Imaginairement, la Photographie . . . représente ce moment très subtil où, à vrai dire, je ne suis ni un sujet ni un objet, mais plutôt un sujet qui se sent devenir objet: je vis alors une micro-expérience de la mort (de la parenthèse): je deviens vraiment spectre.

[In terms of image-repertoire, the Photograph . . . represents that very subtle moment when, to tell the truth, I am neither subject nor object but a subject who feels he is becoming an object: I then experience a micro-version of death (of parenthesis): I am truly becoming a specter.] (*CC*, 30/13–14)

12. The deictics of the photograph are self-designating and self-contained; it is the photograph's reality to be exactly just as it is and thus to reduce expression to a linguistic minimum, to empty words:

Pour désigner la réalité, le bouddhisme dit *sunya*, le vide; mais encore mieux: *tathata*, le fait d'être tel, d'être ainsi, d'être cela; *tat* veut dire en sanskrit *cela* et ferait penser au geste du petit enfant qui désigne quelque chose du doigt et dit: *Ta, Da, Ça!* Une photographie se trouve toujours au bout de ce geste; elle dit: *ça, c'est ça, c'est tel!* mais ne dit rien d'autre.

[In order to designate reality, Buddhism says *sunya*, the void; but better still: *tathata*, the fact of being this, of being thus, of being so; *tat* means *that* in Sanskrit and suggests the gesture of the child pointing his finger at something and saying: *that, there it is, lo!* but says nothing else.] (*CC*, 15–16/4–5)

See also Barthes's description of the lover's desire to designate the other in its essential being, its "suchness," without recourse to either image or adjective, in the chapter "Tel" in *Fragments d'un discours amoureux*, pp. 261–64 ["Thus," in *A Lover's Discourse: Fragments*, pp. 220–23].

Looking at oneself in a photograph, one is struck by the otherness of what is represented, by the reality of difference which reveals itself. It does not correspond to the image one has of oneself. The impression of strangeness comes from a new dimension that has been added; namely, the immobility of death: "What I see is that I have become Total-Image, which is to say, Death in person; others—the Other—do not dispossess me of myself, they turn me, ferociously, into an object" (*CC*, 31/14). Having taken from a living being his mobile and protean self, death causes it to be replaced by a petrified image, which, because it is now affixed to a piece of photographic paper, can circulate, can pass from hand to hand, like currency. Death is as much the end of life as it is the paralysis of signification, which the image-repertoire accomplishes. I now see myself as I am seen from the perspective of death. I am embodied in an image that dispossesses me of both body and self, divesting me of what I truly am in the passing moments of a day, a month, a life.

When we say that "we have *taken* a picture," our use of language is revealing; it indicates our confidence in the power to possess and capture an object of perception. Barthes observes that the part he loves best about being photographed is the sound the shutter makes. This sound symbolizes the last moment of life before it is fixed for all time in a changeless representation that nothing can undo. The click of the shutter is the last and short-lived moment of reprieve from the death that the photograph realizes. It is the sound of time passing just as that passing is about to be arrested, just as the glue of the Imaginary is about to set. The click signifies a threshold between life and death, movement and immobility, present and past. Because one of the qualities of the photograph is its representation of the reality of the "Ça-a-été," the "It-has-passed," the click of the shutter is the voice of the "It-is-passing," the last gasp of a still living moment. And the click has an almost erotic effect on Barthes; it expresses a possession, a taking hold that has not yet become final, that has not yet expended itself, and so for a microsecond still lives. It is thus like the ephemeral flash of the haiku, without meaning and beyond representation. The click of the shutter is the ejaculatory moment preceding the nothing, the extinction, and the death that the camera accomplishes when it takes possession of the subject in the thanatographic image.[13]

13. It is interesting to compare Barthes's description of the erotic and ejaculatory dimension he associates with the shutter's click of death—in which plenitude and loss, presence and absence, possession and dispossession, appearance and disappearance, and, finally, passion and death momentarily coincide—to his discussion of the erotics of

Every photograph, therefore, presents an image for which it is already and always in mourning. It represents a being who continues to live in the present not as a person, not as a self, but as a thing. Because of the authenticity of reference which the image certifies—the fact that what we see did at one time exist—the photo has the force of the real but neither the presence nor the immediacy of the real. Thus, the photograph reveals the vast expanse and unfathomable depth of loss. Between mother and son, the experience of unmediated oneness has vanished. All that remains of her intense presence is a piece of paper imprinted with a pale and faded image. Photographed, the mother has become an entombed miniature, an object no larger than the hand holding it. She dwells in the realm of Signification. Barthes contemplates this immobilized image like a dreamer endlessly searching for a place he cannot find or vainly seeking entry to a room where there are no doors: "The same effort, the same Sisyphean labor: to reascend, straining toward the essence, to climb back down without having seen it, and to begin all over again" (*CC,* 104/66).

The Photograph of an Absence/The Absence of a Photograph

The reality of photography for Barthes lies in its power to present and ratify its referent as real. Photograph and referent are like two pages of paper glued together; the removal of one ruins the other. They are attached, Barthes remarks in a strikingly apt comparison, like a condemned man chained to the dead body of a fellow prisoner (*CC,* 17/6). The photograph is not a copy of its referent but an emanation, the sediment of the past deposited on the soil of the present:

> D'un corps réel, qui était là, sont parties des radiations qui viennent me toucher, moi qui suis ici; peu importe la durée de la transmission; la photo de l'être disparu vient me toucher comme les rayons différés

---

textual pleasure: "The pleasure of the text is like that untenable, impossible, purely *novelistic* instant so relished by Sade's libertine when he manages to be hanged and then to cut the rope at the very moment of his orgasm, his bliss" (*PT,* 15/7). From another point of view, Metz interprets the click of the shutter as a figure of castration and thus the beginning of a fetishistic defense that keeps the frightening reality of the off-frame from being represented in the photograph. Where the off-frame signifies lack, loss, and absence, the in-frame, the photograph itself, represents fullness, plenitude, and presence: "The photographic *take*," he writes, "is immediate and definitive, like death and like the constitution of the fetish in the unconscious, fixed by a glance in childhood, unchanged and always active later. Photography is a cut inside the referent, it cuts off a piece of it, a fragment, a part object, for a long immobile travel of no return" ("Photography and Fetish," p. 84).

d'une étoile. Une sorte de lien ombilical relie le corps de la chose photographiée à mon regard: la lumière, quoique impalpable, est bien ici un milieu charnel, une peau que je partage avec celui ou celle qui a été photographié.

[From a real body, which was there, proceed radiations which ultimately touch me, who am here; the duration of the transmission is insignificant; the photograph of the missing being . . . will touch me like the delayed rays of a star. A sort of umbilical cord links the body of the photographed thing to my gaze: light, though impalpable, is here a carnal medium, a skin I share with anyone who has been photographed.] (*CC*, 126–27/80–81)

This description, unlike other passages in *La Chambre claire*, attests to the power of the photographic image to revive the presence of the other. The link between the spectator and the subject of the photograph is physical and sensual. My hands touch, my eyes see, and my skin grazes, Barthes seems to suggest, a surface that the body of the other as radiated light, as luminous emanation, truly touched at a particular moment in the past, marking it with the intensity of its physical presence. The photographic image is an "umbilical cord" linking past and present. The metaphor is appropriate not only because it suggests a sustaining attachment between the referent and the spectator but also because it translates Barthes's desire to recover the mother and, more precisely, to reexperience phantasmatically a certain physical unity with her. The longing for fusion with the referent is at the center of Barthes's desire. It bears witness to the illusory hope that, across the gap of time and through the void of death, he can regain contact with what has been lost. The awareness of loss is momentarily placed in parentheses, suspended, as the thought of the realness of the referent dominates. Barthes's fantasy of recuperation—his desire to repossess the mother through the mummified intermediary of the photographic image and to reestablish the presence of the past— derives from a state of melancholic longing. In melancholy, explains Freud, the image of the lost object is internalized in the unconscious, where it continues to live, thus blocking the awareness of a loss too devastating to accept. Similarly, the photograph works to achieve the melancholic preservation of the lost object. It presents a picture of the past so real, so graphic, so irrefutable as to appear to deny that any absence or loss ever occurred.[14]

14. One of the most powerful of photography's many illusions is the sense of presence it gives, as Rosalind Krauss points out: "Photography's vaunted capture of a

Yet, Barthes knows that the realness of the photographic referent, its physical presence as an image of the past, is negated by his awareness of its real absence; "what the Photograph reproduces to infinity," he writes, "has occurred only once: the Photograph mechanically repeats what could never be repeated existentially" (*CC*, 15/4). Photography thus designates the absence of a moment it cannot help but commemorate. On the one hand, it affirms that the referent appears exactly as it once was; this is the "thereness" of the photograph, its stubborn permanence and intractability, its irrefutable presentness as the "*Ça-a-été*" (*CC*, 120/77). On the other hand, the photograph states that this "fait d'être tel, d'être ainsi, d'être cela" ("fact of being this, of being thus, of being so"; *CC*, 15/5), this *punctum*, is an irreversible and ineradicable fact of loss, of absence. What the photo preserves is, therefore, not a body but an image. Decorporealized by death, the photographed being has as its material substance only what is imparted to it by the yellowing paper on which it is printed for all time. He who looks at this figure, even if he is a loving son, is compelled by death to become a reader, only slightly more knowledgeable ultimately than the reader of *La Chambre claire*, for whom the invisible winter garden photograph is a text, the textualized presence of an unseen image. Thus, to read a photograph of absence is also to read an absent photograph.

The Photograph as Fetish

In his 1927 essay "Fetishism," Freud describes how the child, reacting to the perception that the female genitalia lack a penis, finds a symbolic substitute for the missing phallus and thus succeeds in denying the reality of what he believes to have been a terrifying event of

---

moment in time is the seizure and freezing of presence. It is the image of simultaneity, of the way that everything within a given space at a given moment is present to everything else; it is a declaration of the seamless integrity of the real. The photograph carries on one continuous surface the trace or imprint of all that vision captures in one glance. The photographic image is not only a trophy of this reality, but a document of its unity as that-which-was-present-at-one-time" (p. 23). Thus, Krauss concludes that the photograph, because it is "a kind of deposit of the real itself" (p. 26), is not an icon in the way drawings and paintings are, but an index: "For photography is an imprint or transfer off the real; it is a photochemically processed trace causally connected to that thing in the world to which it refers in a manner parallel to that of fingerprints or footprints or the rings of water that cold glasses leave on tables. . . . On the family tree of images it is closer to palm prints, death masks, the Shroud of Turin, or the tracks of gulls on beaches" (p. 26). ("The Photographic Conditions of Surrealism," *October* 19 [Winter 1981]: 3–34).

castration. "The fetish," Freud writes, "is a penis-substitute . . . for a particular quite special penis that had been extremely important in early childhood but was afterwards lost. That is to say: it should normally have been given up, but the purpose of the fetish precisely is to preserve it from being lost. To put it plainly: the fetish is a substitute for the woman's (mother's) phallus which the little boy once believed in and does not wish to forego."[15] The boy denies the absence of a penis in the woman because to fail to do so is to put his own phallus in danger. But the perception of the lack persists, and in reaction to it the child finds a surrogate object to replace it. "Something else has taken its place," Freud writes, "has been appointed its successor, so to speak, and now absorbs all the interest which formerly belonged to the penis. But this interest undergoes yet another very strong reinforcement, because the horror of castration sets up a sort of permanent memorial to itself by creating this substitute."[16]

The phallus is, therefore, both present (in the form of the fetish object) and absent (in the form of the lack for which the fetish compensates). Against the fact of an absence and the reality of loss, the child fantasizes a fictional wholeness, which paradoxically he succeeds in creating by means of a partial object, either a part of the body or a piece of clothing. The fetish works through metonymic substitution; a part-object signifies what is an unrepresentable and phantasmatic whole. Because the fetish object blocks out consciousness of castration, interceding at "the last moment in which the woman could still be regarded as phallic,"[17] it preserves the status quo as perceived by the child. The fetish object, thus, denies an awareness of the reality of loss. But this denial is never complete, because the fetishist is of two minds. There is a splitting of the ego between two independent and contrary attitudes. The fetishist's "disavowal is always supplemented by an acknowledgment."[18] Knowing that the woman has no phallus, he nevertheless signifies his desperate denial of this knowledge through the fetish. The fetish, therefore, like the photograph, is simultaneously an acknowledgment and a disavowal of loss.

At certain times in *La Chambre claire*, Barthes reacts to the loss inscribed in the winter garden photograph by averting his glance, by looking away from an emptiness and a lack that are too frightening for

15. Philip Rieff, ed., *Sexuality and the Psychology of Love* (New York: Collier Books, 1963), p. 215.

16. Ibid., p. 216.

17. Ibid., p. 217.

18. Sigmund Freud, *An Outline of Psycho-Analysis* (1940), trans. and ed. James Strachey, rev. ed. (New York: W. W. Norton, 1969), p. 61.

him to acknowledge. Death forces him to find something else that he can put in its place so as to make the absence of the mother seem like a presence. Barthes hallucinates this presence by fixing his attention on the photographic image *as image*. The figure of the mother as presented by the photograph becomes the fetishized substitute for the absent person who was his mother. The image becomes the hallucination by which the absence of the mother's body is supplanted by her representation, as if this were her only true reality. The fetishized photograph fights off the consciousness of a void and instead works to fill it with a hallucinated presence.[19] But this surrogate presence, while denying the loss, also memorializes its reality. The very presence of the compensating fetish attests to the fact that something has been lost. Loss is the precondition for fetishization. The photographic image denies the lack of the mother but, by taking her place, acknowledges that her loss is real and absolute.[20]

Photography, because it confuses the truth of an event or a person (*"C'est ça!"*) (*"there-it-is!"*) with the reality of its having taken place or existed (*"Cela a été"*) (*"it has been"*; *CC*, 176/113) is, Barthes concludes, a form of madness. Photography is mad in the way it blurs the distinction between presence and absence. It reveals that something intensely present can also be intensely absent. Photography is, therefore, a new form of hallucination: "false on the level of perception, true on the level of time: a temporal hallucination, so to speak, a modest, *shared* hallucination (on the one hand 'it is not there,' on the other 'but it has indeed been'): a mad image, chafed by reality" (*CC*, 177/115). The

19. In "Photography and Fetish," Metz associates the place of terrifying absence, of castration, with the off-frame of the photograph. The off-frame is the lack that the fetish by its presence seeks simultaneously to replace and to ward off: "The character who is off-frame in a photograph, however, will never come into the frame, will never be heard—again a death, another form of death. The spectator has no empirical knowledge of the contents of the off-frame, but at the same time cannot help imagining some off-frame, hallucinating it, dreaming the shape of this emptiness. . . . The off-frame effect in photography results from a singular and definitive cutting off which figures castration and is figured by the 'click' of the shutter. It marks the place of an irreversible absence, a place from which the look has been averted forever" (p. 87). According to Metz, Barthes's *punctum* is the only part of the photograph which "entails the feeling of an off-frame space" (ibid.).

20. A more psychoanalytic interpretation of the fetishistic reality of the winter garden photograph might emphasize the phallic nature of both the photograph and the mother: first, because the pale and not too well preserved photograph has undergone a kind of mutilation; second, because given his intense identification with the mother throughout *La Chambre claire*, Barthes may unconsciously think of her as being endowed with his own phallus; and third, because in this photograph the phallic child-mother is shown holding (and hiding) the finger of one hand in the other, a pose also captured in the only photograph of the mother as child which Barthes does publish in *La Chambre claire* (entitled "La Souche," p. 163 ["The Stock," p. 104]).

photograph is a phantasm, simultaneously false and true, absent and present. It is, to be sure, an image, but one that has been touched by the real. The photograph is a kind of *frottage:* the trace of something that was sufficiently present to leave its imprint but, having subsequently disappeared, is no longer knowable except through the imprecise markings it has left behind.

In attempting to define more clearly what he means by the particularity of the hallucination as it relates to photography, Barthes offers a personal anecdote. One day, after spending several hours looking through photographs of his mother, he goes to see Fellini's film *Casanova.* He finds the movie boring, except for one scene where Casanova dances with an automaton. Barthes is fascinated by this automaton because it represents what is simultaneously and paradoxically mechanical and human, inert and compassionate. It reminds him of what he finds most seductive in all the photos of his mother he loves: the enigmatic juxtaposition of life and death. Watching the dancing automaton, he realizes that there is just "*un peu* de corps sous la robe aplatie" ("the *slightest* of bodies under the flattened gown"; *CC*, 178/ 116). Barthes is hallucinating a *soupçon* of life and flesh where in reality, given the mechanical nature of the automaton, there should be none at all. His hallucination is fetishistic because he senses that under the dress perhaps there is a body part ("*un peu* de corps"), a phallus, that would otherwise be absent from what is, after all, only a machine. As images of lack, both the photograph and Fellini's automaton are endowed by Barthes's fetishistic imagination with a recuperative presence. Such "madness," such hallucinatory fetishism, is without question the province of the photograph; for it invests death with life, absence with presence, loss with repossession, and image with being. The encounter with absence stimulates the imagination of both the writer and the lover, provoking them to hallucinate the presence of the absent other they have lost, not only like the fetishist guarding the delusion of a maternal phallus but also, to quote Barthes's very telling analogy, like "un mutilé qui continue d'avoir mal à sa jambe amputée" ("an amputee who still feels pain in his missing leg"; *FDA,* 49/39).

The Child Is Father of the Woman

Barthes inscribes the mother through writing. He attempts to free her from the image-system in which she is shrouded by transforming the winter garden photograph into a text, a play of signifiers. Only writing can unravel the woof and warp of the Imaginary because the text is "language without its image-reservoir, its image-system" (*PT*, 55/33). It is significant that he has chosen as the title for his study of photography *La Chambre claire*, the name given to a technique of mimetic representation, by means of which one writes or, more precisely, traces the image of an object of perception. Barthes traces his mother on the pages of his text in accordance with the optics of "la chambre claire," the *camera lucida*. Yet, by "writing" the mother Barthes's text re-creates her, or, as he states repeatedly, gives birth to her. As reader of the mother's photographic image and then as writer of the text that tries to undo that image, that signified, Barthes endows the mother with a new corporeality, a new textuality. Because he is a writer, and because writers find pleasure in the play of language, especially that of "la langue maternelle," it follows that the writer

> est quelqu'un qui joue avec le corps de sa mère . . . : pour le glorifier, l'embellir, ou pour le dépecer, le porter à la limite de ce qui, du corps, peut être reconnu.

> [is someone who plays with his mother's body . . . : in order to glorify it, to embellish it, or in order to dismember it, to take it to the limit of what can be known about the body.] (*PT*, 60/37)

To play with the maternal body and its image is thus to foil the Imaginary. It is to inscribe the body within a force field of changing, indeterminate, and plural signifiers through the *erotics* of writing.[21]

Throughout *La Chambre claire*, Barthes engenders his mother. She becomes his one and only child. At the end of her life, she is so weak

21. For Barthes, the erotics of writing and teaching are associated with maternal presence (and paternal absence). The writer/teacher resembles a child, actualizing his desire by bringing to the mother a present, which is a text. The text revolves playfully around the mother; it is a *speaking to* the mother, the writer's gift to her. Writing and teaching are activities in which the ludic possibilities of digression or, more important still, of "excursion" activate the movement of desire; that is, the comings and goings of

> un enfant qui joue autour de sa mère, qui s'en éloigne, puis retourne vers elle pour lui rapporter un caillou, un brin de laine, dessinant de la sorte autour d'un centre paisible toute une aire de jeu, à l'intérieur de laquelle le caillou, la laine importent finalement moins que le don plein de zèle qui en est fait.
> Lorsque l'enfant agit ainsi, il ne fait rien d'autre que de dérouler les allées et venues d'un désir, qu'il présente et représente sans fin. Je crois sincèrement qu'à l'origine d'un enseignement comme celui-ci, il faut accepter de toujours placer un fantasme, qui peut varier d'année en année. . . . C'est à un fantasme, dit ou non dit, que le professeur doit annuellement revenir, au moment de décider du sens de son voyage; de la sorte il dévie de la place où on l'attend, qui est la place du Père, toujours mort, comme on le sait; car seul le fils a des fantasmes, seul le fils est vivant.

that Barthes begins to live within the orbit of her feebleness. So great is this identification that he begins to find the world of health, of dynamic urban life, and of intellectual and university activity unbearable. During his mother's illness, Barthes cares for her; he feeds and watches over her like a parent: "She had become my little girl, uniting for me with that essential child she was in her first photograph" (*CC*, 112/72). Barthes's fantasy of the mother as child, as *his* child, reveals the great significance of the winter garden photograph, in which childhood is synonymous with the maternal. Having, late in his own life, cared for *the child-in-the-mother*, Barthes after her death returns to the distant past of the winter garden photograph, where he discovers *the mother-in-the-child*. He fantasizes that no distinction—and no separation—exists any longer between mother and child: "She who had been so strong, had been my inner law, ultimately I experienced her as my feminine child" (*CC*, 113/72).[22] This is his way of countering death, of resolving it "à

[a child playing beside his mother, leaving her, returning to bring her a pebble, a piece of string, and thereby tracing around a calm center a whole locus of play within which the pebble, the string come to matter less than the enthusiastic giving of them.

When the child behaves in this way, he in fact describes the comings and goings of desire, which he endlessly presents and represents. I sincerely believe that at the origin of teaching such as this we must always locate a fantasy, which can vary from year to year. . . . It is to a fantasy, spoken or unspoken, that the professor must annually return, at the moment of determining the direction of his journey. He thereby turns from the place where he is expected, the place of the Father, who is always dead, as we know. For only the son has fantasies; only the son is alive.]
(*Leçon* [Paris: Seuil, 1978], pp. 42–44) ["Inaugural Lecture, Collège de France," trans. Richard Howard, in *A Barthes Reader*, ed. Susan Sontag (New York: Hill and Wang, 1982), pp. 476–77]

22. A similarly interesting reversal of roles in which the adult child imagines himself the parent of his parent is expressed by André Frénaud in the poem "Tombeau de mon père" (1939–52):

Mon père, depuis que tu es mort
c'est toi qui est devenu mon petit enfant.

. . . . .

O père, c'est ma vie qui te garde en vie
pour que tu l'éclaires.
Tu disparaîtras quand je ne serai plus.

Toujours liés, nous deux. Jusque là on ne se quitte pas.

[Father, since your death
it is you that have become my little child.

. . . . .

Oh father, it is my life that keeps you alive
so that you may enlighten it.
You will disappear when I no longer exist.

Forever bound, one to the other, we do not part.]
(*Il n'y a pas de paradis*, Collection Poésie [Paris: Gallimard, 1962], pp. 195, 200)

ma manière" (ibid.). If the disappearance of the individual assures the survival of the species, then Barthes, who has no progeny, feels that he has produced an offspring who will give him a future:

> Si, après s'être reproduit comme autre que lui-même, l'individu meurt, s'étant ainsi nié et dépassé, moi qui n'avais pas procréé, j'avais, dans sa maladie même, engendré ma mère.

> [If after having been reproduced as other than himself, the individual dies, having thereby denied and transcended himself, I who had not procreated, I had, in her very illness, engendered my mother.] (*CC,* 113/72)

Barthes's future will come about through the act of re-creating the mother: the engendering of her body in writing. It is the son who now gives birth to the mother. Her death removes any possibility of pro-creation, other than that of writing. By substituting themselves for the mother, texts now become the new progeny Barthes fathers. The wound and the pain of loss demand such an endless outpouring of signifiers. There is no other way to revive the mother's body, to breathe new spirit into the mother tongue, and to struggle against the Signified that death establishes. The passing away of Barthes's mother engenders, then, an incessant, fetishized writing because the signifiers, under ever-increasing pressure to fill the void that has opened in his life, run to greater and greater excess. Confronted by the reality of death, writing becomes uncontrollable. Where once for Barthes there existed the *mère-enfant,* and then the *mère-photo,* there now remains only the endlessly repeated *mère-écriture.*[23]

23. The winter garden photograph, not only because it represents the child-mother but also because it incarnates the essence of childhood and, more particularly, the nurturing and mothering dimensions of childhood (childhood-as-mother, one might say), could be seen as presenting Barthes with the image of *himself* as child. His identification with the mother is thus tightened even further; the anaclitic relationship between child and mother reaches its most perfect form. Barthes's perception of *his* own body in the "specular" image of the mother as "reflected" in the winter garden photograph can be interpreted as a hallucinated experience of what Lacan calls the mirror stage: that period between the ages of six and eighteen months when, in reaction to the unconscious needs, drives, and demands the infant cannot control, he experiences imaginary relations of harmony and wholeness with the self, the mother, and a surrogate other that Lacan names *l'objet a.* In his fantasy, however, Barthes goes a step beyond the child's mirror stage identification with the mother. He not only sees his mother both as mother and as child but also sees himself as mother and child. Unlike the infant, moreover, who perceives in the mirror before which the mother is holding him an image of her which is either to the side of or merely proximate to his own, Barthes seems unaware of the mother as a separate other. The fusion of their specular images *as children* in the winter

To the appeal of the sign and of writing, Barthes's absent mother remains mute. In death she has become a signified that no signifier can recall or fully recover. This does not imply, however, that Barthes's study of photography ends on a note of failure or despair. Although he may not be able to articulate what the winter garden photograph has whispered to him, there is, nevertheless, something that emanates from it. Because it is the photograph's function to authenticate the physical existence of what it represents, especially the body and face of a loved being, Barthes finds affirmed in the winter garden photograph something essential, although inexpressible and indeterminate, to which he gives the name "*l'air.*"

The "air" of the photograph is the spirit of the photographed being. It cannot be analyzed or decomposed. It is the truth adhering to the maternal image in the winter garden photograph. At the instant he discovers this truth in the only photograph of the mother where it exists, Barthes utters a cry of surprise. This is because the "air" stops the flow of words; it is "ce cri, fin de tout langage" ("this cry, the end of all language"; *CC,* 167/109). Encountering the "air" for the first time, Barthes, like an excited child pointing to a coveted object, cannot keep himself from shouting "*C'est ça!*" ("That's it!"; *CC,* 167/109). In the winter garden photograph he suddenly discovers the flash of an ephemeral, ineffable presence—in which meaning, continuity, and language are abruptly suspended and depleted—that he associates with Japanese satori (and in another, more erotic, context with the experience of

---

garden photograph appears total. No longer does the specular image of the mother's body appear positioned slightly to the side of the child's or her face blocked by the child's reflected image. The slight gap or space between the mirror reflections of mother and child has been eliminated in Barthes's fantasy. Images of mother-as-child and son-as-child perfectly overlap and coalesce because mother and son are the same specular child. They have become fused in an indissoluble oneness through the childhood they now phantasmatically share.

On the mirror stage, see Jacques Lacan, "Le Stade du miroir comme formateur de la fonction du Je telle qu'elle nous est révélée dans l'expérience psychanalytique," in *Ecrits,* 2 vols., Collection Points (Paris: Seuil, 1966, 1971), 1:89–97; and Anthony Wilden, "Lacan and the Discourse of the Other," in Jacques Lacan, *The Language of the Self: The Function of Language in Psychoanalysis,* trans. Anthony Wilden (New York: Dell, 1968), pp. 159–92. For an interesting discussion of the influence of Lacan's theory of the mirror stage and his concept of "*l'imaginaire*" on Barthes's work, in particular *Roland Barthes par Roland Barthes* and *Fragments d'un discours amoureux,* see Gregory L. Ulmer, "The Discourse of the Imaginary," *Diacritics* 10 (March 1980): 61–75, esp. 68–72. Finally, for Barthes's own allusions to the mirror stage, as it applies to his own childhood and the creation of the Imaginary, see *RB,* 25 and 156/21 and 153, and his "Barthes puissance trois," *La Quinzaine littéraire* 205 (1–15 March 1975): 3–5; here, he writes that the photographs of his mother reproduced in *Roland Barthes par Roland Barthes* designate "the only Nature, acknowledged by one who has never stopped denouncing 'the natural' everywhere" (5).

la jouissance). The "air" turns the mother into a haiku, into a poetic concentration of fugitive reality, surging into being at the very same second it vanishes:

Enfin la Photographie du Jardin d'Hiver, où je fais bien plus que la reconnaître (mot trop gros): où je la retrouve: éveil brusque, hors de la "ressemblance," *satori* où les mots défaillent, évidence rare, peut-être unique du *"Ainsi, oui, ainsi, et rien de plus."*

[Finally the Winter Garden Photograph, in which I do much more than recognize her (clumsy word): in which I discover her: a sudden awakening, outside of "likeness," a *satori* in which words fail, the rare, perhaps unique evidence of the "So, yes, so much and no more."] (*CC,* 167–68/109)

The truth of the mother is perceived in a moment of intense revelation, where presence and plenitude, hovering tenuously on the edge of absence, emptiness, and depletion, momentarily coalesce. So, the desire for fusion with the mother, everywhere present in *La Chambre claire,* comes to rest on this revelation of the perfect correspondence between the image of the child-mother and the truth of her life. Barthes, however, keeps himself from falling too deeply into the trap of transcendental idealism by acknowledging that the experience of satori, of loss of meaning, which the "air" gives him, is, like the haiku and the *punctum,* a temporal event. Fugitive and ephemeral, this experience cannot be put into writing, it cannot be represented, it cannot be framed by the Imaginary.

The "air," therefore, envelops the maternal body in the luminous aura of subjective truth—"la vérité pour moi" (*CC,* 171/110)—a first step perhaps toward "la science impossible de l'être unique."[24] The

24. Barthes's perception of the "air" that englobes his mother's image resembles Walter Benjamin's concept of *aura,* the decline of which the latter associated with the rise of photography: "What was inevitably felt to be inhuman, one might say deadly, in daguerreotypy was the (prolonged) looking into the camera, since the camera records our likeness without returning our gaze. But looking at someone carries the implicit expectation that our look will be returned by the object of our gaze. Where this expectation is met (which, in the case of thought processes, can apply equally to the look of the eye of the mind and to a glance pure and simple), there is an experience of the aura to the fullest extent. . . . To perceive the aura of an object we look at means to invest it with the ability to look at us in return" (*Illuminations,* trans. Harry Zohn [New York: Schocken Books, 1969], pp. 187–88).

It is Barthes's desire that the photographic image of his mother return his gaze. Both the *punctum* and the "air" function to animate the immobilized image, to restore aura to it, and to provoke it to look back at him. Furthermore, Barthes's experience of the "air" rescues the subject from the paralysis of absolute death and from the mummification of the Imaginary. Through the power of the "air," the dark tomb of photography for an instant opens itself to the clarity and lightness of being. The *camera obscura (la chambre noire)*, whose image must be developed in darkness, gives way to the *camera lucida (la chambre claire)*, where the act of representation occurs in the light of day and in the openness of existence. It is thus that Barthes traces the luminous shadow—"l'ombre lumineuse," "l'ombre claire" (*CC*, 169/110)—of maternal being.

Tracing the Luminous Shadow: *Camera Lucida*

Photography has no depth, no dark and hidden regions. Everything about it is evident and visible. Because the photographic image is seen in the open, in light, it is a mistake, Barthes suggests, to associate photography with "la chambre noire," the "camera obscura." The photo is a transparence, a clear light; in it one sees the referent directly. Indeed, it is the *camera lucida*, Barthes observes, that best represents the way we see and read photographs:

C'est *camera lucida* qu'il faudrait dire (tel était le nom de cet appareil, antérieur à la Photographie, qui permettait de dessiner un objet à travers un prisme, un oeil sur le modèle, l'autre sur le papier).

[It is *camera lucida* that we should say (such was the name of that apparatus, anterior to Photography, which permitted drawing an object through a prism, one eye on the model, the other on the paper.)] (*CC*, 164/106)

---

paradoxical mixture of intimacy and distance, presence and absence, which is embodied in the winter garden photograph, accords with another aspect of aura as Benjamin defined it: "a strange weave of space and time: the unique appearance or semblance of distance, no matter how close the object may be" ("A Small History of Photography," in *One-Way Street and Other Writings*, trans. Edmund Jephcott and Kingsley Shorter [London: NLB, 1979], p. 250). Moreover, in the winter garden photograph Barthes searches for traces of a presence that will have meaning for his life in his own moment in time, a phenomenon that Benjamin identifies with the unique magic of photographic representation: "No matter how artful the photographer, no matter how carefully posed his subject, the beholder feels an irresistible urge to search such a picture for the tiny spark of contingency, of the Here and Now, with which reality has so to speak seared the subject, to find the inconspicuous spot where in the immediacy of that long-forgotten moment the future subsists so eloquently that we, looking back, may rediscover it" (ibid., p. 243). Benjamin's "tiny spark" of the "Here and Now" which has seared the subject of the photograph resembles Barthes's *punctum*, which, emerging from the image in which it has been preserved, burns its way through the consciousness of the spectator.

Invented in 1807 by the Englishman William Hyde Wollaston, the *camera lucida* (or "lucie," for short) was not really a photographic apparatus, but rather an optical instrument designed as a mechanical aid in drawing. *Camera lucida* is a misnomer because there is no chamber or box in which the image appears. It is an instrument in which the acts of seeing and inscribing predominate. A draughtsman or artist would set up the *camera lucida* in front of the object or subject to be copied. Placing the pupil of his eye directly above the edge of a prism, which rested on a long rod extending upward from a flat board that held a piece of drawing paper, the artist could see the image of the object reflected in the prism with one half of the eye and the pencil and paper with the other half. Thus, he could simultaneously study the image reflected in the prism and the image traced on the paper.[25] In the *camera lucida,* seeing and writing coincide.

The great importance of the optics of the *camera lucida* is evident for Barthes's *La Chambre claire.* He looks at the image of the mother at the same time he tries to put that image into writing. Like the operator of the *camera lucida,* Barthes keeps his eye both on the reflected image (the winter garden photograph) and on the tracings and inscription of that image on paper (his text). The book, *La Chambre claire,* is truly what its title indicates: an apparatus for seeing the mother and a mechanism for inscribing her reflection. Barthes attempts to draw the image of the mother as he sees her in the winter garden photograph and as he remembers her from life. But he soon discovers that writing an image, whether photographic or mnemonic, does not extend it, does not enhance it, does not even capture it. *La Chambre claire* is a failed attempt to write a new image of the mother, an image that would capture her truth as the "unique être." Writing the mother's body has become for Barthes an endless operation of tracing. He can do nothing but repeat her image by copying it again and again. For an artist looking through the *camera lucida* and for a writer, like Barthes, using words to produce a textual *"camera lucida,"* the object of study is always a reflection, never a person. Writing, drawing, and tracing begin, therefore, not with the thing itself, but with its image.[26]

25. For a more detailed description of the *camera lucida,* see Beaumont Newhall, *The History of Photography: From 1839 to the Present Day,* rev. and enl. ed. (New York: Museum of Modern Art, 1964), pp. 12–15; and John H. Hammond, *The Camera Obscura: A Chronicle* (Bristol: Adam Hilger, 1981), p. 7.

26. It is curious that in Barthes's description of the *camera lucida* he imagines the artist using both eyes; the apparatus allows the artist to "draw an object through a prism, one eye on the model, the other on the paper" (*CC,* 164/106). Most descriptions of the *camera lucida* suggest, however, that the artist, looking through the prism, sees the model and

Like the artist using the *camera lucida,* Barthes has his eye both on the mother and on the pencil, on the photograph and its textual reflection. Writing is his way of magnifying the photographic image, of scrutinizing its details, of enlarging its elements, and of decomposing its features in order to learn more about the mystery of the reflection that was his mother. But, ultimately, Barthes realizes that there is no going beyond the enigma of this reflection. There is no reality outside of the image. It is the visible "nothing" that cannot speak, that "cannot *say* what it lets us see" (*CC,* 156/100)—the "intractable reality" with which the writing, the tracing, of *La Chambre claire* ends.

The Intractable Reality

Loss immobilizes everything. Suddenly, time stands still like the frozen hands on the clock of the devastated tower in the city of Hiroshima, which mark to this day the exact moment of the atomic explosion. Thereafter, nothing can be the same. The catastrophe of loss becomes the reference point for a life, the new marker on the private calendar of an existence, the new milestone on the road of existence. It is the great tear that cannot be repaired, the wound that leaves an indelible scar. A new life begins, which, having at one time been centered around the presence of a loved person, must now be built upon his or her absence. Barthes knows that one lives with loss; that one comes to inhabit it like a residence; that one's identity is soon synonymous with it. After his mother's death, he feels the almost physical presence of her absence, as earlier during her lifetime he had experienced the physical presence of her body. Lack is endowed with a corporeal reality, which is also textual; it becomes the dwelling place for a life dominated by the anguish of separation and mourning. About this space of emptiness, this hole in the real which loss has opened in his life, Barthes writes movingly in a passage that is unique in the way it uses a fissured, fragmented, punctuated discourse, full of parentheses and other breaks, to create an iconic syntax of the *punctum:*

On dit que le deuil, par son travail progressif, efface lentement la douleur; je ne pouvais, je ne puis le croire; car, pour moi, le Temps

---

the paper with one eye only. What Barthes does not mention in his description of the *camera lucida*'s operation, but of which he was undoubtedly aware, is the presence of the reflected image in the prism. The *camera lucida* is definitely an instrument of mediation. The perception of the subject to be drawn, traced, or, in Barthes's case, written is not direct, but mediated by the optics of the prism.

élimine l'émotion de la perte (je ne pleure pas), c'est tout. Pour le reste, tout est resté immobile. Car ce que j'ai perdu, ce n'est pas une Figure (la Mère), mais un être; et pas un être, mais une *qualité* (une âme): non pas l'indispensable, mais l'irremplaçable. Je pouvais vivre sans la Mère (nous le faisons tous, plus ou moins tard); mais la vie qui me restait serait à coup sûr et jusqu'à la fin *inqualifiable* (sans qualité).

[It is said that mourning, by its gradual labor, slowly erases pain; I could not, I cannot believe this; because for me, Time eliminates the emotion of loss (I do not weep), that is all. For the rest, everything has remained motionless. For what I have lost is not a Figure (the Mother), but a being; and not a being, but a *quality* (a soul): not the indispensable, but the irreplaceable. I could live without the Mother (as we all do, sooner or later); but what life remained would be absolutely and entirely *unqualifiable* (without quality).] (*CC*, 118/75)

Barthes experiences the *punctum* of loss, the piercing wound of absence which designates, punctuates, and punctures the midpoint of his life. He confronts what in photography he identifies, in the final words of *La Chambre claire*, as "l'éveil de l'intraitable réalité" ("the wakening of intractable reality"; *CC*, 184/119). Barthes's struggle to wrest meaning from the image of his dead mother, as well as his search to recover and inscribe the radiant truth of maternal being through the writing of light (*camera lucida*), ultimately stumbles against the fundamental reality of death and nothingness: a reality of loss beyond which there is no telling and no seeing, but only the intractable presence, the ineffable "air," of a faded photograph, which somehow endures.

Index

Library of Congress Cataloging-in-Publication Data

Stamelman, Richard.
  Lost beyond telling : representations of death and absence in modern French poetry /
Richard Stamelman.
    p. cm.
  ISBN 0-8014-2408-9 (alk. paper)
    1. French poetry—20th century—History and criticism. 2. French poetry—19th
century—History and criticism. 3. Separation (Psychology) in literature. 4. Death in
literature. I. Title.
PQ443.S74   1990
841.009'354—dc20   90-55127

DATE DUE

DEMCO 38-297